PLAYGROUNDS

This book compares the theatrical cultures of early modern England and Spain and explores the causes and consequences not just of the remarkable similarities but also of the visible differences between them.

An exercise in multi-focal theatre history research, it deploys a wide range of perspectives and evidence with which to recreate the theatrical landscapes of these two countries and thus better understand how the specific conditions of performance actively contributed to the development of each country's dramatic literature. This monograph presents an innovative comparative framework within which to explore the numerous similarities, as well as the notable differences, between early modern Europe's two most prominent commercial theatre cultures. By highlighting the nuances and intricacies that make each theatrical culture unique while never losing sight of the fact that the two belong to the same broader cultural ecosystem, its dual focus should appeal to scholars and students of English and Spanish literature alike, as well as those interested in the broader history of European theatre. Learning from what one 'playground' – that is, the environment and circumstances out of which a dramatic tradition originates – reveals about the other will help solve not only the questions posed above but also others that still await examination.

This investigation will be of great interest to students and scholars in theatre history, comparative drama, early modern drama, and performance culture.

David J. Amelang is an assistant professor in English Literature at the Department of English Studies of the Universidad Autónoma de Madrid. He currently serves on the board of directors of the Madrid Institute for Advanced Study (MIAS) and of the Spanish and Portuguese Society for English Renaissance Studies (SEDERI).

Studies in Performance and Early Modern Drama
Series Editor: Helen Ostovich
McMaster University, Canada

This series presents original research on theatre histories and performance histories; the time period covered is from about 1500 to the early 18th century. Studies in which women's activities are a central feature of discussion are especially of interest; this may include women as financial or technical support (patrons, musicians, dancers, seamstresses, wig-makers) or house support staff (e.g., gatherers), rather than performance per se. We also welcome critiques of early modern drama that take into account the production values of the plays and rely on period records of performance.

Shakespeare's Hobby-Horse and Early Modern Popular Culture
Natália Pikli

From Playtext to Performance on the Early Modern Stage
How Did They Do It?
Leslie Thomson

Imitation and Contamination of the Classics in the Comedies of Ben Jonson
Guides Not Commanders
Tom Harrison

Playgrounds
Urban Theatrical Culture in Shakespeare's England and Golden Age Spain
David J. Amelang

For more information about this series, please visit: https://www.routledge.com/Studies-in-Performance-and-Early-Modern-Drama/book-series/SPEMD

PLAYGROUNDS

Urban Theatrical Culture in Shakespeare's England and Golden Age Spain

David J. Amelang

LONDON AND NEW YORK

Cover image: Detail of Wenceslaus Hollar, A View from St. Mary's, Southwark, Looking Towards Westminster (ca. 1638). The Yale Center for British Art, Paul Mellon Collection

First published 2023
by Routledge
4 Park Square, Milton Park, Abingdon, Oxon OX14 4RN

and by Routledge
605 Third Avenue, New York, NY 10158

Routledge is an imprint of the Taylor & Francis Group, an informa business

© 2023 David J. Amelang

The right of David J. Amelang to be identified as author of this work has been asserted in accordance with sections 77 and 78 of the Copyright, Designs and Patents Act 1988.

All rights reserved. No part of this book may be reprinted or reproduced or utilised in any form or by any electronic, mechanical, or other means, now known or hereafter invented, including photocopying and recording, or in any information storage or retrieval system, without permission in writing from the publishers.

Trademark notice: Product or corporate names may be trademarks or registered trademarks, and are used only for identification and explanation without intent to infringe.

British Library Cataloguing-in-Publication Data
A catalogue record for this book is available from the British Library

Library of Congress Cataloging-in-Publication Data
Names: Amelang, David J, author.
Title: Playgrounds : Urban theatrical culture in Shakespeare's England and Golden Age Spain / by David J. Amelang.
Description: New York : Routledge, 2023. | Series: Routledge advances in theatre and performance studies | Includes bibliographical references and index.
Identifiers: LCCN 2022034404 (print) | LCCN 2022034405 (ebook) | ISBN 9781032399447 (hardback) | ISBN 9781032399461 (paperback) | ISBN 9781003352112 (ebook)
Subjects: LCSH: English drama--Early modern and Elizabethan, 1500-1600--History and criticism. | English drama--17th century--History and criticism. | Spanish drama--Classical period, 1500-1700--History and criticism. | Theater--England--History--16th century. | Theater--England--History--17th century. | Theater--Spain--History--16th century. | Theater--Spain--History--17th century. | English drama--Spanish influences. | Spanish drama--English influences.
Classification: LCC PR651 .A625 2023 (print) | LCC PR651 (ebook) | DDC 822.309--dc23/eng/20221017
LC record available at https://lccn.loc.gov/2022034404
LC ebook record available at https://lccn.loc.gov/2022034405

ISBN: 978-1-032-39944-7 (hbk)
ISBN: 978-1-032-39946-1 (pbk)
ISBN: 978-1-003-35211-2 (ebk)

DOI: 10.4324/9781003352112

Typeset in Bembo
by MPS Limited, Dehradun

To my parents, Jim and Elena

CONTENTS

List of Illustrations ix
Acknowledgements xi

Introduction 1

1 Cities 8
   England and Spain's Theatrical Capitals 9
   Early Urban Theatre Districts 16
   The Place of Theatres in English and Spanish Society 25
   Playhouse Locations after Consolidation 29

2 Playhouses 43
   Why did English and Spanish Theatres Look so much Alike?
     A Few Genealogical Conjectures 44
   The Organic Corral vs the Immutable Theatre 50
   Seeing and Hearing (and Being Seen) in England and Spain's
     Playhouses 55
   Beyond the Bare Stage: Machines, Candles, Multi-Platforms 60

INTERLUDE 1
Why Did Madrid Not Have a Blackfriars? 73

3 Players 78
Professional Playmakers in Early Modern Society 79
Company Models, Structure and Organisation 83
Touring Practices 88
Who Played the Female Roles? Women and Children on the Commercial Stage 92

4 Dramatists 102
The Making of a Professional Playwright 103
Verse, Prose and Polymetry 106
Dramatic Genre(s) 110
Quantities of Writing and Notions of Artistry 115

INTERLUDE 2
Professional Actresses: To Have and Have Not (and How It Made a Difference) 127

5 Playbooks 143
Playbook vs Play: Printing Theatre in England and Spain 144
Publication Strategies, Licensing and Censorship 149
The Playbook in the Literary Marketplace 152
Other Documents of Performance 157

Conclusion 167

Works Cited *175*
Index *206*

ILLUSTRATIONS

Figures

1.1	Map of the British Isles highlighting the urban centres with documented venues built or adapted to serve solely or primarily as performance spaces	13
1.2	Map of the Iberian Peninsula highlighting the urban centres with documented *corrales de comedias*	15
1.3	Map of sixteenth-century London and its commercial playhouses (circles) as well as the inns frequently used for performances (squares)	17
1.4	List of known *corrales de comedias* built in Spain during the sixteenth century	21
1.5	Map of sixteenth-century Seville and its *corrales de comedias*	22
1.6	Map of sixteenth- and seventeenth-century Madrid and its *corrales de comedias*	24
1.7	Map of seventeenth-century London and its commercial playhouses	30
1.8	Map of seventeenth-century Seville and its *corrales de comedias*	33
2.1	The stage of the reconstructed *Almagro* Copyright: *Corral de Comedias de Copyright: Concejalía de Cultura y Turismo. Ayuntamiento de Almagro*	45
2.2	Antonio Lafréry's engraving of the Roman colosseum, with the caption "*Theatrvm Sive Colisevm Romanvm*" in his *Speculum Romanae Magnificentiae*. Copyright: The Trustees of the British Museum	49

2.3 Estimated plans of the first (left) and second (right) designs of the Rose playhouse in Southwark Copyright: The Museum of London Archaeology 51
2.4 Plans of various Iberian *corrales de comedias* from the sixteenth and seventeenth centuries Copyright: Peter Lang (Allen) and Grupo de Investigación Siglo de Oro. Modified with permission of the authors 53
2.5 Acoustic projections of London's Globe (left) and Blackfriars (right) playhouses Copyright: University of Chicago Press 59
5.1 Length distribution of commercial plays in Shakespearean England (left) and Golden Age Spain (right) 148

Interludes

1.1 Acoustic projection of Madrid's *Corral del Príncipe* with the canvas *toldo* Copyright: University Presses of Florida. Modified with permission of the author 75
2.1 Total proportion of lines allocated to female (dark) and male (light) characters in Shakespearean England and Golden Age Spain's commercial plays 128
2.2 Proportion of lines allocated to female (dark) and male (light) characters in the corpora of Shakespearean England and Golden Age Spain's dramatists (min. five plays) 129
2.3 Proportion of lines allocated to female (dark) and male (light) characters in Shakespearean England and Golden Age Spain's commercial plays divided into dramatic genres 130
2.4 Proportion of lines allocated to female characters (dark), male characters (light) and female characters in breeches (striped) in the ten English and Spanish plays with the largest share of lines spoken by female characters 131

ACKNOWLEDGEMENTS

This book would not have been possible without the support by many people; many people, too many to whom I can do justice here. It is the evolution of my doctoral dissertation, carried out under the auspices of the Erasmus Mundus Joint Doctoral Programme Text and Event in Early Modern Europe (TEEME) at the University of Kent and the Freie Universität Berlin. My first thanks, thus, must go to my supervisors Marion O'Connor and Andreas Mahler. Each in their own way kept me sane, on track and in shape during this tenure, and without their mentoring, feedback, directives and advice I am not sure where I would be right now. I consider myself extremely lucky that they took me on as an apprentice of their craft. I would also like to thank all the TEEME partners and instructors, in particular the coordinators Bernhard Klein, Sabine Schülting, Rui Carvalho Homem and Martin Procházka for keeping us always busy, entertained and well-provided for during those three years.

Taking a step back, I owe much to my professors at the Universidad Autónoma de Madrid who first sparked my interest in Renaissance literature. During my graduate studies, the English Department at King's College London pushed my passion for everything early modern further, with particular thanks to Lizzie Scott-Bauman, Gordon McMullan, my tutor Sarah Dustagheer and my academic advisor Ann Thompson. Not only was their dedication contagious, but they were also extremely helpful in counselling me on how to take my first steps towards applying to TEEME. Regarding the project itself, the inspiration for my research topic has two clear sources: John Jay Allen and Margaret Greer. Meg's article "A Tale of Three Cities" was the spark that lit the flame, and Jay's stagecraft studies teemed with an energy and passion that made me want to partake in his endeavour. Throughout all these years, I have been able to get to know each of them quite well, and the greatest compliment I can offer is to say that their scholarly work, to which I often return and look upon with the same level of admiration, pales in comparison with their kindness and helpfulness.

Additionally, many other people have helped me out by providing feedback, advice, insight and support. Carlos Aladro, Rachael Ball, Laura Bass, Jimena Berzal de Dios, Brigitte Blanco, Sònia Boadas, Fernando Bouza, Julian Bowsher, Graham Caie, Antonio Castillo, Callan Davies, Carla Della Gatta, Teresa Ferrer, Alejandro García Reidy, Laura Gianetti, Guillermo Gómez, Clive Griffin, Eva Griffith, Brean Hammond, Stefan Hulfeld, Suzanne Jones, Richard Kagan, Andy Kesson, James Knowles, Beat Kümin, Donald Larson, Russ McDonald, Harry Newman, Tanya Pollard, Joan Oleza, Alexander Samson, Bruce Smith, Louise Stein, Jonathan Thacker, Jesús Trónch, Alejandra Ulla and Betsy Wright are among those who have provided their invaluable (and much more than) two cents when I approached them with queries and doubts. I would also like to thank the members of the Association for Hispanic Classical Theatre, Deutsche Shakespeare Gesellschaft, Grupo ProLope, SEDERI, Shakespeare Association of America, Theater Without Borders and many other early modern scholars and enthusiasts across the world for sharing their thoughts and advice with me as I presented parts of my project at different conferences and events. And lest I forget the all-too-often-unsung heroes that are the librarians: in my case, many thanks to the staff at the Staatsbibliothek zu Berlin (particularly to Dr Jochen Haug), the Iberoamerikanisches Institut, the British Library, the Biblioteca Nacional de España, the Templeman Library, the FU Philologische Bibliothek, the Biblioteca de Humanidades at the UAM, the Folger Library and the Huntington Library, all of whom were very generous with their time and expertise.

On a more personal level, I will always cherish the days and nights spent trekking the different confines of the world with the other members of TEEME's third cohort: Diviya, Djamila, Jelena, (Kate,) Natacha, Somnath, Tiago and YiChun. In Berlin, I was lucky to share apartments and countless conversations over a bottle or two of beer/wine with Alison Marie Plock, who along with Laurin Schöneman and Tiphaine Ferry put up with their share of PhD-induced tantrums and offered both psychological and physical shelter whenever I needed it. I am now back in my hometown of Madrid, surrounded by my childhood friends and my family, who were the necessary support group to carry this project across the finish line. There is Daniel, Lidia and (not so) little Nora. There is also my dad Jim and my má Elena: not many among us can say that their intellectual and professional parent figures are in fact their actual parents, and it would be absurd for me to try to list all the ways in which they have helped me throughout the years. My partner Bea has the uncanny sense of when to drag me out of my cave and force me to enjoy life beyond work, and consequently, life has been much more enjoyable since I met her. And now that all of this is said and done, I will go back to scratching behind the ears of my dog Silvestra as she guffaws happily knowing that this is what we both most enjoy.

INTRODUCTION

For one reason or another, Ezra Pound did not like Shakespeare. Instead, he looked to Chaucer as the beacon of English literary achievement. Whenever he had the chance, Pound tried to tone down the general public's enthusiasm for Shakespeare by highlighting the early modern playwright's shortcomings in comparison with his medieval predecessor. "Chaucer had a deeper knowledge of life than Shakespeare", he wrote in the *ABC of Reading* (1934), and "let the reader contradict that after reading both authors, if he chooses to do so".[1] Pound's was an uphill battle, trying to change the deified perception of the writer history had dubbed 'the Bard' over all other candidates. This owed much, according to the modernist poet, to the fact that

> English opinion has been bamboozled for centuries by a love of the stage, the glamour of the theatre, the love of bombastic rhetoric and of sentimentalizing over actors and actresses; these, plus the national laziness and unwillingness to make the least effort, have completely obscured values.[2]

Pound's harsh words for the theatre come as a surprise since this had not always been his attitude toward the stage. In fact, in 1906 he had plans to write his doctoral thesis on a prominent early modern dramatist, Spain's Lope de Vega. Before he ended up discarding the academic enterprise altogether, the young Ezra Pound was thinking of dedicating his life not only to the study of Renaissance and Baroque drama, but also to do so by focusing on a playwright very often compared to the Bard he so insistently sought to undermine later in his career.[3]

When delving into the rich world of European Renaissance and Baroque literature, only very rarely does one encounter anyone as eager to sidestep Shakespeare's dominance as was Pound. And just as it is difficult, if not impossible,

DOI: 10.4324/9781003352112-1

to discuss the literature of early modern Europe without coming across references to Shakespeare and Elizabethan and Jacobean theatre, the same could be said about the plays of Golden Age Spain and its two household-name dramatists, Lope de Vega and Calderón de la Barca. Molière, Racine and their peer playwrights from seventeenth-century France are similarly unavoidable, as are nods to the popular Italian *commedia dell'arte* street theatre. What is more, the dramatic works of the Renaissance and Baroque occupy a privileged position within the period's larger scope of literary studies. The Spanish scholar Carlos Gutiérrez explains that this is the case because drama was

> the touchstone upon which the other literary fields of the European (Spanish, English, and French) Renaissance were built. The main reasons behind this are three, which in combination gave the theatre a certain halo of heterodoxy: its distinctive commercial and/or aristocratic character, the quickest strategy for rapid and direct success in the world of letters; its spectacular and large-scale appearance; and, lastly, its complex relationship with poetry, the literary arch-genre of the time.[4]

Of the three countries Gutiérrez lists, France can be set apart due to its theatre's markedly aristocratic character, particularly beginning in the 1630s. England and Spain's early modern theatre, on the other hand, stand out for their unique commercial and populist nature, meant to appeal to the tastes of the higher and the lower classes alike. In fact, that is just one of the long list of striking similarities between the English and Spanish theatrical worlds of the time, especially in their metropolitan centres of London, Madrid or Seville. With these resemblances in mind, this study comparatively surveys the development of urban theatrical culture in Shakespearean England and Golden Age Spain in order better to understand how the social fabric was seamlessly woven into the texts of two of Europe's most iconic dramatic traditions.

In the late 1980s, when seeking to consolidate his fledgling 'poetics of culture', Stephen Greenblatt argued that Shakespeare's plays,

> it seemed, had precipitated out of a sublime confrontation between a total artist and a totalizing society. By a total artist I mean one who, through training, resourcefulness, and talent, is at the moment of creation complete unto himself; by a totalizing society I mean one that posits an occult network linking all human, natural, and cosmic powers and that claims on behalf of its ruling elite a privileged place in this network. Such a society generates vivid dreams of access to the linked powers and vests control of this access in a religious and state bureaucracy at whose pinnacle is the symbolic figure of the monarch. The result of this confrontation between total artist and totalizing society was a set of unique, inexhaustible, and supremely powerful works of art.[5]

David Scott Kastan and Peter Stallybrass concur when they describe dramatic texts as "sites rather than the exclusive sources of meaning, places where audiences, readers, actors, writers (not to mention scribes and compositors) construct and contest meanings".[6] These texts were just one of the many elements that played a role in the composition of a theatrical event, all of which are worth studying. "It would be a terrible mistake", José María Díez Borque cautions when discussing the theatre of seventeenth-century Spain, "to imprison the works of our playwrights in crystal palaces of reverential respect; the truth is that theatrical production in the early modern period was teeming with life".[7] Indeed, there was much more to – for instance – the playhouses of the golden ages of English and Spanish theatre than plaster and timber: cities, audiences, players, playwrights and text converged in these buildings to give shape to an activity of enormous cultural importance. Even more intriguing is that theatrical events in Shakespeare's England almost inexplicably resembled those of Golden Age Spain. Much has already been written about the resemblances between the English Globe-like amphitheatres and Spain's *corrales de comedias*. That comparison can be extended to discuss how the playmaking communities of both countries had to endure similar political and religious pressures that sought to undermine their very existence. Such parallels continue in the structure and working patterns of their acting companies, as well as in the position and reputation of players and playwrights in the social order of each country, the growth of printed theatre in English and Spanish book markets, and the increasing involvement on the part of dramatists in the publication of their own works.

Clearly, seen from a distance of slightly over four hundred years, the 'playgrounds' of early modern Spain and England – that is, the environments in which these two theatrical cultures developed and thrived – appear to have been very similar, if not the same. And to a certain extent, this comparative study promotes the idea of these two playmaking communities facing rather comparable realities. Yet, by taking a closer look at the two side by side, this study also highlights the nuances and intricacies that make each playground unique, while never losing sight of the fact that both belonged to the same broader cultural ecosystem. Even though the two theatrical cultures existed in relative if not total ignorance of each other – this is especially true when talking of English drama, which did not reach southern European countries to a significant extent until much later – it does not mean that they lived in complete isolation from each other: they both drank from the same well of early modern Renaissance and Baroque culture.[8] By identifying not only the elements in common but also the particularities of the theatrical worlds of Shakespearean England and Golden Age Spain, this overview sets forth a comparative framework for exploring early modern European dramatic traditions that for the most part have been analysed separately, each in its own domestic sphere. It organises and presents the pillars of these two playgrounds' histories both to students as well as to specialists who, by nature, will be more familiar with one of the two traditions and are interested in learning more about the other.

There is also a very practical reason for promoting more comparative work on the English and Spanish theatrical cultures of the Renaissance and Baroque. Not only must the remarkable similarities between the two playgrounds be accounted for, but also the scholarship devoted to analysing the two objects of study – that is, the two playgrounds – is eerily complementary. They fit together like two linking pieces of a same puzzle. José María Ruano de la Haza sums it up best:

> The tenacity and passion of the Elizabethan theatre historians, who have managed to build impressive monuments of erudition with very little documentary evidence, is admirable to behold. In Spain, on the other hand, we enjoy a wealth of information, including playhouse plans, building and leasing contracts, municipal ordinances, documents about repairs carried out, [...] hundreds of manuscript plays (many of them written by the playwrights themselves), player and company and performance contracts, and numerous and somewhat faithful descriptions of what plays would have been like at the time.[9]

However, other than a handful of monographs, book chapters and articles, little has been done to further the understanding of the original circumstances in which the Spanish commercial theatre thrived, at least in comparison with Elizabethan and Jacobean England, a field of study with considerably less documentary evidence. The recent archaeological discovery in 2016 that the Curtain playhouse may have been square-shaped and not circular as it was traditionally thought, almost perfectly timed to honour the four-hundredth anniversary of Shakespeare's passing, highlights the dearth of Elizabethan and Jacobean England's theatrical paper trail, especially when compared to Golden Age Spain and its *corrales*. Greater awareness of the theoretical approaches to or the documentary evidence behind the other country's theatre history studies would help raise scholarly pursuit to a different level.[10]

This study follows the trail blazed by a short but invaluable series of publications that, starting in the mid-1980s, have engaged in a comparative analysis of the English and Spanish early modern theatrical cultures. Walter Cohen's *Drama of a Nation* (1985) and John Loftis' *Renaissance Drama in England and Spain* (1987) were the first long-format studies to compare the dramatic production of Shakespearean England and Golden Age Spain and to examine specific themes of the two corpora within a shared historical context.[11] *Comedias del Siglo de Oro and Shakespeare* (1989) edited by Susan L. Fischer, *Vidas paralelas* (1993) edited by Anita K. Stoll and *Parallel Lives* (2001) edited by Peter and Louise Fothergill-Payne, collect the works of a growing number of scholars from diverse academic fields and communities in the first collective multidisciplinary efforts to connect the two theatrical traditions.[12] In 2005 Iván Cañadas pushed the ball forward with his *Public Theater in Golden Age Madrid and Tudor-Stuart London* by placing particular emphasis on the dynamics of gender on the commercial stages of the two countries' capital cities. Since then, the comparative analysis of female characters in English and Spanish plays has garnered a significant amount of scholarly attention, including Gemma Delicado Puerto's *Santas y Meretrices* (2011) and the collection of essays *Heroines of the Golden Stage* (2008) edited by Rina Walthaus and Marguérite Corporaal.[13] Barbara Fuchs brought to the fore the considerable debt of Jacobean dramatists to their Spanish counterparts in her engaging *The Poetics of Piracy* (2012), and more recently Rachael Ball's *Treating the Public* (2017) extended the comparative approach by contrasting early modern England and Spain's theatrical cultures from a colonial and trans-Atlantic point of view.[14] Finally, various topics currently in vogue attract the attention of both English and Spanish theatre historians and have inspired a considerable number of publications in the last decades. These include the never-yielding Black Legend, the lost play *Cardenio* that Shakespeare supposedly co-wrote based on a passage from Cervantes's *Don Quijote*, and the four-hundredth anniversary of the deaths of Shakespeare and Cervantes that was celebrated worldwide in April 2016.[15] Still, many major questions have yet to be addressed. To this end, this study surveys the theatrical contexts of Elizabethan-Jacobean England and Habsburg Spain from a broad comparative perspective and provides a wide-ranging interpretation of the relationship between the performance cultures of these two dramatic traditions.

The book is divided into five chapters. The first two, "Cities" and "Playhouses", analyse the most prominent theatrical urban centres and neighbourhoods in late-sixteenth- and early-seventeenth-century England and Spain, as well as the playing venues themselves, their architectural characteristics and conditions of performance. Chapters 3 and 4, "Players" and "Dramatists", explore the similarities and differences between the two countries' professional playmaking communities. The final chapter, "Playbooks", deals with the transformation the theatre of Elizabethan-Jacobean England and Golden Age Spain underwent from live spectacles to printed textual artefacts. Additionally, two interludes (located between Chapters 2 and 3, and Chapters 4 and 5) address two particularly distinctive and revealing idiosyncrasies of England and Spain's theatrical traditions: the absence in Madrid of a public-yet-elite indoor playhouse à la London's Blackfriars, and the consequences of the lack of professional female players in the main commercial theatres of England as opposed to Spain.

The primary objective of such a wide-ranging exploration is to provide an overview of the central issues as a means of encouraging and guiding future Anglo-Spanish comparative theatre research, a field of study that is currently attracting ever greater attention among early modern students and scholars alike. More than any other two European theatrical cultures in the sixteenth and seventeenth centuries, England and Spain share a long list of similarities that go considerably beyond the merely coincidental, and in the majority of cases also beyond the superficial. Closer familiarity with these commonalities will provide the foundations needed to continue enhancing our collective understanding of what it was like to create commercial theatre in some of early modern Europe's most important cities. This survey also draws attention to the benefits of cross-cultural comparative theatre history: contemplating the larger picture is the best way to understand what makes each theatrical culture distinctive. As we grow increasingly aware of the interconnectivity of early modern Europe's dramatic traditions, it becomes ever more important to look beyond the confines of national borders in order to test existing theories within transcultural frameworks.[16] By challenging ourselves to answer what justifies, or at least explains, the similarities and in particular the differences between the theatrical worlds of Shakespearean England and Golden Age Spain, we become more acutely aware both of the broader shared culture as well as the singularities that marked the achievements of the communities behind the texts we continue to enjoy today.

Notes

1 Pound, *ABC of Reading*, p. 99.
2 Pound, *ABC of Reading*, p. 99.
3 Rogers, "Ezra Pound, 'lopista'", p. 219.
4 Gutiérrez, *La espada, el rayo y la pluma*, p. 43 [my translation].
5 Greenblatt, *Shakespearean Negotiations*, p. 2.
6 Kastan and Stallybrass, "Staging the Renaissance", p. 2.
7 Díez Borque, *El teatro en el siglo XVII*, p. 27 [my translation].
8 Although Shakespeare and his contemporaries did have some level of presence in northern Europe in the seventeenth century, Richard Andrews points out that "the same tale cannot be told of France, Italy, or Spain: it seems that there was a significant linguistic division in this respect between the Europe of Germanic and Slavic languages on the one hand, and the Europe of Romance languages on the other. From what has been discovered so far, we cannot argue that [*commedia dell'arte* standard-bearer] Flaminio Scala, or any other theater practitioner of the sixteenth and seventeenth centuries, had even heard of Shakespeare or of any other English dramatist". Andrews, "Resources in Common", pp. 37–38.
9 Ruano de la Haza and Allen, *Los teatros comerciales del siglo XVII y la escenificación de la comedia*, p. 248 [my translation].
10 Precisely with this intention in mind, in 1998 John J. Allen summarised the vast and ever-growing collection of *Fuentes para la historia del teatro en España* [*Sources for the history of Spanish theatre*], initiated by John E. Varey and Norman Shergold, for the English-speaking readership of the *Cardenio is covered in more* in his "Documenting the History of Spanish Theatre".
11 Cohen, *Drama of a Nation*; Loftis, *Renaissance Drama in England and Spain*.
12 Fischer (ed.), *Comedias del Siglo de Oro and Shakespeare*; Fothergill-Payne and Fothergill-Payne (eds.), *Parallel Lives*; Stoll (ed.), *Vidas Paralelas*.
13 Cañadas, *Public Theater in Golden Age Madrid and Tudor-Stuart London*; Delicado Puerto, *Santas y Meretrices*; Walthaus and Corporaal (eds.), *Heroines of the Golden Stage*. See also Ihinger, "The Mirror in Albion".
14 Ball, *Treating the Public*; Fuchs, *The Poetics of Piracy*.
15 Scholarship regarding the lost *Cardenio* is covered in more detail in p. 173, n. 3. Publications that stem from the Cervantes – Shakespeare connection and/or their shared 2016 quatercentenary include González (ed.), *Cervantes – Shakespeare 1616-2016*; Gregor, "Transversal Connections"; Luis Martínez and Gómez Canseco (eds.), *Entre Cervantes y Shakespeare*. Additionally, a growing number of journal articles and book chapters delve into the Anglo-Spanish theatre comparison. Especially noteworthy

contributions include Cohen's "The Artisan Theatres of Renaissance England and Spain", Margaret Greer's "A Tale of Three Cities" and "Move Over Shakespeare", John J. Allen and his various publications on Madrid and London's public playhouses (more in chapter 2), and the wide-ranging cross-cultural explorations of Alexander Samson ("A Fine Romance", "Cervantes on the 17th Century English Stage", "Exchanges", "'Last Thought Upon a Windmill'", among others).

16 Especially influential in my transcultural approach is the research collective *Theatre Without Borders*. This informal association of scholars who gather annually to promote and partake in interdisciplinary and transnational research in early modern theatre studies has for the past three decades been shedding light on the various modes of exchange, influence and mobility of ideas among Renaissance and Baroque Europe's playmaking communities. Their publications, in chronological order, are Henke and Nicholson (eds.), *Transnational Exchange in Early Modern Theater*; Henke and Nicholson (eds.), *Transnational Mobilities in Early Modern Theater*; Katritzky and Drábek (eds.), *Transnational Connections in Early Modern Theatre*.

1
CITIES

In his 1657 city guide to London, historian and political writer James Howell asks himself and his readership a loaded rhetorical question:

> If it was esteemed an honour among the *Greeks*, to be born in *Athens*; If among the *Italians*, to be a *Roman*; If among the *Spaniards* to be a *Toledano*: why should it be lesse honour for an *Englishman* to be born in *London*?[1]

The implication here is that seventeenth-century London was comparable to some of the most revered cities in the history of western civilisation. Athens, Rome and – curiously – Toledo are in Howell's opinion the mirrors in which the capital of England could or should see itself reflected. This query raises two questions of its own. The first is whether London was indeed comparable to Athens or Rome, generally regarded as the birthplace of western culture. The other is why Toledo, the medieval capital of Castile, and not Madrid comes across Howell's mind.[2] The importance of the first two cities was and is evident to readers then and now, but Toledo might stand out in this select list, especially since Madrid had been the seat of the Spanish court for almost a century by that time. Howell's question, whether purposefully or not, speaks volumes about the unclear mapping of Spain's political, economic and cultural centres. The significance of the Spanish capital within its borders had by no means been comparable to London's absolute dominance in England, as other cities in the Iberian Peninsula challenged Madrid for a place in the national spotlight. These two very different national dynamics, one of focalised monopoly and the other of predominance among plural centres, was also reflected in their theatrical landscapes. This chapter charts the most important urban centres and districts in the development of commercial theatre in early modern England and Spain, and explores how the identities of these cities and neighbourhoods

DOI: 10.4324/9781003352112-2

played a part in the making of Renaissance Europe's most dynamic popular theatre cultures. But first, it is important to understand how and why London and Madrid became capitals in their respective countries, and how they carried their political capitality into the cultural (and by extension, theatrical) domain as well.

England and Spain's Theatrical Capitals

London's becoming the cultural and theatrical centre of early modern England is not surprising. It had been the main commercial, political and social nucleus of the island since the thirteenth century, and no other city could rival its supremacy.[3] Referred to as a metropolis as early as the twelfth century, even if the definition of the term at the time was vague and literary, London exercised an informal hegemony in the social and cultural spheres as well as in the economy. Despite the fact that the adjacent city of Westminster was the official seat of the monarchy (and it would be a mistake to understand the two cities as two parts of a whole), London exercised substantial influence over the court while maintaining its autonomy – and vice versa.[4]

In fact, in terms of population size, commercial strength and overall productivity, as well as its considerable political autonomy, London's self-sufficiency and dominance equalled that of an early modern city-state.[5] And such was its growing national and international pre-eminence that, from a continental perspective, England's capital slowly progressed from being the most important city of the British Isles to becoming one of the leading cities in Europe. In the early seventeenth century around 200,000 people lived in the London area, making it the third largest city in western Europe after Paris and Naples. By 1700 the city had swollen to over 500,000 inhabitants, approximately 75% of England's city dwellers. Soon dwarfing all competitors, it emerged as the western European metropolis par excellence.[6] The exponential growth in population during this period also affected the capital's size and topography, which as late as 1561 consisted of a relatively small walled nucleus with a narrow ring of suburbs. The Venetian traveller Alessandro Magno provides a concise description of his first impression of the city when he arrived in 1562:

> London is a very beautiful city, rich and populous. There are abundant supplies of woollen cloth and *carisee* (kerseys). The circuit of the walls is five miles, and nine including the suburbs which are very fine. It has nine gates, eight with suburbs outside, while the other has a beautiful common where every Sunday men and women gather to meet and play.[7]

This description would soon be dated, since in the following century the city stretched into a shapeless metropolis, with the extramural ditches and the surrounding green fields becoming urbanised to the extent that the original layout was almost completely dissolved. If in the 1300s more than 80% of

London's population could be found living within the City walls, by 1650 already half of the capital's inhabitants lived in the suburbs – and by the nineteenth century, the latter share was as high as 85%.[8] The city's population and geographical size kept (and keeps) on growing every year, with betterment migrants trying to find a new staircase to climb within a city of endless opportunities, and subsistence migrants settling for trying to survive one day at a time.

Madrid's evolution, on the other hand, differed substantially from that of London. Whereas early modern London was, as historian Derek Keene reminds us, defined by its "physical inheritances from earlier times" and already a city of significance in the sixteenth century, Madrid did not have such a solid foundation to look back on when Philip II decided to make it the new capital of the Hispanic empire in 1561.[9] Tired of dealing with all the political, social and ecclesiastical pressures that marked an established Castilian stronghold such as Toledo, the spiritual epicentre of the kingdom since the Middle Ages and the informal capital at the time, Philip decided to start afresh in Madrid, a *villa* (which translates best into 'town') he could shape to his royal will.[10] Before 1561, Madrid was a small-to-medium-sized urban centre that catered to royal and aristocratic leisure, thanks to its proximity to some of the most renowned Crown-owned hunting grounds in the kingdom. Other than that it was unremarkable, and as dissimilar from London as one can imagine. It had no cathedral, no institutions of higher education, and no important tribunal or seat of authority. Its population in the mid-sixteenth century was small in comparison with that of the larger cities in Spain; moreover, it had no important river, and its closest port – Valencia – was over 350 kilometres away, thus restricting the possibilities of its developing beyond the role of a regional economic centre.[11] In short, London and Madrid followed visibly different trajectories in the decades that preceded the opening of their commercial playhouses.

Thus one begins to understand why, even as late as 1657, Howell talks about Toledo and not Madrid in his list of celebrated capitals. But from 1561 onward Madrid caught up quite quickly with its new status as the epicentre of the most important European empire of its day. Its population increased at an impressive rate thanks to the immigrants who hoped to make a living for themselves in or around the court.[12] For instance, the number of registered baptisms in Madrid grew from around 300 in 1561 to over 1,000 in 1563, and reached 1,315 by 1571.[13] At the turn of the century, the capital had around 65,000–70,000 inhabitants, and these numbers continued to grow throughout the early modern period with the sole exception of 1601–1606, when Philip III briefly relocated the capital and court to Valladolid.[14] During that five-year interval, Madrid lost one-half of its inhabitants and registered one-third fewer baptisms.[15] But when the king and court returned in 1606, it quickly recovered and reclaimed its former role as the head of the body politic. This episode speaks volumes of Madrid's dependence on its status as the country's capital; Philip II clearly longed to have a royal seat dependent on the crown's interests, and he got his wish. Local and central government merged in Madrid in a way that cannot be said of Tudor-Stuart

London, in which the royal seat of Westminster – a city in its own right – maintained its autonomy within an expanding metropolitan area that soon dwarfed the City itself. Above all, London had other sources of strength beyond its capitality, and had the English court moved elsewhere it would still have remained in essence Britain's leading *urbs*.

Madrid's economy also differed from that of London. Most crucially, its productive base was weak, and moreover played a subordinate role within a luxury-oriented economy that was highly dependent on foreign imports. Indeed, the strength of royal and aristocratic consumption did relatively little to stimulate local production: not surprisingly, the largest proportion of the active population of the capital worked in what we now refer to as the service sector. Habsburg Madrid joined many other early modern cities that functioned on balance as an "economic parasite", in David Ringrose's words, much like imperial Rome had been previously and early modern Rome and Naples continued to be. Its socio-economic profile reflected

> a perennial relationship between its urban functions and the larger world. Its most prominent features were a large, poorly paid service sector and a landed and bureaucratic elite that controlled a huge share of urban income and constituted the focal point for the city's economic life. Madrid's function as a producer of political and social services is starkly outlined in its occupational structure.[16]

Despite Madrid's impressive demographic and commercial growth after it was named the capital, Seville continued to serve as the leading economic centre of Habsburg Spain. And while Madrid caught up with its population of around 120,000 inhabitants in the 1620, the Andalusian city maintained its role as the commercial hub of the Hispanic empire, especially since all trade with the American colonies had to pass through its Casa de Contratación [Board of Trade]. Madrid's commerce was oriented above all toward satisfying the needs of local consumers – which explains why some of the fastest growing trades in the capital were those that dealt with luxury textiles and other courtly products. Madrid thus resembled other European capitals such as Vienna, Lisbon, The Hague, as well as the aforementioned Naples and Rome; London, and to a lesser extent Paris, were exceptional cases in which the court coexisted with an unusually vibrant industrial sector.[17]

Yet even if its capitality did not entail the same level of across-the-board supremacy as London's, being the tent for the Court meant that Madrid was, like London, the main stage for artistic display and dissemination for the rest of the nation. London had been England's cultural showpiece for at least two centuries and was portrayed as its most significant emblem of education and civility.[18] Some admittedly saw the capital as a nest of ungodliness: "For when the Country cannot find out sinnes to fit his humour," the poet Francis Lenton wrote in 1629,

"London doth invent Millions of vices, that are incident to his aspiring mind".[19] But no one failed to acknowledge its status as England's sole perennial and cornucopian source of entertainment. Thus the writing-master John Davies of Hereford defined early modern London as "the Faire" that "lasts all year", an image that fits in well with Peter Burke's depiction of the capital as the Elizabethan equivalent of the city that never sleeps:

> It is probably accurate to imagine the inhabitants of English villages and small towns in the seventeenth century as living out their year in remembrance of festivals past and in anticipation of festivals to come. In London, on the other hand, there was no lack of shows to fill up the spaces between festivals.[20]

Elizabethan Londoners could partake in many forms of popular entertainment, including a colourful mixture of traditional events with new and innovative spectacles. Formal literature – and specifically poetry – was closely linked to the aristocratic circles of the capital, but it slowly made its way into the larger public sphere. Although poetry was not performed in public spaces in early modern London the way it was in Italy and especially the Low Countries, some recitals took place in semi-public venues (taverns, the Court, etc.).[21] In addition, the booksellers in St. Paul's Churchyard ensured that printed literature enjoyed broad public presence as well. Markets and fairs proved to be natural *loci* for popular entertainment, but so were all the processions throughout the city. These included both the religious ones, most of which disappeared after the Reformation, and the secular parades such as the annual *fête* in honour of the Lord Mayor of the City. Executions, as grim as they might appear to audiences nowadays, were another reason to congregate and celebrate in public, as were other forms of public exhibition of cruelty, chiefly animal baiting.

And, of course, there was the stage. The earliest documentary traces of the existence of a public, commercial theatre in London date to the late 1530s and early 1540s; prior to this, performances were for the most part confined to the liturgical and civic calendars, as well as being ostensibly amateur and non-profit in nature.[22] The boom-decade of the 1570s marked the consolidation of the commercial theatre enterprise, and culminated in the construction of the first venues primarily built with the business of playing in mind (which I will refer to as 'purpose-built' from now on). These were not the only spaces London's theatrical community resorted to, since many of the City's inns had long hosted regular performances and continued to do so until the end of the century. Nevertheless, the emergence of buildings "made specifically for plays, capable of holding many more people than inns or other city venues" speaks to the popularity of this form of entertainment, and remained a fixture in the capital until the Civil Wars of the 1640s.[23] This is not to say that there was no performance culture beyond London, nor were purpose-built playhouses exclusive to the capital; there is documentary evidence of venues built or adapted to serve primarily as performance spaces in Bristol, York, and the then Lancastrian market town of Prescot in the early seventeenth century, in addition to the Werbugh Street Theatre in Dublin of the late 1630s (Ireland at the time was under English control). What is more, the *Records of Early English Drama (REED)* and the *Before Shakespeare* projects, in addition to Callan Davies' recent paradigm-shifting study of English playhouses, shed light on many other locales that, despite not having been built exclusively for theatrical spectacle, had in some ways even greater standing as performance spaces than some of the purpose-built structures listed above and shown in the map below.[24] Notwithstanding these significant discoveries, their existence does not contest the overarching truth that during this period London's predominance in all things theatrical was never in question.[25]

FIGURE 1.1 Map of the British Isles highlighting the urban centres with documented venues built or adapted to serve solely or primarily as performance spaces

Theatre in London during this era was unquestionably popular. By the turn of the century, between 18,000 and 24,000 Londoners flocked every week to see the plays performed in playhouses throughout the city, making it the main leisure attraction of the time along with animal baiting.[26] The fact that John Stow in his wistful 1599 *Survey of London* only fleetingly mentions the playhouses reflects the novelty of playgoing in early modern London. After all, the *Survey* – described by J.F. Merritt as "a paean of praise of his own city, but also a heavily nostalgic one which lingers lovingly over the past but (more often than not) deplores more recent events" – was written only three decades after the first commercial playhouses opened in Shoreditch. This left Stow little enough time with which to process this new cultural trend as he was still busy reflecting on how much greener the grass was when he was a child.[27]

Madrid's cultural development in the sixteenth century also differed noticeably from that of London. Just like every other medium-sized town in Renaissance Spain, prior to 1561 Madrid's calendar was marked with numerous *fiestas* and events for popular celebration, much like the English villages to which Peter Burke alludes. But before the *villa* was transformed into a capital it had housed few known poets, *autores de comedias* [actor-playwright-managers of the Spanish Golden Age theatre], or artists of any kind. Lope de Rueda, Garcilaso de la Vega and the other leading wordsmiths of Spain during Charles V's reign spent their time in the main cities: Toledo, Seville, Valencia, Valladolid … but not Madrid. Roving troops of players and street performers made stops there, but it was more of a pass-through than a destination. Once the crown and court relocated to Madrid in 1561, however, among the migrant families which followed were those of Lope de Vega, Tirso de Molina, Calderón de la Barca and many others who would eventually become the icons of Spain's literary Golden Age.[28] The *villa*'s new status as the first fixed seat of the Hispanic empire's court not only ensured visibly increased investment in entertainment and cultural activity, but also transformed its festive calendar from that of a regional town into one more appropriate for one of the most active and renowned urban centres in western Europe.[29]

The temporary relocation of the court to Valladolid from 1601 to 1606 once again serves to highlight Madrid's dependence on its newfound capital status. When Philip III – or, more accurately, his *valido* [favourite] the Duke of Lerma – moved the court to northern Castile, most of the more prominent *literati* followed suit and migrated to the new capital: Góngora, Quevedo, Cervantes … virtually all the standard bearers of Spain's Golden Age of literature except Lope de Vega abandoned Madrid.[30] The days of Valladolid as the capital were short-lived, however, and the king and court returned to Madrid for good just five years later in 1606. From then on, the *villa* established itself as an indisputable focal point for Spanish theatrical culture, and one that exercised increasing influence on other forms of cultural activity throughout the rest of the country.[31]

Yet at no point did Madrid's dominance become a cultural monopoly.[32] Even if the capital was the most important centre for cultural activity, it was by no means the only one; the composite nature of Habsburg Spain and relatively high levels of urbanisation encouraged the decentralisation and dispersal of wealth and cultural activities and entertainment, including theatre. Every provincial centre had its own independent festive calendar, and religious processions – the most important and frequent form of popular cultural display in early modern Spain – in various towns and cities held their own against or even eclipsed those of the capital.[33] Also, while by the seventeenth century, Madrid was the most important printing centre in the country, it did not enjoy the publishing monopoly for Spain that London exercised in England. And regarding theatre, the pattern repeats itself: whereas the theatrical calendar and infrastructure of London had no rival in early modern England, a respectable number of cities and market towns in Golden Age Spain had their own recognisably own theatre infrastructures and traditions. In addition to Madrid, Seville had a notably vibrant stage scene, as did – albeit to a lesser extent – other cities such as Valencia, Lisbon (Portugal formed part of the Habsburg Empire from 1580 to 1640), Toledo or Valladolid. Moreover, smaller and/or temporary *corrales* opened up in cities and market-towns across the peninsula in the seventeenth century, partially countering the centripetal pull of the larger urban centres.[34]

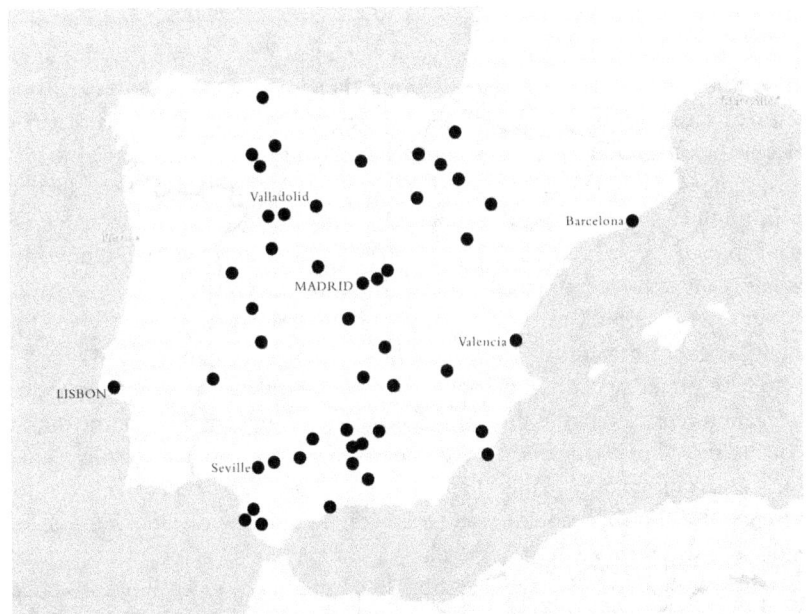

FIGURE 1.2 Map of the Iberian Peninsula highlighting the urban centres with documented *corrales de comedias*

So decentralised was early modern Spain's theatrical landscape that some scholars have gone as far as to say that Seville was the country's "undisputed capital" for theatre, and not Madrid.[35] Hyperbole apart, that a case can be made for Seville's early theatrical supremacy over Madrid already signals a major difference between the English and Spanish theatrical milieux. When boiled down to a simple exercise in pairing numbers and balancing out the scales, no single city in early modern Spain could match London's singular standing in England's commercial theatre scene. Instead, what I suggest here is that, in ways similar to developments in the political and the economic spheres, it would have taken the combined cultural and theatrical activity of its largest urban centres – with particular emphasis on Madrid and Seville – to match both the standing and the population numbers of the English metropolis, which raises questions of timing as well as of spatial predominance.

Early Urban Theatre Districts

All across Europe, but especially in England and Spain, the second half of the sixteenth century witnessed a change in the relationship between the commercial theatre enterprise and the most important cities. Throughout the Middle Ages and until the beginning of the century, the few individuals who dedicated themselves exclusively to the business of playing were rootless, itinerant, and above all lacking in purpose-built venues wherein to practice their craft. Cities provided the most important shelters during their travels, but they lacked the infrastructure that acting companies needed in order to take up permanent residence in them. Most spectacles, whether sacred or secular, were performed in taverns, squares, churches, marketplaces and other makeshift spaces. Yet, as cities grew in number and size during this period of major urban expansion, some of their inhabitants and institutions began to invest in more adequate and ultimately profitable venues for commercial theatre. Many of the earliest efforts to raise permanent, purpose-built playhouses proved to be short-lived; most survived by doubling as multi-functional spaces that housed other activities; all were extremely bare-boned and primitive when compared with what came later. Still, their creation represented the first step taken to establish stable environments for two of the most important theatrical traditions in western popular culture. This section focuses on where in cities these early playhouses were built, the better to understand the social, economic, and topographical place the theatre and its practitioners occupied within the broader urban context.

Present wisdom holds that the first short-lived attempt to erect a purpose-built playhouse in London can be traced back to the northeastern suburb of Mile End, where in 1567 John Brayne converted a patch of farmland into a rudimentary scaffolded yard for performances of plays and other forms of entertainment which they called the Red Lion. Callan Davies has recently suggested that it seems increasingly likely that other performance venues existed in the London area as early as the 1520s, but in any case none of these buildings had a lasting impact.[36] The situation soon changed, though: a decade after the Red Lion, in 1576, the same John Brayne along with his wife Margaret and his brother-in-law James Burbage built the Theatre playhouse in the neighbouring suburb of Shoreditch, which would be the main home for Shakespeare's company until the end of the century. At around the same time another playhouse, the Curtain, opened its doors nearby. These were neither the first nor the only performance venues active at the time; indeed, as alluded to above, at this early stage the most important *loci* for theatrical shows were the City's inns, such as the Bell Savage, the Bull, the Bell and the Cross Keys Inn, which remained active well into the 1590s. Moreover, we know of at least one extramural playhouse operating a couple of years earlier in the hamlet of Newington Butts in the southern outskirts of the capital.[37] The Theatre and the Curtain were nevertheless among the first long-lasting structures purposefully and primarily built for the performances of plays in England, thus making Shoreditch an early hub of the growing public theatre enterprise. By the end of the sixteenth century, however, new acting venues began to emerge in other suburban districts of the capital, especially the bankside borough of Southwark.[38]

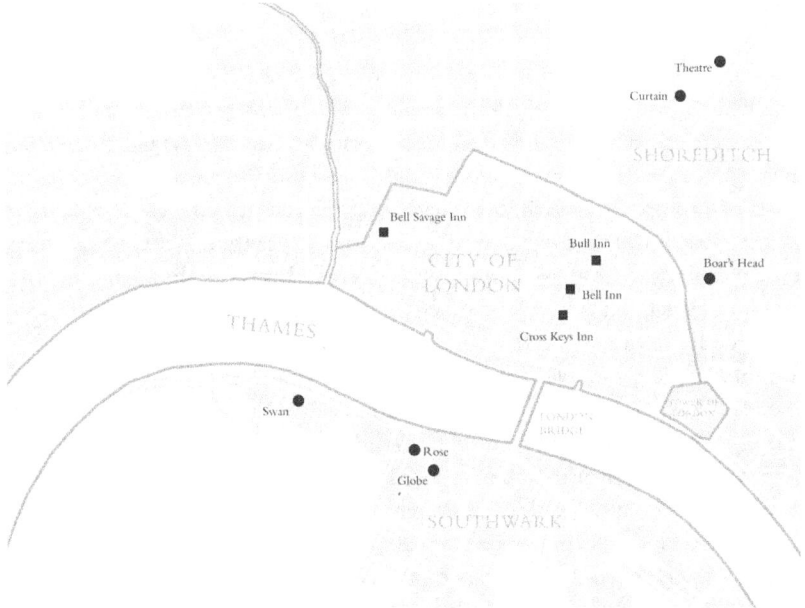

FIGURE 1.3 Map of sixteenth-century London and its commercial playhouses (circles) as well as the inns frequently used for performances (squares)

All these early playhouse locations in the extramural suburbs of London had many traits in common. The most obvious among such shared features is that the districts in which they operated housed some of the poorer neighbourhoods in the greater London area. As the intramural City reached an almost unmanageable population density, the better off migrants preferred to move to the West End near the Inns of Court and Westminster, whereas the 'middling sort' – the period term for the middle class – and the poorer inhabitants settled in the remaining suburbs, especially those to the east and south of the City.[39] The economic landscape of each neighbourhood was shaped by these migration and settlement patterns: the western suburbs and the City served as the political and the legal quarters of the capital (i.e., elite and service sector), while the east and south housed the manufacturing and maritime districts as well as warehousing sites.[40] These poorer neighbourhoods in which the playhouses were built also shared similar architectural features and arrangements. Whereas the western suburbs slowly took on an "ordered appearance" due to landowning patterns favouring the consolidation of larger buildings and a growing demand for a more formalised urban landscape, the East End and southern bank struck observers as anarchic and untidy. The City and the West End favoured multi-storey buildings in order to make the most out of such highly coveted terrain: the land between London and Westminster thus started to fill up with fancy shopping streets, upscale housing projects, parks and other spaces for urban leisure.[41] On the other hand, most of the new dwellings built in the poorer neighbourhoods were either small single-family units made with cheap materials or larger but older properties that were subdivided and slowly converted into slum-like residences. The number of tenements, as such buildings were called (due to the type of lease typically associated with them), is one of the first features that catches John Stow's attention as he narrates his perambulation through Southwark, along with the "diuers streetes, wayes and winding lanes" that Derek Keene eloquently describes as a labyrinthine network, in sharp contrast to the more neatly organised west.[42] There land was cheap and not too densely populated, making the suburbs ideal locations for constructing large buildings with even larger needs such as amphitheatres.

Another similarity all playhouse districts shared, and very closely connected to the previous one, was their association with other licentious pleasure industries. This is particularly true of Southwark, the most important and best-known theatrical district during Shakespeare's lifetime. The Borough of Southwark, on the south bank of the Thames opposite the City of London, was home to the Globe Theatre, the principal open-air playhouse of Shakespeare's playing company from 1599 onward. It also housed two of the other amphitheatres of the time, the Rose and the Swan, in addition to the aforementioned animal baiting arena, or bear garden, as it was also known. Just as Westminster was a city in its own right and separate from London, Southwark too differed from the City and the other extramural districts. This is of particular relevance to the neighbourhood's becoming the theatrical site of choice for many Londoners because, more than any of the other boroughs outside the City walls, Southwark had a reputation for being the "pleasure-ground for the more closely regulated community to the north", as Jessica A. Browner puts it.[43] The seemingly endless opportunities for leisure in the district went a long way in shaping the understanding of what playgoing meant to early modern Londoners.

According to Browner, the origins of Southwark's singular reputation as London's primary leisure district "almost universally predated the jurisdictional and demographic developments of the sixteenth and seventeenth centuries".[44] Southwark controlled the only land-based access point to the City from the south; its two main parishes, St. Saviour's and St. Olave's, flanked the road that connected London Bridge and the counties of Kent and Sussex – and, by extension, the continent. It is perhaps because of this threshold quality that Southwark, an almost obligatory first stop for many newcomers to London, quickly became the leading suburb of the capital by the turn of the century (almost 10% of the area's population lived there) and the second largest urban area in the country after the City itself.[45] Due to the Kent thoroughfare road and the City's policy of closing the London Bridge gates at nightfall, the borough had been full of inns housing travellers since the Middle Ages. Some of these inns were famous enough to make it into Stow's *Survey*, such as the Tabarde, which Geoffrey Chaucer had previously mentioned in *The Canterbury Tales*.[46] Hand in hand with the innkeeping world came another set of closely related businesses, prominently the victualing industry and prostitution. London became a leading site for brewing for export as well as domestic consumption, and its suburbs had a remarkably high number of alehouses when compared with the City and many other extramural districts (one in every six buildings in Southwark were watering holes, as opposed to the one in every 30 or 40 within City walls).[47] Brothels and stew-houses "for the repair of incontinent men to the like women", very often hidden under the veil of alehouses, had also been a traditional staple of poorer suburbs in general and of Southwark in particular (even though Henry VIII's 1546 closure of licensed brothels did see much of the area's prostitution drastically reduced).[48] These two 'leisure' industries had close ties with the theatrical world (in that these services were offered also in and around the playhouses), and played an important part in creating the ecosystem in which commercial playhouses flourished.

The final feature these theatrical locations shared was that they were not directly under the jurisdiction of the City of London. All Elizabethan amphitheatres were erected in 'liberties', that is, areas within London's wards that were jurisdictionally independent from the City. This factor is extremely important because in 1574 London's civic authorities looked on theatrical activity as a possible source of revenue, and subjected innkeepers and other hosts of for-profit performances to a licensing fee whose proceeds were earmarked for the city's hospitals and poor relief. However, theatre impresarios successfully evaded this levy by building their new playhouses in London's 'liberties' instead, which the City could not tax.[49] The term 'liberty' does not mean that the districts lacked regulation, as it might misleadingly suggest; in this case, it simply meant that these territories belonged to a different jurisdiction. For example, the three playhouses and the baiting arena in the Borough of Southwark were located in two administrative districts under the jurisdiction of the county of Surrey, the liberties of Paris Garden and the Clink. In the northern suburbs, the Theatre and the Curtain were part of the liberty of Shoreditch, which in turn belonged to Middlesex County. To be sure, one must never lose sight of the fact that, despite technically being outside their legal control, the City of London's aldermen exercised a significant amount of power over these suburban liberties in one way or another;

these zones were, as Janette Dillon reminds us, "free of city controls, but crucially determined by the city".[50] However, these administratively confusing (and confused) districts played a crucial role in the building of the early modern English playhouses, since the first theatre impresarios took advantage of the relatively loose ties of the liberties with the City to thwart the local authority's desire to levy taxes and other constraints on commercial theatre-making in London.[51]

The existence of liberties in the greater London area led to an impressive homogeneity regarding the locations of the first public commercial amphitheatres in the capital's poorer extramural suburbs. One could even venture to say that if investors wished to open a large performance venue to cater to all classes of London society (larger than the City inns, at least), there was no other viable alternative location. However, this was not the case in early modern Spanish cities. There it is much more difficult to identify one or another type of neighbourhood as the natural playground of choice. It was not unusual for cities with more than one *corral* to find them dispersed in very different areas, such as in Seville; and even where all the playhouses were located in the same district, as is in the case of Madrid, the popular identity of the neighbourhood was not as sharply defined as it was in London. From early on this broader social complexity marked the districts where Spanish theatres took root and quickly demonstrated their ability to lure playgoers from a wide range of backgrounds.

In Spain, the building of spaces specifically – or at least primarily – intended to host public theatre started slightly before similar efforts in England. As early as 1554, the famous actor and playwright Lope de Rueda arranged for some scaffolding to be put up near the Gate of San Esteban in the Castilian city of Valladolid, not far from the main square. That Valladolid frequently housed the Spanish court during Charles V's reign made it one of the most attractive and lucrative venues for itinerant commercial performers and thus an obvious candidate for a first try at sedenterisation. Lope de Rueda was well known for his performances at court, and would usually take his show out to the streets as a secondary source of income. In these early years, that meant setting up a cart in the streets, squares, inns and yards in cities throughout the peninsula.[52] What little information there is suggests that this was the first attempt to establish a theatre-specific infrastructure in Spain. In the following decades, more or less permanent acting spaces were opened across the country, both in large cities and in smaller market towns, in order to provide venues for liturgical performances as well as the shows of itinerant troupes. A list of known commercial public acting venues in the Iberian Peninsula built during the sixteenth century is included in Figure 1.4.

From an initial comparative perspective, the difference in diversity of locations and the sheer quantity of playhouses between England and Spain is remarkable. The disparity can be partly attributed to the fact that many of these *corrales de comedias* were in truth, at least in the beginning, little more than courtyards with

NAME	CITY	DATES
Patio de Comedias	Badajoz	c. 1592 – <1630
Patio de Comedias de los Niños de la Doctrina	Burgos	1587 – 1752
Coliseo/Casa de Comedias	Granada	1593 – 1781
Corral/Patio/Casa de Comedias	Jaén	1595/1605 – c. 1656
Pateo das Arcas	Lisbon	1593 – 1755
Corral del Lobo/Puente	Madrid	1568 – c. 1579
Corral de la Pacheca	Madrid	1569 – 1574
Corral de Burguillos	Madrid	1574 – ?
Corral de la Valdivieso	Madrid	1579
Corral de la Cruz	Madrid	1579 – 1737
Corral del Príncipe	Madrid	1582 – 1735
Corral del Trinquete	Murcia	c. 1597 – 1713
Corral del Zoco/Azoque	Murcia	16th C. – 1713
Corral de Don Pablo	Seville	1560s – ?
Corral de las Atarazanas / del Arenal	Seville	1576/8 – 1585
Corral de Doña Elvira	Seville	1577 – 1631
Corral de San Vicente / del Duque / de las Higueras	Seville	1581 – 1597
Corral de la Alcoba	Seville	1585 – 1589
Corral de Don Juan / de los Zurradores / del Marqués de Villamediana	Seville	c. 1570 – 1589/95
Mesón de la Fruta	Toledo	1576 – ?
Patio de las Comedias	Tudela	1597 – ?
Casa de la Cofradía de San Narciso	Valencia	1582 – 1584
Casa del Santets	Valencia	1584 – 1614
Casa de la Olivera	Valencia	1584 – 1618
Corra de la Puerta de Santisteban / de la Cruz Verde	Valladolid	1559 – 18th C.
Corral de la Longaniza	Valladolid	1574 – 1579
Teatro de la Comedia	Valladolid	1574 – 19th C.
Patio del Hospital	Zamora	1574 – 1606
Casa de las Comedias	Zaragoza	1590 – 1808
Casa del León	Zaragoza	<1584 – 1591

FIGURE 1.4 List of known *corrales de comedias* built in Spain during the sixteenth century

stages (or makeshift carts) placed at one of their ends. The *corral de vecinos* – that is, a multi-household housing structure organised around a common patio – was one of the staples of the Castilian urban landscape and could be reycled into a performance venue with relative ease (see p. 52). It was definitely easier and less expensive to convert an existing *corral de vecinos* into a fully functioning playhouse than to produce a new one ideally designed for the purposes of playing and playgoing. As a result, the line separating temporary performance spaces and fully functioning playhouses in Spain was much more blurred than in England, especially in the early years of commercial theatre.[53]

22 Cities

One consequence of this practice of repurposing as a performance venue a relatively common urban structure that could be found in virtually all Spanish cities was that there was no fixed pattern as to where the first *corrales* were located. It seems as if, especially in the earliest years, the most important precondition for opening such a venue in this or that district was for it have a *corral de vecinos* available to be leased and converted; that is, the decision to build a *corral de comedias* in this or that part of a city depended on the availability of a suitable structure more than any other factor. However, with time, certain areas were successfully transformed into theatrical districts while other such projects failed. The case of Seville, the city with the most *corrales* throughout the second half of the sixteenth century, poignantly illustrates that the reasons for this were far from random.

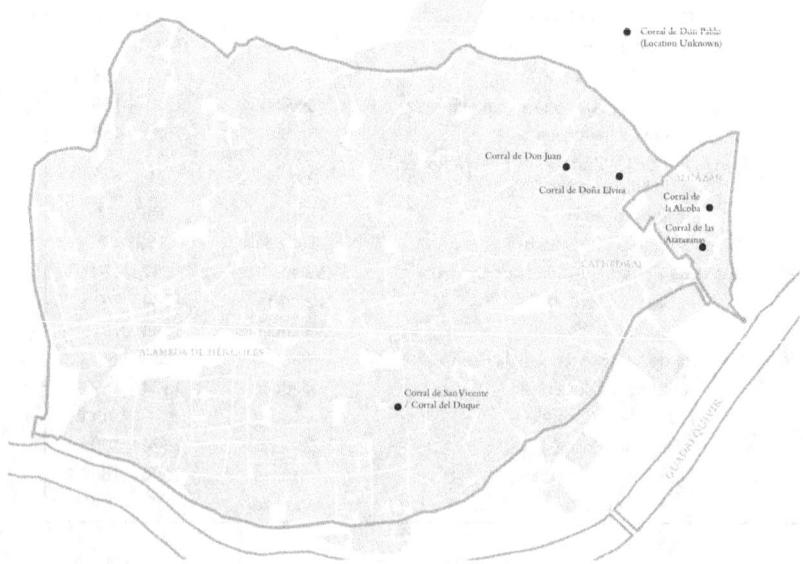

FIGURE 1.5 Map of sixteenth-century Seville and its *corrales de comedias*

The first documented courtyard used for theatre in Seville was the Corral de Don Pablo, presumably during a very brief spell in the late 1560s. From then until the turn of the century, at least six different *corrales* were active in the Andalusian city. The level of success and the lifespan of each *corral* depended in large measure on its location. For instance, the most popular playhouse was the Corral de Doña Elvira, on the eastern edge of the city. Located in the relatively quiet parish of Santa Cruz, it stood right next to the main commercial and waterfront district of the city and under the towering gaze of both the cathedral and the royal palace known as the Alcázar. This meant that, as Jean Sentaurens explains, the Corral de Doña Elvira was host to a uniquely large and heterogeneous crowd and its success was for the most part due to its geographic situation, which permitted it to attract not only the clergy, aristocrats, merchants, ship-owners and artisans who made up the everyday *demos* of the neighbourhood, but also travellers, *indianos* [returnees from the Americas], seafarers and the naval personnel.[54]

Its serving as the geographical and demographical intersection between the popular and the elite, between the centre and the periphery, guaranteed Doña Elvira's long life. The Corral de Don Juan opened in the same area, and thrived as a profitable playhouse for over 20 years before returning to its original purpose as a *corral de vecinos*. Other *corrales* were not as lucky; the Corral de la Alcoba – built from the timbers of the Corral de las Atarazanas, widely considered the first purpose-built theatre in Spain and which had to be torn down when the lease over the land expired – was not as successful as its predecessor since, even though both were located within the Alcázar district, the Alcoba was tucked "further away and in an area with a worse reputation".[55] The very poorest section of Seville, the extramural suburb of Triana, never even had a *corral*. On the other end of the spectrum, the Corral de San Vicente, a private locale on the premises of the former palace of the Dukes of Medina Sidonia in one of the wealthiest parishes of the city, opened to the public in 1581; it had a successful 16-year run, but after it shut down no other playhouse was built in that area. All this suggests that the Sevillian *corrales* that were located in districts that could draw visitors from all social strata had the best chance of succeeding. Thus, when theatre impresarios and local officials decided it was time to build new *corrales* in the city in the seventeenth century, they chose to do so in the neighbourhoods that were seen as common ground shared by all strata of local society.[56]

The same approach was found in Spain's other major sixteenth-century theatrical centre, Madrid. As in Seville, the first and most immediate concern was available space. Then, if conditions allowed for a steady stream of across-the-social-spectrum playgoers a location would go on to solidify its status as a theatrical district. Unlike in Seville, however, all of Madrid's *corrales de comedias*, starting with its precarious *corral* on the Calle del Sol of the late 1560s all the way up to the fabled Corral de la Cruz and the Corral del Príncipe, were located in a single area of the city: the macroparish of San Sebastián. That said, when looking closely at the characteristics of the districts in Seville in which theatre ultimately flourished and the area in which the Madrid *corrales* were located, one begins to detect certain similarities that in turn reveal much about the social and cultural profile of commercial theatre culture in the peninsula.

San Sebastián was the second largest parish in the capital, and at first glance, it displayed a markedly popular and artisan identity not unlike that of London's poorer suburbs. This humble reputation, which can be traced back to medieval times, merely deepened when Madrid was made the capital in 1561, since logistical constraints forced most of the flood of new immigrants to settle in the peripheral parishes. San Sebastián, which stretched southward all the way to the

FIGURE 1.6 Map of sixteenth- and seventeenth-century Madrid and its *corrales de comedias*

villa's natural boundary at the Manzanares River, was one such locale and thus one of the preferred destinations for new settlers. However, it is important not to forget that its northern border reached the very heart of the capital, and that a significant portion of the parish formed part of the wealthier city centre as well.[57] San Sebastián was by no means an indivisible quarter housing a homogeneous community. Instead, it stood out as a district of social, occupational and financial contrasts, and it is quite safe to affirm that there was a clear difference between its northern half, where all the *corrales* were located, and the southern.

The Calle de Atocha was (and is) a street running diagonally from the city's centric Plaza Mayor [Main Square] to the south-eastern outskirts of the capital. Atocha divided the early modern parish of San Sebastián, both geographically and ethnographically, into two distinct halves. Most of the area south of it was located outside the medieval city limits, and anything that was not part of the old city was considered an *arrabal* [shantytown, or suburb in the Southwark or Shoreditch sense], the once empty stretch of land new-coming families and minority communities made their own.[58] This southern half was where new immigrants and the lower classes settled, as rental prices in the northern sector would have been largely beyond their means. This in turn explains why most of the commercial activity in the neighbourhood took place in the southern side of the parish, as well as why all the known nobles and better-off residents inhabited its northern half, including the streets of the *corrales* themselves.[59] Even with regard to prostitution (a factor often brought-up when assessing a neighbourhood's reputation) there was a clear distinction between the sort of brothels located north of Atocha, which catered mainly to elites, and those in the south.[60] Thus the northern sector of San Sebastián, while not being completely disassociated from the parish's overall reputation and identity, was where two different sides of Madrid met to converge in the *corrales*, just as they did in Seville's Doña Elvira.

A delicate balance between resemblance and distinction governed the location of playhouses in the emerging theatre systems of sixteenth-century England and Spain. Much the same – superficial similarity overlaying the existence of important differences – also marked the role the up-and-coming commercial theatre industry played in contemporary religious and moral discourse and practice. For this reason, before moving on to the next set of commercial playhouses and their geographical and social coordinates, we should pause to consider the crucial question of how each country's moralist spheres reacted to the growing popularity of public theatre.

The Place of Theatres in English and Spanish Society

The opening of permanent playhouses in London and the major Spanish cities stirred a wave of resentment and animosity against the business of playing, mostly on religious and moralistic grounds. It was not that theatre in itself was the problem; educational, religious or aristocratic drama did not generate the same level of anger and opposition. It was the markedly popular, commercial and for the most part secular nature of this new form of entertainment that was condemned. And nothing, in the eyes of moralists, was a more poignant symbol of such decadent and illicit cultural activity than the theatres themselves. The fact that professional players, until that point regarded as no better than vagabonds and prostitutes (see pp. 79–83), were starting figuratively and literally to buy real estate in your city and become your neighbours was for some like pouring salt in the wound.

In both countries, the loudest and fiercest critics of the growing urban commercial theatre belonged to the most rigorist factions within their respective religious and ideological landscapes. In England, Puritans and the more radical members of the Church of England led the charge against anything related to commercial playing. From the opening of the first purpose-built theatres in the 1570s up until their closure in 1642 by Parliament, the prohibitionist movement actively criticised the lewdness and iniquity of those who participated in or endorsed the performance of plays for profit. The moralist pamphleteer Philip Stubbes offers one of the most aggressive condemnations of the corrupting power of the playhouse in his 1583 tract *The Anatomie of Abuses*:

> Do they not maintaine bawdrie, insinuat folery, & renew ye remembrance of hethen ydolatrie? Do they not induce whordome and unclennes? nay, are they not rather plaine deuourers of maydenly virginitie and chastitie? For proofe whereof, but marke the flocking and running to Theaters & curtens,

daylie and hourely, night and daye, tyme and tyde to see Playes and Enterludes, where such wanton gestures, such bawdie speaches: such laughing and fleering: such kissing and bussing; such clipping and culling: Suche winckinge and glancinge of wanton eyes, and the like is vsed, as is wonderful to behold.[61]

The Jesuits in Spain matched the English Puritans in playing the surprisingly similar part of anti-thespians following the emergence of large-scale urban theatre in the later sixteenth century.[62] Even though commercial secular theatre before Lope's time was not a very popular form of entertainment and could only be found in the larger cities and towns of the country, with the arrival of the new wave of *comediantes* and *corrales* the theatre soon became the preferred spectacle of Spaniards. "Therefore we should not be surprised", the well-known literary historian Emilio Cotarelo y Mori reflects, "that grave and pious men became concerned with such entertainments and asked for their immediate closing".[63] One such grave and pious man of the time was the Jesuit scholar Juan de Mariana, whose criticism of the theatre drew on the same ancient tropes as Stubbes', and thus rings eerily similar: "the licentiousness that rules the playhouse ... makes it nothing but an institution for lewdness and scandal, where men and women of all sorts of class and age go to deprave themselves with the feigned acts that portray real vices ... Thus it is my opinion, the theatre's licentiousness is a true calamity for good Christian customs and a public offense to such values".[64]

And while displays of fervent condemnation such as these targeted the entire commercial secular theatre enterprise, particular animosity was reserved for the venues themselves. The playhouses embodied the heathenish playworld, and metonymically stood for all that was wrong in the theatrical culture. The Anglican pastor Thomas White described the Shoreditch theatres as "a continual monument of London's prodigality and folly", while Henry Crosse compared them to "a sinke in Towne, whereunto all the filthe doth runne"; in his collection of sermons *Fruits of Honest Work and Damages of Idleness* (printed in 1614), the Spanish Jesuit Pedro de Guzmán dedicates a lengthy portion of his anti-drama rant to the playhouses themselves, which he repeatedly describes as 'schools of vice' and laments that "we should have silenced and shut [them] down by now".[65] While the Spanish Jesuits were not very successful at quieting the *corrales*, London's moralists had reasons to celebrate when they secured the banishment of the first playhouses to the capital's suburbs, even if – as explained above – this was more likely an unintended consequence of a plan by the local government to tax the theatrical enterprise and not the result of an active campaign to rid the City of players and their playhouses.

Indeed, such moralistic animosity toward theatre and the theatres did not gain much traction, as all strata of society came together in accepting and embracing the commercial performance of plays. "The *corral de comedias*", José María Díez Borque explains, "is an exact mirror, and economically quantifiable as well, of the social structure of Habsburg Madrid: a social microcosm that reflects to perfection the insurmountable distance between the classes, even though they all illusorily co-exist for a couple of hours in the same space, participating in the same spectacle"; Andrew Gurr asserts much the same for the London playhouses prior to 1600, and he backs up the argument with an appendix listing the surviving accounts of London playgoers from a wide range of social backgrounds.[66] Furthermore, it is telling that following the establishment of the first permanent performance spaces, the commercial theatre infrastructure in both countries did not fail to grow, in terms both of the appearance of new venues as well as an increase in the frequency of performances.

If anything, the condemnation of the theatrical industry by the more extreme religious factions backfired by motivating different ways for the authorities to give legal and moral shelter to the increasingly popular shows. In England, the acting companies sought the patronage and protection of willing nobles and even members of the royal family, and their support was instrumental to the broader survival and eventual success of the business of playing. One of the pivotal moments came in 1585, when the City Fathers of London produced a "modest list of requirements for the toleration of players", as Andrew Gurr puts it. This brief acknowledged the possibility of a licit commercial theatre culture in the capital, which in turn encouraged private individuals to invest in permanent theatre venues and other means of elevating an entertainment culture that not too long before was synonymous with vagrancy in the eyes of the law.[67] With time, the country's most important acting companies and theatre impresarios secured sufficiently good standing with the authorities to be able to open various forms of commercial playhouses in areas previously out of bounds and out of reach, including within City limits.

The legitimisation of theatre and theatres in Spain was an easier case to argue from the very beginning. Unlike in England, where the playhouses were private enterprises, most of Spain's *corrales* were run by local authorities and the officers of religious brotherhoods, who used part of the profits to fund hospitals, shelters and other charitable efforts. (As noted above, in 1574 London's Common Council attempted to tax theatrical performances in a similar fashion, but their plans were thwarted by the exodus of the theatre-builders to areas outside the City's direct control; in Spain, the lack of an equivalent to London's 'liberties' prevented any such evasion.) Madrid provides the most prominent example of this crucial difference. There the crown granted two confraternities, the Cofradía de la Soledad and the Cofradía de la Pasión, a joint licensing monopoly over all commercial theatrical activity in order to finance the capital's hospitals.[68] Thus, Madrid's health literally depended on a thriving public theatre, which is why whenever the *corrales* had to shut down operations – due to public safety concerns (i.e., plague) or in order to mourn the passing of a royal family member – the *villa*'s hospitals suffered greatly. Such was the case in 1597 and 1598, when theatrical activity was halted following the deaths of the princess Catalina Micaela and king Philip II: even though it was a plague-ridden period, Madrid's city officials wrote letters to the crown imploring it to lift the ban on public theatre that was depriving the hospitals of the *limosnas* [alms] the religious brotherhoods collected at the *corrales*. This petition runs counter to the logic displayed by London's local government, which was quick to close the theatres every time the plague visited the English capital so as to avoid large public gatherings. In Madrid, on the other hand, public officials argued that keeping the theatres closed in such times not only would affect the morale of the populace, but it would also be akin to killing a sick man instead of curing him.[69]

The arrangement to subsidise public health institutions via the theatres spread throughout Spain and its territories abroad, which is why most local governments showed strong support and even enthusiasm for the theatre industry, and devised a variety of ways of obtaining the approval of the clerical estate for public theatre performances.[70] In the case of Madrid, the administrators of the brotherhoods procured a written brief in 1589 from the main theologians of the nearby University of Alcalá in defence of the theatre: this text illustrates how the authorities and the Church managed to resolve the dilemma posed by what they perceived as a generous and yet immoral source of revenue.[71] A decade later the royal favourite the Duke of Lerma charged a council of the capital's theologians to set the parameters for the writing and playing of morally acceptable *comedias*. The resulting document, very much like the Alcalá brief, reveals constant negotiation between unswerving faith and necessary pragmatism. The dictum begins by conceding that "the *comedias* written and performed up until this day in the theatres, with the lascivious and dishonest jesting and acting and wiggling and dancing and singing, were unlawful and performing them was mortal sin".[72] However, the council moves on to provide five keys in order to make said 'mortal sins' into acceptable shows: 1) no lascivious material; 2) only four companies at the same time allowed in the city; 3) no female players; 4) no shows during Lent or on Advent Sundays and 5) religious theatre could only be performed in churches and convents.[73] This list was strikingly similar to that of London's City Fathers from 1585, which also included restrictions on performing during holidays and on the authorised number of companies. The existence of such documents was crucially important because it meant that, even though the English and Spanish players did not fully comply with these rules (most notably, women did act professionally in Spain), the possibility that performing plays could be tolerated by the religious authorities was publicly acknowledged.

Additional steps were also put in place to make sure that all plays performed met a minimum standard of morality, and thus guaranteed the integrity and overall respectability of the theatres. In England, prompt copies of the plays – that is, the texts used during rehearsals – had to pass through the hands of the Master of the Revels before making it onto the stage. In Spain, the playtext had to be approved by the *censor*, the *fiscal* [prosecutor] and the *protector del hospital* [hospital administrator] – with the occasional supervision of the Inquisition – in order to guarantee its moral viability.[74] With all these safeguards and with overwhelming across-the-board endorsement from all strata of society, the theatres quietly held their own in the face of most reservations and restrictions, particularly those prohibiting the establishment of playhouses in certain areas of the cities. Only crucial events in the middle decades of the seventeenth century – royal mourning in Spain, and revolution in England – would succeed in temporarily closing the playhouses. Indeed, as time went by the geographical and social limits once imposed on the theatrical community became more and more permeable, which is why the map of playhouse locations of the seventeenth century, as illustrated and explained in the following section, looks completely different from that of the commercial playgrounds' early years.

Playhouse Locations after Consolidation

The slow but progressive relocation of commercial secular theatrical practice which took place during the early modern period, from the social margins of vagrancy to the centre of culture and entertainment, was reflected in the topographical changes of the early modern English and Spanish theatrical landscapes. The calculations behind opening a playhouse for a group of little-better-than-vagabonds or for players with widespread popular support and (more often than not) political, aristocratic or royal patronage differed substantially. Both in England and in Spain, the turn of the seventeenth century saw new opportunities flourish for the theatrical community. Above all, the social acceptance of commercial performance culture from the opening of the first purpose-built playhouses onward became increasingly manifest in the expanding geographical boundaries of the playgrounds, as previously inaccessible or uncharted areas – on both a local and national scale – slowly became available for theatrical terraforming. And nowhere was this trend better exemplified than in the emergence of indoor public theatres within the previously out-of-bounds City of London.

The early seventeenth century saw the incorporation into London's commercial theatre circuit of a handful of new venues, two of which looked nothing like the rest: these were small, roofed and candlelit purpose-built venues in the heart of the City. Not that the Blackfriars playhouse and the playhouse in St. Paul's, as they were commonly known, were newly built: they first opened in the late 1570s, more or less around the same time as the Shoreditch amphitheatres. However, there were some significant differences between these intramural venues and their suburban counterparts. For starters, instead of for commercial purposes they were initially established as the spaces in which city's boy choirs rehearsed their material in front of a paying elite audience before taking their show to court before the queen, and only the capital's aristocracy was allowed to witness these performances. It must be noted that these choirs were not the only ones that charged for access to their 'rehearsals': according to Andy Kesson, the Queen's Men were "allowed to perform in and around London in 1583 for exactly the same reason (nor was this unusual: in 1581 the city aldermen allowed an unnamed adult company to play in London 'for that they are to present certayne playes before the quenes Ma[jesty]')", which suggests that there may have not been much difference between rehearsing in front of a paying audience and performing publicly.[75] Much more importantly, though, is that the style of playwriting for the Blackfriars and St. Paul's playhouses catered to a different audience than that of the open-air theatres in Shoreditch. According to the prologue of John Lyly's *Sappho and Phao* (c. 1584), the plays written for those spaces and audiences looked to "moue inward delight, not outward lightnesse" (which we can assume was Lyly's opinion of what was taking place in the Theatre and Curtain).[76] Eventually, the two indoor theatres closed their doors, and during the 1590s the only active purpose-built theatre venues in the capital were the suburban amphitheatres, which continued to operate alongside the City's inns. However, the re-emergence of the St. Paul's and Blackfriars playhouses in 1599 and 1600 respectively yet this time catering to a broader public – and, in a way, taking up the baton of the inns, which had by then closed their doors as well – changed London's theatrical landscape forever.

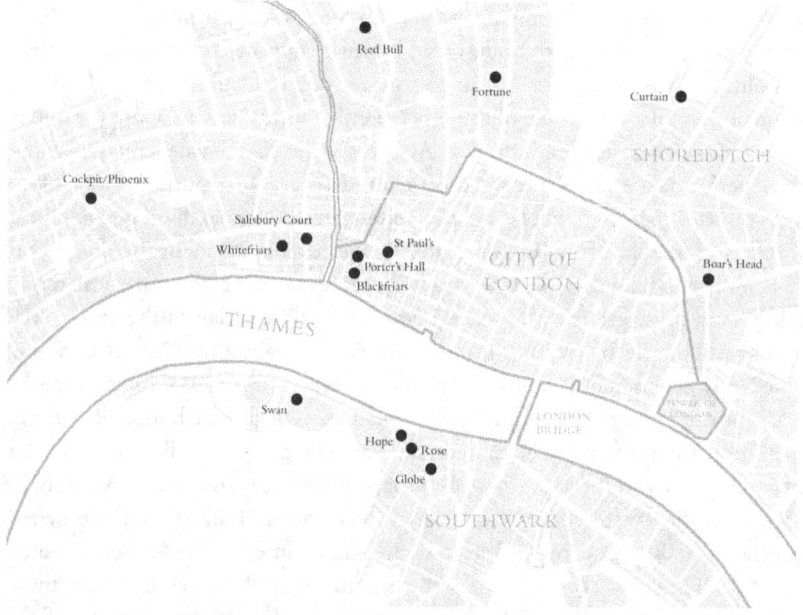

FIGURE 1.7 Map of seventeenth-century London and its commercial playhouses

Even though this time around the playhouses opened under new management and with new artistic and/or commercial objectives, a lot of the old theatres' conceptual foundations were recycled along with the buildings themselves. In reactivating the decade-long quiet indoor playhouses, the St. Paul's and Blackfriars impresarios took advantage not only of the architectural but also – and more importantly – the legal framework set up for the benefit of the previous tenants. Much like their suburban open-air counterparts, the intramural indoor venues were located in districts of London with unusual jurisdictional properties, known as 'ecclesiastical liberties'. As the name suggests, these areas were – at one point, in any case – property of the Church, and thus outside the City's rule. This was the case of the Blackfriars precinct, once the home to the City's Dominican Order's priory; after Henry VIII expropriated the land in 1538, the monarchy used the buildings in the district either for administrative purposes, to reward loyal subjects, or to make a steady profit out of renting or selling the properties to wealthy individuals. The precinct, however, did not fall under somebody else's control after the expropriation: it was, so to speak, on its own, even if loosely overseen by the City fathers. This allowed a man by the name of Richard Farrant to lease out and reconvert some of the rooms of the west end of the old Blackfriars' Priory into a performance venue, the first Blackfriars theatre, at about the same time the Theatre and Curtain amphitheatres in Shoreditch opened their doors.[77] The first St. Paul's playhouse also was built in the late 1570s, and even though it remains unclear exactly where it was located, most scholars concur that it was somewhere within the cathedral's grounds and thus "in the jurisdiction of the dean of the Cathedral, not the City".[78] These two locations were among the very few areas of the City in which a playhouse could be located, and even then their creation involved lengthy negotiations and skilful defensive action against the enemies of the theatre. In the end, and much like the Theatre and Curtain playhouses in Shoreditch, it took a particular set of legal circumstances for the St. Paul's and Blackfriars theatres to succeed in their early exclusively aristocratic days. This success provided an important precedent for future plans to bring commercial theatrical activity inside the City walls.

Precisely because impresarios were allowed to take advantage of the legal precedents thanks to which the first St. Paul's and Blackfriars were built, they also inherited all the other social and financial foundations of the old venues that set them apart from the popular playhouses outside the City walls. With these new spaces available in the heart of the capital, upper-class theatregoers no longer had to travel to the suburbs to enjoy popular theatre shows. Even more importantly, they would have no more need to rub shoulders with their poorer neighbours during performances: the entrance fees to Blackfriars and St. Paul's – up to five times those of the amphitheatres – ensured somewhat of a distinctive atmosphere in comparison to what the suburban playhouses had to offer.[79] This is why these theatres were oftentimes referred to as 'private': despite being theoretically public, their prices were so restrictive that few people outside the capital's elite would have been tempted to spend an average Londoner's full day's wages to attend a play.[80]

The Blackfriars playhouse is the best-known example of this new array of elite spaces that had become available within England's commercial theatre landscape with the turn of the century. The closest point within the City walls to the Court in Westminster and the Inns of Court (the city's law schools), the Blackfriars precinct's history as a favoured location of the crown and the aristocratic character of the district's leading inhabitants became one of the 'private' theatre's calling cards. In addition to its legal uniqueness as a former ecclesiastical liberty, the Blackfriars – along with the Whitefriars, the other such liberty – also enjoyed a special social standing: "in the minds of Londoners, the liberties were distinct from the city itself" and found mention as such in public discourse.[81] Moreover, the former priory had an extraordinary amount of green space for a district within the City due to the two cloisters and the many gardens that went back to the Friary's earlier days. In a city that was seen as claustrophobic, smoky and contagious, Blackfriars was one of the few such pockets one could find, along with the neighbouring Inns of Court and the expanding layout of new squares in the western suburbs.[82] Additionally, the whole district was surrounded by walls, a rarity within the City, and served as an elitist gated community that unequivocally separated those few within from the many without.[83] Needless to say, the ecology of the privileged Blackfriars precinct, and to a lesser also that of the neuralgic urban centre that was St. Paul's Churchyard, had very little to do with that of the suburban playhouses that held a monopoly in London's commercial playing during the second half of the sixteenth century. Together they provided England's capital's playing and playgoing communities alike with a new set of allures.[84]

The emergence of the commercial 'private' theatres in London, located somewhere in between the aristocratic court and the demotic open-air playhouses, seems to have addressed the particular needs of the growing wealthy non-aristocratic middle class of the city. They were not seen as replacements for the amphitheatres, at least not immediately; new amphitheatres kept opening in the extramural districts of the capital, mostly as a way of replacing the ageing ones of the sixteenth century. The indoor playhouses were instead complementary venues that allowed the theatrical community to engage in different ways with the city, and to tap into both old and new audience markets with a broader range of theatrical supply.[85] In fact, many impresarios or companies who owned amphitheatres began to lease the new indoor playhouses as a way of extending their reach on the theatrical map.[86] The second Blackfriars and St. Paul's were followed by the opening of the briefly-lived Porter's Hall indoor theatre (1615), also in the Blackfriars precinct, and the Whitefriars (c. 1606–1607), Cockpit/Phoenix (c. 1616) and Salisbury's Court (1629) indoor playhouses in the upper-end western suburbs between the City and Westminster, in what would eventually become London's preeminent theatrical hub, the West End, thus ending the City's and elite suburbs' attempts to prevent hosting public playhouses.[87]

That history did not exactly follow the same path as London's in Spain's larger cities was especially noticeable in Madrid. There the Spanish theatrical community had access to a relatively well-regarded district from the very beginning, to which neither the upper nor lower classes had any significant objections; as a result, the locations did not change. In Seville, where during the sixteenth-century playhouses had opened throughout the city and in very diverse neighbourhoods, when it came time to replace their old *corrales* with two new state-of-the-art venues, the Coliseo (1607) and the Corral de la Montería (1626), their owners chose to do so in those areas in the city that could attract audiences from both ends of the social spectrum equally.[88]

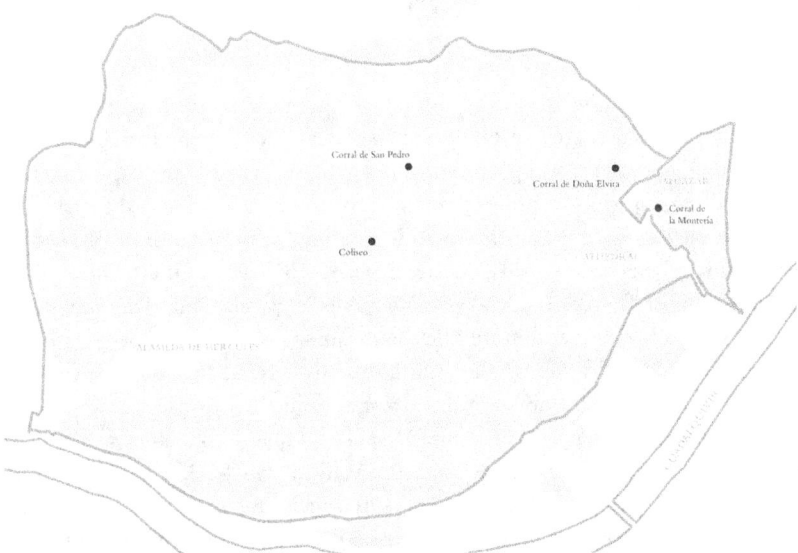

FIGURE 1.8 Map of seventeenth-century Seville and its *corrales de comedias*

Where the paths of early modern England and Spain's theatre history did meet during their phases of social consolidation, however, is in the emergence of peripheral playhouses outside the main theatrical centres. Commercial secular theatre, now an established cultural and artistic practice rooted in the large cities that was slowly but steadily shedding the stigma that weighed it down in its early years, began to extend its presence to smaller cities and large market towns that were striving to acquire some of the cultural capital of the metropolis. This effort culminated in several of these smaller centres opening their own purpose-built theatrical venues and thus quickly becoming attractive destinations for acting troupes touring the country or looking for a new home. That we know of, in the first decade of seventeenth-century England theatres were built in the cities of Bristol and York, and in the market town of Prescot. Their number is modest because, as Siobhan Keenan explains in her book about touring theatre in Shakespeare's time, regional towns and their surrounding populations were not great enough to provide the kind of large, regular, and profitable audiences afforded by the metropolitan community. Raising money to build a playhouse or to convert an existing building into a theatre was also potentially more difficult in a provincial town. There were generally fewer wealthy people who could be approached to act as investors in such a venture. It is probably no coincidence that two of the three provincial towns recorded as being home to a Renaissance playhouse were among England's largest and wealthiest regional towns.[89]

London's clear predominance in the cultural and artistic landscape, in addition to the country's theatrical culture being for the most part privately financed, did make opening permanent and purpose-built playhouses outside the capital before the 1660s a rare and risky venture: that somebody eventually decided to take on those odds highlights the good health and standing of the business of playing in England during the Stuart years. Were England to have registered more institutional support for commercial playing in its regional centres at the time, perhaps it would have looked more like the theatre-studded landscape of Golden Age Spain. Thanks to its decentralised nature, as well as the regular involvement of local governments and publicly funded charities in the theatrical business and the relatively simple process of recycling a *corral de vecinos* into a *corral de comedias*, there were many more playhouses outside Madrid and Seville in Spain than outside London in England. Indeed, there is solid documentary evidence for *corrales* and *casas de comedias* built during the late sixteenth and early seventeenth centuries in over twenty cities and towns (as shown in the map on p. 15) and that is counting only those in the Iberian Peninsula and not in Spain's large overseas empire.

Numbers aside, it is important to recognise that the emergence of non-metropolitan purpose-built theatres in both countries at roughly the same time is not a coincidence. Seen as more legitimate thanks to their association with the courts and capitals, the opposition to the building of playhouses in smaller cities and towns was less effective than in London or Madrid. Moreover, it was common to see them located in centric and important streets or squares in ways beyond the reach of the theatre impresarios of the capitals. The Bristol playhouse was located in the relatively centric Wine Street, and the one in Prescot was on the town's High Street; Dublin's Werburgh Street indoor playhouse stood at the heart of Ireland's capital right next to the city's castle, and while the precise location of the short-lived York playhouse is not known it almost surely stood within the city walls.[90] This was also the case in most of Spain's secondary cities and towns: Alcalá, Toledo and Almagro went as far as to locate their theatres in their *plazas mayores* [main squares], with the support and even the active involvement of the local government in helping to make available such prime real estate.[91] The same even applied to a territory outside of Spain that was also part of the Habsburg Empire: the Pateo das Arcas (1593), a Castilian-style *corral* built in Lisbon by a Spaniard and intended for Spanish touring troupes visiting the Portuguese capital, was located a mere block away from city's popular market square, the Praça do Rossio.[92]

The visible acceptance – and in some cases endorsement – of the building of playhouses in various cities and towns in both England and Spain is another manifestation of the shifting perception society had of commercial theatre, as it moved steadily from the darkness of the margins toward the spotlight. In terms both of the growing number of playhouses at a local and national level, as well as the location of these venues within their own specific environments, the final decade of the sixteenth and the first half of the seventeenth centuries witnessed the entire commercial secular theatre industry ascending the social, economic and cultural ladder to the higher rungs of wealth and prestige. That this display of collective upward mobility found additional reflection in the architectural features of the playhouses themselves will be examined in detail in the following chapter.

Notes

1 Howell, *Londinopolis*, sig. A2v.
2 Castile was the largest kingdom within the conglomeration of territories that made up the 'composite monarchy', to use John Elliott's expression, that was Habsburg Spain. Madrid, as the capital of Castile and seat of the monarchy since 1561, was therefore the *de facto* capital of the Spanish kingdoms. More in Elliott, "A Europe of Composite Monarchies", as well as Feros, *Speaking of Spain*, pp. 12–47.
3 Keene, "Material London in Time and Space", p. 57.
4 Such was the geo-ideological distance between London (and its suburbs) from the city of Westminster that, despite their physical proximity, Elizabethan cartographer John Norden decided to present them in separate maps in his *Speculum Britanniae* (1593), pp. 31, 59. Anecdotally, even as late as 1658, the founder of the Quaker movement George Fox refers to Westminster and London as separate entities in his journal; after staying at the Earl of Newport's house on the Longacre in Westminster, he "passed to London". *The Journal of George Fox*, p. 262.
5 More on London as an early modern city-state in Keene, "Metropolitan comparisons", pp. 466–476. Additionally, James Robertson analyses the unusual nature of Stuart London's capitality in his "Stuart London and the Idea of a Royal Capital City".
6 See Beier and Finlay, "The Significance of the Metropolis", p. 4; Boulton, "London 1540-1700", p. 315; Clark, *European Cities and Towns*, pp. 120–122; Harding, "City, capital, and metropolis", p. 117; Rappaport, *Worlds within Worlds*, pp. 61–86; Sacks, "London's Dominion", p. 23. More on the demography of early modern London in Finlay and Shearer, "Population Growth and Suburban Expansion", and Harding, "The Population of London, 1550-1700".
7 "The London Journal of Alessandro Magno, 1562", p. 141.
8 Harding, "City, capital and metropolis", pp. 118–129; Keene, "Growth, Modernisation and Control", pp. 8, 11. For a vivid narration of London's demographic and geographic growth during Shakespeare's lifetime see Porter, *Shakespeare's London*, pp. 33–58.
9 Keene, "Growth, Modernisation and Control", p. 7.
10 Here I paraphrase Jesús Escobar's *The Plaza Mayor and the Shaping of Baroque Madrid*, p. 26. Other reasons for wanting to leave Toledo, which included the city's lack of

housing and its topographical challenges, are listed in Kagan, "The Toledo of El Greco", p. 37.
11 Alvar Ezquerra, "Todo empezó en 1561", pp. 118–119; Río Barredo, *Madrid, Urbs Regia*, pp. 5–11. Alvar Ezquerra's "La villa de Madrid vista por los extranjeros en la Alta Edad Moderna" briefly depicts what Madrid was like before it became the capital by drawing on period accounts and descriptions. The lack of an important port may well be the most important contrast between Madrid and London as capital cities, since it is often suggested that it was the Thames that made London the metropolis it was and still is. Joseph Ward paraphrases John Stow when he writes that "London was the capital city of England primarily because of its location on the Thames – far enough inland that it was protected from foreign invasion and yet close enough to sea for the ships to take advantage of the tides" (Ward, "The Taming of the Thames", p. 57).
12 Clark, *European Cities and Towns*, p. 162. During the early modern period, Madrid never officially became a city despite its being the largest urban centre in the country, keeping instead its official title of *villa y corte* [town and court]. From now on I will refer to Madrid as either *villa* or city indistinctly.
13 Alvar Ezquerra, "Todo empezó en 1561", p. 133. A more detailed breakdown of immigration to Madrid in the sixteenth and seventeenth centuries can be found in Carbajo Isla, *La población de la villa de Madrid*, pp. 115–131 and Alvar Ezquerra, *El nacimiento de una capital europea*, pp. 15–104.
14 In 1600, the combined population of the central regions of Spain (Castile, León, Guadalajara, Toledo and Madrid) was roughly 2,930,000 persons, nearly 31% of the Kingdom. These numbers reflect Spain's highly ruralised demographic patterns, since only 2% of the country's population lived in the capital despite its considerable growth. In contrast, London amassed 5% of England's population in 1600 and around 10% in 1700. More in Díez Borque, *Sociedad y teatro en la España de Lope de Vega*, p. 120; Finlay and Shearer, "Population Growth and Suburban Expansion", pp. 38–39; Marín and Mas, "Madrid", pp. 31–61. More on London's 'magnetic' power in early modern England in Finlay, *Population and Metropolis*, pp. 1–19.
15 Carbajo Isla, *La población de la villa de Madrid*, p. 6; Marín and Mas, "Madrid", p. 36.
16 Ringrose, *Madrid and the Spanish Economy*, pp. 4, 66. "The implications of that role", David Ringrose writes in a different publication, "are embedded in the phrase 'Solo Madrid es Corte', which translates as 'Only Madrid is the seat of the Court'. Yet it can also be read to say 'Madrid is no more than the royal court,' a translation with many ambiguities. The Ancien Regime's concept of monarchy defined bureaucracy and aristocracy as personal subordinates of the King, and therefore as parts of his household. Since Madrid consisted largely of that court, and of the artisans, priests, entertainers, servants, labourers, and merchants who served the court, both meanings were accurate. Thus, we cannot understand Madrid as a transmitter of values without seeing this identity between King, courtier, bureaucrat, and citizen of Madrid". Ringrose, "The Paradoxes of a Royal City", p. 20. For differing points of view on Madrid's regional, national and international role see López García (ed.), *El impacto de la Corte en Castilla*, pp. 151–229, 300–322, 377–487; Madrazo and Pinto (eds.), *Madrid en la época moderna*; Zofío Llorente, *Gremios y artesanos en Madrid, 1550-1650*, p. 117.
17 Albardonedo Freire, *El urbanismo de Sevilla durante el reinado de Felipe II*, p. 63; Bolaños Donoso, "Reescritura de la vida y memoria del corral de comedias de San Pedro", pp. 301–305; Clark, *European Cities and Towns*, pp. 112–113; Collantes de Terán et al., "Sevilla", pp. 188–189; Zofío Llorente, *Gremios y artesanos en Madrid*, pp. 132–149; Zofío Llorente, "Trabajo y emigración en el Madrid de los siglos XVI y XVII", pp. 98–99. For a detailed summary of early modern Seville's demography see Sentaurens, "Séville dans la seconde moitié du XVIe siècle".
18 Gail Kern Paster aptly describes London as a "world-city" in *The Idea of the City in the Age of Shakespeare*, p. 6.

19 As cited in Finkelpearl, *John Marston of the Middle Temple*, p. 13.
20 Burke, "Popular Culture in Seventeenth-Century London", p. 39; Davies as cited in Sacks, "London's Dominion", p. 20. A good and thorough explanation of the Elizabethan festive calendar – with particular emphasis on its relation to the world of theatre – can be found in Laroque, *Shakespeare's Festive World*, pp. 78–175.
21 More on public recital of poetry in the Netherlands in Cohen, *Drama of a Nation*, pp. 89–96; Marnef, "Chambers of Rhetoric and the Transmission of Religious Ideas in the Low Countries"; Sanz Ayán, *Hacer escena*, pp. 84–90; van Bruaene, "'A wonderfull tryumfe, for the wynnyng of a pryse'".
22 Kathman, "The Rise of Commercial Playing in 1540s London".
23 Kathman, "The London Playing Bust of the Early 1580s and the Economics of Elizabethan Theater", p. 46.
24 Davies, *What is a Playhouse?*. For the main portal of the REED project see http://reed.utoronto.ca. The *Before Shakespeare* project is housed in http://www.beforeshakespeare.com.
25 Andrew Gurr explains that "London was the only really large market for the peculiarly portable commodity that the playing companies had to sell". Gurr, *The Shakespearian Playing Companies*, pp. 12–13.
26 Burke, "Popular Culture in Seventeenth-Century London", p. 39.
27 Merritt, "Introduction", p. 4; Stow, *A Survey of London, Vol. I*, p. 92. As Jean Howard notes, daily life in early modern London is better understood by reading Stow's *Survey* side by side with Thomas Dekker's pamphlet *The Gull's Hornbook* (1609), the other side of the coin to Stow's pessimistic depiction of London decay. "If Stow's text is steeped in nostalgia", Howard writes, "Dekker's pamphlet is entirely of the moment. If Stow hardly mentions the theater, Dekker makes it central to the daily life of the London gallant". Howard, *Theater of a City*, pp. 6–7. More on Stow's writing style in Archer, "The Nostalgia of John Stow".
28 Rey Hazas, "El Madrid literario en la Edad Moderna", pp. 362–365. See also Gutiérrez, *La espada, el rayo y la pluma*, pp. 35–42. The writer Alonso de Salas Barbadillo (1581–1635) sourly described Madrid's continuous influx of immigrants in the seventeenth century as that of "a shared and universal mother to all foreigners, yet a step-mother to her own children" ["patria común y madre universal de los extranjeros, madrastra de sus hijos propios"], as cited in Barbadillo de la Fuente, "Madrid en la obra de Salas Barbadillo", p. 241 [my translation].
29 For more on cultural and festive activity in Habsburg Madrid see Río Barredo, *Madrid, Urbs Regia*; Escobar, *The Plaza Mayor and the Shaping of Baroque Madrid*, pp. 174–186; Thomas, *Madrid: A Traveller's Companion*, pp. 395–410.
30 Why Lope did not follow the court to Valladolid remains a mystery even today. Elizabeth Wright suggests that his staying behind in Madrid, where the best and largest *corrales* in the country were located, was the catalyst that propelled his career as a commercial playwright. More in Wright, *Pilgrimage to Patronage*, pp. 67–73.
31 As Josef Oehrlein points out, Madrid was the only place in which actors could exercise their profession in all three of its branches: public *corral* theatre, court theatre, and Corpus Christi dramatic performances. Oehrlein, *El actor en el teatro del Siglo de Oro*, p. 12.
32 While it is unquestionable that Madrid was the single most important concentration of urban architectural investment during the Habsburg era – on this see above all Escobar, *The Plaza Mayor and the Shaping of Baroque Madrid* – its image lagged behind that of many other capital cities of the time. Above all, it had to compete for royal funds with many neighbouring royal properties as well, most prominently the El Escorial palace northwest of the capital; in fact, it was not until the later eighteenth century, under the Bourbon king Charles III, when Madrid began to be rebuilt according to an ambitious, planned program of construction, infrastructural improvements, and urban embellishment. More

in Cervera Vera, *Las mejoras urbanas en el Madrid de Carlos III*; Ringrose, "A Setting for Royal Authority", p. 232; Equipo Madrid, *Carlos III, Madrid y la Ilustración*, especially pp. 125–151.
33. The major study on this subject is García Bernal, *El fasto público en la España de los Austrias*, pp. 263–392.
34. For a full list of the *corrales de comedias* in the Iberian Peninsula visit *SdOCORRALES: Corrales de Comedias del Siglo de Oro Español* (http://www.sdocorrales.com), an interactive map and database locating and documenting all the Spanish and Portuguese playhouses of the sixteenth and seventeenth centuries.
35. Sentaurens, "Los corrales de comedia de Sevilla", p. 71.
36. Davies, *What is a Playhouse?*, pp. 5–7; Wickham et al. (eds.), *English Professional Theatre*, pp. 290–294.
37. For more see Kathman, "The London Playing Bust of the Early 1580s and the Economics of Elizabethan Theater", pp. 45–49; Kesson, "Playhouses, Plays, and Theater History", pp. 29–30.
38. More on the Shoreditch playhouses in Cruickshank, *Spitalfields*, pp. 75–87; Ingram, *The Business of Playing*, pp. 182–238.
39. In addition to the previously cited population statistics, it is worth noting that the City of London was relatively small in geographical size: approximately 3 km from east to west, and considerably less from north to south. See Browner, "Wrong Side of the River", s.n.; Clark, "The Multi-Centred Metropolis", p. 251; Keene, "Growth, Modernisation and Control", p. 11. More on the term 'middling sort' and social ranks in England and London in Earle, "The Middling Sort in London"; Wrightson, "'Sorts of People' in Tudor and Stuart England".
40. Schofield, "The Topography and Buildings of London", p. 297.
41. Howard, *Theater of a City*, p. 3. For a classic account of western London's residential development see Brett-James, *The Growth of Stuart London*, pp. 151–186, as well as Lawrence Stone's "The Residential Development of the West End of London in the Seventeenth Century", which builds on Brett-James' study.
42. Stow, *A Survey of London, Vol. II*, p. 52; Keene, "Growth, Modernisation and Control", pp. 24–25. More in Schofield, "The Topography and Buildings of London", p. 309.
43. Browner, "Wrong Side of the River", s.n.
44. Browner, "Wrong Side of the River", s.n.
45. Boulton, *Neighbourhood and Society*, pp. 9–12, 20–21.
46. Stow, *A Survey of London, Vol. II*, p. 63.
47. Keene, "Material London in Time and Space", pp. 65–66; Browner, "Wrong Side of the River", s.n.
48. Stow, *A Survey of London, Vol. II*, p. 54. More in Browner, "Wrong Side of the River". Nevertheless, Paul Griffiths is right in pointing out that although there is no doubt that some of London's neighbouring areas were considered 'suburbs of sin' (Aldgate, Clerkenwell, Southwark, East Smithfield and St. Katherine's, to name a few), a significant amount of prostitution activity took place within the City walls. Griffiths, "The Structure of Prostitution in Elizabethan London", p. 54. For a counterpoint to the conventional narrative of Southwark as being Elizabethan London's red-light district see Salkeld, *Shakespeare Among the Courtesans*, especially ch. 3.
49. Kathman, "The London Playing Bust of the Early 1580s and the Economics of Elizabethan Theater", p. 45. For the source argumentation see Ingram, *The Business of Playing*, pp. 121–145.
50. Dillon, *Theatre, Court & City*, p. 33.
51. A clear summary of early modern London's liberties, a topic much debated ever since Steven Mullaney foregrounded it in his seminal *The Place of the Stage* (1988), is Kozusko, "Taking Liberties".

52 García de León Álvarez, "El corral de comedias de Almagro", p. 20; García de León Álvarez, "La construcción del Corral de Comedias de Almagro", pp. 17–18; Mouyen, "Las casas de comedies de Valencia", p. 93; Sentaurens, *Seville et le théatre*, pp. 82–83.
53 More in Amelang, "¿Qué es un teatro?".
54 "… se debía ante todo a su situación geográfica, que le permitía ejercer una atracción no sólo en los eclesiásticos, los aristócratas, los tratantes, los navieros o los artesanos que formaban la población habitual del barrio, sino también en los viajeros, los indianos, los marinos, los soldados de la armada". Sentaurens, "Los corrales de comedia de Sevilla", pp. 75–76 [my translation].
55 "… no alcanzó el éxito y la fama de su predecesor, a causa del alejamiento y la mala reputación del barrio en que estaba ubicado". Sentaurens, "Los corrales de comedia de Sevilla", p. 75 [my translation]. As for the Corral de las Atarazanas being the first purpose-built playhouse, what is meant here is that, unlike its predecessors, the playhouse was built in an empty orchard, instead of repurposing an existing *corral de vecinos*. More in Bolaños Donoso, "Acerca de la ubicación del corral de las Atarazanas"; Sentaurens, "Los corrales de comedia de Sevilla", p. 75; Shergold, *A History of the Spanish Stage*, pp. 191–192.
56 A detailed account of Seville's theatrical life in the sixteenth and seventeenth centuries can be found in Ball, *Treating the Public*, pp. 50–67. For an overview of the different neighbourhoods in sixteenth-century Seville see Albardonedo Freie, *El urbanismo de Sevilla durante el reinado de Felipe II*, pp. 55–115.
57 Larquié, "Barrios y parroquias urbanas", pp. 59–61.
58 Pinto Crespo and Madrazo Madrazo (eds.), *Madrid. Atlas histórico de la ciudad*, p. 115.
59 More on the social and economic disparities between these two sections of the parish in Alvar Ezquerra, *El nacimiento de una capital europea*, pp. 246–254; García Sánchez, "Pobreza, desigualdad y redes sociales en dos ciudades europeas", pp. 121–132; García Sánchez, "Urbanismo, demografía y pobreza en Madrid", pp. 74–75.
60 Villalba Pérez, "Notas sobre la prostitución en Madrid a comienzos del siglo XVII", pp. 516–517; Villalba Pérez, *¿Pecadoras o delincuentes?*, pp. 252–254. Baroque writer Alonso de Castillo Solórzano refers to the parish's sexual and theatrical activities as prominent and interconnected attractions for the capital's *mozos* [gallants] in his satirical novel *Las harpías en Madrid* (1631). "The neighbourhoods near San Sebastián," he writes, "were the most frequented in all of Madrid by the gallant youth, due to both its proximity to the two *corrales de comedias* as well as to the many ladies of the profession who live there" ["los barrios cerca de San Sebastián eran los más frecuentados de todo Madrid de la gente moza, así por estar cerca de los dos corrales de comedias, como por vivir en ellos muchas damas de la profesión"]. Castillo Solorzano, *Las harpías de Madrid*, p. 53 [my translation].
61 Stubbes, *The Anatomie of Abuses*, sigs. L8-L8v. For a detailed analysis of the rhetoric of religiously motivated anti-theatrical manifestos see Streete, *Protestantism and Drama in Early Modern England*, pp. 129-139. For an explanation as to why a playwright such as Anthony Munday also participated in the writing of anti-theatrical pamphlets see Hill, "'He hath changed his coppy'".
62 It is worth noting that, except in a handful of cases, their attacks are directed strictly against commercial performances. In fact, the Jesuit schools in Spain and other Catholic countries were well known for their instruction in dramatic theory and practice, as long as it was oriented toward a better understanding of Christian doctrine. More in Brockey, "Jesuit Pastoral Theatre on an Urban Stage"; Greer and Junguita, "Economies of the Early Modern Spanish Stage", pp. 34–35; and most importantly Menéndez Peláez, *Los Jesuitas y el Teatro en el Siglo de Oro*, pp. 11–97. Similarly, in England, the first indoor private performances in playhouses such as the pre-1606 Blackfriars were condoned on grounds of their benefiting the boy actors' education. More on this below in pp. 87–88.

63 "Por eso no debemos de extrañar que los varones graves y piadosos comenzasen á preocuparse de semejantes diversiones y llegasen á pedir algunos su cesación inmediata". Cotarelo y Mori, *Bibliografía de las controversias sobre la licitud del teatro en España*, p. 18 [my translation]. This large volume collates a rich and diverse set of texts written by a wide range of authors for and (especially) against the theatre in early modern Spain. Other than Cotarelo y Mori, a detailed summary of religious publications for and against the theatre under Philip II can be found in Suárez García, "La licitud del teatro en el reinado de Felipe II".

64 "... la licencia que reina en el teatro, de la que especialmente hablaremos, hace que no sea otra cosa que una oficina de liviandades y escándalo, donde se depravan las gentes de toda condición, edad y sexo, en la que con acciones simuladas se enseñan los vicios verdaderos". Mariana, "De los espectáculos", pp. 426-427 [my translation]. More on Juan de Mariana and his criticism of commercial theatre in Suárez García, "Enemigos del teatro en el Siglo de Oro". Another important Jesuit theologian, the Portuguese Pedro de Fonseca, wrote very similar texts against the theatre, which can be found summarised in Granja, "Un documento inédito contra las comedias en el s. XVI". Additionally, a detailed analysis and transcription of a similarly anti-theatrical anonymous treatise is Marino, "*Del peligro de oír comedias lascivas y asistir a bailes y danzas*". For a broader survey of Jesuit opposition and activism against the commercial theatre of the Golden Age see Menéndez Peláez, *Los Jesuitas y el Teatro en el Siglo de Oro*, pp. 105–133.

65 "... los theatros, que ya auian de estar callados, donde estas representaciones se hazian ...". Guzmán, *Bienes de el honesto trabajo*, pp. 272–301, quotation on p. 272 [my translation]; White as cited in Wilson, *Life in Shakespeare's England*, p. 228.

66 "El corral de comedias es un reflejo exacto, y cuantificable en dinero, de la estructura social del Madrid de los Austrias; un microcosmos social que refleja, a la perfección, la inasequibilidad de los estratos superiores, aunque, ilusoriamente, todos convivían, por dos horas, en un mismo lugar, participando de un espectáculo común". Díez Borque, *Sociedad y teatro en la España de Lope de Vega*, p. 141 [my translation]; Gurr, *Playgoing in Shakespeare's London*, pp. 65–66, 191–204. A good joint summary of the anti-theatrical traditions in England and Spain is Ball, "'Beautiful Serpents' and 'Cathedras of Pestilence'".

67 Gurr, *The Shakespearean Stage*, p. 36.

68 Ball, *Treating the Public*, pp. 21–25. See also Díez Borque, *El teatro en el siglo XVII*, pp. 20–21; Oehrlein, *El actor en el teatro del Siglo de Oro*, p. 210; Sanz Ayán and García García, *Teatros y comediantes en el Madrid de Felipe II*, p. 5, 10–11.

69 More in Mackay, *Life in a Time of Pestilence*, pp. 258–260. In fact, the intertwining of Spain's commercial theatre industry and the public institutions, Rachael Ball argues, generated more anti-theatrical sentiment in Spain than in England, as the theatre's detractors viewed this connection as representative of the country's civic degeneration. More in Ball, *Treating the Public*, pp. 130–146.

70 Other major Spanish cities in which the *corrales* were used to finance charities, hospitals and other public welfare institutions include Valencia, Barcelona, Burgos, Toledo and Valladolid; for most smaller towns with playhouses the same can be said. More in Fernández Martín, "Construcción de nueva planta del antiguo teatro de Valladolid", pp. 106–110; Mouyen, "Las casas de comedies de Valencia", pp. 94–95; Sánchez Rubio, "Mesón de la Fruta y Teatro Rojas de Toledo", p. 185 The only notable exception is Seville, in which most theatres were privately run until 1609, after which the local government took control over the licensing of performances. More in García Gómez, "Los espacios teatrales y su campo de irradiación", pp. 21–25; Sentaurens, "Los corrales de comedias de Sevilla", pp. 72–75.

71 This text, signed by one Doctor Garnica and other members of the theology faculty of Alcalá, can be found in Cotarelo y Mori, *Bibliografía de las controversias sobre la licitud del*

teatro en España, p. 325. Further discussion on the matter in Sanz Ayán and García García, *Teatros y comediantes en el Madrid de Felipe II*, pp. 11–12.

72 "las comedias conforme hasta alli se habían representado y solían representarse en los teatros, con los dichos y acciones y meneos y bailes y cantares lascivos y deshonestos, eran ilícitas y era pecado mortal representarlas". As cited in Cotarelo y Mori, *Bibliografía de las controversias sobre la licitud del teatro en España*, p. 208 [my translation].

73 Cotarelo y Mori, *Bibliografía de las controversias sobre la licitud del teatro en España*, p. 208.

74 Granja, "Comedias del Siglo de Oro censuradas por la Inquisición"; Greer, "The development of national theatre", p. 243; Kinney, *Shakespeare by Stages*, pp. 141–156; White, *Renaissance Drama in Action*, p. 38.

75 Kesson, "Playhouses, Plays and Theater History", p. 28.

76 Lyly, *Sappho and Phao*, sig. A2. A brief overview of the first indoor theatres' plays in Gurr, *Playgoing in Shakespeare's London*, pp. 129–132; McCarthy, "The Influence of Children's Stagecraft".

77 Kozusko, "Taking Liberties", pp. 41–49. For the history of the Blackfriars precinct and the first Blackfriars playhouse see Dustagheer, *Shakespeare's Two Playhouses*, pp. 31–42; Shapiro, *Children of the Revels*, pp. 1–17; Smith, *Shakespeare's Blackfriars Playhouse*, chs. 1–6.

78 Berry, "Where was the Playhouse in Which the Boy Choristers of St. Paul's Cathedral Performed Plays?", p. 101. More on St. Paul's Cathedral's churchyard and the possible location of its theatre in Gair, *The Children of Paul's*, pp. 2–43, 69–72; Pérez Díez, "The 'Playhouse' at St Paul's", pp. 204–209.

79 Many references to entrance fees for the private playhouses suggest that it could have cost somewhere between six pence and two shillings (a private box went as far as half a crown, which is two and a half shillings). More in Smith, *Shakespeare's Blackfriars Playhouse*, pp. 299–301.

80 The first reference to indoor playhouses being qualified as 'private' can be found in John Marston's *The Malcontent* (1604). Additionally, as Sarah Dustagheer notes, the social connotation of what the term 'private' should not go understated, since its opposite – 'public' – could also mean 'common' and 'vulgar', in addition to its literal sense. More in Dustagheer, *Shakespeare's Two Playhouses*, pp. 30–51; Smith, *Shakespeare's Blackfriars Playhouse*, pp. 130–132; White, *Renaissance Drama in Action*, pp. 144–145. In a recent publication about theatrical activity in St Paul's during the 1560s and 70s, Callan Davies challenges this long-held assumption by referring to W. Reavley Gair's speculation of the price of entrance to the first St Paul's being as affordable as two pence. "There is therefore no reason to assume", Davies concludes, "that Paul's was, like later indoor venues, open only to 'elite' audiences". Davies, "Elizabethan Commercial Playing at St Paul's", p. 224.

81 For more on how the Blackfriars and Whitefriars liberties were discussed in early modern drama see Bly, "Playing the Tourist in Early Modern London" (citation taken from p. 62).

82 Williams, "'To recreate and refresh their dulled spirites in the sweet and wholesome ayre'", pp. 187–196. In fact, what was once the Great Cloister had been the largest Dominican cloister in the country (110 square feet). The western yards, through which one could access the stairs to the playhouse, were also of considerable size. More in Smith, *Shakespeare's Blackfriars Playhouse*, pp. 36–37, 72–73, 99, 107. In her Red Bull playhouse monograph, Eva Griffith also picks up on how much City Londoners "would value the wider space" that some of the suburbs had to offer (in her case, Clerkenwell and the green in front of St. James' Church) and would frequently visit them in their leisure hours. Griffith, *A Jacobean Company and its Playhouse*, p. 30.

83 Smith, *Shakespeare's Blackfriars Playhouse*, p. 59. More on gates and gardens as signs of status and distinction in Shakespeare's London in Crawforth et al., *Shakespeare in London*, pp. 79–86.

84 For more on the spatial and cultural geography of the Blackfriars precinct see Sanders, "'In the Friars'".
85 For an interesting exploration of the different relationships between an open-air and an indoor playhouse (the Globe and the Blackfriars), their dramatic repertories and the City of London see Dustagheer, "'And here in London, where I oft have beene".
86 For a thought-provoking contrarian take on the general assumption that outdoor and indoor playhouses were viewed as complementary see Knutson, "What was James Burbage *Thinking*???".
87 For a concise summary of London's indoor playhouses in the sixteenth and seventeenth centuries see Ichikawa, *The Shakespearean Stage Space*, pp. 8–12. For a thoughtful explanation of why these venues came to be, touching on many of the points covered in this and the following chapter (albeit without the comparative angle) see Astington, "Why the theatres changed".
88 Sentaurens, "Los corrales de comedia de Sevilla", pp. 76–79.
89 Keenan, *Travelling Players in Shakespeare's England*, p. 144.
90 More on England's provincial playhouses in Keenan, *Travelling Players in Shakespeare's England*, pp. 144–164. A brief description of theatrical practice in early modern Dublin can be found in Ball, *Treating the Public*, pp. 97–100.
91 Allen, "The Teatro Cervantes in Alcalá", pp. 148–151; García de León Álvarez, "El corral de comedias de Almagro", p. 21; García de León Álvarez, "La construcción del Corral de Comedias de Almagro", pp. 17–29; Higuera Sánchez-Pardo et al., "Alcalá de Henares", pp. 80–82; Sánchez Rubio, "Mesón de la Fruta y Teatro Rojas de Toledo", pp. 185–187.
92 Calado et al., "Lisboa", 98; Reyes Peña and Bolaños Donoso, "El Patio de las Arcas de Lisboa", pp. 267–268.

2
PLAYHOUSES

Among the many aspects of the Shakespearean and Golden Age theatrical cultures that are said to have led 'parallel lives', what most resemble each other are their playhouses. At least at first sight, it seems almost impossible to tell the two structures apart. Theatre historian John J. Allen eloquently illustrates this in the following passage:

> We are in the central box in the third story of an open-air playhouse, facing the stage that rises some five or six feet off a yard or pit. The paved yard slopes gently downward toward the stage from ground level beneath our box. Some sixty or seventy feet from us at the back of the stage is the tiring-house wall, and a curtain or arras hung from the forward edge of the floor of an upper gallery masks double doors in the center, flanked by another door at each side. Spectators are seated on benches or stools on either side of the central stage, and standees fill the yard below, between us and the stage, which is roofed by a shadow or cover supported by two posts or pillars. It is three o'clock in the afternoon, the play has just begun, and we see a character rising from beneath the stage through a trapdoor; he parts the central pair of curtains, revealing that the double doors are open to a sort of tableau. Are we in London or in Madrid? I think it is impossible to say.[1]

That the English Globe-like theatres were on the surface so similar to the Spanish *corrales de comedias* is all the more remarkable when one takes into consideration the apparent lack of communication between the two countries' playmaking communities. With this in mind, this chapter opens with a survey of the possible shared connections and points of encounter between the theatrical cultures of the two countries, in pursuit of the most likely explanation as to why the commercial theatre venues in England and Spain looked so much alike. This brief incursion into the conjectural is followed by a walkthrough of the physical characteristics of the various building types, and of the performance conditions in each. The chapter ends by exploring the role and experience of theatregoers in such unique performance settings, in contrast, both with each other as well as with present-day playhouses.

Why Did English and Spanish Theatres Look So Much Alike? A Few Genealogical Conjectures

It is important to note here that many theatres both in England and in Spain had roofs; indeed, not all English theatres had a polygonal plan. The images of the roofless *corral de comedias* and the o-shaped English playhouse come readily to mind not only because they were the best-known and most iconic (if not necessarily the most common) types of playhouses in each country, but also thanks to the popularity of the Shakespeare's Globe and the Corral de Almagro reconstructions.[2] That said, it is also important to keep in mind that many theatres both in England and Spain were indeed roofless, and a good number of London playhouses apart from the Globe were also polygonal. As to why these English roofless theatres and Spanish *corrales de comedias* looked so much alike, and so much unlike the popular or elite playhouses in other early modern European countries, we can merely speculate. If it were a coincidence, it is an extremely odd and eye-catching one, only heightened by the fact that the first long-lasting purpose-built amphitheatres in both countries appeared only a couple of years apart. For this reason alone, it is worth exploring possible points of encounter, whether genealogical or conjunctural, between the two otherwise non-communicating theatrical cultures in order to dispel the mystery that surrounds this particular aspect of Renaissance England and Spain's comparative theatre history.

An often evoked, and by far the most plausible, conjectural common ancestor is the practices of Italian *commedia dell'arte* troupes travelling abroad and exporting ideas – or requirements, rather – to both countries at the same time. All of Europe registered the transnational presence of Italian street theatre companies, not only as a backdrop for many of the structural and plot-building techniques in English and Spanish secular commercial theatre but also perhaps for the types of attributes the acting spaces featured. The influence and importance of Italian comedians, and in particular the troupe manager Alberto Naselli (or Naseli), better known as Ganassa, in the development of commercial theatre in Golden Age Spain has been widely documented. After participating in the early days of the Spanish theatrical boom in Valladolid and Seville, he became one of the earliest investors in the furnishing of Madrid's Corral de la Pacheca in 1574, for which he famously demanded the construction of "a stage [meaning a stage backdrop] and a platform, each of them roofed". Many other Italian *commedia* troupes, inspired by Ganassa's success, also relocated to Madrid, Seville and the

FIGURE 2.1 The stage of the reconstructed *Almagro* Copyright: *Corral de Comedias de* Copyright: *Concejalía de Cultura y Turismo. Ayuntamiento de Almagro*

other important theatrical centres in Spain, and were a common sight in the country's mid-sixteenth century entertainment industry.[3] In England, while the traces of *commedia* presence are not as strong, we can still find passages of unimpressed playwrights and poets such as Ben Jonson and Thomas Nashe scorning the occasional visiting Italian troupes and their craft. Not only were *commedia* performances reduced in their words to simple antics, but these critics also vehemently disapproved of professional actresses, not allowed on the English stages and whom Nashe described as "whores and common Curtizens".[4] The indisputable amount of shared theatrical practice, whether it was on a dramatic or an entrepreneurial level, among all three countries suggests an emanation of ideas flowing from Italy to the rest of the Europe through more or less direct channels, which may have led to England and Spain's playhouses to adopt such similar architectural features simultaneously yet independently.[5]

The other main explanation has been to trace the two theatrical traditions to a common intellectual heritage based on the values of the classical theatre reclaimed during the Italian Rinascimento. Frances Yates championed this loftier proposition in her influential books *The Art of Memory* (1966) and *The Theatre of the World* (1969). In the latter she went as far as to associate the structure of the English playhouse, specifically its stage disposition (more on this below), with the Serlian memory theatre Giulio Camillo designed as a mnemonic device, a goal the Paracelsian philosopher Robert Fludd similarly pursued in mid-seventeenth century England. Moreover, the almost round shape of John Brayne and James Burbage's

Shoreditch amphitheatre is, in her opinion, a purely Renaissance phenomenon with a semi-religious geometrical composition much like that of the Vitruvian man:

> And this suggested plan [of the Theatre] draws near to the Vitruvian image of man within the square and the circle, that basic Renaissance image which [John] Dee knew so well and popularized in his Preface, as a statement in symbolic geometry of man's relation to the cosmos, of man the Microcosm whose harmonious constitution relates him to the harmonies of the Macrocosm.[6]

To a certain extent, the arguments Yates presents for the classicism of English amphitheatres also apply to the *corrales* of Spain, although not as strongly. The fact that the Braynes and Burbage named their playhouse the 'Theatre', an unusual moniker that echoed the thespian culture of classical Greece and Rome, reinforces this narrative in a way that the Spanish venues cannot match.[7] Furthermore, Bruce Smith equates the circular design of the Globe and the other o-shaped theatres in London with the human vocal tract, in an effort to link the shape of the English amphitheatre to a humanistic conception of buildings; English public playhouses would have been conceived, in Smith's words, as "instruments for producing, shaping, and propagating sound". This interpretation goes hand in hand with the classical approach to architecture, inspired by the Roman architect Vitruvius, that dominated in Renaissance Europe in which the human being served as the fundamental unit of measurement.[8] These hypotheses regarding the intellectual process behind the building of these popular structures for the most part have become outdated, although they still raise some unanswered questions.[9] Above all, if either of these two genealogical theories were true, why were there no structurally similar theatre venues in Italy, France, and the rest of the countries that participated both in the Renaissance and/or in the *commedia dell'arte* network? Builders in the Middle Ages already employed the architectural technique of inserting squares into circles and vice versa, known as *ad quadratum* and used by both Vitruvius and the Bolognese Mannerist architect Sebastiano Serlio in their theatre designs. In other words, it is not necessary to travel back in time to classical days to justify the circular design of the English playhouse.[10]

The most probable scenario is that the circular design of the Theatre, the Globe and similar London playhouses derived from practical and time-tested building knowledge. For example, Andrew Gurr agrees with Smith when he argues that the polygonal o-shape was chosen in order to improve the building's acoustics and audibility. "Before audio amplification, the essence of listening was proximity to the speaker", he writes, and theatre was an art form conceived "not for people to see, but to hear".[11] Gurr's reading of the polygonal design has a clear pragmatic bent, which many other scholars share.[12] And even though in cities such as London, Madrid or Seville the odds of finding 'architects' – in opposition to mere highly skilled builders and carpenters – were higher than in most elsewheres, the popular nature of the building suggests that these early modern playhouses were a product of a vernacular tradition with surface allusions to classical motifs, names and figures as ornament. Janette Dillon's description of the English amphitheatre as a dual-nature building, equally elite and popular, must be nuanced by emphasising the predominance of the latter over the former.[13] After all, many of the features that the English and Spanish public playhouses shared have a distinctly practical purpose: an open-air space surrounded by scaffolding or other forms of boundaries seems like the ideal design with which to house a large group of people in a closed space for which an entrance fee can be charged and without having to invest in artificial lighting. Varey, who discusses Yates' theory regarding memory theatres in connection with both the English and Spanish playhouses, points out that many of these performance venues were "built in spaces determined by buildings" and thus the craftsmen were probably addressing practical issues instead of humanist ideals.[14] This fact is glaringly obvious in the case of Spain's courtyard *corrales*, but it also applies to many of their English counterparts, since the structure of some of the London playhouses was also constrained by external boundaries, including very probably the first purpose-built theatre of the city, John Brayne's Red Lion.[15] The Theatre in Shoreditch was similarly designed with strong awareness of and interrelation with the surrounding buildings. Essentially, the first performances in the rudimentary playhouses of the 1560s and 1570s in both countries could be compared with street performances, the major differences being a slightly higher level of comfort for some of the attendees, and more likely greater economic success for the performers.

In addition to the practical and classicist conjectures that connect the infrastructural similarities between English and Spanish playhouses, there are also some local theories one must take into account. The most important and intriguing of these is, by far, Richard Southern's study that connects the disposition of the Elizabethan public playhouse with the interior decoration of English country houses. In his 1973 monograph, *The Staging of Plays Before Shakespeare*, Southern very convincingly explains how the backdrop walls in Elizabethan theatre stages, with their discovery spaces, side doors and overlooking galleries, looked remarkably similar to the screens typically found in the great halls of Tudor England country houses. These large rooms were the centre of the social and administrative life of the estate, and one of their multiple functions was to hold performances of interludes prior to or in place of the development of purpose-built theatrical spaces. In the lower end of the great hall, a series of screens covered the two doors that led to the kitchen and storerooms. "In the earlier period the screens were generally without galleries", Southern explains, "but sometime in the late fifteenth century the entry passage behind began to be roofed over and the top adapted as a gallery, and as a consequence the contemporary interluders might have to work in surroundings that varied from hall to hall"; these screens, his study illustrates, grew and evolved into structures that indeed resembled an early modern stage wall.[16] Exciting as his research is, Southern's theory cannot answer why the tiring house walls of Spanish theatres were arranged in this same way. In a period in which the playmakers of both countries did not communicate directly, one would need to find an alternative yet comparable source of inspiration for the façade of the Spanish playhouse *vestuario* [tiring house], but thus far the search has yielded few results.[17] Theatre historians of early modern Spain have so far deemed Italian troupes as the likely source for why the *vestuario* looked the way it did; hence the episode cited above in which the *capocomico* Ganassa petitioned to have a stage with an arras and a canopy built in Madrid's Corral de la Pacheca, since this was the ideal stage structure for the performance of *scenari*. In addition, some Venetian-style façades designed by Sebastiano Serlio, well-known for his involvement in Italian theatrical architecture, also remind us of this tripartite tiring house disposition.[18] Could it be possible, then, that English and Spanish theatre entrepreneurs concluded that they needed the exact same stage disposition despite their having reached it by following two completely different paths?

A pragmatic reading of the conception process, which would favour the *commedia dell'arte* conjecture, nevertheless fails to explain why the Braynes and Burbage decided to use the impractical *ad quadratum* building technique for their popular playhouse. And if there truly had not been any common antecedent or any direct communication between England and Spain's commercial theatre designers, it is quite difficult to explain how the stage-platforms' dimensions in both countries were roughly the same in most playhouses (the length being approximately double the width).[19] This latter question has a rather easy, yet unsatisfactory answer: that some theatrical agents, very possibly *commedia* troupes, embedded some of their performance considerations or conventions into the English and Spanish stagecrafting process. Yet this is a cultural transfer for which we have no tangible proof. Regarding the classical motifs and/or underlining mentioned above, most theatre historians believe that the London amphitheatres owe their round design to the popular animal-baiting arenas, which could in turn have a classical inspiration of their own: the Roman Colosseum, well-known for hosting animal baiting shows as well as gladiator combats and Christian martyrdom. This is precisely the line of thought both E.K. Chambers and Glynne Wickham champion in their separate exhaustive studies of early English stages, as do David Brandon and Alan Brooke in their popular history of the Bankside district.[20] The later builders of o-shaped playhouses could have modelled their designs after Burbage's, in an attempt to follow in the footsteps and enjoy the same success of the Chamberlain's Men and their home venue. J.W. Saunders was surely right to conclude that "the design of an Elizabethan playhouse was determined less by rational choice than by the accumulation of tradition".[21]

If one however prefers to leave the arenas out of the equation, a possible explanation for the round design is that the Braynes and Burbage might have confused the Latin concepts of *theatrum* and *amphitheatrum*. After all, their playhouse had structurally more in common with the Flavian Amphitheatre than it did with the Vitruvian theatre venue. Illustrations or engravings such as that of the Roman amphitheatre in Antoine Lafréry's widely circulated *Speculum Romanae Magnificentiae,* which has the misleading caption "*Theatrvm sive Colisevm Romanvm*" (["Roman Theatre or Coliseum"] c.1558), make this abundantly clear. Lafréry's, or Lafreri's, *Speculum* was widely collected throughout Europe in the form of single standing print-sheets to be arranged as owners pleased, and soon became one of the leading examples of the 'print collecting' phenomenon. The wondrous Colosseum, Rebecca Zorach writes, "was included in almost every guidebook to Rome" in one format or another (various prints represented it, either in its accurate ruinous state or in fictional reconstruction). It is thus not unlikely that the Theatre's builders would have seen a print of the symbolic Roman building and been deceived by its caption, and that the Shoreditch playhouse may very well owe its odd polygonal shape to a muddled muse.[22]

FIGURE 2.2 Antonio Lafréry's engraving of the Roman Colosseum, with the caption "*Theatrvm Sive Colisevm Romanvm*" in his Speculum Romanae Magnificentiae. Copyright: The Trustees of the British Museum

It does appear that Thomas Heywood, in his genealogy of classical theatres in *An Apology for Actors* (1612), believed that Julius Caesar's "Amphitheatre, *Campo Martio*, in the field of *Mars*" belongs to the same category as the "semi-circle, or halfe-moone" theatres of Greece and Rome in which dramatic performances were given (and which most closely resembled God's round-shaped theatre).[23] This mistaken belief appears to have extended across Europe: a tourist visiting

Bankside in 1600 wrote in his journal that he had "heard an English play; the theatre was constructed in the style of the ancient Romans, out of wood. It was so built that spectators could very easily see from every part".[24] The Spanish poet Agustín de Rojas repeats the same myth in one of his *loas* in *El Viaje Entretenido*, first published in 1603. According to Rojas, comedies were part of society

> Since the dawn of time
>   founded, used and composed
>   by the Greeks, and the Latins,
>   and other diverse nations.
> Enlarged by the Romans,
>   who built for them
>   theatres and coliseums,
>   and the Amphitheatre, which was
> Where they would always go,
>   to listen to plays like these,
>   eight hundred thousand people,
>   and those are only the ones worth counting.[25]

While the animal-baiting arena explanation seems more probable, these theories are not mutually exclusive and to a greater or lesser degree the classical world undeniably played a role in the Braynes and Burbage's deciding for a round-like plan for their Theatre. With time, as the playgrounds of Jacobean-Caroline England and late Habsburg Spain gained in reputation, theatre impresarios of both countries introduced more and more elements of high architecture into the design of their buildings. Giulio Parigi's alumni Inigo Jones in England and Cosimo Lotti in Spain, to name the best known two, reinserted the court-environment playhouses into the classical tradition of erudite buildings (more on this below). What is more, the sophistication of public theatres rose sharply a decade or so into the seventeenth century. Andrew Gurr classifies the 1614 reconstructed Globe as belonging to a 'late', more baroque style of English amphitheatres quite unlike its 'early style' predecessor.[26] In Spain, the *corrales* built in Cordoba in 1602, Valencia in 1618 and Seville in 1626 boasted much more complex semi-circular and oval gallery arrangements than did the public theatres of the late sixteenth century.[27] That said, this ascension into high architecture would not have been possible, as I argue in the following section, if a vernacular tradition had not done the heavy lifting in the early and less reputable years of these theatrical cultures.

The Organic *Corral* vs the Immutable Theatre

Naturally, the original source designs for the early modern English and Spanish public playhouses, whatever they may have been, underwent changes in order to adjust to their new uses. Theatre builders, like any other type of craftsmen of both then and now, groped their way to success through trial by error: the motto of the Galilean scientists at the Accademia del Cimento in seventeenth-century Florence, the Dantean '*provando e riprovando*' ['try and try again'], is a testament to the value placed on empiricism even at the highest social levels. This willingness to build on the original plans, with scarce attention to a theoretical design, was even more visible in popular building, and thrown into sharpest relief when said original plans were palpably flawed. A well-known such case in England's theatre history was that of the Rose playhouse in Southwark. The Rose first opened its doors in 1587, yet it very quickly had to be closed and would not reopen until 1592. Evidence uncovered during the 1989 archaeological digs indicates that theatre impresario Philip Henslowe financed a costly and time-consuming renovation in order to deal with some significant flaws in the initial design. The yard floor's aggressive slant was levelled, and the galleries nearest to the stage were widened in order to create better visual lines with the stage after the addition of the roof or heavens, a required element in many Elizabethan plays that the first design lacked. The widening of the galleries also increased the audience capacity, and the stage itself was also modified to give it more prominence and 'thrust' as well as to place it in better geometrical relation with the rest of the building. The acting space, nevertheless, remained roughly the same (47.6 square metres).[28]

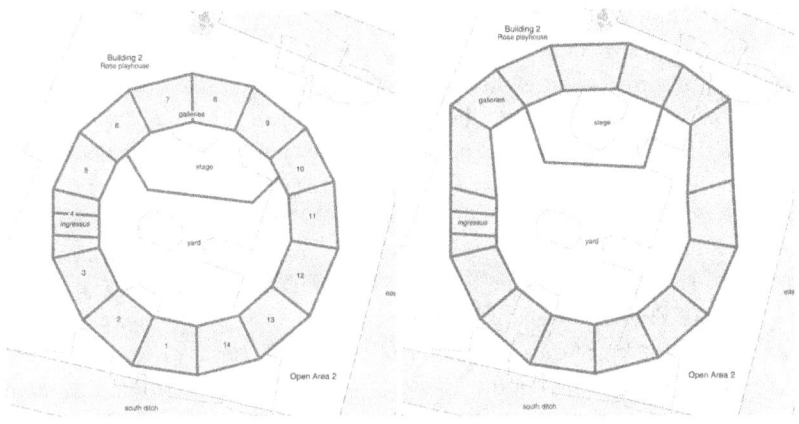

FIGURE 2.3 Estimated plans of the first (left) and second (right) designs of the Rose playhouse in Southwark Copyright: The Museum of London Archaeology

The reason why this particular incident of playhouse rebuilding is often brought up in Shakespearean theatre history is because it is practically the only one known to us, at least when discussing the iconic o-shaped amphitheatres of Elizabethan London; at least two innyards, the Boar's Head (1559–1605) and the Red Bull (1604-1642), were converted progressively and "in an *ad hoc*, pragmatic way" into rectangular amphitheatres, for instance.[29] Other than the Rose, however, the only known accounts of stand-alone, purpose-built and open-air playhouses being partially rebuilt in early modern England were the Curtain in 1612/1613 and the King's Men's Globe after it burned down in 1613 thanks to a pyrotechnical malfunction during a performance of *Henry VIII*.[30] In other words, all significant alterations to Elizabethan playhouses seem to have been motivated by inescapable necessity: barring a few exceptional exceptions, significant design malformations or a cannon accidentally setting the playhouse roof on fire, London's open-air theatres stayed roughly the same throughout their existence.

This is where the lives of England and Spain's otherwise strikingly similar-looking amphitheatres most notably departed, since the *corrales de comedia* were defined by their continuous evolution. In fact, they owe their name – *corrales* – to the building structures from which they evolved. Much as London's Boar's Head and Red Bull were converted inns, the first commercial playhouses in Spain's were recycled *corrales de vecinos*, one of the most typical urban housing typologies in the kingdom of Castile beginning in the Middle Ages. With roots in the North-African *adarve* and the Sephardic *curral*, the typical *corral de vecinos* was (and still is) a group of one-to-three storey buildings divided into small houses with shared communal services and arranged around a four-sided patio. One could find *corrales de vecinos* of all sizes, building quality and social attributes, although as a whole they leaned more toward the populace than the elite.[31] The way in which these housing structures were transformed into performance venues was simple enough: theatre impresarios would lease out the façade and back buildings of the *corral* – which gave access and control to the patio on one side and a tiring house for the performers on the other – and set up a stage at the far end of the yard. Then, if the venture proved profitable, they acquired the lateral buildings and turned them into viewing boxes or galleries for the wealthier patrons. After that, their options included opening a refreshment stand in the ground floor of the façade building and adding wooden bleachers on the sides of the patio. And so on. Thus, a *corral de comedias*, unlike a London amphitheatre, should be thought of less as a building than a space between buildings that slowly assimilated the surrounding properties into its function. And, unlike the relative – or at the very least apparent – immutability of the London amphitheatre, the Spanish playhouse was organic, to paraphrase John Orrell, and ever-changing.[32]

It is true that the appearance of inalterability of the London amphitheatres and of continuously morphing Spanish *corrales* may be at least partially related to the outstanding imbalance between period documents preserved from one and another countries' playhouses. Whereas theatre historians in Spain work with a documentary embarrassment of riches regarding its performance spaces, very little of the English playhouses' paper-trail has survived. It is, therefore, quite probable that the amphitheatres in London also underwent minor modifications and improvements throughout their existence in a fashion similar to that of most of Spain's *corrales*.[33] Nevertheless, in addition to these smaller developments,

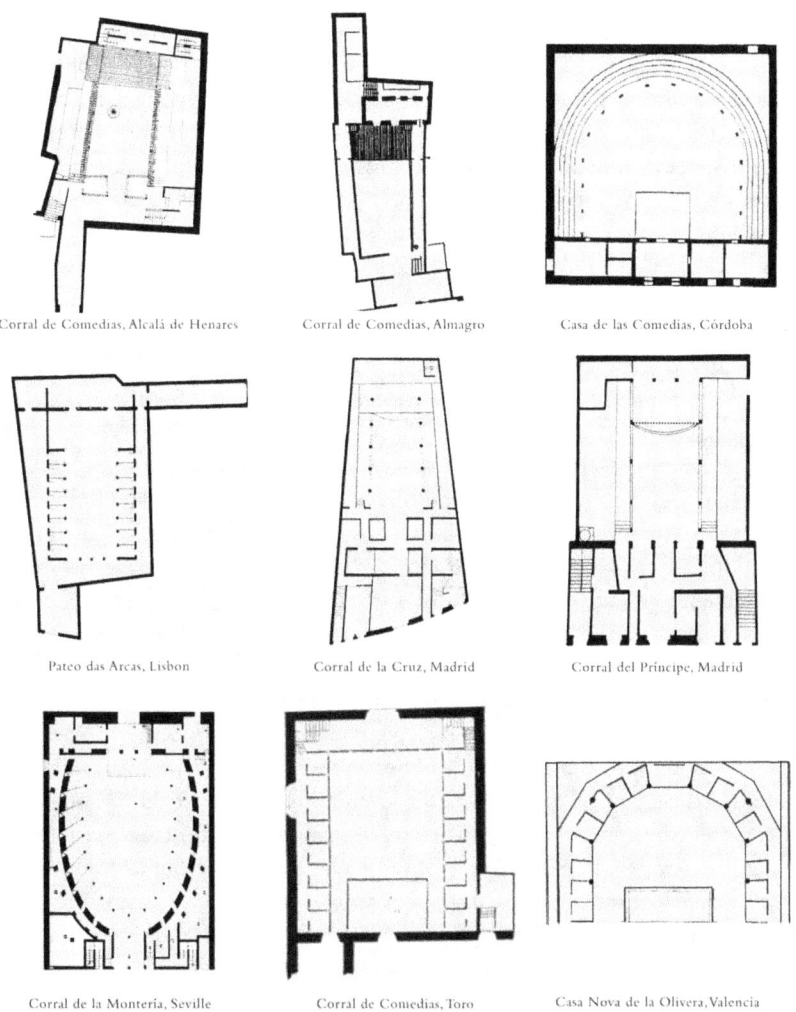

FIGURE 2.4 Plans of various Iberian *corrales de comedias* from the sixteenth and seventeenth centuries Copyright: Peter Lang (Allen) and Grupo de Investigación Siglo de Oro. Modified with permission of the authors

throughout their existences many Spanish playhouses experienced significant, even remarkable changes that we are fairly sure did not take place in their English counterparts. The two most drastic were the addition of benches and seats to the empty patios previously reserved for the standing *mosqueteros* [groundlings], and the covering of the open-air courtyards with full roofing. A good example combining these two innovations was the Casa de la Olivera playhouse in the Mediterranean port city of Valencia. In 1582, the administrators of the General Hospital leased a property near the city's university after the Crown granted them a local monopoly over commercial playing. They turned the venue into a rudimentary yet serviceable playhouse, distinct in shape from the Castilian *corrales* of the period but endowed with basically the same infrastructural features: open-air, with a cobblestone yard for standing spectators, and galleries for women and better-off playgoers. In the following decades, they added more and more comfortable *cadires* [seats] at the front of the patio, with rows of benches behind them, shrinking the space for the rowdy *mosqueteros* with every passing opportunity. Finally, in 1618 the playhouse shut down for a full year to conduct major renovations, and all performances were temporarily relocated to the nearby Casa del Santets. When the Olivera reopened in 1619, not only was the standees' space reduced to the bare minimum at the back of the yard, now in the shape of a semi-circle to improve visibility, but the new *casa de comedias* also boasted a complete roof, immediately turning the front row *cadires* into a very attractive location for the Valencian playgoing aristocracy.[34] And like the Casa (now known as Casa Nova) de la Olivera, playhouses across the peninsula similarly roofed themselves and/or changed their design: the Mesón de la Fruta in Toledo, the Patio del Hospital de San José y los Niños Expósitos in Valladolid, the Coliseo in Seville and the Pateo das Arcas in Lisbon went from roofless to roofed, and many of the new *corrales* in the seventeenth century – such as those in Badajoz, Burgos, Calahorra, Ciudad Rodrigo, Salamanca, Seville (a different playhouse, the Corral de la Montería), Toro and Zamora – were built with a roof from the very beginning.[35]

The purpose of having or not having a roof went beyond the strictly pragmatic desire to protect customers from an inclement climate. Much like the relocation of the playhouses into more centric and better-to-do areas of the cities, this was yet another clear sign of the upward social mobility the theatrical industry was both experiencing and promoting. The same could be said of the replacement of standing *mosqueteros* with sitting *mosqueteros* in the patio. The popular and rudimentary *corrales* of sixteenth-century Spain were evolving into, or in some instances were being replaced by, performance venues that catered more and more to aristocratic sensibilities. Or, at least, that could satisfy both ends of the social spectrum within a single venue, and could periodically reinvent themselves if need be. This is why the *corral de comedias* in Alcalá de Henares has managed to survive until today, although it is difficult to glimpse the original design under the many layers of change it has suffered throughout the years.[36] In England, on the other hand, it would not be unreasonable to infer that the fabric of the London amphitheatres remained fundamentally the same from start to finish, rooted to a specific moment in time. The gap between what the suburban amphitheatre had to offer and what the upper classes were demanding led to the reanimation of a completely different venue type for the higher palate taste of the urban elite: the indoor public playhouses that had previously been home to the children choir companies and John Lyly's plays.

In addition to their central and more prestigious locations, as discussed in the previous chapter, the major architectural differences between these elite commercial playhouses and their popular suburban siblings hamfistedly point to an aristocratisation of the theatrical enterprise not unlike the changes observed in the Spanish *corrales*. These were smaller venues, roofed, with no yard for standing groundlings. Not only were the performances put on in these playhouses different than those in the amphitheatres, but so were the experiences of both playing and playgoing. The following sections explore the conditions of performance as well as what it would have been like to attend a show at one of these venues, so as to nuance our understanding of the differences and similarities between English and Spanish early modern playhouses from the perspective of those who brought life to these buildings: the players and playgoers of Shakespeare and Lope de Vega's time.

Seeing and Hearing (and Being Seen) in England and Spain's Playhouses

Students of early modern theatre have long debated whether the plays of Shakespeare, Lope and their contemporaries were meant to be seen as opposed to being heard. The dispute originates in descriptions of theatregoers as the 'audience', from the Latin '*audire*' [to listen], as well as in the frequent references to 'hearing plays' one can find in period documents from both theatrical cultures. The insinuation is that Renaissance theatregoers had to use their ears more than their eyes in the playhouse; not necessarily implying that one was intrinsically more important than or preferable to the other, but rather that good visibility was not always guaranteed and thus the act of listening carried oversized weight in comparison with the modern playgoing experience.[37] Nevertheless, and as this section illustrates, there is ample evidence that theatregoers in the commercial playhouses of the two countries had no choice but to be both auditors and spectators, and that theatremakers built their performance spaces with this duality in mind. Moreover, it also seems clear that with the passage of time both English and Spanish playhouse managers worked toward improving the conditions of performance in their venues for players and playgoers alike. The following pages describe what could have been seen and heard in the public theatres of early modern England and Spain, as an additional way of marking the similarities and differences in the configuration of the venues of these two countries.

As Allen's reverie at the beginning of this chapter suggests, what London's amphitheatres and Spanish cities' *corrales de comedias* offered from a visual standpoint was strikingly similar. This is especially true of the stages, i.e., the spaces in which the actors performed and on which all eyes were fixed. In both countries, the convention was to have a thrust or apron stage surrounded by audience members on at least three sides. The dimensions of stage platforms were roughly the same, the length being somewhere near double the depth (a proportion found in other theatres across Europe and possibly associated with the practices of touring *commedia dell'arte* troupes). The platform, or *tablado* in Spanish, stood approximately six feet above the yard level in both countries alike, which allowed for a trapdoor entrance from which characters could enter or exit the stage. More often than not, a canopy of one sort or another covered the platform, and served as an access point as well as shelter for the performers. Finally, the English and Spanish tiring house walls were practically identical, with a large discovery space in the middle flanked by a door on each of the two sides, and a gallery above that doubled as an acting balcony or as audience boxes, depending on the needs of each production (see p. 43).[38]

In terms of acoustics, the amphitheatres of both countries resembled each other as well. These buildings shared the same architectural features, the most important of which – as far as sound is concerned – was their open-air arrangement. The lack of a roof meant that hearing in these theatres, much like seeing, was more challenging than what modern audiences are used to nowadays: sounds coming from the neighbourhood made their way uninvited into the performance at the same time that a portion of the actors' voices escaped through the gaping hole that presided over every show.[39] Another similarity they shared is that they were made from the same base materials, wood and plaster. These are high-quality transmitters of sound, as their reverberation levels are not too high and they provide a reasonably ample frequency reception (i.e., a wide pitch range).[40] The polygonal shape of many of London's theatres may have offered slightly better acoustics than the rectangular *corrales* (since the more surfaces on which the sound could reflect the better); on the other hand, records suggest that the average London playhouse could fit more playgoers than the largest *corrales* in Spain's major cities, and more playgoers translates into more difficulties for the actors' voices to carry properly.[41] In either case, the differences between the two types of playhouses, aurally as well as visually, were relatively insignificant.

Not only was what one could see and hear in English and Spanish public theatres virtually the same, but so were the types of 'tickets' and vantage points at the playgoers' disposal. In both countries, playhouses operated under a layered fee-collecting system, in which the further up in comfort and style a playgoer wished to go the greater the price he or he would end up having to pay. A first fee granted access to the yard or patio. There, the patrons – known as groundlings and *mosqueteros,* respectively – had to stand on their feet during the entire show. Moreover, they were often the victims of overcrowding, inclement weather, occasional rowdiness and/or brawling, which made their zone a less-than-ideal location from which properly to appreciate the performances, despite its relative proximity to the stage and the players. An additional fee allowed playgoers to use one of the sheltered benches along the walls of the patio; another bought entry into the gallery above, which was more quiet and removed from the bustling standees; another yet into the upper gallery, the most prestigious vantage point in the house. To the modern theatre patron, this arrangement would appear counter-intuitive, since in contemporary venues the front of the pit is a very desirable, and oftentimes expensive, location. Both aurally and visually, the first rows of the auditorium provide the best performance conditions the modern playhouse has to offer.[42] But because in the amphitheatres of early modern England and Spain this location required standing uncomfortably in an overcrowded and unsheltered yard, closely following the play may have struck some playgoers as less important than their comfort, not to mention their desire for visible separation from those who they considered their social and economic inferiors. Each playhouse had its own idiosyncratic admissions procedure, some more refined than others, but they all worked along these lines and the cost was roughly the same in both countries as well.[43] In this regard, the only significant difference between the English and Spanish amphitheatres is that whereas in the former men and women stood together as groundlings in the yard (as long as a woman was escorted by a man, that is), in the latter non-aristocratic women were not allowed to enter the yard's main viewing area. Instead, a separate box known as the *cazuela*, or stew-pot, housed them on the first level so as to avoid any untoward mingling between the sexes.[44] The rest of the upper galleries at the *corrales* remained restricted to the wealthiest patrons, men as well as women, along with some boxes permanently reserved for the clergy and for local politicians.

In addition to the standard audience locations, there was one additional place from which the most privileged playgoers could witness the play, and that is the stage itself. In both countries, it was customary for elite audience members to sit on the sides of the platform or in the balcony above.[45] This practice mirrored that of monarchs and the higher nobility in court performances and private shows, who as audience members were positioned in a spot so visible that it would effectively make them part of the spectacle.[46] And this was precisely the goal of many wealthy patrons at the public playhouses: not only did being on the stage guarantee good visibility and audibility of the performance, but the conspicuous nature of the public playhouse provided theatregoers with an unparalleled opportunity to buy their way into the play and from there better to display their wealth and privilege. Thus, many sought to take advantage of the theatrical limelight by sitting on or right above the stage while wearing expensive clothing, smoking and/or chewing (then still) exotic tobacco, and other ways of flaunting their economic and social status. In doing so they literally created visible distance between themselves and their less-deserving neighbours. English and Spanish playhouses were places in which one went to see as well as to be seen. In them, playgoers as well as players were expected to put on a performance, which is why the most prime locations in the playhouse seating chart were invariably the most conspicuous as well, even if this at times meant that one could not see the play from there as well as from a cheaper vantage point.[47]

While it is true that being seen was very important for English and Spanish playgoers, elite and otherwise, to say that they showed no interest in enjoying the play as much as possible as well – and that theatre impresarios made little effort to improve the conditions of both their players and their patrons – would be absurd. Especially from the seventeenth century onward, guaranteeing better visibility and acoustics became a driving principle in the construction (and reconstruction) of public theatres. Indeed, this was one of main attractions of the newly refurbished 'private' playhouses in the City of London. Along with their central location, seating for the entire house and elite clientele, these venues were also smaller and roofed, ensuring a more comfortable and intelligible playgoing experience for all spectators.[48] In his influential *The Acoustic World of Early Modern England* (1999), Bruce Smith illustrates how much better the sound quality was in a venue such as the Blackfriars theatre as compared to the Globe. Not only was the former's auditorium significantly smaller and thus more manageable, but also the actors' voices reverberated off the roof creating a round sound, much preferable to the broad and flatter projection of the open-air playhouses.[49] It is particularly revealing that whereas in the amphitheatres the yard was the most affordable (yet disagreeable) location, the same space in London's private playhouses – in which, conversely, its inhabitants sat comfortably right in front of the stage – was prime real estate, suggesting that nearer and better viewing and listening conditions were becoming increasingly sought after, especially when this did not require sacrificing comfort and status.[50]

In Spain, as discussed in the previous section, many of the *corrales* – being either newly built or renovated from the turn of the century on – began to add roofs, set up benches for the *mosqueteros* and/or discarded the traditional rectangular design for new layouts that improved the galleries' view of the stage. These modifications were meant to raise the prestige and social profile of the venue, of course, but they also addressed what were increasingly seen as the deficient conditions of performances of their more primitive predecessors. Even in the *corrales* that never became fully roofed or changed their initial plan, such as the ones in Madrid, steps were taken to upgrade the viewing and listening quality for the spectators. In addition to progressively elongating the roofs of the galleries to shelter more and more of the yard, it was customary for theatre managers to cover the remaining roofless space with a canvas awning during performances. The deployment of a *toldo*, as it is known in Spanish, served to prevent possible *chiaroscuri* on the stage as well as to improve the venue's soundscape; it even protected the *mosqueteros* from occasional showers.[51] In both countries, the primitive amphitheatres of the sixteenth century were being redesigned as, and even replaced by, performance environments that directly anticipated the modernised coliseums of eighteenth- and nineteenth-century Europe.

In summary, performance conditions in the public playhouses of the major English and Spanish cities were almost identical. For the most part, the stages looked the same, the acoustic properties of the buildings were similar, and the locations and perspectives from which playgoers witnessed the plays were also comparable. As the decades went by and commercial theatres grew in numbers and importance, playmakers worked on improving their facilities. The net result was the transformation of rudimentary open-air theatres into spaces that better preserved the integrity of plays, the players and the playgoers. These developments moreover extended beyond the playgoing conditions to affect staging

Playhouses **59**

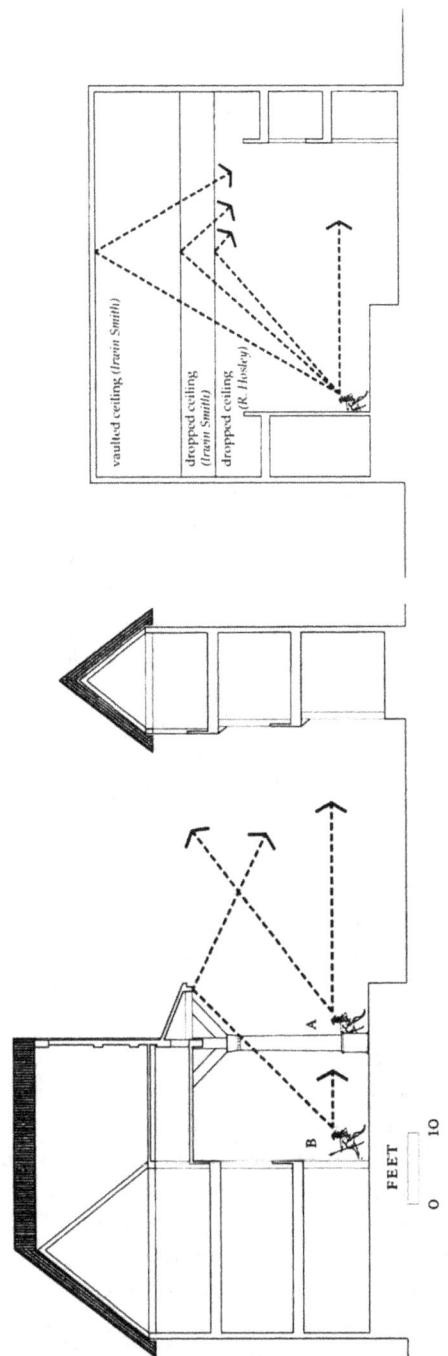

FIGURE 2.5 Acoustic projections of London's Globe (left) and Blackfriars (right) playhouses Copyright: University of Chicago Press

practices and facilities as well: what started as a form of entertainment that relied on few staging amenities slowly gave way to a full-fledged performing culture endowed with much more elaborate tools and techniques. The final section of the chapter examines more closely some of the more interesting transformations that took place on England and Spain's commercial stages during the first half of the seventeenth century, and which served further to move the two respective dramatic traditions away from the minimalist staging practices of the previous generations of playmakers.

Beyond the Bare Stage: Machines, Candles, Multi-Platforms

A roofed platform, a stage backdrop and a paying audience. As noted above, those were the only requirements the Italian *capocomico* Ganassa listed when he decided to invest in Madrid's Corral de la Pacheca in 1574. He and his company needed nothing else to put on a successful show; having just recently migrated from playing in the streets to performing in the country's first temporary *corrales*, their repertory was meant to work well despite not having many specific props and staging utilities at their disposal. And even in the years following the opening of the first permanent theatres, with their additional features and amenities, commercial performances in Spain relied on a minimalist scenography and playgoers' willingness to suspend their disbelief and re-imagine a mostly bare stage into the varying milieux described by the characters' words. England saw the same: dramatists in Shakespeare's time made sure that their plays could translate from one stage to another without affecting the delivery of the spectacle. Even in the case of regional theatres, as well as in the smaller private theatres in London, the overall design and proportions were retained as much as possible so as to have all the necessary staging features required in plays originally written with the larger amphitheatres and *corrales* in mind.[52] Regardless of the playhouse or the city or even the country, a company would be able to put on – and an audience would be able to enjoy – the same, or at least a very similar, production regardless of the specific locale.

That late sixteenth-century English and Spanish playwrights wrote their works to survive, or to thrive, on even the most barren of stages does not mean that commercial performances at the time lacked visual appeal. What it means is that, due to practical constraints and limitations, in these productions a metaphoric or metonymic relationship linked what was been represented with how it was being staged. A couple of players dressed as soldiers stood for an army; a staircase signified a mountain or a tower; if somebody carried a candle it meant that it was nighttime in the play-world. And it rested on the playgoers' shoulders to ignore the sunshine pouring over the stage if that was the case. Or to accept that, with what can only be described as symbolic effort, what had been a field in France five minutes before had suddenly become the interior of an English alehouse.

And so on. What could be seen was part of a carefully curated aspect of the performance; after all, in both countries a playing company's most valuable possessions were its costumes and dresses, which attests to their production's visual as well as aural allure.[53] Instead it reveals that these shows required the audience's collaboration for them to seem believable. Visual verisimilitude was not on offer in early modern England and Spain's commercial playhouses, especially in their early days, and the visual took its cues from the aural as the playwrights' words imbued the bare staging with their intended meaning.[54]

This dynamic began to change with the arrival of Italian-trained theatre practitioners in the seventeenth century. Engineers such as the aforementioned Inigo Jones and Cosimo Lotti, both educated in the same Florentine stagecrafting workshops, were hired to incorporate more sophisticated machinery and perspective scenography in palace theatres of England and Spain, respectively. This new technology allowed them to stage masques and other more baroque and visually striking productions that had become so popular with elite audiences in Italy.[55] Eventually some public playhouses, especially those in large cities and that catered to the higher echelons of society, figured out ways to host shows resembling those at Court, even if somewhat watered down. While not necessarily casting away the practices of the 'bare stage' theatre altogether, performances at London's indoor playhouses and the seventeenth-century *corrales* of Madrid, Valencia and Seville placed more emphasis on the use of discoveries [*apariencias*] and flight systems [*tramoyas*] that were so commonly used in court spectacles. In other words, these playhouses offered an alternative way of staging plays that leaned more heavily on the visual and relied less on the aid of verbal cues and the generous imagination of the audience. English and Spanish dramatists took note of the new staging possibilities – as well as playgoers' positive attitude towards them – and began to incorporate them into their works, and in doing so transformed however slightly the semiotic relationship between the matter and style of what was being staged into one that migrated increasingly toward the verisimilar (albeit spectacularly so) and away from the symbolic.[56]

The addition of spectacular machinery and the adoption of certain conventions associated with aristocratic entertainment in commercial playhouses led to these public venues, and the plays written with them in mind, becoming windows through which to look into the privileged performance practices of the palace theatres. This was the case of Ben Jonson's *Cynthia's Revels* (c. 1600), the first play performed in the rehabilitated Blackfriars; as Sarah Dustagheer explains, with this piece Jonson turned the commercial venue into "a space of royally approved performance and gives the audience a tantalising opportunity to experience an exclusive court masque".[57] Another, perhaps better-known, example of an aristocratic spectacle inserted into an otherwise traditional popular dramatic work – at least as far as staging is concerned – takes place in the fourth act of Shakespeare's *The Tempest*.[58] In Spain, Calderón stood at the forefront of blurring the lines between court and commercial entertainment by integrating the new scenery technology into the *comedia nueva*. His plays were meant to be performed both in the palace theatres and public playhouses, and even if in productions for the latter some of the more elaborate staging choices had to be watered down it was nevertheless evident that visually driven spectacles were taking over the more traditional aural drama of Lope and his generation. Indeed, at the tail-end of his career Lope famously lashed out against the growing reliance on flights and props, and dedicated the preface to the sixteenth volume of his plays (1621) to attacking what he described as the *comedias de tramoya* [spectacular plays]; all in vain, however, as Calderón, who was much more attuned to courtier tastes, replaced him as the nation's stage-poet laureate.[59]

Another court-performance convention introduced into the English and Spanish commercial theatre mainstream was the use of artificial lighting. Originally, the public theatres in both countries relied exclusively on natural light during their performances. The logistics of properly illuminating large spaces for the full duration of a play were challenging, not to say expensive, which is precisely why the venues were roofless and the shows were always scheduled in the early afternoon. In court and private shows, however, it was customary to light the room with candles. Whether it was because most of these performances took place indoors (and sometimes not during daytime) or because being able to afford this added expense was a sign of distinction, artificial lighting became a common feature of aristocratic entertainment.[60] The same was true of the children companies that performed in elite playhouses in London, as well as the adult players when they took over the City's indoor theatres toward the end of the first decade of the seventeenth century. In fact, many scholars believe that the use of artificial lighting influenced the way English playwrights and players wrote and performed theatre: in the indoor venues, unlike in the open air theatres, actors could manipulate the levels of visibility by lighting and extinguishing candles, which means that darkness and nighttime were no longer necessarily figments of the theatregoers' imagination. The upper gallery of the Blackfriars had windows to allow as much natural light in as possible (and acting companies still held their performances during the day apparently with this purpose in mind), but these could be blocked with shutters if the performance required it.[61] This does not mean that plays taking advantage of this possibility could not be staged in the amphitheatres. As a matter of fact, John Webster's *The Duchess of Malfi* (1613-1614) – a play that invokes pitch darkness several times throughout – was first performed at the Blackfriars and at the Globe in the same season, and as far as we know both performances were successful and no one was disappointed that the amphitheatre was not really as dark as the text suggests. Still, for the indoor venues, candlelight offered new opportunities for more elaborate staging choices that inched away from the minimalistic bare stage practices of old and toward a performance culture that was less taxing on the audience's willing suspension of disbelief.[62] In Spain, despite there being no evidence of artificial lighting used to illumine venues for the entirety of shows, candlelight was introduced along with resort to discoveries and similar visual props. Even as more and more *corrales* started adding roofs throughout the seventeenth century, much like the English private theatres they made sure to have enough windows for the stage to be naturally lit.[63] And yet, when *apariencias* were brought out onto stage at the climactic apex of the show, they would often be surrounded with candles in order for everyone to see them in all their splendour.[64] As was the case in palace theatres or in London's indoor playhouses, artificial lighting in Spain's commercial playhouses came hand in hand with the elevation of the visually spectacular, which in turn was both cause and consequence of the progressive aristocratisation of the two countries' popular theatre scenes.

As this chapter illustrates, most of the major innovations in the commercial playhouses and staging practices of one and another country found similar if not identical replicas in the other's. That said, there was one novel feature unique to certain Spanish *corrales* that had no counterpart in the English theatres, which nevertheless spoke to this same dynamic of trending towards a more elaborate staging culture: the development of *tablados laterales*, or lateral stages. Sometime in the late sixteenth century, the managers of the Corral del Príncipe and the Corral de la Cruz in Madrid set up smaller platforms that flanked the thrust *tablados* to allow privileged playgoers to be closer to the action, much like the gallants sitting on stools on the side of the stage in the London theatres.[65] As noted previously, being on the stage, or by the stage, was a way for the richest patrons to see as well as to be seen more clearly. But this was not the only purpose of these platforms: they were also used to perform *autos sacramentales* in the *corral* setting.[66] These religious plays were normally staged on three *carros* [carts] in the squares and streets of the cities, and each *carro* was adorned with a spectacular feature or decoration of one sort or another. They were visually striking and prop-riddled spectacles, and were by far the most popular and lucrative form of theatre in early modern Spain. It made sense, thus, for *corral* impresarios to want to adapt their venues in order to be able to host *autos* as well.[67]

It must be noted that not all Spanish theatres had *tablados laterales*. In fact, other than Madrid's Corral del Príncipe and Corral de la Cruz, there is only evidence of permanent *tablados laterales* for the *corral* in Almagro and perhaps the one in Alcalá de Henares.[68] However, that the capital's playhouses – those which most of the period's dramatists kept in mind when writing – did so had a tangible impact on the production of secular plays in Golden Age Spain. Just as the use of court machinery made its way into the popular drama of both countries, Spanish playwrights started to experiment in their *comedias* with the possibilities these additional stages had to offer. By clearly signalling that the lateral platforms represented locations distinct from those of the main stage, for instance, the plot of the play could transition seamlessly from one locus to another completely different setting without having to call in the stagehands. In other words, this innovation facilitated their having different active locations on stage at the same time. This was the case, according to John J. Allen, of Calderón's *La vida es sueño*

(1631), which would have been represented with a hill on one lateral platform and a tower on the other, while the palace and battle scenes would have been carried out in the central stage and the tiring house wall galleries. Frequent references to hills and towers in other theatrical pieces written during the same period suggest that the use of this type of split stage design became commonplace in the *corrales* that had side platforms.[69] These plays could still be performed in the smaller *corrales* outside Madrid, most of which did not have *tablados laterales*; in this sense, this bifurcation resembles that of the indoor and open-air theatres in England. However, the Spanish public playhouses that did have side stages allowed for performances there to rely less on audiences' willing suspension of disbelief to help them redefine the bare stage into one or another location, and more on the increasing use of visual aids and the deployment of richer and more elaborate settings.[70]

All of the staging features described in this section first took form outside England and Spain's public playhouses. Both the use of stage machinery and artificial lighting originated in court theatres and similar venues, while the Spanish lateral platforms owe their existence to the *auto sacramental* genre of religious street theatre. Nevertheless, English and Spanish commercial playwrights and players – who were, after all, also in charge of scripting and putting on the court shows and *autos* – introduced and adapted some of these features into their popular venues and performances. Thus, by virtue of proximity, commercial theatre became increasingly more reliant on these new possibilities at their dramatists' and performers' disposal, and began to inch slowly away from the bare stage and towards a new culture of theatrical verisimilitude that defined the centuries to follow. The reopening of playhouses in England after the fall of Cromwell's Commonwealth in 1660 marked an inflection point in the theatrical practices in the country, as plays written from the Restoration period onward were intimately associated with the indoor proscenium theatres of London's West End. No such inflection point took place in Spain, and its *corrales* survived well into the eighteenth century, slowly becoming démodé in the eyes of foreign travellers; this seems to have been the opinion of Thomas Williams, an Englishman who visited Seville in the 1670s and in his diary sounds taken aback by the fact that in both of the city's theatres "they act by daylight" as well as their lack of elaborate scenography and costumes, almost as if such practices had never been seen on English soil.[71]

Notes

1 Allen, "The Disposition of the Stage in the English and Spanish Theatres", p. 55.
2 In the introduction to his recent monograph *What is a Playhouse?* Callan Davies convincingly links the predominance of the Globe-like amphitheatre in historical descriptions of Elizabethan theatrical culture to the figure of Shakespeare. "There is a parallel", Davies writes, "between Shakespeare as poster-boy for English literature and the Theatre and then the Globe as his architectural counterparts". Davies, *What is a Playhouse?*, p. 1.

3 Ganassa translated by and cited in Varey, "Memory Theaters, Playhouses, and *Corrales de Comedia*", pp. 44–45 [my gloss]. More on Ganassa and *commedia dell'arte* companies in Spain in Allen, *The Reconstruction of a Spanish Golden Age Playhouse*, pp. 115–116; Fernández Martín, "Construcción de nueva planta del antiguo teatro de Valladolid 1609-1610", pp. 106–112; Gramegna, "Actores italianos en España en los siglos XVI y XVII"; Greer, "A Tale of Three Cities", pp. 392–393; Henke, "Border-Crossing in the *Commedia dell'Arte*"; McKendrick, *Theatre in Spain 1490-1700*, pp. 46–50; Sanz Ayán, *Hacer escena*, pp. 57–74; Shergold, "Ganassa and the *Commedia dell'Arte* in Sixteenth-Century Spain"; Thacker, *A Companion to Golden Age Theatre*, p. 132.
4 Nash [sic.] as cited in Katritzky, *The Art of Commedia*, pp. 89-90. Tiffany Stern recapitulates the debate among theatre and book historians regarding the origin of plots of English plays, which in John Payne Collier's always doubtful opinion could have derived from the *scenarii* of *commedia dell'arte* performances; more in Stern, *Documents of Performance in Early Modern England*, p. 204.
5 More in Andrews, "Resources in Common".
6 Yates, *The Theatre of the World*, p. 133.
7 Gurr, *The Shakespearean Stage*, p. 31. More on the Theatre's name and its association with classical concepts and motifs in West, "The Idea of a Theater".
8 Smith, *The Acoustic World of Early Modern England*, pp. 206–208. For an explanation of Vitruvius' standing in early modern architectural theory see Hart, "Introduction", pp. 18–29.
9 A brief summary of the long-lasting tensions between the two scholarly theories of sixteenth-century playhouse genealogy can be found in Vince, "Historicizing the Sixteenth-Century Playhouse".
10 Bowsher and Miller, *The Rose and the Globe*, p. 121; Orrell, *The Human Stage*, pp. 130–149. For instance, a specifically round theatrical performance design in the Middle Ages is the sketch for the staging of the morality play *The Castle of Perseverance*, in which a ditch of water surrounded the circular place of performance. The scaffolds on the outside of the ditch were not round themselves, but quadrangular, a much easier building design. More in Southern, *The Medieval Theatre in the Round*, pp. 17–27.
11 Gurr, "Why was the Globe Round?", p. 3.
12 In their book detailing the archaeological excavations of the Rose and Globe theatres in the 1980s and 1990s, Julian Bowsher and Pat Miller differentiate between 'high' and 'vernacular' architecture. "To an architect", Jon Greenfield pertinently reminds us, "the relationship between the use and form of a building is fundamental". William Turner writes about how the development of 'practical knowledge' in sixteenth-century England (to which I add the rest of Europe), "a specific intellectual formation [...] that resulted from a convergence between the predominantly linguistic epistemologies of European humanism, on the one hand, and the quantitative and iconic modes of representation characteristic of the spatial arts, on the other". Bowsher and Miller, *The Rose and the Globe*, pp. 108–109; Greenfield, "Reconstructing the Rose", p. 23; Turner, *The English Renaissance Stage*, p. 43.
13 Dillon, *Theatre, Court & City*, pp. 40–41. A good example of what is meant here by 'vernacular' building techniques would be Leonard Digges' best selling *Tectonicon* (1556). This quarto publication, which went through 18 editions between 1556 and 1656, displays the sophistication of what Anthony Gerbino and Stephen Johnston define as "practical mathematics" for the Elizabethan mechanic's measurement techniques. Its distinctive pragmatic approach, as well as its intended readership ("Surueyers, Landmeters, Ioyners, Carpenters and Masons") sets it apart from the style that Inigo Jones would later import into the country from his education in Florence under Giulio Parigi. The early Elizabethan playhouses would have been built if anything with the *Tectonicon*, and not Palladio, in mind. Not even in Italy, where the

profession of the architect was much more developed at the time and the theoreticians were much more vocal, one can find many popular buildings with an elaborate and intellectually driven design. The one exception was Palladio's Teatro Olimpico in Vicenza, the most elaborate/intellectually designed theatre in Renaissance Europe, but it was built and theorised about too late (in the 1580s) to have been able to influence the first generation of English and Spanish amphitheatres. "Buildings for purposes of public entertainment", writes Jacob Burckhardt in one of his influential studies of the Italian Renaissance, "probably had, as yet, no distinctive architectural form, or were merely temporary buildings, or, if handsome, have in any case perished". Burckhardt, *The Architecture of the Italian Renaissance*, p. 162. Moreover, when one looks at the list the 18th-century Scottish architect Colen Campbell made of English buildings he considered to be influenced by classical and/or Italian Renaissance forerunners, they all have distinctive aristocratic or ecclesiastical marking. However large a part one believes the classical influence played in the design of Burbage's Theatre, its presence paled so much in comparison with that in other buildings of its spatial and temporal vicinity that the Theatre would unquestionably stand out in that list. Not even the playhouse designs attributed to John Webb (a member of the architectural network of Inigo Jones, who in turn features prominently in the second volume) were included in Campbell's collection. See Campbell, *Vitruvius Britannicus*; Digges, *A Boke Named Tectonicon*; Gerbino and Johnston, *Compass and Rule*, pp. 45–64.

14 Varey, "Memory Theaters, Playhouses, and *Corrales de Comedias*", p. 45. See also Marías, "Teatro antiguo y corral de comedias en Toledo", pp. 1629–1636. A lively description of the construction process of an early modern theatre (the seventeenth-century *corral de comedias* of Alcalá de Henares) can be found in Allen, *La Piedra de Rosetta del teatro comercial europeo*, pp. 17–21.

15 Janet S. Loengard's theory that the Red Lion was a *de novo* construction and not a converted innyard is very convincing, but the shape of the courtyard in which the playhouse was circumscribed would have nonetheless conditioned the shape of the galleries erected within it. Loengard, "An Elizabethan Lawsuit", p. 305. Regarding the Theatre, as Herbert Berry explains, it was a timber building "built among other timber buildings which had existed for a long time and many of which continued to exist. The Theatre depended on these other buildings in many ways. The same phrases were sometimes used to describe physical aspects of them all. At least two workmen worked on them all. At the beginning of the Theatre's history it could incorporate building materials from the other buildings, and at the end of its history building materials from the Theatre could be used in the other buildings." Berry, "Aspects of the Design and Use of the First Public Playhouse", p. 30.

16 Southern, *The Staging of Plays Before Shakespeare*, p. 98. For his full explanation see pp. 48–100. See also Tittler, *Architecture and Power*, pp. 139–150.

17 A short background study of the Spanish country estates and houses in sixteenth-century Castile can be found Bustamante and Marías, "Algunas consideraciones sobre la casa rural en Castilla en el siglo XVI".

18 D'Evelyn, *Venice and Vitruvius*, p. 19 [fig. 5].

19 Ruano de la Haza and Allen, *Los teatros comerciales del siglo XVII y la escenificación de la Comedia*, p. 49; Smith, *Shakespeare's Blackfriars Playhouse*, p. 308. According to Allen, *commedia dell'arte* street platforms with similar dimensions can be traced throughout several European countries during these years. More in Allen, "Los primeros corrales de comedia", pp. 14–15, 22.

20 Brandon and Brooke, *Bankside*, pp. 94–95; Wickham, *Early English Stages 1300 to 1660: Volume Two 1576 to 1660, Part I*, pp. 161–163 (Chambers' study also as cited here by Wickham). For a critical survey of the common ground shared by London's theatrical community and the practice of animal baiting see Scott-Warren, "When

Theaters Were Bear-Gardens". More on the archaeological discoveries of the Tudor-Stuart baiting arenas in Bowsher, *Shakespeare's London Theatreland*, pp. 151–159; Mackinder et al., *The Hope Playhouse, Animal Baiting and Later Industrial Activity at Bear Gardens on Bankside*, pp. 10–25.

21 Saunders as cited in Allen, *The Reconstruction of a Spanish Golden Age Playhouse*, pp. 33–35. The design descriptions and contracts of the Fortune and the Hope theatres explicitly refer to the Globe and the Swan theatres, respectively, as the prototypes after which to model the new theatres. In Spain, the *corral* in Alcalá was also explicitly modelled after Madrid's Corral de la Cruz. More in Ruano de la Haza and Allen, *Los teatros comerciales del siglo XVII y la escenificación de la Comedia*, p. 212; Smith, *Shakespeare's Blackfriars Playhouse*, p. 291.

22 The Flavian Amphitheatre was also referred to as the "hunting theatre", due to its famous spectacles involving gladiators and ferocious animals. All the ancient Roman references to the Amphitheatre, collected by Donald R. Dudley in *Urbs Roma*, refer to the building as a gladiator and animal-baiting arena only, and never to theatre being performed there. The term Coliseum, or Colosseum, is a medieval term for the structure "perhaps based on a nearby colossal statue of Nero", as Rebecca Zorach notes. More in Dudley, *Urbs Roma*, pp. 142–145; Zorach, *The Virtual Tourist in Renaissance Rome*, p. 105.

23 Heywood, *An apology for actors*, sigs. D2-D2v. A summary of what little is known of Rome's first permanent amphitheatre in Campus Martius, and to which Heywood alludes, can be found in Dodge, "Amphitheaters in the Roman World", pp. 547–548. More on Heywood's religious interpretation of the English amphitheatre in Ruge, "Having a Good Time at the Theatre of the World", pp. 35–37.

24 As cited in Orrell, *The Human Stage*, p. 45.

25 "Desde el principio del mundo / hallada, usada y compuesta / por los Griegos, y Latinos, / y otras naciones diuersas. / Ampliada por los Romanos, / que labraron para ella / teatros y coliseos, / y el anfiteatro, que era, / Donde se encerraban siempre, / a oyr comedias destas / ochocientas mil personas, / y otras que no tienen cuenta". Rojas, *El viage entretenido*, p. 47 [my translation]. Confusion regarding the venues of entertainment in ancient Rome appear to be quite common ever since the Middle Ages. The much-copied medieval guidebook to Rome, *Mirabilia Urbis Romae*, includes the Flaminian Circus among its list of theatres (rechristened as the Flaminian Theatre). The Colosseum is described as the pagan temple of the Sun, and the text makes no mention whatsoever of the animal baiting and gladiator practices for which it was best known. More in *The Marvels of Rome: Mirabilia Urbis Romae*, pp. 10, 28–29.

26 Gurr, *The Shakespearean Stage*, pp. 121–153.

27 Bolaños Donoso et al, "El Corral de la Montería de Sevilla", pp. 221–230; Díez Borque, *El teatro en el siglo XVII*, pp. 19–20; García Gómez, "La casa de las comedias de Córdoba"; Gentil Baldrich, "Sobre la traza oval del Corral de la Montería"; Mouyen, "Las casas de comedies de Valencia", pp. 106–122; Pineda Novo, *El teatro de comedias del Corral de la montería del Alcázar de Sevilla*; Ruano de la Haza and Allen, *Los teatros comerciales del siglo XVII y la escenificación de la Comedia*, pp. 200–203; Sentaurens, "Los corrales de comedia de Sevilla", pp. 76–78. A virtual reconstruction of Seville's oval-shaped Corral de la Montería is available at the *Grupo de Investigación Teatro Siglo de Oro*'s website (https://investigacionteatrosiglodeoro.com).

28 Bowsher, "The Rose and its Stages"; Bowsher and Blatherwick, "The Structure of the Rose"; Bowsher and Miller, *The Rose and the Globe*, pp. 22–62. Jon Greenfield suggests that the 1587 Rose, due to its structure and separation between galleries and yard, may have been initially conceived as a multi-purpose arena, only later converted into a full-time playhouse. More in Greenfield, "Reconstructing the Rose".

29 Orrell, "Spanish *Corrales* and English Theaters", p. 26. For the Red Bull playhouse, Eva Griffith provides a detailed account of the progressive transformation of the inn,

which started off as "a 'howse' with 'stables and other roomes' set around a 'square Court'", into a theatre venue in *A Jacobean Company and its Playhouse*, pp. 93–107; Herbert Berry's canonical *The Boar's Head Playhouse* does the same for its namesake. The original description of the leased property that would be converted into the Red Bull playhouse is cited in Griffith, *A Jacobean Company and its Playhouse*, p. 66.

30 It should be noted that the King's Men, by far the most popular and successful playing company in Jacobean England, took advantage of this unfortunate event to improve their open-air playhouse. The building costs of the second Globe doubled those of the first, which might suggest a level of baroque opulence and comfort never seen before in the suburban playhouses. More in Bowsher and Miller, *The Rose and the Globe*, p. 91.

31 More on *corrales de vecinos* in Seville (the birthplace of this infrastructure) in Carloni Franca, "La cultura de los corrales sevillanos, a través de la utilización del espacio", pp. 559–562; Morales Padrón, *Los corrales de vecinos de Sevilla*, pp. 11–18; Morell Peguero, *Mercaderes y artesanos en la Sevilla del Descubrimiento*, pp. 123–124. For a detailed and one-of-a-kind study of two early modern *corrales de vecinos*, in this case in Toledo, see Passini, *Casas y casas principales urbanas*, pp. 93–95, 115–116, 311–322.

32 Orrell, "Spanish Corrales and English Theaters", p. 28. Allen compares the development of a *corral* with the growth of a tree, slow yet seamlessly steady, in Allen, *La Piedra de Rosetta del teatro comercial europeo*, p. 13.

33 For a description of the most detailed English playhouse construction contract that survives, see Orrell, "Building the Fortune". Moreover, the organic process of evolution of Habsburg Spain's theatres cannot be said to be specific to the country or the period. In Richard and Helen Leacroft's *Theatre and Playhouse* we find conjectural illustrations of how from 1548 to 1717 France's Confrérie de la Passion slowly converted the tennis court of the Parisian Hôtel de Bourgogne into a fully functioning and sophisticated indoor playhouse (pp. 49–51).

34 Mouyen, "Las casas de comedies de Valencia", pp. 94–108. A virtual reconstruction of the final appearance of Valencia's Casa de la Olivera playhouse is available at the *TC/12: Red del Patrimonio Teatral Clásico Español* project's website (https://tc12.uv.es).

35 Bolaños Donoso et al., "El Corral de la Montería de Sevilla", pp. 235–237; Domínguez Matito, *El teatro en la Rioja*, pp. 100–118; Fernández Martín, "Construcción de nueva planta del antiguo teatro de Valladolid 1609-1610", pp. 120–121; Marcos Álvarez, "Los teatros fijos de Badajoz en el siglo XVII", p. 249; Marías, "Teatro antiguo y corral de comedias en Toledo", pp. 1626–1627; Miguel Gallo, *El teatro en Burgos*, pp. 78–80; Reyes Peña y Bolaños Donoso, "El Patio de las Arcas de Lisboa", pp. 279–315; Sánchez Rubio, "Mesón de la Fruta y Teatro Rojas de Toledo", pp. 187–190. A virtual reconstruction of the final appearance of Lisbon's Pateo das Arcas is available at the *Grupo de Investigación Teatro Siglo de Oro*'s website (https://investigacionteatrosiglodeoro.com).

36 Today the Teatro Corral de Comedias de Alcalá provides archaeological testimony to four centuries of performance activity. The renovation efforts have successfully managed to display simultaneously all the layers of reconstruction and reinvention throughout the venue's history. A detailed evolution of said phases can be found in Allen, *La Piedra de Rosetta del teatro comercial europeo* (an English-language version of this monograph has been serialised by the *Bulletin of the Comediantes* journal under the title "The Teatro Cervantes in Alcalá de Henares"); Higuera Sánchez-Pardo et al., "Alcalá de Henares".

37 For summaries of this line of thought regarding English theatre see Gurr, "Why was the Globe Round?", p. 3; Kinney, *Shakespeare by Stages*, pp. 76–90; White, *Renaissance Drama in Action*, pp. 3–8. For Spain see Dixon, "La comedia de corral de Lope como género visual".

38 Allen, "El corral de comedias de Almagro", pp. 199–201; Allen, *The Reconstruction of a Spanish Golden Age Playhouse*, pp. 29–31; Gurr, *The Shakespearean Stage*, pp. 122–123;

Ichikawa, "Continuities and innovations in staging", pp. 79–80; Ruano de la Haza and Allen, *Los teatros comerciales del siglo XVII y la escenificación de la Comedia*, pp. 49, 160, 226–227; White, *Renaissance Drama in Action*, pp. 110–117.
39 Smith, *The Acoustic World of Early Modern England*, pp. 213–214.
40 Bolaños Donoso et al., "El Corral de la Monteria de Sevilla", pp. 226–229; Ruano de la Haza and Allen, *Los teatros comerciales del siglo XVII y la escenificación de la Comedia*, p. 151; Smith, *The Acoustic World of Early Modern England*, pp. 209–210.
41 Smith, *The Acoustic World of Early Modern England*, pp. 207–211. For the seating (and standing) capacity of England and Spain's most important playhouses see Allen, *The Reconstruction of a Spanish Golden Age Playhouse*, pp. 95–100; Gurr, *The Shakespearean Stage*, pp. 115–118; Sentaurens, "Los corrales de comedias de Sevilla", p. 71; Thacker, *A Companion to Golden Age Drama*, p. 127.
42 As Andrew Gurr explains when discussing the Globe theatre's layout, "the social mix of an audience totalling 450, the cheaper half of them positioned facing the stage and the richest two hundred, all the most celebrated and highest in social rank, sitting beside and behind it, is completely alien to any modern auditorium design". Gurr, "Why was the Globe Round?", p. 7.
43 For England see Gurr, *The Shakespearean Stage*, pp. 134–135; Manley, "Why did London Inns Function as Theatres?", p. 184; White, "William Poel's Globe", p. 154. For Spain see Albrecht, *The Playgoing Public of Madrid in the Time of Tirso de Molina*, pp. 54–55; Díez Borque, *El teatro en el siglo XVII*, pp. 23–27; Ruano de la Haza and Allen, *Los teatros comerciales del siglo XVII y la escenificación de la Comedia*, pp. 33–35, 40–43; Varey and Shergold, *Teatros y comedias en Madrid*, pp. 33–35.
44 Certain evidence suggests that in the very beginning women and men did coexist in the same spaces of the *corrales*. Very early on this became the target of moralists' complaints, which led to the playhouses being required to segregate the paying audience according to their sex. More in Allen, *The Reconstruction of a Spanish Golden Age Playhouse*, p. 28; Ruano de la Haza, "Una nota sobre la cazuela alta del corral del Príncipe"; Sanz Ayán and García García, *Teatros y comediantes en el Madrid de Felipe II*, p. 7. For more on female playgoers in the English amphitheatres see Gurr, *Playgoing in Shakespeare's London*, pp. 60–64; Keenan, *Acting Companies and their Plays in Shakespeare's London*, pp. 137–138.
45 Allen, *The Reconstruction of a Spanish Golden Age Playhouse*, pp. 24–25; Gurr, *Playgoing in Shakespeare's London*, pp. 36–40; Gurr, *The Shakespearean Stage*, p. 147; Ruano de la Haza and Allen, *Los teatros comerciales del siglo XVII y la escenificación de la Comedia*, pp. 160–163.
46 For the location of monarchs in court entertainment see Greer, "Playing the Palace", pp. 90–91; Kernan, *Shakespeare, the King's Playwright*, p. 19. Occasionally, members of the high nobility – and, in Spain's case, even King Philip IV – attended the public theatres, and would sit in very conspicuous private boxes next to or above the stage; in England, the gallery above the stage was referred to as the Lords' Room because that is where they often were seated. More in Bowsher and Miller, *The Rose and the Globe*, pp. 115–116; Díez Borque, *Sociedad y teatro en la España de Lope de Vega*, pp. 157–158; Yachnin, "The Reformation of Space in Shakespeare's Playhouse", pp. 275–276.
47 For an exploration of the social connotations of theatregoing in the commercial theatres of England and Spain, and early modern playgoers' use of the theatrical event as an opportunity to cast themselves publicly in a favourable light, see my "A Day in the Life". See also Ball, *Treating the Public*, p. 25; Dustagheer, "'Our scene is London'", pp. 98–103.
48 Gurr, "The move indoors", pp. 8–10.
49 Smith, *The Acoustic World of Early Modern England*, pp. 212–230. See also Dustagheer, "Acoustic and visual practices indoors", pp. 137–143. Moreover, in a recent monograph, Will Tosh reports on his interviews with players and playgoers in London's

reconstructed open-air Globe and Jacobean-like Sam Wanamaker playhouses during the 2014 and 2015 seasons, and finds that they corroborate Smith's acoustic assessment of the two types of venues. More in Tosh, *Playing Indoors*, pp. 71–74. For more on the Sam Wanamaker Playhouse project in general see Gurr and Karim-Cooper, "Introduction", pp. 1–3; Greenfield and McCurdy, "Practical evidence for a reimagined indoor Jacobean theatre".

50 Smith, *Shakespeare's Blackfriars Playhouse*, pp. 290–296. It is worth noting that, responding to Tosh's surveys for *Playing Indoors*, playgoers at the Sam Wanamaker Playhouse generally perceived the pit, along with the side-stage boxes, as the preferred (and most prestigious) vantage point for audiences in a Jacobean indoor theatre (pp. 135–139).

51 Allen, *The Reconstruction of a Spanish Golden Age Playhouse*, pp. 88–92; Ruano de la Haza and Allen, *Los teatros comerciales del siglo XVII y la escenificación de la Comedia*, pp. 29, 50, 141–148; Varey and Davis, "The Corral del Principe in 1609", p. 53. In addition to Madrid's *corrales*, other Iberian theatres known to have used *toldos* and similar covers include the first Casa de la Olivera in Valencia, the Pateo das Arcas in Lisbon, the Casa de las Comedias of Córdoba and the *corral* in Valladolid. More in Fernández Martín, "Construcción de nueva planta del antiguo teatro de Valladolid 1609-1610", p. 109; García Gómez, "Casa de comedias de Córdoba", p. 26; Mouyen, "Las casas de comedies de Valencia", p. 99; Reyes Peña and Bolaños Donoso, "El Patio de las Arcas de Lisboa", p. 279.

52 For the stage dimensions and disposition in England's regional playhouses and London's indoor theatres see Gair, *The Children of Paul's*, pp. 56–60; Gurr, *Playgoing in Shakespeare's London*, pp. 31–32; Gurr, *The Shakespearean Stage*, pp. 156–157; Keenan; *Travelling Players in Shakespeare's England*, pp. 148–149; Pérez Díez, "The 'Playhouse' at St Paul's", pp. 208–213; Smith, *Shakespeare's Blackfriars Playhouse*, pp. 306–338. For Spain see Ruano de la Haza and Allen, *Los teatros comerciales del siglo XVII y la escenificación de la Comedia*, pp. 218–225.

53 Gurr, *The Shakespearean Stage*, pp. 194–198; Ruano de la Haza, *La puesta en escena en los teatros comerciales del Siglo de Oro*, pp. 73–77.

54 In his influential *Shakespeare and the Popular Tradition in the Theater*, Robert Weimann describes this phenomenon as 'word scenery', in that the "general absence of scenery on the large acting area of the Elizabethan platform stage placed rigorous demands on the dramatist's use of language, the actor's use of gesture, and the audience's attentiveness and imagination" (pp. 215–216). For a description of the traditional *mise-en-scène* in English public playhouses see Gurr, *The Shakespearean Stage*, pp. 172–191. For Spanish *corrales* see Ruano de la Haza, *La puesta en escena en los teatros comerciales del Siglo de Oro*, pp. 101–221.

55 For more on Inigo Jones' theatre work see Anderson, *Inigo Jones and the Classical Tradition*; Astington, *English Court Theatre*, pp. 110–124; Gurr, *The Shakespearean Stage*, pp. 201–208; Harris and Higgott, *Inigo Jones*, pp. 13–51, 270–284; Leacroft and Leacroft, *Theatre and Playhouse*, pp. 59–66; Orrell, *The Theatres of Inigo Jones and John Webb*. For Cosimo Lotti see Brown and Elliott, *A Palace for a King*, pp. 203–219; Díez Borque, *Sociedad y teatro en la España de Lope de Vega*, pp. 159–162; Egido, *El gran teatro de Calderón*, pp. 106–118; Greer, "Playing the Palace", pp. 95–97; Shergold, "Documentos sobre Cosme Lotti, escenógrafo de Felipe IV"; Thacker, *A Companion to Golden Age Theatre*, p. 129.

56 Dustagheer, "Acoustic and visual practices indoors", pp. 143–151; Greer, *The Play of Power*, pp. 12–15; Ruano de la Haza, *La puesta en escena en los teatros comerciales del Siglo de Oro*, pp. 223–264; Stern, "'A ruinous monastery'", pp. 108–114.

57 Dustagheer, *Shakespeare's Two Playhouses*, p. 45.

58 For more instances of plays combining popular and aristocratic staging practices on the Jacobean stage see Stern, "'A ruinous monastery'", pp. 113–114; Weimann, *Shakespeare and the Popular Tradition in the Theater*, pp. 202–216.

59 Vega, *Comedias de Lope de Vega. Parte XVI*, pp. 43–51. For more see García Santo-Tomás, "Introducción", p. 81; Greer, "A Tale of Three Cities", pp. 393–394. For a more general analysis of the blurring of lines between court and *corral* entertainment see Shergold, *A History of the Spanish Stage*, pp. 360–382.
60 Díez Borque, *Sociedad y teatro en la España de Lope de Vega*, p. 159; Ruano de la Haza, *La puesta en escena en los teatros comerciales del Siglo de Oro*, pp. 268–269; White,"'When torchlight made an artificial noon'".
61 Dustagheer, *Shakespeare's Two Playhouses*, p. 15; Smith, *Shakespeare's Blackfriars Playhouse*, pp. 301–303.
62 Martin White at the University of Bristol's Wickham Theatre, followed by the researcher and performers at the Sam Wanamaker Playhouse, have been experimenting with candlelight in reconstructed Jacobean playhouses, including the aforementioned darkness scenes in *The Duchess of Malfi*. More in Tosh, *Playing Indoors*, pp. 91–118; White, *The Chamber of Demonstrations*.
63 Bolaños Donoso et al., "El Corral de la Montería de Sevilla", pp. 235–237; Marcos Álvarez, "Los teatros fijos de Badajoz en el siglo XVII", p. 49; Mouyen, "Las casas de comedies de Valencia", p. 108.
64 Ruano de la Haza, *La puesta en escena en los teatros comerciales del Siglo de Oro*, pp. 266–268.
65 For more see Davis and Varey (eds.), *Los corrales de comedias y los hospitales de Madrid*, pp. 45–57.
66 Allen, "The Reemergence of the Playhouse in the Renaissance", pp. 27–30; Allen, "The Spanish *Corrales de Comedias* and the London Playhouses and Stages", pp. 214–215; Allen, "The World of the *Comedia*". pp. 24–25; Greer, "Playing the Palace", p. 79.
67 More on the *auto* and its place in seventeenth-century Spanish society in culture in Shergold and Varey, *Los Autos sacramentales en Madrid en la época de Calderón*, pp. xi-xxxii (period illustrations of *auto* staging in pp. 160–161).
68 Allen, "El corral de comedias de Almagro", pp. 202–203; Allen, "The Disposition of the Stage in the English and Spanish Theatres", pp. 56–57; Allen, "Los primeros corrales de comedia", p. 15; Coso Marín et al., *El Teatro Cervantes de Alcalá de Henares*, p. 201; Ruano de la Haza and Allen, *Los teatros comerciales del siglo XVII y la escenificación de la Comedia*, pp. 225–226.
69 Allen, "La importancia de la restauración y la reanimación del Teatro Cervantes", pp. 15–18. Moreover, Ursula Aszyk reconstructs the staging of Lope's *Lo fingido verdadero* with the use of tablados laterales in Aszyk, "'… pon el teatro, y prevén / lo necesario …'".
70 In fact, there is evidence of a provincial performance text for *La vida es sueño* in which all stage direction allusions to the *monte* [hill] of the original Madrid production were taken out. More in Allen, "Los corrales de comedias y los teatros coetáneos ingleses", pp. 18–19. For more on the use of hills, towers and other scenery props in the Spanish *comedia* see Ruano de la Haza and Allen, *Los teatros comerciales del siglo XVII y la escenificación de la Comedia*, pp. 404–446.
71 As cited in Chaytor, "The travels in Spain of Thomas Williams", p. 62.

INTERLUDE 1
Why Did Madrid Not Have a Blackfriars?

While never explicitly asked and therefore also never directly addressed, the question why Madrid did not develop a centric, smaller and roofed public playhouse for its elite theatregoers has loomed over the first two chapters of this book. Throughout the span of Spain's Golden Age of drama, the two long-lasting open-air playhouses of the capital – the Corral del Príncipe and the Corral de la Cruz – were neither replaced by nor complemented with a more sophisticated type of commercial performance venue, in terms of both acting facilities and technologies as well as audience comfort. That an equivalent to London's Blackfriars did not exist in Madrid is a surprising difference that distinguishes two urban theatrical landscapes which were otherwise remarkably alike. While briefly revisiting the main points presented in the first two chapters, this interlude also offers further observations that help explain this unusual departure in the close comparative trajectories of the two cities' theatrical cultures.[1]

First, while early modern London and Madrid are obvious candidates for comparative study thanks to the numerous similarities between them, two fundamental asymmetries also appear from the beginning. The first is that the Spanish theatrical scene was much more decentralised than the English one, which meant that Madrid did not carry as much weight in its national public theatre scene as did London. The second is that London was a considerably larger and more diverse city than its Iberian counterpart. This is of particular relevance to this query, since it probably meant that the English capital had too large an upper-class audience – especially if one adds to it the substantial wealthy middle class whose ranks were considerably leaner in Madrid – to fit all of it into the Court and Court-adjacent private performances. A high-end-yet-public playhouse may well have solved the problem of how to accommodate the wealthier patrons without access to palace entertainment. In Madrid, on the other hand, for the few

DOI: 10.4324/9781003352112-4

cases in which the *corrales* did not satisfy the social needs of Madrid's upper-class playgoers, the combination of frequent performances at Court and even more frequent *particulares* [private performances] would have proved more than sufficient to fill the gap. At least in this respect, there would have been less need for an additional exclusive performance venue for Madrid's wealthy theatregoers than there was in London.

The location of the playhouses within specific neighbourhoods of the cities of London and Madrid, and their respective reputations, would have been another determining factor when deciding whether a completely new type of performance venue for elite audiences was necessary. That London's amphitheatres were built in the poorer suburban liberties surrounding the City, in response to the licensing fees the Common Council tried to levy on theatre builders who wanted to raise playhouses within the capital's territory, probably encouraged the eventual construction (or, in the case of St. Paul's and Blackfriars, rehabilitation) of playhouses in more respectable areas of the English capital. In contrast, Madrid's *corrales de comedia* were located in the northern half of the parish of San Sebastián, an area of decent enough reputation for there to be no need for a upper-class alternative. Since *corrales* were built in pre-existing spaces, there would have not been any motivation to move further out of the city in search of ample building lots, which was one of the underlying factors behind the location of London's amphitheatres. Furthermore, the lack of separate jurisdictional liberties in Madrid – and the fact that the civic and religious authorities wound up actively supporting the theatrical enterprise – removed any possible incentive for Spanish theatre impresarios to build the playhouses in the outskirts of the city in the first place, where the foot traffic and respectability would have been lesser. Whether the fruit of coincidence or consciously planned, the settlement of Madrid's theatrical community in the upper side of San Sebastián, as explained earlier (pp. 23–25), turned out to be an ideal environment from which to attract the full social breadth of the capital's potential playgoers.

One other element that played in the *corrales*' favour in this respect is that, even though all strata of society would gather and coexist in these spaces (as they did in London's amphitheatres), within the Madrid playhouses themselves the different sections of playgoers were more thoroughly isolated from each other than in the London ones. The *corral de comedias* was in essence a yard surrounded by various different houses, a space between buildings and not a building itself. Because of this arrangement, each building had a different entrance and the audience members in the upper levels of the theatre – women, aristocrats, politicians, clergy and other elite patrons – did not access the venue through the main doorway reserved for the remainder of the audience. This system of separate entry and exit doubtless fostered a greater sense of social segregation within the supposedly shared ecosystem that did not always exist in London's suburban theatres. Moreover, once inside the *corrales* the elite audience members continued to be insulated. Unlike in the Globe-like amphitheatres, the upper levels of a *corral* were not open galleries from which everyone could comfortably see; instead, they were rooms with windows overlooking the yard, often covered with gratings or lattices so as better to preserve the intimacy of their occupants. While in the eyes of the members of London's upper classes there may have been a need for a commercial theatre venue in which they could enjoy a show surrounded only by their peers and not by all the social strata of the metropolis, the insulated segregation Madrid's *corrales* offered facilitated the cohabitation – at a certain distance – of its elite theatregoers with the city's other social classes.

From the standpoint of the performance (and playgoing) conditions, the constant renovations the Spanish *corrales* underwent guaranteed that the venue kept up to speed with the rising acceptability of the theatrical event. Subtle but persistent architectural tinkering by theatrical entrepreneurs in Madrid made sure that the playgoing and playmaking conditions were able to accommodate audience expectations. Among the many aspects of their venues Madrid theatre impresarios worked to improve, in addition to the general comfort of their patrons, was the acoustic quality of their venues. By progressively elongating the roofs to cover a larger percentage of the yard, in addition to covering the remaining roofless space with a canvas awning, the aural environment of the Spanish capital's *corrales* was far superior to that of London's amphitheatres. These measures, combined with the fact that the Corrales de la Cruz and del Príncipe were smaller and less densely populated (1.100 and 1.500 spectators, respectively) than theatres such as the Globe or the Swan (which could reportedly fit up to 3.000), endowed these performance spaces with an acoustic profile much closer to that of London's indoor playhouse than the open-air suburban amphitheatres.

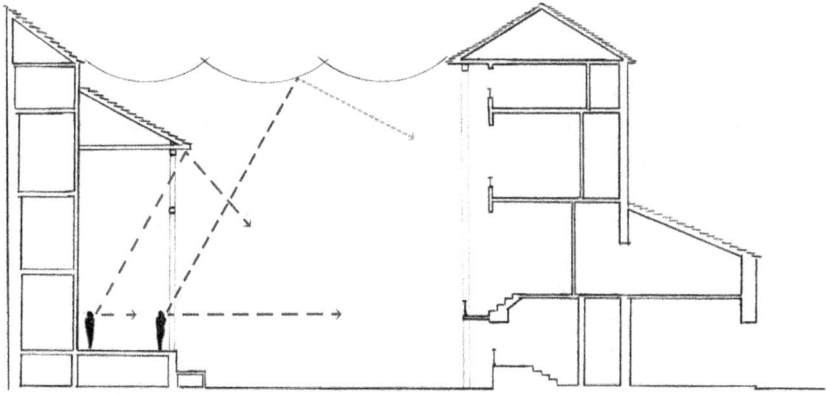

INTERLUDE 1.1 Acoustic projection of Madrid's *Corral del Príncipe* with the canvas *toldo*
Copyright: University Presses of Florida. Modified with permission of the author

Indeed, Madrid's *corrales* offered performers and playgoers alike a level of comfort and a range of staging possibilities that its London counterparts did not match. The Corrales del Príncipe and de la Cruz's incorporation of lateral platforms meant that the once primitive innyards had gradually become spaces capable of hosting the visually striking and crowd-favourite *autos sacramentales*, as well as much more sophisticated *comedia* productions and tampered-down court spectacles of the second half of the seventeenth century. Systematic improvements such as these were not as common in the London amphitheatres, and stagnation in their performance conditions may have been a significant factor in the emergence of higher-quality indoor theatres within the public theatre landscape. The Corral del Príncipe and the Corral de la Cruz remained active throughout the entire early modern period, continuously evolving and adapting to the speed of Madrid's theatrical customs and practices. Throughout their tenure they were the only fully public playhouses of the capital, and Madrid's theatrical community – both playmakers and playgoers – never seemed to long for newer, more centric or more sophisticated venues. In their eyes, a Madrid Blackfriars was not necessary.

That said, in February 1640 the *madrileños* did get something new, in a better location, and much more sophisticated: the Coliseo theatre of the Buen Retiro Palace. This performance venue, part of the new luxurious royal complex built in the 1630s on the eastern outskirts of the city, was initially conceived as a space in which Philip IV and his court could enjoy theatrical spectacles without having to leave the comfort of their new home. It was fully furnished with state-of-the-art stage machinery, the most avant-garde perspective scenography (in Spanish known as *mutaciones*), and its roof and artificial lighting allowed the monarchs to attend spectacles all year long no matter the weather conditions. It was clearly not intended to function as a public theatre. However, not long after it first opened the royal household decided to allow the Coliseo to be used for public functions as well. This does not mean that the masses were welcome to attend the same shows as the king and queen, but rather that the theatre was leased to the same theatre impresarios and acting companies that ran the city's *corrales* as a way of making some additional income for a Crown in an increasingly precarious financial situation. The amenities and prestige of the Coliseo quickly made it the most sought-after venue in Madrid, and the Corrales del Príncipe and de la Cruz gradually became obsolete in the eyes of the capital's playmakers and playgoers.[2] The two public playhouses survived until the the mid-eighteenth century, when they were finally torn down in order to make way for performance spaces more appropriate for the new incoming dramatic culture that regarded both the *comedia nueva* and its accompanying *corral de comedias* as reminders of an outdated albeit glorious past. The Corral de la Cruz was replaced by the Teatro de la Cruz in 1735-1737, and remained one of the most important playhouses in the country until it was demolished in 1859. The Teatro del Príncipe was built in the lot vacated by theCorral del Príncipe in 1735, where it still stands today in the centric Plaza de Santa Ana under its new name Teatro Español. It is the longest continuously-serving site for the performance of theatre in Spain; in its atrium one can find a model of the *corral* that once stood in its place.

Notes

1 This interlude summarises many of the principal points of the book's first two chapters, as well as the main arguments of my article "Comparing the Commercial Theaters in Early Modern England and London", published in *Renaissance Quarterly* 71.2 (2018). Complete documentation for the observations made below can be found therein.
2 More on the Coliseo of Madrid's Buen Retiro Palace in Brown and Elliott, *A Palace for a King*, pp. 74, 95, 105, 111 and fig. 148; Flórez Asensio, "El Coliseo del Buen Retiro en el siglo XVII".

3
PLAYERS

"Are you crazy? What are you saying? You want to start an acting company?". In the opening scene of his extremely popular *El viaje entretenido* (1603), a fictionalised version of Spanish writer Agustín de Rojas chides a friend of his who has just told him he wishes to become a *comediante*.[1] Both his opinion and the opinion of his avatar would have carried some weight in Spanish society, as Rojas was a well-known writer of *loas* [prologues and induction scenes] that served as appetisers for the works of Lope, Tirso de Molina and other playwrights. In other words, here a famous insider of the Golden Age Spanish theatrical world (or someone enacting him) appears on a public stage and declares in front of many hundreds of playgoers that one must be mad to want to become a professional actor. And Rojas was neither the first nor the last to bemoan the arduous nature of the business of playing, as one can hear echoes of this same lament reverberate through practically every dramatic culture in history, including that of Shakespeare's England.

Chapters 3 and 4 of this book offer an exercise in diagnosis: why did one have to be crazy to want to be a professional actor or dramatist in early modern England and Spain? And what were those crazy someones to do if they wanted to make their mad dreams come true? I seek to answer these questions in the following two chapters, the first devoted to players and the second to playwrights (although, as one will be able to see soon enough, there was considerable overlap between these two collectives at times). Chapter 3 opens by identifying the place and reputation of the playmaking community in early modern European society. Thereafter follows a breakdown of the organisational models and structures of acting troupes in England and Spain. Then, after mapping the different touring practices of the companies in the two countries, the chapter ends by focusing on perhaps the most visible difference between the two theatrical cultures: whereas in England women were not allowed to perform on the commercial stage and female roles were customarily represented by young cross-dressed boys, in Spain the professional actress was one of the most prominent figures in the industry.

Professional Playmakers in Early Modern Society

Rojas' "Are you crazy?" outburst shifts meaning as it proceeds. In the first of the many *loas* that populate his collage-like *El viaje entretenido*, the Spanish writer tries to explain, through a rough exchange between a fictionalised version of himself and an unspecified man by the (last) name of Gómez, how an acting troupe's success depended on the fame of its performers:

> **Ro.** Are you crazy? What are you saying?
>   You want to start an acting company?
>   Which famous lead man do you have?
>   And which other players did you come with?
> With Villegas and Rios already in town
>   and their excellent troupes
>   putting on so many plays and shows,
>   So much good music and so many good players,
> You decide to come here to perform:
>   I don't start to understand
>   What may have made you do that.
> **Go.** The desire to please.
> **Ro.** What costumes? Which players?
>   Which renowned musicians?
>   Which actress to play the lead lady?
>   What fool to play the Cisneros?
> What Morales, what Solano?
>   What Ramírez? What León?
>   Or which famous actor do you
>   Bring? **Go.** The story is good, at least.[2]

Actors were popular figures in early modern Spain, and by the beginning of the seventeenth century there was a star system in place that allowed some of them to achieve what we now describe as 'celebrity' status. Villegas and Ríos were the last names of two of the main company leaders associated with the theatrical scene in Seville, the city for which this *loa* was originally written; Cisneros, Morales, Solano, Ramírez and León were well-known players whose acting had become synonymous with excellence, and any frequent theatregoer listening to Rojas' prelude would have been familiar with these names.[3] Similarly, Shakespearean scholars are quite used to hearing how Richard Burbage and Edward Alleyn, star performers in London's primary theatre ensembles, were repeatedly acclaimed for their 'protean' talent and amassed significant wealth and celebrity as a result. In

Ben Jonson's *Bartholomew Fair* (c. 1614) the character of Cokes inquires a puppet-master after his troupe's "Burbage", by which he clarifies he meant his "best Actor"; as in Rojas' *loa*, the names of certain players were synonymous with excellence in Elizabethan and Jacobean England.[4] But this was not always the case: for a very long time working as a player in either of these two countries was considered nothing short of being a vagrant (and in the case of England, the *Act for the punishment of vacabondes* of 1572 turned this popular perception into criminal law). The concept of early modern Golden Age commercial theatre of turn-of-the-century England and Spain with which we are familiar, John Astington reminds us, "was the result of at least fifty years of continuing enterprise" and a slow but relentless – even if not always successful – chipping away at this built-in prejudice against the playing community.[5]

What brought into being this aversion towards the professional performer? In the decades leading up to our timeframe, dramatic texts and performances for the most part originated among amateurs, even if amateur could mean completely different things. It comprised on the one hand members of the wealthy classes who wrote high poesy and closet drama for the benefit of small audiences and coterie readership; on the other it included artisans and members of the lower orders of society who put on short plays in nobles' houses and at fairs and other festivities for money as well as for their own enjoyment. In both England and Spain the earliest professional performers hailed from this second group. Growing up and out of the ranks of the artisan class, these amateur players and playwrights gradually left their day professions for the more lucrative, if considerably more risky, theatrical enterprise.[6] And even though everyone enjoyed watching these shows in one or another context, the humble provenance of the professional playmaking community also meant that they could never count on full acceptance in the social sphere. As John Astington summarises:

> Though [the theatre] was highly regarded by many, its popularity made suspect, in certain eyes, any pretensions it might have to being an especially serious or meaningful human endeavour, while certain stripes of religious fundamentalism, by no means solely 'puritan', regarded its appeal to the senses and its arousal of pleasure as morally corrupting.[7]

This stigmatisation of the theatre-for-profit industry affected not only the players but also the playwrights. Despite the fact that many of the latter attended university and had a professional skillset that would theoretically set them apart from the players, the public standing of professional dramatists was always lower than that of specialists in other literary genres. This is mainly because, especially in its nascent years, the commercial stage was a space of collaborative creation among members of unprivileged social backgrounds, an "artisanally dominated, composite mode of production" as Walter Cohen puts it, and this would not have escaped social judgement.[8] Another prevailing reason to group actors and performers into a single cohort is that very often playwrights would also be players and players would turn into playwrights. In Francisco de Quevedo's picaresque novel *El Buscón* (1626), the narrator at one point joins an acting company, and is surprised to find out that a show it performed was written by one of the troupe's players:

> We performed a *comedia* written by one of our players, and I was taken aback to learn that players were playwrights as well, since I thought that only very wise and learned men could be poets and not such ignorant people; but in truth nowadays there is not a player who does not write *comedias*, nor a performer who does not put on his own mummers' farce about Christians and Moors; I remember the days in which if it were not for the *comedias* by the excellent Lope de Vega [...] there would be nothing at all.[9]

England also had its share of player-playwrights, the most notable being Thomas Heywood and William Shakespeare. The blurry line separating the two professions often led to them being grouped, referred to, and judged as one. When Heywood – the longest serving professional dramatist of the time – wrote his *Apology for Actors* (1612), he hardly distinguishes between them, which might stem from his own situation of having a foot in both fields. Thus, the "City-Actors" to whom he dedicates the book are his "good Friends and Fellowes".[10] For better or worse, as G.E. Bentley remarks in his influential *The Profession of Dramatist in Shakespeare's Time*, "the status of the dramatist was closely related [...] to the status of players and theatres, both of which improved under the notably increasing patronage of King James I and the members of his court".[11] The same can be said of Spain after the ascent to the throne of Philip III, a greater enthusiast of the *comedias* than his father.

The gradual shift in the public perception also took place semantically, as people changed the way they referred to the playmaking professions. Even though I have been using 'actor' and 'player' indistinctly here, the truth is that the use of these terms differed markedly. It would have been more correct to refer to them as 'players', because that is how they were described in the public sphere at the time. For starters, saying 'player' highlights the fact that these performers did much more than just act, since they also were expected to sing, dance, mime, jest, and entertain in a multitude of ways.[12] But perhaps more importantly, 'actor' was a Latinism inherited from the classics that was associated with a professionalism and respect that in the eyes of the public had yet to be earned. With time, the professionals proactively began to claim the loaded moniker for themselves, and one could see the term 'actor' used more and more in the printing of plays. To recycle an example, Heywood would have been positioning himself quite openly when he dedicated his work to his fellow "Citty-*Actors*", as he finds the need "to approue our Antiquity, ancient Dignity, and the true use of our quality".[13] The same could be said of Ben Jonson, who fashioned himself an "Author" and not a mere writer, and who addressed the performers of his plays quite deliberately as "Comoedians" and "Tragoedians" in his 1616 collected works.[14] In Spain, even the most established of players were referred to as *representantes*, *farsantes*, *comediantes*, *recitantes* ... only a select few were unequivocally described as *actores* and *actrices*.[15] All these marked expressions, which only slowly caught on with the rest of society, sought to evoke an unequivocal link to the well-reputed dramatic literature of ancient Greece and Rome, from which both Heywood's *Apology* and Rojas' eighth *loa* in *El viaje entretenido* (see p. 50) claim direct lineage.

Although Heywood affirms that he wrote the *Apology* because the theatrical world did not have the "sufficient countenance to bolster it selfe by his owne strength", the truth is that the life of the playmaker had by that point improved considerably in comparison with the first decades of commercial theatre.[16] While it is true that most players in Jacobean England remained "poor men, as they have been in almost all ages of the theater", the landscape had changed enough to allow a certain few even to become considerably wealthy; indeed, acting became one of the "few avenues of free enterprise open to an Elizabethan of modest means".[17] Shakespeare, along with fellow King's Men John Heminges and Henry Condell, were members of a successful company and had managed their investments well enough to be considered affluent. Others, such as Christopher Beeston, Thomas Greene, and the more popular performers of London's companies also fared well. Edward Alleyn became extraordinarily rich, to the point that he was able to open his own charity school in Dulwich in 1619. These cases were no doubt exceptional, but what trickled down from their success and celebrity was that, the relentless enemies of the theatre notwithstanding, players were no longer looked upon as the vagrants and vagabonds described in the 1572 dictum.[18] And this ascent in status of England's theatrical culture found a perfect mirror in Spain: the more hands-on patronage model of both James I and Philip III, and especially the significant increase in court performances, changed the public perception of the playmakers who found themselves performing more frequently in front of, and mingling more and more with, members of the court and the urban elite.

This growing comfort and association with the upper echelons of society notwithstanding, the stigma of professional playmaking endured. As noted earlier, if someone with aristocratic ties or aspirations desired to venture into the playground it would be best to do so as an amateur, or at least to appear as one. Professional acting, more so than writing, was definitely not considered acceptable for the upper classes. One telling example is what has come to be known in Shakespeareana as the Clifton Affair. A London neighbour by the name of Henry Clifton was outraged after the Children of the Blackfriars abducted his son to become a member of their reputed boy company. The abduction in itself was not the issue, as this was both legal and common practice. But the father of young

Thomas Clifton thought becoming a player was below his son's worth. Clifton complained that his son had been taken "unto the said playhouse in the Blackfriars aforesaid and there to sort him with mercenary players and [...] there to detain and compel to exercise the base trade of a mercenary interlude player to his utter loss of time ruin and disparagement [...] amongst a company of lewd and dissolute mercenary players".[19] No doubt Clifton's reaction represented an extreme position towards the profession of playing, just as Heywood and Rojas represented the polar opposite. A meeting point between the two edges would have been the most populated territory. Or a straight mixture of both, sometimes: in a 1593 legal transcript of a Sevillian trial – famous for having Cervantes himself among the witnesses listed – the figure of the *comediante* awakened admiration and disgust in equal measures within the same person.[20] In 1628, the caricaturist John Earle summarised this sentiment best when he wrote that the profession of playing "ha's in it a kind of contradiction, for none is more dislik'd, and yet none more applauded".[21]

To sum up, players and playwrights were the objects of growing praise, but ran into a firm ceiling in terms of social aspirations. Even if English dramatist Robert Greene's alter-ego poet in *Groats-worth* was praised for his rhetoric and "his labours were so well esteemed", he never wins respect as a serious businessman and is conned time and again by those around him.[22] Travel writer Fynes Moryson (1617) praised the London players as they, in his opinion, "excel all others in the world", and in doing so he signalled that performers and playwrights were cultural patrimony and a source of pride.[23] And yet Quevedo's Buscón, who ends up becoming a rich and well-regarded *comediante* – both as player and playwright – finally quits the job and uproots his life to try something else; after all, he was leaving behind a "bad life: the life of a player".[24]

Company Models, Structure and Organisation

The links between the commercial playmakers and the artisan class went beyond social perception and prejudices; in fact, the very structure of the early modern professional playing company reflected the socioeconomic reality of the period. Although it was not recognised as an official guild – the dominant labour model in early modern European cities – from the beginning the theatremaking community organised itself according to the same hierarchical structure. Both in guilds and in acting companies a first echelon of members emerged, followed by a second tier of hired hands of all sorts, and finally a group of apprentices. Developing such an internal structure made sense, since most of the early professional players in both countries grew up within the ranks of this workforce system. "For the Alleyns and Burbages, the most familiar model of commerce was the guild", writes Roslyn Knutson before providing a substantial list of many early modern English theatrical entrepreneurs and their original guild affiliations. Carmen Sanz and Bernardo García offer a similar list to Knutson's for the first professional *comediantes* in Spain, and it is precisely because of the strong ties between the guild and play worlds that Sanz and García refer to the first generation of players as *"artesanos de la comedia"* ["artisans of the theatre"].[25] Furthermore, in the case of Spain one can argue that the influence of the guild model on the acting community was even stronger, since the first commercial theatre performances in the country derived from the practice of guilds participating in contests to win the privilege – and monetary prize – of performing their religious pageants during the annual Corpus Christi festivities.[26] The ghost presence of an unofficial guild-like regulation and structure in Spain led to the creation in 1630 of the Cofradía de la Novena, a prominent religious brotherhood located in the parish of San Sebastián which eventually became the official corporate organisation for the *comediantes* in the Spanish capital. The confraternity – to which all actors and playwrights were required to belong – behaved exactly like a guild, not just ensuring them a proper Christian burial but also representing its members before the municipal government and jostling for prestige with the other liveries.[27]

The most telling parallelism between the playing company and the guild was their almost identical hierarchical structure. Like all guilds, the playing companies recognised different levels of membership, ranked according to experience and talent in acting. However, there also had to be a manager of sorts running the business end of things. Spanish companies referred to this figure as the *autor de comedias*, a player-manager who oversaw the company as his (at the beginning they were always men) individual enterprise.[28] The company was named after him, planned by him and built around him.[29] He was often the lead actor, and his wife was often the lead actress (more on this later). The *autor* took the full share of the company profits, and from them paid the remaining players wages agreed upon in advance, with an additional *per diem* stipend when the company was on tour. Additionally, the *autor* owned the repertory of plays (by either writing the *comedias* himself or purchasing them from other *poetas*), the wardrobe, and all the company equipment. Thanks to this rigid hierarchy, the typical Spanish playing company was known as a *compañía de autor* or *compañía de ración* [manager/waged company].[30]

In England every company had a manager as well, even if he did not always have the same amount of power as the *autor* did in Spain. The most prominent representative of the English company managers was the Admiral's Men's Edward Alleyn, who doubled as lead player and brains behind the business. Alleyn's company exemplifies what Andrew Gurr labels an 'impresario system', the closest equivalent in England to Spain's *compañía de autor*. But England also offered an alternative model: in some troupes it would have been difficult to single out a single leader and/or business owner, as they were run by a group of players instead. Gurr and other theatre historians have described this type of company as a 'share company', with Shakespeare's own Chamberlain's/King's Men standing tallest among them. Sharers would have been percentage owners of the enterprise, endowed with a certain amount of executive authority regarding company matters as well as being entitled to a portion of the profits. Sharers were fellows, partners and colleagues. Gurr writes that the "sharer system" of Shakespeare's company was "a strikingly democratic system in a deeply patriarchal and authoritarian age".[31] That said, it would have been also impossible to conceive such an intricate business operation without at least one managerial figure in every troupe:

> The complexity of the affairs in which Elizabethan, Jacobean, and Caroline repertory companies were necessarily involved required that some one or two players be in charge, at least to the extent of authorizing the purchase of new costumes and costume materials; paying for new plays by freelance dramatists; getting scripts approved by the Master of the Revels, paying him for licenses for the theater and for occasional privileges, like playing during parts of Lent; paying the company's regular contributions to the poor of the parish, assessing fines against sharers or hired men for infringement of company regulations; calling rehearsals; collecting fees for court and private performances, supervising the preparation and distribution of playbills; and perhaps for paying the hired men.[32]

In other words, even in the King's Men – so often portrayed as an ideal democratic joint-stock company in which all the sharers had equal say – sooner or later someone had to carry out the decisions. One such figure was John Heminges, the King's Men's "God" to the other fellows' "angels" (an analogy attributed to John Donne).[33] Some cases of sharer system companies also emerged in Spain, chiefly among the the Italian troupes. But even in these *compañías de partes* [companies of parts or partners] a *capocomico* [head comedian] was elected – democratically – to give the company a name, a face, and a leader. This would have been the case of the company led by Ganassa, frequently referred to throughout the first section of this book. That said, the *compañía de partes* model was not all that successful among the Spanish companies, which overwhelmingly preferred the *compañía de autor* model instead.[34]

Another quintessential guild characteristic also present in the early modern playing company was its reliance on the family. Fraternal bonds and camaraderie united professional players in general, and the members of each company in particular. This is palpable in the surviving documents from the English acting community, such as wills and testaments, which clearly show that the lines that separated the personal and the professional were often too blurred for us to distinguish. Many sons of actors became actors, many daughters of actors married other actors, and many widows of actors remarried their late husbands' former colleagues.[35] In Spain there were professional stage actresses as well (see pp. 92-96), and numerous companies were formed around a marriage or family consisting of the company manager, the lead actress, and their siblings and/or children. A prominent example of this company model, commonly known as the *familia de cómicos* [family of players], was that of the manager Jerónimo Velázquez, who became the most successful theatre manager of the 1570s and 1580s along with his wife, daughter and son.[36] In England such a company model was not possible, of course, but the wives of the players were often an integral part of the business as well. Relatives of the companies' visible faces often undertook all the work off the stage and behind the curtains. Such was the case of the Chamberlain's/King's Men, a company with a high degree of intermarriage, and in which the wives performed the duties of gatherers and stagehands.[37] Professional playmaking in the early modern days was, in short, a family business.

The companies were organised internally into three distinguishable levels of performers. The first tier was that of the lead players (or *primeras figuras* in the case of Spain), the "most distinguished and popular performers in the troupe", which normally included the player-managers and/or sharers as well as a handful of indispensable actors and actresses. Whether they were sharers or hired hands, players of this calibre earned significantly more, and they frequently specialised in roles such as the gallant, the lady, the fool, or the old man or *barba* [pantaloon]. The more proficient (and fortunate) among them could even aspire to celebrity status. In Spain hired players of this level of importance were known as the *oficiales*, and each company had around three or four such figures around which the rest of the cast was built and rebuilt on a yearly basis. The remaining hired adult performers followed this first tier: their level included not only actors and actresses, but also specialist musicians and dancers. The company contracted their services on a temporary basis, mostly depending on the needs of that year or season's repertory. And in the lowest echelon each company had a group of apprentices who learned the trade of playing from the lead players, just as in any other guild profession.[38] Apprentices were especially important in England because they were charged with playing the female parts since women were not allowed on the professional stage.[39] An apprentice was often the son – occasionally the daughter, in the case of Spain – of a company player; after honing their skill with a troupe, they could aspire to ascend the ranks and become a regular player or *oficial*; after that, an important *oficial* or a sharer; and eventually, even a manager or *autor de comedias*.[40]

One should never forget all the hired hands – and in some cases slaves – who worked for the companies even if they did not see any acting time themselves. These were the offstage theatre functionaries: fee collectors, stage keepers, wardrobe keepers, bookkeepers, musicians, prompters and, of course, playwrights.[41] The types of relationship between early modern playwrights and companies were very diverse, almost as diverse as playwrights themselves. For the most part, both in Spain and in England the playwright was an external hire commissioned to write a play or plays for the company. In very few cases, playwrights in England became part of a company and wrote exclusively – or almost exclusively – for one troupe, as was the case of Shakespeare and the King's Men. But the underlying principle never changed: the company or *autor* who commissioned and paid for a text, and not the playwright, became the legal and intellectual owner of the play and could do with it as he or they pleased. This ownership included the exclusive rights of performance, the rights to change the play according to their performance needs, and even the right to sell the manuscript (or a copy of it) to other companies or to printers as a way of recovering some of their initial investment, all without the need to consult the dramatist. Roslyn Knutson explains the London situation best: "playing companies relied on a cooperative workforce of playwrights who could readily supply scripts on popular topics in fashionable genres that were marketable on stage and, when some advantage to the companies presented itself, at the bookshop".[42] Once that premise is set, every playwright-company agreement imaginable took place within these two theatre systems, ranging from selling plays by the act to playwrights becoming sharers in companies. This last scenario – the ever-recurring case of Shakespeare as a single company's in-house dramatist – was admittedly unusual.[43] Still, English companies appear to have created longer lasting bonds with specific writers than Spanish troupes, where 'freelancing' was the most common practice.[44]

A word must also be said about London's professional children acting companies. As noted earlier, thanks to their guild-like hierarchical structure most early modern acting troupes in both countries included boys and adolescents among their ranks. However, only England formed professional companies comprised exclusively of younger performers. These groups emerge as the natural commercial outcome of what was once an exclusively didactic exercise: as a way of improving their Latin, children across Renaissance Europe – including England – were taught in grammar schools the art of eloquence and oratory through the performance of short dialogues and colloquies. Their ranks also included the children of Tudor London's main choirs, who ever since the mid 1550s were invited every Christmas to perform in court. In order to prepare these court shows, choir masters had them 'rehearse' – as it was insistently referred to – in front of paying, aristocratic audiences. By the early 1580s, London's two most important children choirs, the Children of St. Paul's and the Children of the Chapel, had their own playhouses and house dramatists (additionally there apparently was also the Oxford's Boys, a composite troupe drawing youths from both Paul's and the Chapel).[45] Although by this point in essence these were professional players and performances, the company masters kept their original education-related choir names "in order to foster the illusion that they were amateur children's troupes, the traditional purveyors of dramatic entertainment to the court".[46] It was morally much less problematic for public figures openly to endorse private performances and the rehearsals of children troupes than public performances for commercial gain. William More, who in the late 1570s had leased his property in the Blackfriars priory to Richard Farrant for his choir, complained about the obvious deceit: "Ferrant pretended unto me to use the house only for the teaching of the Children of the Chapel but made it a Continual house for plays".[47]

Following some years of prominence and success, both boys' companies had dissolved by the late 1580s. After a decade of silence, the Children of Paul's came back in 1599, and shortly thereafter so did the Blackfriars troupe. The new lessor of the old Blackfriars priory playhouse, Henry Evans (who had worked under Farrant in the first Blackfriars and briefly took over the company after his employer's death), recruited the choir master of the Children of the Chapel Royal at Windsor in order to benefit from both the reputation associated with his post, which also evoked the original Blackfriars troupe of the 1580s, and his license to abduct children for educational purposes (the Clifton affair referred to in the previous section of this chapter is an example of one of many forced conscriptions the company carried out). Evans' group, which in 1603 was re-baptised the Children of the Queen's Revels after acquiring a royal patent, would become the "most enduring and influential of the Jacobean children's companies".[48] Under his direction, the Children of the Queen's Revels, as well as their rivals at St. Paul's, set aside any didactic considerations and became aggressively market-oriented. Their controversial repertory and style, regularly spiced with commentary on the affairs of the court and its denizens, would make them favourites among the wealthier London playgoers. It also eventually led them to lose their royal patronage in 1606 and their Blackfriars lease in 1608 for ruffling the wrong feathers one too many a time. With the help of some makeovers they managed to survive, and performed at court and in the Whitefriars playhouse throughout the following decade. However, the all-boy companies lost a lot of ground to the adult players when the King's Men took over the Blackfriars in 1608.[49] The performance conventions that had once set them apart – especially the interlude music and dancing – survived this changing of the guard as staples of central London's indoor playhouses even after the adult companies took over.

Touring Practices

This book focuses primarily on the playgrounds of the major cities of Shakespearean England and Golden Age Spain, for and from which the most well-known commercial dramatic output was initially conceived. These are where the major playhouses were located, where the dramatists usually lived, and where the acting companies hoped to work. Nevertheless, since plays in both countries were also put on elsewhere, this theatre deserves its own section here as well, especially since the performance practices of the regional and travelling companies exerted considerable influence over how the theatrical communities in England and Spain's large urban centres conducted themselves. Touring played an indispensable role in the shaping of these two theatrical cultures, even if – as this section illustrates – the ways and means of touring in the two countries were motivated by different factors, charted by different interests, and ultimately directed towards different goals.

Before the emergence of London as the theatrical centre of Elizabethan England, the most successful way of making a living as a player was by touring. And even after the first permanent playhouses were built in the capital, touring remained an important part of English playing practice in the early decades of professional theatre, as Scott McMillin and Sally-Beth MacLean explain: "the actors were in circulation – that is the best way to think of them. London was the centre of the circulation, with its rapidly growing population, its new playhouse, and its proximity to court".[50] From 1590 to 1642 approximately twenty commercial troupes performed in London, of which only the Chamberlain-King's Men were consistently present; that is twenty out of the over 100 troupes that existed in England during that period, most of which never set foot in London. Despite London's all-important status within the early modern English theatrical landscape, decentralisation was stronger than the traditional narrative suggests.[51]

There were enormous differences between performing in post-1570s London and elsewhere. Other than the capital, only Bristol, York and Prescot had permanent purpose-built acting spaces in England before the 1660s (see pp. 12-13). Gurr encapsulates best this paradoxical situation when he writes that "London was the only really large market for the peculiarly portable commodity that the playing companies had to sell".[52] Therefore touring troupes had to perform in repurposed spaces that did not always meet the technical standards and comfort of the London playhouses.[53] Siobhan Keenan's research locates secular theatre performances in town-halls, large country houses, inns and even town churches, since these tended to be among the largest indoor public spaces in which a community could hold such an event; in a different publication she goes on to suggest that "without permanent places to perform these travelling troupes were accustomed to performing in a variety of spaces from market-places and town-halls to monasteries and country houses; a fortunate few were also invited to perform at court".[54] Moreover, the practice – or tradition – of touring did not end for the London companies with the building of permanent theatres in Shoreditch and Southbank. Frequently these troupes had to leave the capital for financial or public health reasons. Touring the countryside meant new income for plays that had worn out their welcome on the London stages after having been performed there time and again. And even when the playhouses were not officially shut down by the Master of the Revels during plagues, the fear of epidemic could still be felt: "[m]any Londoners voted with their feet when the plague figures rose, leaving London if they could afford to, and avoiding crowds so far as they could, including those gathering at playhouses".[55] In such situations, the company with the means and *savoir-faire* to tour took to the road, even if that meant leaving life in the metropolis behind for an extended period. As the writer of *The Rich Cabinet Furnished with Variety of Excellent Descriptions* (1616) succinctly put it: "[the p]layer is afraid of the plague, as much as a coward of a musket: for as death is formidable to one, so is poverty and want to the other".[56]

Deciding where to go was easy for most of the London companies, since they could fall back on their routes and networks from earlier touring days. McMillin and MacLean have traced seven different touring circuits across early modern England: East Anglia, south east, south west, Midlands, west Midlands, north east and north west.[57] Each troupe picked its region according to the company's popularity there, the economic potential (i.e., the size of the markets, fairs and the towns themselves), and whether the name of the company's patron carried any local weight. In a modern sense, there was neither an obligation for companies to take to the road nor any restrictions on where the company could tour as long as the proper local licences were acquired. In fact, touring eventually became less important for the London companies and they ended up abandoning the practice altogether, which gave rise to a 'London troupe' versus 'travelling troupe' dichotomy. As this gap grew London players and touring players developed different mind-sets, and in a way worked in completely different professions. The always-polemical John Marston distinguishes in his works between the two types of performers when he shows contempt for touring players, who were in his always critical eye still very much the vagrants described in the aforementioned 1572 dictum.[58] The schism between the London-based companies – which included the boy companies at Blackfriars and St. Paul's as well as the major adult ones – and the travelling troupes was in no small part due to the paucity of licences London issued for companies to perform in the city. According to Keenan, "the story of acting companies in Shakespeare's London is partly a story of growing professionalization and commercialization but it is also one of increasingly tight regulation".[59] In 1611, after eight years of close supervision under James I, only six companies had permission to play in the capital. This proved too many for the commercial market, and by 1615 only four companies were allowed in London. This left the other troupes either to tour for a living or dissolve. Also, the growing association between the practice of playing and provincial views of the capital as a den of sin stiffened opposition in outlying towns to theatre and travelling players. By the 1620s all practice of touring in England had decreased significantly, and with it so did the activity of the travelling troupes.[60]

Touring practices in Spain resembled those found in England, starting with the major cities' restricted issue of licences. Companies without a license to perform in any Spanish municipality – this applies not just to metropolitan centres such as Madrid and Seville, but in theory to all urban centres – were required to remain at least one league away so as to not compete directly with the licensed troupes. This led to a recognisable hierarchy among theatre professionals. Unlicensed performers were known as *cómicos de la legua* [league actors], to set them apart from the much more formal *compañías de título* [licensed companies], also referred to as *compañías reales* [royal companies]; moreover, the most important licensed troupes were known as *grandes compañías* [large companies].[61] In a way, the two tiers of performing troupes in England find an almost exact equivalent in early modern Spain. Similarly, the social standing of the two company structures also differed. Society regarded the *cómicos de la legua*, often referred to as *chocarreros* [buffoons] and *histriones* [mummers], as no better than *volteadores*, *buratines* or *titiriteros* [acrobats and puppeteers], and thus much inferior to performers in the main cities.

However, one major difference marked the two systems. From the beginning a license to perform in one of the Spanish cities, unlike a license for London, was not permanent: after a couple of months of performing in the same place, the license expired and the company had to leave the host city and relocate. That meant that all Spanish companies, regardless of their wealth and fame, had to live 'on tour'.[62] Thus in 1600, for example, only four licensed companies were allowed to perform in Castile's various *corrales*, a figure which happens to coincide with the maximum number of troupes the council of theologians appointed by the Duke of Lerma that same year ruled as morally acceptable. And while there were four troupes with official permission to perform in Castile, only two of them could be in the capital city of Madrid at the same time, one for each playhouse. This restriction was "due more to an interest in maintaining an economic monopoly rather than any kind of moral compunction", since one of the main beneficiaries of the *corrales* was the local governments themselves. By 1603 the rapid increase in popularity and demand for commercial theatre doubled the number of companies with permission to perform in the capital. The peak was reached between 1625 and 1641, when twelve troupes shared Castile's theatrical calendar and Madrid's two main *corrales* among them.[63] The solution reached was for the *compañías* to leave the city after two or three months, and to play in other cities and towns across the country during the remainder of the year. The same policy was adopted in Seville, the other main theatrical stronghold in seventeenth-century Spain. It was this itinerancy, a blend of government imposition and the allure of the *fiestas* of other cities and towns (especially since playing the religious *autos sacramentales* at specified moments in the liturgical calendar proved to be much more lucrative than regular everyday *comedias*) that made the Spanish theatrical scene much more decentralised, dispersed and multifocal than its English counterpart.[64]

The fact that every Golden Age playing company – large or small, licensed or not – toured left deep tracks for all troupes to follow. The same principles for choosing where to visit and perform in Elizabethan England applied to Habsburg Spain: the targets were important urban centres, routes regularly favoured by the court, flagship fairs, and territories in which the *autor* and/or players had greater presence and reputation. And with Spain's greater demographic decentralisation, the alternatives to Madrid were many and almost equally profitable, especially during holiday seasons. However, and unlike England, the circuits of Spanish troupes could be influenced by changing political and administrative conditions. The Iberian Peninsula housed several kingdoms, each with its own physical and legal boundaries and jurisdictions, which could pose problems for outsiders. Thus, a Castilian company would have to pay customs taxes when crossing the border into Portugal or Aragon, and vice versa. According to Sanz Ayán and García García, this gave rise to five major territorial subdivisions: the main theatre centres – Madrid, Valladolid, Toledo, Seville and Valencia – most of which were located in the central kingdom of Castile; Portugal; Navarre; the crown of Aragon, which included Catalonia and Valencia; and the Andalusian provinces.[65]

Choosing one or another travel route depended largely on the location of the company's headquarters; choosing whether to travel or not, however, was not an option in Golden Age Spain as it was in late Elizabethan and Jacobean England. Thus, since companies in Spain could not reside in Madrid or Seville the way English companies did in London, geographic stability was nearly impossible for a Spanish troupe. The Augustinian friar Juan González de Critana openly lamented this reality in 1610, since the constant travelling made it impossible for the players to hold their less-egregious previous job during weekdays:

> ... and let us not allow these bands of men and women to travel across our realm; the company at court should remain at court, and the company of Toledo should stay in Toledo, so that the player can see to his trade during the week, as Lope de Rueda, Navarro and Cisneros did at the beginning, even if eventually they started to form *compañías* and go from town to town.[66]

In one way or another, the practice of touring was a pivotal element in the development of the commercial theatre sector in early modern England and Spain's theatrical hubs. Touring players connected the country's major urban centres with the peripheral pockets of professional playing. In reciprocal fashion, the conventions and habits of one play culture influenced the other and vice versa. Any overview of the theatrical cultures of Shakespearean England and Golden Age Spain must include their troupes' regular interaction with towns and cities beyond the theatrical capitals among the most significant characteristics they shared.

Who Played the Female Roles? Women and Children on the Commercial Stage

So far, each element of playmaking in one country has found a more or less stable equivalent in the other. The final section of this chapter takes a detour from this narrative and addresses what is, in my opinion, the most significant difference between Shakespearean England and Golden Age Spain's playmaking communities: that whereas England's commercial playing companies were exclusively comprised of male players and thus all female roles were performed by young cross-dressed boys and adolescents, the professional actress was a central figure in the Spanish theatrical landscape. Triggering this divergence were the efforts of authorities and theologians to prevent the increasingly popular theatrical enterprise promoting lewdness. The obsession with lust comes across in practically every surviving anti-theatrical sermon or treatise from the period (see pp. 25-29), and the figure of the on-stage female – both as performer and as character of a fiction – was always at the heart of their concerns. In his treatise *De Spectaculis* (1599), the Spanish

Jesuit Juan de Mariana laid bare the debate: on one hand he was aware that "women have the talent and ability to attract men, in the way a magnet attracts iron, even if they do not want to be moved", and that actresses on stage always tended to dress in the most inappropriate of ways (or so he had been told). On the other, the danger of banning actresses would result in having "little children dressed and adorned in women's clothing, which might tempt the people to feel a different, much more deranged and criminal lustful temptation".[67] The dilemma of choosing between these two unacceptable options marked the crossroads at which both England and Spain's playgrounds found themselves.

For the English, having female performers was the more dangerous option. Women enjoying the limelight of the public stage would have given "prominence to sexuality and the female body, precisely those entities that most demanded – and threatened – patriarchal domination".[68] Consequently, cross-dressed boy actors were tapped to play the female parts in order to mitigate the femininity of both performer and performance. Seeing young boys on stage alongside adult actors would not have shocked Elizabethan Londoners; as explained earlier, the guild-like nature of the playing companies was predicated on experienced veterans shepherding a cohort of apprentices through the ins and outs of the trade. Furthermore, the existence of London's children companies speaks to the period's appreciation for the skillset of many of these younger performers. Casting their trainees, who ranged approximately from ten to twenty-years-old, as the female characters – in addition to the juvenile roles – allowed English adult companies to have their youthful and higher-pitched performers hone their talents while at the same time respecting the female-free regimen of the English stage.[69] Or, as Pamela Brown succinctly puts it, "the English stage took boys for actresses because they wanted everything the actress offered, except the player itself".[70] While there was still some notable opposition to the cross-dressed boy actors – the Puritan William Prynne infamously described them in his polemic *Histrio-Mastix* (1633) as "our English Man-woman monsters" – on the whole they were seen as a more palatable alternative to permitting women to play the female roles.[71]

It should be noted that the 'prohibition' (more cultural than strictly legal) of actresses in England applied only to commercial performances in public theatres. Early modern English women "had long appeared as players in a variety of arenas, and at every level of society", with gentle ladies often taking on the main roles in court masques, female citizens performing in parish plays and civic pageantries, and lower-class women often earning a living as itinerant entertainers (ballad singers, dancers, etc.).[72] Moreover, occasional visits from French and Italian troupes to London allowed company actresses to play their parts in the capital's public venues.[73] The actress-less predicament of Shakespearean England's public playhouses could thus be described as a 'cultural interregnum' in the performance practices of a nation that otherwise fell squarely within Europe's theatremaking tradition.[74]

Spain, like the rest of western continental Europe and unlike England, had professional actresses. Their presence on the boards began with the arrival of the first Italian *commedia dell'arte* troupes, and their involvement increased gradually over time. In 1580 the Italian *capocomico* Ganassa's company included nine members, only one of whom – his wife, Barbara Flaminia – was a woman; she shared the responsibility for playing the female roles with two of the company's male performers. There is also evidence of men playing the female parts in other early productions in Spain, including in those by Lope de Rueda (who is widely considered to be Spain's first home-grown *autor de comedias*). In other words, countries such as Spain or Italy allowed for an certain familiarity with both men and women representing female characters on the public stage.[75] These early episodes of transvestism in continental performances may help explain why none of the foreign travellers who visited the English playhouses and wrote about their experiences bothered to remark on the unusual sight of cross-dressed boys playing all the female roles. Nevertheless, the involvement of women in the Spanish theatrical enterprise eventually grew to the point that male actors no longer had to play female parts on a regular basis, rendering it the polar opposite of the situation in England.

This does not necessarily mean, however, that the Spanish and the English thought differently regarding the presence of women on the nation's boards. In fact, the idea of women being allowed to parade their bodies so publicly outraged Spain's moralists as much as cross-dressed men and boys playing female roles. From the very beginning, religious leaders lobbied to ban women from performing in the *corrales*, and even managed to get the Council of Castile to do so on at least two separate occasions. The first was in 1580, although apparently all the parties involved – acting companies, audiences and even the local authorities – ignored the edict and women continued to perform on stage despite the new ruling. The second prohibition was decreed in 1586, and this time the law was enforced albeit briefly, since the following year the Council reassessed this measure and officially lifted the ban.[76] Two main driving forces explain this change of heart. The first was the sincere social consternation caused by young boys performing the female parts in cross-dress. As Ursula K. Heise's research shows, the Spanish authorities' fear of homosexuality was much stronger than in other European countries, particularly compared to England. Having young boys pretending to be women in public, rendering them as potential objects of desire for the predominantly male theatre-going body, was seen by many as the more disturbing alternative. In fact, a group of prominent actresses, led by Mariana de O and Mariana Vaca, took advantage of this discomfort to circulate a public complaint denouncing the moral problem of letting young boys play female roles. Trapped between a rock and a hard place, the Council determined that allowing women to appear onstage was the lesser of the two evils.

The second reason was financial. As explained earlier (pp. 27-28), Spain's public theatres were regularly used to finance local charities and public health institutions, and a company's strongest attraction was its celebrity female performers. The *primera dama* [first lady] was always among the most admired and best paid members of the troupe in frank recognition of her star power and audience pull; indeed, only the *autor de comedias* himself earned more than the company's lead actress. Moreover, the *segundas damas* [supporting ladies] received the same level of remuneration and esteem as the *segundos galanes* [supporting gallants] and other second-tier male perfomers.[77] Additionally, each company hired a significant number of musicians and dancers, many if not most of whom were women. The 1586 ban caused the nation's playgoing body to react negatively to this casting change, which led to a perceptible drop in revenue coming from the *corrales* during the following year. The measure struck a direct blow against the funding of public hospitals and charitable institutions, which led many anti-theatrical theologians and politicians to reconsider their original stance against allowing women to appear onstage. On November 17th 1587 the ban on professional actresses was lifted, and the revenue stream of the nation's *corrales* went back to its original vigorous flow. Both moralists and legislators accepted this reversal on the condition that all actresses should be married (to ensure their virtue) and that the *autores* provide the authorities with lists of all the women under their employment each season. The marriage requirement gave rise to the aforementioned troupe model known as the *familia de cómicos*, in which the *autor* and lead actress were husband and wife. It also predictably resulted in an array of sham marriages and other loopholes associated with widowhood.[78] The following passage in Quevedo's *El Buscón*, which follows the protagonist as he and his acting troupe make their way to Toledo, provides a poignant illustration of how the effect of these 'well-intended' laws ran only skin deep:

> Men and women travelled all mixed together, and one of the women, the dancer (who also played the queen and other somber roles in the plays), seemed to me to be very flirtatious. I happened to be sitting next to her husband, and I, not knowing to whom I was talking, overcome with desire to love and enjoy her, said to him: 'this woman ... what must one do to be able to spend twenty *escudos* on her? I find her beautiful'. 'I should not be telling you this, since I am her husband', the man replied, 'nor should I be dealing in such matters ... but the truth is, and no passion moves me to say this, you can spend on her as much as you want, and that the world has not seen such loins, and such playfulness'. And, after saying that, he jumped off the wagon and hopped onto a different one, as if to give me the chance to talk to her. The man's answer amused me, and then I understood that these were people of whom one could say are married only on paper, turning license into malice.[79]

There were subsequent attempts to ban actresses, including a successful one in 1596 that lasted longer than previous efforts due to the shut-down of the theatres in 1598 following Philip II's death. But from the reopening of the *corrales* in 1600 onward the Spanish actress took centre stage never to depart. Her physical presence was moreover marked explicitly within the plays written by or after the fashion of Lope de Vega, whose burgeoning *comedia nueva* invested female characters with newfound levels of protagonism and agency. Many seventeenth-century actresses became household names, celebrated for their talent and their beauty. Sir Richard Wynn, an English courtier who travelled to Madrid in 1623 as part of Prince Charles' entourage, visited one of the capital's famous innyard theatres and noted that

> [t]he players consist of men and women: the men are indifferent actors, but the women are very good, and become themselves far better than any that ever I saw act those parts, and far handsomer than any women I saw. To say the truth, they are the only cause their plays are so much frequented.[80]

With time, a few of the better known actresses became *autoras de comedias* and led their own troupes. Other women also began to write their own plays for the nation's public playhouses, thus entering a profession, that of the commercial playwright, that had previously been exclusively male.[81] All these steps taken towards the advancement of women in Spain's theatrical culture saw themselves corresponded in the dramatic output, which increasingly privileged female characters, as is explored in detail in the second interlude of this book (pp. 127-142).

In England one would have to await the reopening of the theatres in 1660 to see women return to the commercial stage. The inclusion of both professional actresses and professional female dramatists that spearheaded the reconstituted public theatre of the Restoration laid the groundwork for the ever increasing visibility and protagonism of women in the nation's playmaking community. The brief caesura in female absence/presence that had separated Shakespearean and Golden Age public urban theatres ended then and there, as the second half of the seventeenth century ushered in a new era of comparative Anglo-Spanish theatre history.

Notes

1 "*Ro*. Estays loco? Que dezis? / pues representar quereys?" Rojas, *El viage entretenido*, pp. 4-4v [my translation].
2 "*Ro*. Estays loco? Que dezis? / pues representar quereys? / que autor de fama traeys? / o con que gente venis? / Villegas y Rios presentes / con tan buenas compañias, / tantas farsas, bizarrias, / tan buena música y gentes, / Venis a representar: / yo no acabo de entender, / que os a podido mouer. / *Go*. El deßeo de agradar. / *Ro*. Que galas? que compañeros? / Que musicos de gran fama? / que muger que haga la dama? / que bobo que haga a Zisneros? / Que Morales, que Solano? / que Ramirez? que Leon? / O que

hombre de opinion / traeys? *Go.* El cuento es galano." Rojas, *El viage entretenido*, pp. 4-4v [my translation].

3 The *autores* Rojas refers to are probably Antonio de Villegas, a prominent Seville-born actor, and Nicolás de los Ríos, one of the best known figures in the Spanish theatre scene. The other actors he mentions are Alonso de Cisneros, Alonso or Pedro de Morales, Agustín Solano, Marcos or Miguel Ramírez and Melchor or Jerónimo de León. A complete digital database of Golden Age *comediantes*, including the aforementioned, can be found in Ferrer Valls (dir.), *Diccionario biográfico de actores del teatro clásico español (DICAT)*.

4 Jonson, *Bartholomew Fayre*, p. 74. See also Astington, *Actors and Acting in Shakespeare's Time*, p. 37. My thanks to Tanya Pollard for reminding me of this parallelism.

5 Astington, *Actors and Acting in Shakespeare's Time*, p. 7.

6 García Reidy, *Las musas rameras*, p. 24; Sanz Ayán and García García, *Teatros y comediantes en el Madrid de Felipe II*, pp. 22-23. Nevertheless, the development of a regular theatre for profit did not trump the amateur production of the wealthier writers whose livelihood did not depend on the commercial success of what they wrote. Indeed, being a 'gentlemanly amateur' playwright was socially a much more attractive condition, and even some playwrights who did earn their livelihood by their craft, such as Jasper Mayne or even a young Lope de Vega, made an effort to style themselves as such. More in Bentley, *The Profession of Dramatist in Shakespeare's Time*, pp. 12-14; Clark, *Professional Playwrights*, pp. 4-5; García Reidy, *Las musas rameras*, pp. 107-111.

7 Astington, *Actors and Acting in Shakespeare's Time*, p. 12. Similar sentiments are expressed in Bentley, *The Profession of Dramatist in Shakespeare's Time*, p. 43; Rodríguez Cuadros, "The art of the actor", p. 107.

8 Cohen, *Drama of a Nation*, p. 182. See also Bentley, *The Profession of Dramatist in Shakespeare's Time*, pp. 38-39, 41-42, 50-51.

9 "Representamos vna Comedia de vn Representante nuestro, que yo me admirè de que fuessen Poetas, porque pensaua que el serlo era de hombres muy doctos y sabios, y no de gente tan sumamente lega; y esta ya de manera esto, que no ay Autor que no escriua Comedias, ni Representante que no haga su farsa de Moros y Christianos; que me acuerdo yo antes, que si no eran Comedias del buen Lope de Vega, y Ramon, no auia otra cosa." Quevedo, *La vida del bvscon*, p. 186 [my translation].

10 Heywood, *An Apology for Actors*, sig. A3.

11 Bentley, *The Profession of Dramatist in Shakespeare's Time*, p. 54.

12 Brown and Parolin, "Introduction", p. 4.

13 Heywood, *An Apology for Actors*, sig. A3 [emphasis added].

14 Jonson, *The Workes of Beniamin Jonson* pp. 72-73, 270-271, 354-355, 438-439, 524-525, 600-601, 678-679, 764-765. More in Marcus, *Puzzling Shakespeare*, pp. 3, 21.

15 Rodríguez Cuadros, "The art of the actor, 1565-1833", pp. 109-110.

16 Heywood, *An Apology for Actors*, sig. A4.

17 Dillon, *Theatre, Court and City*, 34.

18 Bentley, *The Profession of Player in Shakespeare's Time*, pp. 5-9.

19 As cited in Bentley, *The Profession of Dramatist in Shakespeare's Time*, pp. 47-48. Selected passages on the Clifton abduction can be found in Wickham et al. (eds.), *English Professional Theatre*, pp. 264-266. More on the topic in Munro, *Children of the Queen's Revels*, p. 17-18, 38.

20 Canavaggio, "Sevilla y el teatro a fines del siglo XVI", 91.

21 Earle, *Micro-cosmographie*, sigs. E3-E3v. I first came across this source in modern-spelling in Wickham et al. (eds.), *English Professional Theatre*, p. 186.

22 As cited in Es, *Shakespeare in Company*, p. 38.

23 As cited in Bentley, *The Profession of Player in Shakespeare's Time*, p. 4.

24 " ... mala vida con no ser Farsante." Quevedo, *La vida del bvscon*, p. 191 [my translation].
25 Knutson, *Playing Companies and Commerce in Shakespeare's Time*, pp. 21-22; Sanz Ayán and García García, *Teatros y comediantes en el Madrid de Felipe II*, p. 22.
26 Jean Sentaurens traces the frequently repeated expression "*que vengan las cofradías de los oficios con sus juegos*" ["let the guild brotherhoods with their shows come and visit us"] in many Sevillian city council edicts throughout the sixteenth century. Progressively, these amateur performers either ended up working full-time in commercial theatre, or were replaced by professional artists. The same can be said of the other main theatre nuclei in the country. Madrid did not become an important city for public drama until the local government raised the prizes for Corpus pageants enough to lure the main companies from the same festivities in nearby Toledo. As a result, Sentaurens convincingly argues that the massive success of the Spanish Baroque theatre owes much to the popularity of the guild performances, since the guilds educated early modern Spanish society to appreciate the theatre. Sentaurens, "De artesanos a histriones", pp. 298-302. More in Greer and Junguita, "Economies of the Early Modern Spanish Stage", pp. 33-34; Sanz Ayán, *Hacer escena*, pp. 194-198; Sanz Ayán and García García, *Teatros y comediantes en el Madrid de Felipe II*, p. 23.
27 Rodríguez Cuadros, "The art of the actor, 1565-1833", p. 105. More on the Cofradía de la Novena in Ferrer Valls (dir.), *Diccionario biográfico de actores del teatro clásico español (DICAT)*; Oehrlein, *El actor en el teatro español del Siglo de Oro*, pp. 241-276; Subirá, *El gremio de representantes españoles y la cofradía de Nuestra Señora de la Novena*.
28 "According to the little information that survives", writes Maria del Valle Ojeda Calvo, "the first professional actors were writing the texts themselves and that is why critics refer to them as *autores-actores*. This is the case of Lope de Rueda, Alonso de la Vega or a man by the name of Navarro". Ojeda Calvo, "Poetas y farsantes", p. 291. For a detailed description of the profession and duties of the *autor de comedias*, see González, "El autor de comedias en el siglo XVII".
29 That said, evidence regarding the internal operations of Alonso de Cisneros' company suggests that there was a considerable amount of delegation and sharing of tasks within the troupe as well. More in Arata and Vaccari, "Manuscritos atípicos, papeles de actor y compañías del siglo XVI", pp. 25-28.
30 Davis and Varey, *Actividad teatral en la región de Madrid según los protocolos de Juan García de Albertos*, pp. lxxxviii-xci; Rodríguez Cuadros, "The art of the actor, 1565-1833", p. 104; Sanz Ayán and García García, *Teatros y comediantes en el Madrid de Felipe II*, p. 22. For a detailed account of the manuscript library of a Golden Age *autor de comedias* see Sanz Ayán, *Hacer escena*, pp. 211-251.
31 Gurr, *The Shakespearian Playing Companies*, p. 9. See also Bentley, *The Profession of Player in Shakespeare's Time*, pp. 25-26, 36-38.
32 Bentley, *The Profession of Player in Shakespeare's Time*, pp. 147-148.
33 As cited in Bentley, *The Profession of Player in Shakespeare's Time*, pp. 152-155.
34 Davis and Varey, *Actividad teatral en la región de Madrid según los protocolos de Juan García de Albertos*, pp. xci-c; Sanz Ayán and García García, *Teatros y comediantes en el Madrid de Felipe II*, pp. 29-30.
35 Astington, *Actors and Acting in Shakespeare's Time*, pp. 2-3; Knutson, *Playing Companies and Commerce in Shakespeare's Time*, pp. 26-28.
36 Noguera Guirao, "Elena Osorio"; Sanz Ayán and García García, *Teatros y comediantes en el Madrid de Felipe II*, pp. 30-31, 48-52. Another famous example was the company led by Jerónima de Burgos and Pedro de Valdés, as described in Gadea and De Salvo, "Jerónima de Burgos y Pedro de Valdés". More on the *familia de cómicos* troupe model in Cañadas, *Public Theater in Golden Age Madrid and Tudor-Stuart London*, p. 43; Oehrlein, *El actor en el teatro del Siglo de Oro*, pp. 216-221.

37 Gurr, *The Shakespeare Company, 1594-1642*, pp. 20-22; Rackin, *Shakespeare and Women*, pp. 42-43.
38 For England see Bentley, *The Profession of Player in Shakespeare's Time*, p. 28; Kathman, "Grocers, Goldsmiths, and Drapers"; Kathman, "Players, Livery Companies, and Apprentices". For Spain see Davis and Varey, *Actividad teatral en la región de Madrid según los protocolos de Juan García de Albertos*, pp. cxiv-cxxi; Noguera Guirao, "Músicos y compañías teatrales en el Siglo de Oro", pp. 310; Oehrlein, "El actor en el Siglo de Oro", pp. 19-20; Rodríguez Cuadros, "The art of the actor, 1565-1833", p. 105; Sanz Ayán and García García, *Teatros y comediantes en el Madrid de Felipe II*, pp. 30, 43; Thacker, *A Companion to Golden Age Theatre*, pp. 131-132.
39 Robert Barrie is right to point out the difference between undergoing a true guild apprenticeship and the apprenticeship in a playing company. Whereas guild masters were sometimes paid for taking up apprentices, acting troupes often had to pay to attract them. Nonetheless, on a superficial level playing companies show a master-apprentice or veteran-rookie relationship within the troupe's ranks that resembled the environment of a guild-like enterprise. More in Barrie, "Elizabethan Play-Boys in the Adult London Companies".
40 For detailed accounts of the Spanish playing companies, their structures and their wages, in Spanish, see Oehrlein, *El actor en el teatro español del Siglo de Oro*, pp. 76-106, 192-207, as well as his "Las compañías de título", pp. 249-252.
41 Bentley, *The Profession of Player in Shakespeare's Time*, p. 29. Tiffany Stern reminds us that sometimes the hirelings and tiremen were used for small and mute roles when a play's cast of characters was too large for the company's regular players. Stern, "The theatre of Shakespeare's London", p. 46.
42 Knutson, *Playing Companies and Commerce in Shakespeare's Time*, p. 46.
43 The other prominent case was that of Thomas Heywood, who was also a sharer, actor, and in-house playwright for Queen Anne's Servants at the Red Bull theatre in Clerkenwell. More on Thomas Heywood and his role in the playing troupe in Griffith, *A Jacobean Company and its Playhouse*, pp. 73-79, Smout, "Actor, Poet, Playwright, Sharer ... Rival?".
44 García Reidy, *Las musas rameras*, pp. 84-101, 116-130, 301-309; García Reidy, "Spanish *Comedias* as Commodities", pp. 204-207; Knutson, *Playing Companies and Commerce in Shakespeare's Time*, p. 48-56; Sanz Ayán and García García, *Teatros y comediantes en el Madrid de Felipe II*, pp. 46-47.
45 Munro, "Children's Companies and the Long 1580s", p. 99; Shapiro, *Children of the Revels*, pp. 1-17.
46 Shapiro, *Children of the Revels*, p. 1.
47 As cited in Shapiro, *Children of the Revels*, p. 15.
48 All historical references here used regarding the Children of the Queen's Revels can be found in Munro, *Children of the Queen's Revels*, pp. 1-25.
49 Smith, *Shakespeare's Blackfriars Playhouse*, pp. 175-197, 244-250.
50 McMillin and MacLean, *The Queen's Men and their Plays*, p. 5. Siobhan Keenan, in her *Travelling Players in Shakespeare's England* (2002), traces touring theatre back to the fifteenth century by combing through the *Records of Early English Drama (REED)* database conceived by McMillin and MacLean. Keenan, *Travelling Players in Shakespeare's England*, p. 2.
51 Bentley, *The Profession of Player in Shakespeare's Time*, pp. 12-13.
52 Gurr, *The Shakespearian Playing Companies*, pp. 12-13. Keenan discusses these non-London playhouses in more depth in *Travelling Players in Shakespeare's England*, p. 144-164.
53 Recent studies have increasingly challenged the long-standing assumption that the touring facilities provided fewer staging possibilities than did the London spaces. More in Thomson, "Staging on the Road".

54 Keenan, *Acting Companies and their Plays in Shakespeare's London*, p. 11. As discussed in the second chapter (pp. 47-48), Richard Southern argues that the structure of the English country house's great hall influenced the disposition of the Elizabethan stage, especially in regard to the tiring-house wall. More in Southern, *The Staging of Plays before Shakespeare*, pp. 48-98.
55 Gurr, *The Shakespearian Playing Companies*, p. 88. Gurr's monograph also includes a chart with all the supposed plague-related playhouse closures between 1563 and 1642 in pp. 91-92. For a thorough and extensive discussion of the topic see Barroll, *Politics, Plague, and Shakespeare's Theater*.
56 As cited in White, *Renaissance Drama in Action*, pp. 21.
57 More in McMillin and MacLean, *The Queen's Men and their Plays*, p. 39.
58 Gurr, *The Shakespearian Playing Companies*, pp. 45-47.
59 Keenan, *Acting Companies and their Plays in Shakespeare's London*, p. 26. A detailed summary of the combined stories of touring and London-based theatrical practices can be found in Schoone-Jongen, *Shakespeare's Companies*, pp. 43-84.
60 Gurr, *The Shakespearian Playing Companies*, pp. 38, 111-121; Keenan, *Travelling Players in Shakespeare's England*, pp. 32-35.
61 Oehrlein, "Las compañías de título", pp. 246-247; Rodríguez Cuadros, "The art of the actor, 1565-1833", p. 104. Jonathan Thacker also suggests that the title *cómicos de la legua* might derive from these itinerant players' need to travel at least a league a day to perform in different towns. Whichever the meaning, the contrast between league players and those of the *compañías reales* was still substantial, and the players of the larger companies were held in higher social regard than the *legua* performers. More in Oehrlein, "El actor en el Siglo de Oro", pp. 18-19; Thacker, *A Companion to Golden Age Theatre*, p. 131. See also Davis and Varey, *Actividad teatral en la región de Madrid según los protocolos de Juan García de Albertos*, pp. lxxiii-lxxxviii.
62 Clara Bejarano provides an illuminating contrast between the itinerant acting troupes that visited Seville in the sixteenth and seventeenth centuries on the one hand, and the city's sedentary musical companies on the other, in her "El oficio de representar y el oficio de la música en Sevilla entre 1575 y 1625".
63 Rodríguez Cuadros, "The art of the actor, 1565-1833", p. 104. More in Ball, *Treating the Public*, p. 30; Cotarelo y Mori, *Bibliografía de las controversias sobre la licitud del teatro en España*, p. 208; Davis and Varey, *Actividad teatral en la región de Madrid según los protocolos de Juan García de Albertos*, pp. lxx-lxxi.
64 Allen, "El papel del vulgo en la economía de los corrales madrileños", pp. 11-12; Rodríguez Cuadros, "The art of the actor, 1565-1833", p. 105; Sanz Ayán and García García, *Teatros y comediantes en el Madrid de Felipe II*, pp. 28-29; Thacker, *A Companion to Golden Age Theatre*, p. 131.
65 Sanz Ayán and García García, *Teatros y comediantes en el Madrid de Felipe II*, p. 33.
66 " ... y que no anden Compañías de hombres y mujeres por el reino; sino que la de corte se esté en la corte y la de Toledo en Toledo, para que el representante atienda á su oficio entre semana, como lo hacían en sus principios Lope de Rueda, Navarro y Cisneros, aunque después comenzaron á juntarse en Compañías y andarse de pueblo en pueblo." As cited in Cotarelo y Mori, *Bibliografía de las controversias sobre la licitud del teatro en España*, p. 326 [my translation].
67 Mariana, "De los espectáculos", pp. 431-433 [my translation].
68 Nicholson, "The Theater", p. 298. See also Greer, "A Tale of Three Cities", p. 402; Mariana, "De los espectáculos", p. 433.
69 For the age of the boy players see Kathman, "How Old were Shakespeare's Boy Actors?". More on the shepherding of children players in London's adult companies in Belsey, "Shakespeare's Little Boys"; Madelaine, "Material Boys"; Tribble, "Marlowe's Boy Actors".
70 Brown, "Why Did the English Stage Take Boys for Actresses?", p. 186.

71 Prynne as cited, along with other similar passages, in Kathman, "How Old were Shakespeare's Boy Actors?", p. 221.
72 Brown and Parolin, "Introduction", p. 1.
73 Nicholson, "The Theater", pp. 309-310; Rackin, *Shakespeare and Women*, pp. 41-42.
74 Stokes, "The Ongoing Exploration of Women and Performance in Early Modern England", p. 13. Other studies correcting the myth of the 'all-male stage' include Brown and Parolin (eds.), *Women Players in England, 1500-1660*; McManus, "Women and English Renaissance Drama"; McManus, *Women on the Renaissance Stage*; Tomlinson, *Women on Stage in Stuart Drama*; as well as the special *Shakespeare Bulletin* issue (vol. 33, n°1) of 2015.
75 Ferrer Valls, "La incorporación de la mujer a la empresa teatral", pp. 141-144. See also Davis, "¿Cuántos actores había en el Siglo de Oro?", pp. 65-66.
76 Ball, *Treating the Public*, p. 26; Oehrlein, "Las compañías de título", pp. 252-253; Sanz Ayán and García García, *Teatros y comediantes en el Madrid de Felipe II*, p. 78.
77 Davis and Varey, *Actividad teatral en la región de Madrid según los protocolos de Juan García de Albertos*, pp. cxxxiii-cxlii; Rodríguez Cuadros, "The art of the actor, 1565-1833", pp. 104-105; Samson, "Distinct Drama?", p. 158; Sanz Ayán, "More than Faded Beauties", pp. 119-120; Sanz Ayán and García García, *Teatros y comediantes en el Madrid de Felipe II*, p. 37.
78 Cañadas, *Public Theater in Golden Age Madrid and Tudor-Stuart London*, p. 43; Ferrer Valls, "La mujer sobre el tablado en el siglo XVII", pp. 92-98; Oehrlein, *El actor en el teatro del Siglo de Oro*, pp. 216-221.
79 "yvamos barajados, hombres y mugeres, y una entre ellas la baylarina, que tambien hazia las Reynas, y papeles graves en la comedia, me pareciò estremada savandija. Acertò a estar su marido a mi lado, y yo sin pensar a quien hablava, llevado del desseo de amor, y gozarla, dixele: esta muger, porque orden le podiamos para gastar con su merced veynte escudos? que me ha parecido hermosa. No me esta bien a mi el dezirlo, que soy su marido (dixo el hombre) ni tratar de esso, pero sin pasion, que no me mueve ninguna, se puede gastar con ella cualquier dinero porque tales carnes no tiene el suelo, ni tal juguetoncita; y diziendo esto saltò del carro y fuesse al otro, segun parecio, por darme lugar a que le hablasse. Cayome en gracia la respuesta del hombre, y echè de ver, que por estos se pudo dezir, que tienen mugeres, como si no las tuviessen, torciendo la sentencia en malicia". Quevedo, *La vida del bvscon*, pp. 184-185 [my translation].
80 As cited in Cañadas, *Public Theater in Golden Age Madrid and Tudor-Stuart London*, p. 49 and Samson, "Distinct Drama?", p. 157.
81 Ferrer Valls, "La mujer sobre el tablado en el siglo XVII", pp. 84-92; Sanz Ayán, "'More than Faded Beauties'", pp. 115-118. For a detailed account of Spain's women playmakers in the seventeenth century see Sanz Ayán, *Hacer escena*, pp. 253-337.

4
DRAMATISTS

Toward the end of a 1620 letter he was writing to his friend and patron the Duke of Sessa, Lope de Vega – by then a veteran playwright who was well known and beloved across Spain – reminds the Duke that he would be meeting him later that same day "so you can relate to me what what the Countess told you, as I fear I am once again to receive bad news".[1] Apparently the Duke's – and by extension also his secretary Lope's – behaviour had been the subject of much gossip and criticism in court those days, which could not have come at a worse time for the dramatist, who had recently applied to succeed Pedro de Valencia as the royal chronicler after his untimely death. It was not the first time Lope had sought the position, having unsuccessfully thrown his hat in the ring in 1611. Despite his status as the nation's most popular dramatist, Lope was beginning to express a certain willingness to leave his playwriting days behind him.[2] Unfortunately (for him), his application once again failed, and Lope continued to write *comedias* until he passed away in 1635.

The reasons behind – and, indeed, the sincerity of – his desire to abandon his career as a dramatist while at the peak of his powers remain unclear.[3] Had he been successful in this aim, though, the history of Spain's Golden Age of theatre would be very different. To begin with, Spain may well have lost its privileged place as Shakespearean England's primary competitor for the title of early modern Europe's preeminent dramatic tradition. Indeed, figures such as Lope, Shakespeare and their playwriting peers have for centuries been the focal point of Renaissance theatre history and drama studies, towering over the rest of the playmaking community despite their being just one cog – albeit an undoubtedly crucial one – in the theatre system's production line.[4] This chapter explores the profession of commercial theatre-writing in early modern England and Spain. It begins with a survey of the role theatre and creative writing played in the school systems of the two countries, and then comparatively analyses the remarkable similarities between the playwriting methods and trends that defined the two dramatic cultures, in terms both of style and content. The chapter ends with a brief ponderation of why a successful dramatist such as Lope – again, at the time the standard-bearer of Spain's *comedia*-writing community – may have entertained the idea of quitting the theatre, or at least publicly pondered that option. I suggest that one of the factors that may have contributed to Lope's proclaimed growing disillusion with the playwriting profession was the torrential overflow of plays being written in Spain in comparison with all other European dramatic traditions at the time or ever since.

The Making of a Professional Playwright

An aspiring playwright's first encounter with dramaturgy would likely have taken place in the schoolroom. At around six to eight years of age, a not-insignificant percentage of England and Spain's male population began its secondary education within institutions commonly referred to as grammar schools (in Spanish the *colegios* or *escuelas de gramática*).[5] Grammar school occupied the space between basic training in reading and writing, whether carried out formally or in a non-institutional venue, and university. And in both countries, as in the rest of Europe and despite national idiosyncrasies, the honing of the students' writing and performance skills stood front and centre in the grammar school curriculum.

Influenced by the developing humanist philosophy and its priorisation of ancient Greek and especially Roman culture, educators across Renaissance Europe turned to the study of the liberal arts as the cornerstone of the schooling of young males. With Latin as its *lingua franca* and leading cultural currency, many of the formative years in grammar school were dedicated to improving the students' handle on the Roman language, with exceptional incursions into Greek if the circumstances allowed it. While there were different paths to learning Latin, the common tenet in its instruction was *imitatio*: following the guidance of Erasmus, Juan Luis Vives and other prominent contemporary pedagogues, students were – in theory – to read and emulate the grammar and style of classical authors as the most effective way of reaching the end-goal of Latinity. This meant close and constant interaction not only with literary texts but also with rhetoric manuals and other guides to polishing one's elocution. Through daily exercises aimed at imitating the styles of Cicero, Terence, Seneca, Virgil and other Roman standouts, the early modern syllabus provided aspiring writers with a substantial foundation for poetic expression in terms of tools as well as themes.[6]

It is important to stress here that Latin was not the only language students, both in England and in Spain, were required to cultivate during their time at grammar school. Their training was meant to help improve their familiarity with their mother tongue as well. As Neil Rhodes explains, Latin was not so much a subject in itself, to be studied alongside mathematics or history, as the vehicle through which an education was acquired and the gateway to all branches of knowledge. [...] The end was eloquence, and the medium was Latin, but the skills acquired were undoubtedly transferable from the classical languages to the vernacular.[7]

Despite the higher regard in which the classical languages were held over more local alternatives, it was understood and expected that thorough training in Latin also favoured proper articulation elsewhere. This became especially obvious with the adoption in the curriculum of double translation. Erasmus championed this pedagogical technique in which students translated a Latin text into their mother tongue only to translate it back into Latin; pupils thus instructed would be able to measure the rhetorical quality and choices of the new rendition against those of the original. This method of learning underlies the transferability of skills the grammar schools taught while it honed the across-the-spectrum eloquence alluded to by Rhodes.[8] Even if the favoured end-goal was Latinity the process wound up brushing up both languages almost to the same extent, and certainly benefitted the tiny minority of students who eventually tried their hand at writing plays, whether it be in the father or the mother tongue.

Of particular relevance to future playmakers was the pedagogical fixation during the Renaissance on oratory and the performative dimension of language. The last of the five canons in classical rhetoric, *actio* or *pronuntiatio*, concentrates on the role the speakers' delivery and oratory style played in enhancing their persuasiveness. Amidst the sixteenth-century rekindling of interest in ancient Greek and Roman oral communication, the period's rhetoricians regarded *actio* as being second only in importance to *elocutio*.[9] Thus, as part of their imitation-based instruction, grammar school students in England learned to mimic the voice, intonation, gestures and passion of their teachers during their frequent exercises in 'loud speaking' as prescribed by the influential English schoolmaster Richard Mulcaster, among others.[10] Oratory was also central to the curriculum of Jesuit schools, widely considered the most important and influential secondary education institutions in Spain – as well as in the rest of Catholic Europe – from the second half of the sixteenth century onward. The Society of Jesus, whose principal mission was to educate the continent's elite youth in the modernised Catholic doctrine of the Counter-Reformation, cultivated their students' ability to debate effectively, and ultimately to persuade and convert others to their cause. It implemented a rigorous curriculum known as the *Ratio Studiorum*, which grounded instruction in Latin in honing students' written and oral eloquence. By the beginning of the seventeenth century, the influence of the Society – which even its fiercest ideological rivals recognised had the best teachers and institutions in Spain – had grown to the point that many of the non-Jesuit schools and universities modelled their syllabi at least in part upon the *Ratio*, resulting in the promotion of the art of oratory in schoolrooms across the nation.[11]

Foremost among the different pedagogical strategies to improve students' public speaking and demeanour was the direct representation of dramatic pieces. From grammar school up to university, educators in both England and Spain relied consistently upon theatre as an integral instrument for oratorial training. According to Rhodes,

> The importance attached to speech skills in education is the reason why drama was encouraged in both schools and universities. Tacit mastery of grammar was insufficient, since humanism tended to regard taciturnity as a dismal inadequacy rather than as a mark of discretion. The end of eloquence was action. Drama offered a means to this end by providing experience in role-playing and by developing self-confidence.[12]

Even the Jesuits in Spain, who famously despised anything related to public theatre and the for-profit performances held in the nation's *corrales* (see p. 26), turned to drama for educational purposes. Indeed, theatre was such a central part of their instruction that they developed a well-known corpus of plays of their own and made substantial investments of time and resources in their performance. These didactic dialogues had little in common with the secular *comedias*, starting with the fact that they were written in Latin and always had at their core a religious theme or message. Still, theatre had clearly won a privileged place close to the centre of the leading teaching programme in the country.[13] The resort to drama in early modern England and Spain's secondary education was without a doubt, as Rhodes explains, the means to an end that had little to do with preparing pupils to enter the playmaking enterprise. It nevertheless did inadvertently provide two countries with successive generations of young men whose training directly connected the art of eloquence with playmaking.

Many dramatists and even some players (although much less frequently) did attend university after completing their secondary education. Ben Jonson, Thomas Heywood and Thomas Middleton are just a few among the English playwrights who spent time studying at either Cambridge or Oxford, following the footsteps of the generation of writers popularly referred to as the 'University Wits' (Marlowe, Greene, Nashe, Lyly, Lodge and Peele). Others frequented London's Inns of Court, the capital's equivalent of Law Schools with strong connections to the theatre world. The three best known dramatists in Spain – that is, Lope de Vega, Tirso de Molina and Calderón de la Barca – all attended at least for some time the University of Alcalá de Henares near Madrid; Calderón later went on to read law at the University of Salamanca.[14] Theatre was often called upon as a pedagogical tool in higher education, and no doubt the playwrights-to-be in attendance benefited from further closer contact with dramatic works at this level as well.[15] However, it is also well known that neither Shakespeare in England nor Cervantes in Spain attended university. Clearly, as far as rhetorical and dramatic training in formal education in these two countries goes, what the grammar and Jesuit schools provided was more than sufficient to set their pupils on the right path for a successful career as commercial writers.

Verse, Prose and Polymetry

After this brief introduction to the educational rearing of England and Spain's professional dramatists, we turn to the plays themselves. What were they like and what did they deal with? Did the business of commercial playwriting call for the same themes and modes in one country and the other, or did dramatic production in England markedly differ than that in Spain? As in the case of the playhouses that hosted them, this all-encompassing question can be roughly boiled down to a matter of predominant kinship: the plays written in England and Spain in the late sixteenth and early seventeenth centuries share many if not most of their primary features, to the point that from a distance one would say they appear as virtually the same. Everything changes, of course (and again much like with the playhouses), on closer inspection, and the differential traits between Elizabethan-Jacobean and Golden Age drama speak directly to the almost-but-not-quite parallel existences of these two theatrical cultures. The following two sections of this chapter explore the craft of commercial playwriting in early modern England and Spain, by analysing first the style and then the substance of the plays written for the two nations' public theatres during this period. The first focuses in particular on the use of verse, along with other modes of writing these dramatic traditions employed, in what can be described as the aspect that best embodies both the broad similitude as well as the nuanced distinctiveness that continuously defines the relationship between these two theatrical cultures.

Constant comparison between English and Spanish plays reveals that, from a structural and aesthetic standpoint, they read and feel remarkably similar, much more so with than any other two dramatic corpora from pre-modern European countries. For starters, the average length of public theatre plays from both England and Spain is fairly comparable, oscilating between 13,000 and 21,000 words (see pp. 147–148). The casts of *dramatis personae*, subject to fluctuations depending on the different dramatic genres (more characters in tragedies and histories, fewer in comedies), are also consistently similar. The one noteworthy structural difference between the two is that whereas the English plays preserved the five-act structure from classical drama, Spanish dramatists overwhelmingly divided theirs into three acts, referred to as either *actos* or *jornadas* [days]; this distinction gains in importance when one considers that in Spain it was customary to perform two long interludes, known as *entremeses*, in between the three acts of a *comedia*, which gave a unique structure to the afternoon's entertainment in the nation's public theatres. Apart from that, though, the list of resemblances continues. English and Spanish public playhouse drama from this period is – unlike, say, court spectacles and street performances – predominantly dialogue-driven, with occasional soliloquies and asides. Stage directions are minimal and inconspicuous, as most of the instructions take place implicitly through the words of the characters. And the brunt of the dialogue – indeed, often all of it – is written in verse, a nod to the Greek and Roman drama being taught and promoted in the schools and universities at the time, as noted earlier. That is, both to the eye and to the ear these plays look and sound very much alike, stylistically speaking.

Two different modes of writing coexisted and co-mingled in the theatre of Shakespeare and his contemporary English dramatists: verse and prose. Despite the occasional encounter with a play written either entirely in verse or (almost) entirely in prose, the vast majority of plays combine the two. That said, the relationship between verse and prose in English drama is an unequal one; in his exploration of Shakespeare's writing style, Russ McDonald explains that "verse is the dominant form and prose the subordinate, a relationship consistent with the practice of most early modern dramatists".[16] This dominance of verse over prose takes place both quantitatively and qualitatively. On the one hand, verse is used much more frequently than prose; in the case of Shakespeare, here very much a representative of the national trend, passages written in prose only account for approximately one fourth of his dramatic production.[17] On the other hand, verse was associated with grandeur and upper-class characters, whereas dramatists preferred to switch to prose for lower-class characters and comic scenes. A change from one mode to another would not be lost on playhouse audiences who, as George Wright describes,

> did understand a difference between the language they heard as verse and the language they heard as prose, that they recognized something of the sacralizing character of verse, at least of the more dignified iambic pentameter in contrast to playful doggerel.[18]

The overwhelmingly favoured verse form at the time was blank verse, an unlimited sequence of unrhyming iambic pentameter lines that sought to confer a certain degree of naturalness upon an otherwise highly artificial medium. Occasionally playwrights resorted to rhyme, and in particular to the incantatory nature of rhyming couplets, as a way of signalling to their audience the extraordinariness of what was taking place: conspicuous sound effects set magical and supernatural scenes, or even uncommon displays of grandeur and/or love, apart from the rest of the play. Other than these sporadic episodes, however, England's dramatists wrote either in blank verse or prose.

The split between the functions of these two registers was particularly pronounced in comedies and history plays from the 1580s and early 1590s. With time, playwrights began to expand and diversify their use of prose, and by the turn of the seventeenth century in some of Shakespeare's plays, as indeed in the plays of many of his contemporaries, "the alternation between verse and prose is so frequent, so unschematic, and so skillful that it is risky to generalize".[19] The two different modes of writing continued to coexist on the pre-1642 English stage, and a change from one to another still was noted by the playgoers and readers even if the underlying message of such a change was not as clear-cut as it once was.[20]

Unlike its English counterpart, the Spanish *comedia* did not feature practically any prose apart from a few exceptions. From the first bucolic colloquies of the early sixteenth century up until the waning days of the Golden Age, Spain's preeminent dramatists wrote almost exclusively in verse. Prose was for the most part kept off the public stage, only very occasionally making a cameo in secondary forms of theatre such as the *entremés* [interlude].[21] Nevertheless, being limited to writing in verse did not result in a lack of diversity. Quite the contrary, Spanish playwrights employed an array of different verse forms not seen before or since in European drama. The most common strophes are collectively described as Spanish strophes thanks to their homegrown provenance as well as, in most cases, their distinctive octosyllabic metre:

> **Romance and Romancillo:** An unlimited sequence of octosyllabic lines of verse in which the even lines rhyme assonantly [-A-A-A-A ...]. The *romancillo* follows the same pattern, but the lines are hexa- or heptasyllabic instead.
>
> **Redondilla:** A quatrain of octosyllabic lines of verse with enveloping perfect rhyme [ABBA].
>
> **Quintilla:** A flexible poetic form consisting of a quintain of octosyllabic lines of verse with two sets of perfect rhyme, in which no three consecutive lines have the same rhyme, nor does it end in a rhyming couplet [ABABA, AABBA, ABBAB, etc.].
>
> **Décima:** A sequence of ten octosyllabic lines that follow a very specific palindromic pattern of perfect rhymes [ABBAACCDDC].
>
> **Silva:** An unlimited sequence of alternating hepta- and hendecasyllabic lines featuring a variety of perfect rhyme patterns.

The shorter length of Spanish strophes sets them apart from the Italian ones, a group of poetic forms either originated by Italian poets during the Renaissance or inspired by their signature use of hendecasyllabic metre:

> **Tercetos Encadenados:** The Spanish term for the Dantean *terza rima*, a unlimited sequence of interlocked hendecasyllabic tercets with perfect rhyme [ABABCBCDC ...].
>
> **Octava Real:** The Spanish term for *ottava rima*, a sequence of six hendecasyllabic lines of verse with perfect alternating rhyme, followed by a hendecasyllabic rhyming couplet [ABABABCC].
>
> **Sonnet:** Following the original Petrarchan design of this popular poetic form, two hendecasyllabic quatrains each with enveloping perfect rhyme

[ABBACDDC] followed by a hendecasyllabic sestet that can present a variety of perfect rhyme patterns [EFGEFG, EFEFGF, EFGFEG, etc.].

Hendecasyllabic Silva: An unlimited sequence of hendecasyllabic lines of blank verse, with occasional couplets peppered throughout the series.

While the strophes listed here are the most prominent, by no means do these account for all the patterns Spanish dramatists employed. Even more striking is the extent to which each individual play mobilised a large number of different verse forms, hence the standard scholarly characterisation of Spanish Golden Age plays as polymetric or multi-strophic.[22]

Such variety of versification did not exist in English drama, and yet the function of polymetry in Golden Age plays closely resembles the relationship between verse and prose in Elizabethan theatre. Much like when English playwrights signalled changes in the story or in the dramatic elements of a play by switching registers (blank verse, rhyming verse and prose), Spanish dramatists used different strophes for different types of dialogues, scenes, atmospheres or characters. In a frequently cited passage of his manifesto *Arte nuevo de hacer comedias* ([*New Art of Writing Plays*], 1609), Lope de Vega breaks down the different forms according to their corresponding matter:

> Use prudence, never let your verse depart
> From what will suit your subject matter best.
> Complaints should be in *décimas* expressed.
> Sonnets are good for those in expectation,
> *Romances* are best suited for relation
> Of actions, though *octavas* have more lustre.
> For grave events, the tercets you should muster
> And *redondillas* for the heart's concerns.[23]

Much like with Shakespeare and his contemporaries' use of verse and prose, the division of labour amongst the different strophes was never as clear-cut as Lope makes it to be, and much ink has been righteously spilled in caveating this listicle. That said, it cannot be denied that playwrights relied on certain verse forms for specific types of discourse, such as the use of *romances* for *relaciones* [long descriptions] or the frequent association of Italian strophes with more solemn matters. What is more, it appears that metric variations also played an important role in dramatists' structuring of works, although there is a healthy ongoing debate regarding how large a role this played.[24] In any case, what is certain is that playwrights from both countries guided performers and audience members through the unfolding of their plays with the help of metric and acoustic cues, drawing out the stylistic similarities between the two national dramatic traditions well beyond the superficial kinship born from their shared preference for writing in verse. The following section shows that the resemblance between English and Spanish playwriting does not end there, but extends further to include the primary dramatic genres, themes and sources that configured the landscape of the Shakespearean and Golden Age theatrical cultures.

Dramatic Genre(s)

Most – more likely all – readers of this book will have heard of *Romeo and Juliet* (c. 1596), Shakespeare's dramatisation of the unfortunate tale of the two star-crossed lovers from Verona. As was freqently the case, Shakespeare himself did not come up with the plot. He based the play on a 1562 narrative poem by Arthur Brooke, which in turn was a translation of Pierre Boaistuau's own adaptation of Matteo Bandello's novella *Giuletta e Romeo* (first published in 1554, itself the re-telling of a tale that winds its way through the centuries and back to Ovid). Fewer readers, though, will be familiar with Lope de Vega's rendition of the same story, *Castelvines y Monteses* (c. 1608-1614).[25] That Shakespeare and Lope decided to take the same Bandello story as the basis for one of their plays is purely coincidental, since in all probability neither of the two knew of the existence of the other. And yet, this stroke of serendipity speaks to the artistic synchronicity that existed between the playmaking communities of early modern England and Spain. That is, not only were their plays stylistically alike, as illustrated in the previous section, but they resembled each other thematically as well.

This is not the only English-Spanish duo of plays from this period that draws on the same sources. Another frequently brought-up case is the tragic demise of the Duchess of Amalfi, again a Bandello story dramatised by both Lope de Vega (c. 1604-1606) and the Jacobean playwright John Webster (c. 1612).[26] What is more, and looking beyond these and other obvious instances of common ground, a similar approach to story-telling and genre – driven for the most part by their shared disinterest in the formal strictures and precepts that dictated Western playwriting since ancient Greece and Rome – informs the two national corpora and binds them closely together. The following pages outline the ways in which England and Spain's commercial playwrights responded to the challenges posed by what they saw as theories of drama rendered outdated by the sweeping success of a new and polymorphic attitude towards writing plays, one in which the separate classical genres of comedy and tragedy as envisioned by Aristotle and his acolytes were swept off the stage by the tradition-defying upstart of the age: tragicomedy.

If one were to put oneself in the shoes of an early modern playwright, holding an inked quill and staring at a blank piece of paper, the first thing that would need to be addressed in order to get started is deciding which type of play to write. In Shakespearean England, there would have been three possible options: a comedy, a tragedy or a history. The first two, as present-day readers will readily recognise, were defined by the types of endings given to the story's main character or characters; a conventional comedy ended with a positive resolution (such as marriage), whereas a tragedy finished with a negative one (such as death). The label 'history' was assigned on the basis of completely different criteria; it marked plays based on real events and episodes – especially if they revolved around the life and times of England's past monarchs, written from a nationalist perspective – regardless of whether the ending was positive or negative. Reference to these three genres of plays keeps recurring, with an endless relay of epithets to accompany them, in the titles of plays printed throughout the Elizabethan-Jacobean period. This is laid bare most famously in the first printed anthology of Shakespeare's dramatic works, the so-called First Folio published in 1623 under the title *Mr. William Shakespeares Comedies, Histories, & Tragedies* and with the 38 plays therein presented divided into those three categories. Despite their vagueness, these labels have made their way through time for the most part unscathed, and current readers (and editors and publishers) of Shakespeare and his contemporaries continue to use them. There have been efforts of varying degrees of success further to profile the generic boundaries of early modern English drama, and to find sub-divisions within these umbrella categories: problem plays, Roman histories, revenge tragedies, domestic tragedies, city comedies, romances ... The truth is that, regardless of however much scholars have helpfully tried to nuance the taxonomy of Elizabethan and Jacobean drama, in practical terms only the specialists dwell on these generic complications. At the end of the day, the modern-day reader (and spectator) falls back on the original three labels of 'comedy', 'history' and 'tragedy' because, notwithstanding their age, they remain the clearest and most universally understood distinctions among the different types of dramatic texts written during this period.

That said, our current understanding of the dramatic genres was not exactly the same as Shakespeare's. Whereas we now ascribe to comedies and tragedies a series of vague and often interchangeable traits, it would be a mistake to think that early modern dramatists shared our flexible interpretation of those two terms, at least initially. A product of the classicist education that dictated the grammar school curriculum, the literary community of Renaissance Europe – including both England and Spain – built its understanding of dramaturgy and story-telling around the theories of genre developed in ancient Greece and Rome. A central tenet in sixteenth-century erudite dramatic instruction, for instance, was the playwrights' need to adhere to the classical unities of action, time and place. According to their proponents, these three prescriptions – first articulated during the Italian *Cinquecento* and supposedly based on the teachings of Aristotle – were necessary safeguards laid out in order to protect playwrights from their own reckless creativity, and ultimately to preserve some sort of cohesion and verisimilitude on the stage. Similarly, erudite circles discussed the two principal dramatic forms in equally restrictive fashion, and emphasised the need to keep both as distinct and far removed from each other as possible. For them, a comedy was not simply a story meant to elicit the audience's laughter and/or marked by a happy ending, but a rigidly codified genre with specific attributes regarding character types (they should be of humble stature), plot construction (centred around everyday affairs), setting and the like. Conversely, tragedies should feature characters of kingly or aristocratic rank, depict events of cosmic instead of individual significance, and lead audiences to experience a cathartic purification of their emotions after witnessing the demise of the protagonist/s. There was little overlap between the two, and any forays across the generic boundaries were to be publicly condemned and ridiculed.[27]

That was the theory. In practical terms, Elizabethan and Jacobean commercial dramatists did not hesitate to flaunt their disregard for the classical precepts. Only in the confines of the schoolroom, university and similar learned contexts does one find conscientious attempts to keep the conventions of Greek and Roman drama alive. Other than rare exceptions, it is very difficult to find public stage-intended plays from this period that follow any of the Aristotelian unities, let alone all three. Regarding genre, most comedies include elements in theory exclusive to tragedies and vice versa, especially in terms of character types. The habitual co-presence of lower and upper-class personages in early modern plays stands among the most visible generic disruptions that the modern reader will hardly even notice, much less register as a boundary-breaking innovation. The same can be said about themes, plot construction, ambience and atmosphere, and didactic intent. Despite the different labels conferred on this or that play, from a classicist perspective the dramatic corpus of early modern England consists almost entirely of generic hybrids, or "mongrel tragicomedies" as Philip Sidney pejoratively described them in his *Defense of Poesy* (c. 1580):

> ... all their Playes bee neither right Tragedies, nor right Comedies, mingling Kinges and Clownes, not because the matter so carrieth it, but thrust in the Clowne by head and shoulders to play a part in maiesticall matters, with neither decencie nor discretion: so as neither the admiration and Commiseration, nor the right sportfulnesse is by their mongrell Tragicomedie obtained.[28]

Sidney's objections – which do not end here – did little to change the minds and hearts of his contemporaries, and in the following decades English dramatists kept writing tragicomedies without using or openly acknowledging the moniker. Eventually Jacobean writers employed the term 'tragicomedy' to describe a collection of plays that, despite the clearly spiralling trajectory of the plot, narrowly avoid ending tragically. The first to embrace the hybrid label was John Fletcher, who in the preface to his *The Faithful Shepherdess* (c. 1608-1609) explained that he considered a "tragi-comedie" not to be "so called in respect of mirth and killing, but in respect it wants deaths, which is inough to make it no tragedie, yet brings some neere it, which is inough to make it no comedie".[29] Fletcher's positive spin on a term that Sidney had initially wielded as an insult set in motion a slow-rolling wave of acceptance of those plays that openly flouted the expectations and strictures of the classical genres, and by the late-nineteenth century a handful of Shakespeare's late plays were re-classified as 'romances' – a term Edward Dowden coined roughly to mean the same as tragicomedy – thanks to how poorly they fit the original three generic boxes in which they were first placed.[30] That said, one should not dismiss Sidney's words simply because of their underlying negativity. He was clearly right to point out that the plays being performed on the London stage were not comedies or tragedies as advertised, but 'mongrel tragicomedies' according to the dramatic theories of the time. To shrug off his discontent would be to underappreciate the wilfully innovative spirit of the period's professional playmaking community.

Spain was different, at least on the surface level. Whereas England's commercial dramatists had to choose among three different genres, even though essentially they were always writing tragicomedies, the option for Spain's playwrights was much more straightforward: they wrote *comedias*. These could be humorous *comedias*, tragic *comedias*, historic/nationalistic *comedias*, romantic *comedias*, religious *comedias*, mythological *comedias* … The term *comedia* here clearly does not mean the opposite of tragedy, as it does in the Aristotelian dispensation. It does not concern itself with the themes, contents or intention of plays. Instead, it is a formal descriptor used to identify the long-form drama intended for performance in the nation's public theatres. *Comedia*, thus, was used to tell this type of spectacle apart from the *auto sacramental* [religious street play], the *entremés* [comic interlude] and the myriad of other forms of theatrical entertainment that coexisted in Golden Age Spain.[31] If one were provide an English translation for it, 'play' comes closest to conveying the original meaning in Spanish.

Yet only to a point. The use of *comedia* to refer to theatre in general coincided with the emergence of the *comedia nueva*, an innovative playwriting style initiated in the late 1580s that took Spain by storm and dominated the nation's theatrical scene for well over a century. In open rebellion against the *comedia antigua* of ancient Greece and Rome, the proponents of this new way of writing plays advocated for more flexibility and freedom in their story-telling, even if that meant flouting the deeply entrenched wisdom of classical dramatic theory by mixing and matching features traditionally ascribed exclusively to tragedy and to comedy.[32] While he did not originate the *comedia nueva*, its highest-profile practitioner and advocate was Lope de Vega, who started writing hybrid plays of this nature very early on in his career after dabbling briefly with the ways of the ancients. By the opening of the seventeenth century almost all dramatists in Spain followed suit, to the point that *comedia* had become synonymous with the Lopean *comedia nueva*. In 1607, decades into his career as the blockbuster standard-bearer of Spanish theatre, Lope was asked to defend his affronts to the classical tradition at the erudite Madrid Academy, a congregation of scholars, literary authorities and aristocratic amateurs from the capital.[33] He obliged by delivering a 389-verse-long speech which he titled *Arte nuevo de hacer comedias en este tiempo* [*New Art of Writing Plays in this Time*].

Throughout his manifesto, which was subsequently printed in 1609, Lope persistently showcases his intimate knowledge of the classical precepts and genres, even as he explains his reasons for forgoing them:

> Tragedy mixed throughout with comedy
> Terence with Seneca – although this be
> Another minotaur or Pasiphaë,
> One section serious, another slight,
> Such varied mixtures lead to much delight.
> For this let nature our example be
> Gaining much beauty in variety.[34]

In the exact same way as their English counterparts, Spanish playwrights showed an overwhelming predilection for what purists decried as boundary-blurring drama, which resulted in the virtual absence of classical comedy and in particular classical tragedy on the commercial stage.[35] Only on the rarest of occasions, and almost always in erudite and academic contexts such as grammar schools and universities, would one encounter a play that adhered to the strictures of Aristotelian doctrine. As the Valencian poet Ricardo de Turia bluntly put it,

> none of the so-called comedies performed in Spain are in fact comedies, but rather tragicomedies, a mixture of the comic and the tragic, taking from the latter the grave personages, the grand acts, the terror and the misery; and from the former the everyday affairs, the laughter and the wit. And nobody should see this mix as improper, since it does not upset neither nature nor poetry that in a single story grave and humble characters appear alongside each other.[36]

Indeed, the few who tried to write within the confines of classicist doctrine found little reward and appreciation among the theatre-going public, who favoured the tragicomic hybridity of the *comedia nueva* at every turn.

Again, the situation in England was remarkably similar. Elizabethan and Jacobean playwrights applied three different labels to their plays, but the expectation was for all commercial drama to be tragicomic, understood to mean a hybrid mixing both Aristotelian tragic and comic features; Spanish dramatists used only one designation, *comedia*, and it was universally understood to mean tragicomedy as well.[37] This in itself is already remarkable, since no other theatre-making community in Renaissance and Baroque Europe dared to defy the classical precepts and traditions in such a sweeping manner. The reasons behind the striking coincidence that both England's and Spain's commercial dramatists wound up breaking with centuries-old traditions at roughly the same time, and with little or no knowledge of the other nation's forward movement, continue to elude theatre historians. What is more, the similarities the plays from these two countries shared extend well beyond mixing the classical genres, since they often deal with the same topics, themes and subjects. In both dramatic traditions one finds revenge tragedies, urban comedies, pastoral dramas, mythological portrayals and depictions of historical events; English and Spanish playwrights alike resorted to well-known plot devices such as cross-dressing and mistaken identities; frequently these stories revolve around the fortunes of a young, attractive heterosexual couple the audience is meant to root for; and, as noted earlier, one can find English and Spanish renditions of the exact same stories, not to mention the plethora of shared theatergrams around which so many of their plays are constructed.[38] The single stand-out point of divergence is that, whereas English commercial drama was primarily secular and the presence of religion as a dramatic anchor or theme was not very pronounced (though not altogether absent), Spanish playwrights based a sizeable portion of their *comedias* on biblical episodes, hagiographies and other plots rooted in Roman Catholic lore. The upfront religiosity of this subset of plays – not to mention that of the Eucharistic *autos sacramentales* that engulfed city streets across the nation during Corpus Christi – clearly contrasts with the absence of overtly spiritual spectacles on the London public stages. Nevertheless, this is one of the most striking differences between two dramatic traditions that were so like-minded that, on more than one occasion, their dramatists were inadvertently yet almost simultaneously writing the same stories, unbeknownst to each other, at roughly 800 miles distance.

Quantities of Writing and Notions of Artistry

In his *El viaje entretenido*, the Spanish prologue-writer Agustín de Rojas dedicated a passage in one of his *loas* to Lope de Vega. In his celebration of "the phoenix of our time, the Apollo of our poets", Rojas commends the rate at which Lope was able to come up with new material: he writes "so many plays, / and all of them excellent, / that I am no longer able to count them all, / nor is any human being capable of pondering them all".[39] Unlike most of the period's flattery, Rojas' comment was probably an uncommonly honest one: Lope claimed to have written 1.500 plays – although scholars moderate that figure down to anywhere between 600 and 800, of which approximately 400 survive.[40] Rojas was not alone in praising Lope's extraordinary prolificacy: Cervantes described him as a "*monstruo de la naturaleza*" ["prodigy of nature"];[41] the Valencian poet Ricardo de Turia wrote that his plays "like from a perennial fountain pour out from his incredible fertile genius";[42] Francisco Pacheco, a painter from Seville, wrote that in Lope's theatre "we admire his natural ease with words, in the abundance of material his exceeding imagination, in the essence of the verses his thorough understanding of discipline and art as working in perfect unison".[43] And while Lope stands out for his unparalleled productivity, he was not the only Golden Age playwright to write drama at a rate hard to fathom by today's standards:

Tirso de Molina claimed more than four hundred plays, of which eighty survive, in spite of the fact that his dramatic career was cut short by his expulsion to a distant monastery of his order. Even Calderón, the consummate craftsman, wrote around 180 plays and 80 *autos*. Many minor playwrights were also extraordinarily prolific: Montalbán himself wrote over 150 plays, while even a now-forgotten dramatist like Alonso Remón, with five extant plays to his name, reputedly wrote well over 200 *comedias*. It has been estimated that the total production of the seventeenth-century Spanish drama was in the region of 10,000 plays and 1,000 *autos*.[44]

This chapter has so far focused on the many similarities dramatists of early modern England and Spain shared, including their classical dramatic upbringing, their aesthetic taste and instincts, and even their comparable approach to genre and story-telling that occasionally led them to rely on the exact same sources and plots for their stories. Some differences between the two exist as well, of course. The most notable is the amount of plays written by the two playwriting communities. Both on a collective as well as an individual level, Spanish dramatists were much more prolific than their English counterparts. "At the turn of the century", F.A. Halliday writes, "there may have been some twenty full-time dramatists writing two to three plays a year, which with the occasional contributions of others would make 60 to 70 a year".[45] Thomas Heywood is by far, and always according to his own claim, the most productive dramatist in England with having had "at least a maine finger" in 220 plays; he is followed at a considerable distance by John Fletcher with 69, Thomas Dekker with 64, and Philip Massinger with 55.[46] The final section of this chapter considers some of the factors behind the disparity in the number of plays written in Shakespearean England and Golden Age Spain, and postulates a series of consequences stemming from this significant imbalance. As will soon become evident, the torrential flow of *comedia*-writing both derived from and contributed to the lower valuation of drama in Spain when compared to its public perception in England, a difference that persisted (and still persists, I contend) well into the future.

That it is not one nor two but so many Golden Age dramatists who wrote such a unwieldy number of *comedias*, oftentimes doubling and tripling the output of their English counterparts, suggests that this discrepancy should not be attributed to individual prolificacy but instead can be traced back to environmental factors. In both countries, plays had unusually short run-times by today's standards, and acting companies operated with large repertories so as to keep their demanding audiences sated with fresh material.[47] However, the ground that Spanish writers had to cover – that is, the number of troupes, playhouses and theatregoers for which they had to provide new plays – was quite simply much larger. Whereas the majority of Elizabethan and Jacobean England's theatrical activity emanated from London, the landscape of professional playmaking in the Iberian peninsula was much more extended and decentralised (pp. 9–16). Moreover, Golden Age drama was regularly performed and read, both in the original and in translation or adaptation, not only in Spain and Portugal but also in other parts of Europe as well as in the Habsburg-controlled territories in the Americas, South Asia and the Pacific Ocean.[48] From a purely practical standpoint, then, Spanish *comediantes* had a significantly larger audience to tend to than any other playwriting community at the time, especially when compared to the strictly insular performance culture of sixteenth and early seventeenth century Britain. This situation lends credence to Melveena McKendrick's assertion that Lope and his peers were party to "probably the most successful theatre ever in terms of the number of plays written and the number of people, proportionate to population of course, who flocked to see them".[49]

One would venture to think that, with this incessant demand for new *comedias*, Golden Age playwrights – especially the more successful ones – would have little time for other literary endeavours. And yet, their astounding productivity extended far beyond the main stage. In addition to contributing to the impressive national corpus of *autos sacramentales*, as well as the various forms of *teatro breve* [minor drama, such as prologues, interludes and jigs] that accompanied the main performances, most *comediantes* were also avid poets and sonneteers, as was customary at the time.[50] Moreover, a fair amount also dabbled in narrative prose fiction, coinciding with the first generation of modern novels written in the Spanish language. Many English dramatists were also prolific poets and prose writers, of course, in addition to working on other forms of dramatic output beyond the public theatre stages; it is also true that their slower playwriting rate – G.E. Bentley estimates that the average full-time professional dramatist wrote two to three plays a year – suggests that they had more time on their hands for their other artistic exploits.[51] If it was already difficult to wrap one's head around the exorbitant number of plays Spanish playwrights were able to produce, adding all these extra-curricular accomplishments boggles the mind even further.

All of which leads us back to Lope de Vega. As has been sufficiently established, Lope was the most popular and prolific writer of *comedias* in Golden Age Spain. At the height of his career, his name was synonymous with excellence, the refrain *"es de Lope"* ["it was made by Lope"] being commonly used to attest to the quality of any sort of product, not the least his own.[52] His success and productivity, though, were not limited to the stage: he wrote over 3,000 sonnets and other *rimas* [short poems], nine long-form narrative poems, three novels and four novellas. Almost all of his non-dramatic writings met with the same popular acclaim, but his *comedias* remained the most lucrative aspect of his career. "For successful dramatists", writes José María Díez Borque, "the theatre was good business when compared to the other literary genres", and nobody was more successful than Lope during his peak (which came in handy, as he was famously prone to splurging).[53] It is thus all the more surprising not only that he dedicated all that time and effort to writing poetry and prose when *comedias* were more profitable, but that on three separate occasions – as mentioned in the introduction to this chapter – Lope applied to become the nation's royal chronicler to no avail.

For someone with his speed and dexterity in playwriting, in addition to his substantial need for money to cover his lofty expenses and pay off his frequent debts, that he so insistently if not necessarily sincerely spoke of desiring a change of scenery is worth reflecting on. His motivation, it seems, for claiming to want to stop writing *comedias* responded to a value system in which being associated with the theatre was something of a hindrance.

The same popularity and profitability that had initially attracted writers such as Lope to the theatrical enterprise, and which caused the ranks of *comediantes* and the number of plays in what would subsequently be known as the Golden Age of Spanish drama to swell so spectacularly when compared to the rest of Europe, backfired in terms of the social respectability and artistic recognition of the profession of commercial playwriting.[54] The *comedia* was regarded as a lesser genre within the reigning literary hierarchy, especially when compared to poetry: poetry was true art, whereas anybody could and did write theatre. One can argue that much of this devaluation derived from Lope's own achievement, the *comedia nueva*, as contemporaries looked down on the new way of playwriting as capitulating to the whims and desires of the unrefined masses. Even Lope himself, albeit somewhat facetiously, acknowledged this reality: "It is true", he mockingly laments in his *Arte nuevo*,

> That I have sometimes written like those few
> Who follow art, but then my eye is caught
> By monstruous works, with painted settings fraught,
> Where flock the crowds and ladies canonize
> By their support such sorry exercise.
> So when I have a comedy to write
> I lock up with six keys out of my sight
> Plautus and Terence, and their precepts too
> For fear their cries will even reach me through
> Dumb books, for I know truth insists on speaking.
> And then I write, for inspiration seeking
> Those whose sole aim was winning vulgar praise.
> Since after all it is the crowd who pays
> Why not consider them when writing plays?[55]

This tongue-in-cheek condemnation of his own work nevertheless speaks to the widespread view among the literati that the plays performed in the nation's *corrales de comedias* were not art, but rather hack entertainment meant to please the undiscerning rabble. Writing *comedias* could lead to wealth and fame but it barred access to a type of recognition that Lope also craved; in the words of his acolyte and first biographer Juan Pérez de Montalbán, Lope was both "the richest and poorest poet of our time".[56] For that reason Lope decried the *comedia nueva* he helped promote and popularise; for that reason he ventured so frequently beyond the confines of the stage and into other more 'artistic' literary realms; for that reason he loudly proclaimed his desire to leave his playwriting days behind altogether and become instead the royal chronicler, a position that brought the social pedigree and stature that being the "poet laureate of the marketplace" – as Elizabeth Wright aptly crowned him – never could.[57]

In England they did things differently. The public stage proved as popular and lucrative there as it was in Spain, with English playwrights earning roughly as much as their Golden Age counterparts, if not more.[58] And while grumbling about the flouted unities lingered within the learned community, the nation's most prominent dramatists never reached the point of having to defend the value of their work the way Lope did before the Madrid Academy. The fact that they did not write an exorbitant number of plays must have clearly played a role in saving them from having to justify themselves as did their Spanish peers. With the ascension of James I in 1603, the Crown took over the patronage of London's top acting companies, forever associating the plays of Shakespeare and his colleagues with the royal family. Such displays of social and artistic respectability for the country's playmaking community would not be seen in Spain until the emergence of Calderón, a generation after Lope.

Notes

1 "Veré a vuestra excelencia hoy para que me diga qué fin tuvo la resolución de la condesa, y si hay algo de mí que me obligue a más disgustos". Vega, *Cartas (1604-1633)*, p. 575 [my translation].

2 More on Lope's sustained interest in becoming royal chronicler in Ferrer Valls, "Lope de Vega y la Corte de Felipe IV", pp. 2086-2090; Florit Durán, "'Vuestra oliva es laurel de mi cabeza'", pp. 70-81; Wright, *Pilgrimage to Patronage*, p. 139.

3 Teresa Ferrer Valls describes Lope's relationship with his own dramatic production as "a very conflicted one, that veered from love to hate, from pride in his creation to disownment". Ferrer Valls as cited in García Reidy, *Las musas rameras*, p. 29 [my translation].

4 Many recent publications on early modern English theatre history have insisted on moving away from using authors as the primary attribute when clustering dramatic corpora in favour of a company repertory-based approach. All evidence suggests that the features and reputation of each troupe dictated the type of play being written much more so than dramatist him or herself. In other words: it makes more sense to group plays together not because they were written by Shakespeare or Ben Jonson or any other dramatist, but instead because they were commissioned and performed by this or that group of actors. The first monographic study to take up this approach was Scott McMillin and Sally-Beth MacLean's *The Queen's Men and Their Plays* (1998). A notable list of subsequent repertory-based studies includes (in chronological order) Gurr, *The Shakespeare Company;* Munro, *Children of the Queen's Revels*; Gurr, *Shakespeare's Opposites*; Manley and MacLean, *Lord Strange's Men and Their Plays*; and Dustagheer, *Shakespeare's Two Playhouses*. For a brief exploration and survey of the "repertory studies" approach and its impact in Shakespearean studies see Rutter, "Repertory Studies".

5 English and Spanish women – including the first female dramatists in their respective countries such as Elizabeth Cary, Mary Wroth, María de Zayas, or Ana Caro – were

not allowed to attend public schools at the time, as was the case throughout most of Europe. It is thus no coincidence that the vast majority of female writers of the sixteenth and seventeenth centuries came from privileged backgrounds that included private tutoring. Moreover, their elite upbringing also explains why England and Spain's first female dramatists authored what is commonly referred to as 'closet drama', i.e., plays meant exclusively to be read or at most performed in small and private settings, never in public nor for commercial purposes (which is why these dramatists and their plays do not feature more prominently in this book). More in Cressy (ed.), *Education in Tudor and Stuart England*, pp. 106-114; Cruz, "Women's Education in Early Modern Spain"; Romero-Díaz and Vollendorf (eds.), *Women Playwrights of Early Modern Spain*, pp. 1-7; Straznicky, "Private drama".

6   Delgado, "Humanismo y Renacimiento", pp. 651-663; Luján Atienza, *Retóricas españolas del siglo XVI*, pp. 47-61; Kagan, *Students and Society in Early Modern Spain*, pp. xx-xxii, 31-35; Rhodes, *Shakespeare and the Origins of English*, pp. 45-52; Rico Verdú, *La retórica española de los siglos XVI y XVII*, pp. 43-47.

7   Rhodes, *Shakespeare and the Origins of English*, p. 48.

8   More on double translation (or *versión directa e inversa*, in Spanish) in Capitán Díaz, *Breve historia de la educación en España*, 97-103; Juhazs-Ormsby, "Dramatic Texts in the Tudor Curriculum", pp. 536-537; López Griguera, *La retórica en la España del Siglo de Oro*, pp. 61-68; Luján Atienza, *Retóricas españolas del siglo XVI*, pp. 197-198; Rhodes, *Shakespeare and the Origins of English*, pp. 62-63.

9   Early modern rhetoricians often narrowed the scope of rhetoric down to these two aspects, especially on the heels of Ramus' observation that neither *inventio* nor *memoria* – two of the other classical canons – were exclusive to the art of developing persuasive speeches. More on *actio* in sixteenth and seventeenth century rhetorical theory and practice in Albuquerque García, *El arte de hablar en público*, pp. 181-185; Enterline, *Shakespeare's Schoolroom*, pp. 38-41; Fernández López, "Rhetorical Theory in Sixteenth-Century Spain", p. 144; Luján Atienza, *Retóricas españolas del siglo XVI*, pp. 184-185; Rhodes, *Shakespeare and the Origins of English*, pp. 27-29. It must be noted here that Vives and many of his followers went further and said delivery should also be detached from rhetoric, for "an orator, by writing, can accomplish his specific function, and be an excellent orator, without gesture". Vives translated and cited in Abbott, "La Retórica y el Renacimiento", p. 97 (see the aforementioned texts for more on this ideological current).

10 Enterline, *Shakespeare's Schoolroom*, pp. 17-18, 38-42; Wesley, "Rhetorical Delivery for Renaissance English".

11 Batllori et al., "Siglo XVI", p. 207; Capitán Díaz, *Breve historia de la educación en España*, pp. 113-122; Kagan, *Students and Society in Early Modern Spain*, pp. 50-54; Rico Verdú, *La retórica española de los siglos XVI y XVII*, pp. 57-72.

12 Rhodes, *Shakespeare and the Origins of English*, p. 24. For more on the use of drama in the English grammar schoolroom see Astington, *Actors and Acting in Shakespeare's Time*, pp. 38-47; Enterline, *Shakespeare's Schoolroom*, pp. 41-48; Juházs-Ormsby, "Dramatic Texts in the Tudor Curriculum".

13 The most exhaustive study of Spanish Jesuit theatre is Menéndez Peláez, *Los jesuitas y el teatro en el Siglo de Oro*, pp. 11-97. More on the use of drama in Jesuit schools in Arteaga Martínez, "El teatro jesuita novohispano"; Ball, *Treating the Public*, pp. 81-82; Batllori et al., "Siglo XVI", pp. 69-70, 213-214; Delgado et al., "Siglo XVII", pp. 424-425; Hernández Reyes, "El teatro de la Compañía de Jesús en las festividades religiosas de la Nueva España"; Shergold, *A History of the Spanish Stage*, pp. 172-174.

14 All biographical information regarding the education of English and Spanish dramatists derives from the *Oxford Dictionary of National Biography (ODNB)* and the "Teatro Clásico Español" portal of the *Biblioteca Virtual Miguel de Cervantes*.

15 Astington, *Actors and Acting in Shakespeare's Time*, pp. 59-75; Blank, "Actors, Orators, and the Boundaries of Drama in Elizabethan Universities"; Finkelpearl, *John Marston of the Middle Temple*, pp. 19-31; Knight, "Literature and drama at the early modern Inns of Court"; Prest, *The Inns of Court under Elizabeth I and the Early Stuarts*, pp. 153-158; Winston, *Lawyers at Play*.
16 McDonald, *Shakespeare and the Arts of Language*, p. 113.
17 Tootalian, "Without Measure", p. 48. Crystal, *"Think on my Words"*, pp. 210-211 offers a detailed breakdown of verse and prose in Shakespeare's plays.
18 Wright, "An Almost Oral Art", p. 167. Hugh Craig and Brett Greatley-Hirsh share Wright's opinion when they affirm that playwrights who changed from verse to prose and vice versa would have been "confident that an audience will recognise the change from one mode to another and make the appropriate inferences, even if subliminally", in Craig and Greatley-Hirsch, *Style, Computers, and Early Modern Drama*, p. 54. An interesting recent study of the association between prose and the language of social comedy is Tootalian, "Without Measure".
19 McDonald, *Shakespeare and the Arts of Language*, p. 114. More on the diversity of prose use in early modern English drama in Burris, "'Soft! Here Follows Prose'"; Craig and Greatley-Hirsch, *Style, Computers, and Early Modern Drama*, pp. 54-78; Wright, *Shakespeare's Metrical Art*, p. 109; Also, place "Vickers, The Artistry of Shakespeare's, Prose, pp. 3-15" before "Wright, Vickers, *The Artistry of Shakespeare's Prose*, pp. 3-15.
20 Two excellent summaries of the question of the co-presence of verse and prose on the English stage are Crystal, *"Think on my Words"*, pp. 208-219; and McDonald, *Shakespeare and the Arts of Language*, pp. 113-117.
21 See, for example, Cervantes' *El juez de los divorcios* [*The Divorce Court Judge*] and *El retablo de las maravillas* [*The Marvelous Puppet Show*], or the *pasos* [dialogues] by Lope de Rueda.
22 For an exhaustive analysis of Golden Age Spain's verse forms, including their various dramatic functions, see Cantero, *Dramaturgia y práctica escénica del verso clásico español*, pp. 212-520. In her study Cantero does not arrange the different strophes according to provenance but rather according to their metre, distinguishing between *arte mayor* (strophes consisting of lines each with nine syllables or more) and *arte menor* (eight syllables or fewer). In addition to Cantero's monograph, the most comprehensive analysis of the dramatic function of polymetry in Spanish drama, centred on the plays of Lope de Vega, is Marín, *Uso y función de la versificación dramática en Lope de Vega*. Additional studies of Spain's multi-strophic drama include – but are not limited to – Bruerton, "La versificación dramática española en el período 1587-1610"; Bryant, "Estudio métrico sobre las dos comedias profanas de Sor Juana Inés de la Cruz"; Crivellari, "¿Las relaciones piden los romances?"; Dixon, "The Uses of Polymetry"; Fernández Guillermo, "Aproximaciones a la versificación en la comedia de Lope de Vega (1611-1615)"; Morley, "Strophes in the Spanish Drama Before Lope de Vega"; Williamsen, "A Commentary on 'The Uses of Polymetry' and the Editing of the Multi-Strophic Texts of the Spanish Comedia".
23 "Acomode los versos con prudencia / A los sujetos de que và tratando: / Las deximas son buenas para quexas, / El Soneto està bien en los que aguardan, / Las relaciones piden los Romances, / Aunque en Otauas luzen por extremo, / Son los Tercetos para cosas graues, / Y para las de amor, las redondillas". Vega, "Arte nvevo De hazer Comedias en este tiempo", p. 373 [translation by Marvin Carslon in Vega, "The New Art of Writing Plays", vv. 294-301].
24 From the mid-1990s on, Golden Age theatre historians have argued about the principal structuring feature playwrights used to provide internal order within their plays. One early proposal was José María Ruano de la Haza's concept of the *cuadro* [scene], an "uninterrupted scenic action that takes place in a single location and moment in time" that ends whenever there is a change of location, time, or when the stage is vacated (Ruano de la Haza and Allen, *Los teatros comerciales del siglo XVII y la escenificación de la*

comedia, pp. 291-292). In 1998, Marc Vitse challenged Ruano's initial proposal by arguing instead that the changes in versification, and not the use of *cuadros*, dictated the playwright's structuring of the play (Vitse, "Polimetría y estructuras dramáticas en la comedia de corral del siglo XVII"). More recently, Daniele Crivellari's 2013 study of Lope de Vega's manuscripts seems to corroborate the preeminence of the *cuadros* in the playwriting process (Crivellari, *Marcas autoriales de segmentación en las comedias autógrafas de Lope de Vega*), acknowledging all the same that the strophes remained an important sign-post for both actors and playgoers. Other publications that have contributed to this debate over the years include Antonucci, "Estructura dramática y función de la polimetría en *La cisma de Ingalaterra* de Pedro Calderón de la Barca"; Antonucci, "La polimetría en *La dama boba*"; Carmona Tierno, "Violencia y versificación en *Renegado, rey y mártir* de Cristóbal de Morales"; and Fernández Rodríguez, "¿Escribió Lope guiones métricos?".

25 Facal, "Sobre *Castelvines y Monteses*", pp. 10-16; Weis, "Introduction", pp. 43-52. In addition to Shakespeare's and Lope's plays, there is yet another Spanish *comedia* based on Bandello's novella, Francisco de Rojas Zorrilla's *Los bandos de Verona* (1640). While it is a new original take on the source story, Rojas Zorrilla would have probably been aware of Lope's play; it is doubtful he would have been familiar with Shakespeare's, though. A select list of publications comparing these plays – whether two of them or all three – includes Friedman, "*Romeo and Juliet* as Tragicomedy"; Pardo Molina and González Cañal, "Prólogo a *Los Bandos de Verona*", pp. 173-181; Rodríguez-Badendyck, "The Neglected Alternative"; Scammacca del Murgo, "Gli amanti di Verona tra Lope de Vega e William Shakespeare".

26 Ferrer Valls, "Prólogo a *El mayordomo de la duquesa de Amalfi*", pp. 326-327; Marcus, "Introduction", pp. 16-23.This duo has attracted more scholarly attention than the Verona plays; more in Baker and Whitenack, "Desire and Social Order in the *Duchess* Plays of Lope and Webster"; Ferrer Valls, "Bandello, Belleforest, Painter, Lope de Vega y Webster frente al suceso de la Duquesa de Amalfi y su mayordomo"; García García, "The *Duchess of Malfi* and *El mayordomo de la duquesa de Amalfi* Revisited"; Holmes, "A Widow's Will"; Loftis, "Lope de Vega's and Webster's Amalfi Plays"; Smith, "Text, Stage, and Public in Webster's *The Duchess of Malfi* and Lope's *El mayordomo de la Duquesa de Amalfi*", Weissbourd, "Spain and the Rhetoric of Imperial Rivalry in Webster's *The Duchess of Malfi*".

27 For a better understanding of the scholastic debates on dramatic theory taking place in early modern Europe in general, and in England and Spain in particular, see Cherry, *The Arden Guide to Renaissance Drama*, pp. 167-184; Hoxby, *What Was Tragedy?*, pp. 8-14, 58-69; Huerta Calvo, "Teorías y formas dramáticas en el siglo XVI"; Sánchez Escribano & Alberto Porqueras Mayo, *Preceptiva dramática española*, pp. 21-36; Vitse, "Teoría dramática y géneros dramáticos en el siglo XVII".

28 Sidney, *The Defence of Poesie*, sigs. I1-I1v.

29 Fletcher, *The Faithfvll Shepheardesse*, sig. A3v. Studies of the history of the concept of 'tragicomedy' and its presence on the early modern English stage include Dewar-Watson, "Aristotle and Tragicomedy"; Henke, "'Gentleman-like Tears'"; Henke, "*The Winter's Tale* and Guarinian Dramaturgy"; Kesson, "Was Comedy a Genre in Early Modern English Drama?"; Kimbrell, "Taste, Theatrical Venues, and the Rise of English Tragicomedy"; Lesser, "Tragical-Comical-Pastoral-Colonial"; Lyne, "English Guarini".

30 For more on the tragicomedy/romance taxonomical debate see Danson, "The Shakespeare Remix"; Hunt, "Romance and Tragicomedy"; McDonald, *Shakespeare's Late Style*, pp. 22-27; McMullan, "Shakespearean Tragicomedy and the Idea of the 'Late Play'". Additionally, for an insightful summary of the use of generic descriptors in anthologies of early modern English drama see Lopez, *Constructing the Canon of Early Modern Drama*, pp. 117-120.

31 Huerta Calvo, "Teoría y formas dramáticas en el siglo XVI", pp. 308-311; Sánchez Escribano and Porqueras Mayo, *Preceptiva dramática española*, p. 25; Shergold, *A History of the Spanish Stage*, pp. 174-175.
32 Greer, "The Development of National Theatre", pp. 238-242. A more extensive profile of the *comedia nueva*, as well as its unique place in the theatrical milieu of Golden Age Spain, can be found García Santo-Tomás, "Introducción", pp. 18-26; and McKendrick, *Theatre in Spain*, pp. 72-83.
33 The Spanish *academias* of the Golden Age, inspired by the Italian tradition best exemplified by the Florentine Accademia della Crusca established in 1583, were "private gatherings of friends who spent their free time cultivating the *belles lettres* so as to enjoy and become more familiar with the literary and artistic production of the period", in Sánchez, *Academias literarias del Siglo de Oro español*, p. 10 [my translation]. More in King, "The Academies and Seventeenth-Century Spanish Literature".
34 "Lo Tragico, y lo Comico mezclado, / Y Terencio con Seneca, aunque sea, / Como otro Minotauro de Pasife, / Haran graue vna parte, otra ridicula, / Que aquesta variedad deleyta mucho, / Buen exemplo nos da naturaleza, / Que por tal variedad tiene belleza". Vega, "Arte nvevo De hazer Comedias en este tiempo", pp. 367-368 [translation by Marvin Carslon in Vega, "The New Art of Writing Plays", vv. 172-178]. More on Lope's approach to genre, and his role in the development and popularisation of the comedia nueva, in Arellano, "Lo trágico y lo cómico mezclado"; Burguillo López, "En los arrabales de Lope de Vega"; Kluge, "A Hermaphrodite?"; Thacker, "Lope de Vega, Calderón de la Barca and Tirso de Molina", pp. 36-49.
35 The existence or lack thereof of tragedy in Golden Age Spain has stimulated an ongoing vibrant academic debate. Some of the more recent interventions include Albrecht, *Stoicism, Seneca, and Seventeenth Century Spanish Tragedy*; Greer, "Spanish Golden Age Tragedy"; Santos de la Morena, "Lope y la tragedia 'al estilo español'"; Sullivan, *Tragic Drama in Golden Age Spain*.
36 "ninguna comedia de cuantas se representan en España lo es, sino tragicomedia, que es un mixto formado de lo cómico y lo trágico, tomando déste las personas graves, la acción grande, el terror y la conmiseración; y de aquél el negocio particular, la risa y los donaires, y nadie tenga por impropiedad esta mixtura, pues no repugna a la naturaleza y al arte poético que en una misma fábula concurran personas graves y humilde". As cited in Huerta Calvo, "Teoría y formas dramáticas en el siglo XVI", p. 312 [my translation].
37 Ever since the seventeenth century, students of the *comedia* have continued to devise useful subgenres to aid readers in navigating the vast landscape of Golden Age drama, with every new generation of scholars finding new ways of describing the plays that kept expanding an evergrowing list of options. With time, the taxonomy of the *comedia* has snowballed to such a point that many casual readers and spectators see it as impractical and unwieldy. As Marc Vitse explains, "we currently find ourselves with an unquestionable will to classify the plays, with a rich if somewhat disorientating variety of categories". Vitse, "Teoría dramática y géneros dramáticos en el siglo XVII", p. 746 [my translation]. For a concise summary of the different subgenres of the Spanish *comedia nueva*, see Thacker, *A Companion to Golden Age Theatre*, pp. 142-152; a thoughtful deliberation on Golden Age Spain's dramatic taxonomy is Oleza and Antonucci, "La arquitectura de los géneros en la *Comedia Nueva*".
38 In addition to the plays about the lovers from Verona and the Duchess of Amalfi, English and Spanish playwrights frequently based their plays on the same literary sources such as the *Decameron* by Boccaccio (Shakespeare's *All's Well that End's Well* and *Cymbeline*; Thomas Middleton's *The Widow*; Lope de Vega's *El ruiseñor de Sevilla*, *La discreta enamorada* and *El ejemplo de las casadas*), historical figures such as Timur (Marlowe's *Tamburlaine* plays; Luis Vélez de Guevara's *La nueva ira de Dios*) and episodes such as the marriages of Henry VIII to Catherine of Aragon and Anne Boleyn

(Shakespeare and John Fletcher's *Henry VIII*; Calderón's *La cisma de Ingalaterra*), festivities such as the Summer Solstice (Shakespeare's *A Midsummer Night's Dream*; Lope's *La noche de San Juan*), the utopic conceptualisation of Arcadia (Samuel Daniel's *The Queen's Arcadia*; Beaumont and Fletcher's *Cupid's Revenge*; John Day's *The Isle of Gulls*, James Shirley's *The Arcadia*; Lope's *La Arcadia*; Tirso de Molina's *La Fingida Arcadia*), in addition to a long and broad-ranging collection of mythological and biblical tales, images and allusions.

39 "Haze sol de nuestra España, / compone Lope de Vega, / (la fenix de nuestros tiempos, / y Apolo de nuestros poetas) / Tantas farsas por momentos / y todas ellas tan buenas, / que ni yo sabre contallas, / ni hombre humano encarecellas". Rojas, *El viage entretenido*, sig. 49v-50 [my translation].

40 Castillejo, *Spanish Classical Drama*, p. 15; Dixon, "Lope Félix de Vega Carpio", p. 259; García Reidy, *Las musas rameras*, pp. 171-174; McKendrick, *Theatre in Spain, 1490-1700*, p. 72. The digital project *ArteLope*, directed by Joan Oleza, hosts an ever-growing and easily accessible collection of Lope's plays; more in http://www.artelope.uv.es.

41 Cervantes, *Ocho comedias, y ocho entremeses nuevos*, sig. ¶¶3.

42 "Príncipe de los poetas cómicos de nuestros tiempos, y aun de los pasados, el famoso, y nunca bien celebrado Lope de Vega [...] que como de fuente perenne nacen incesablemente de su fertilíssimo ingenio". As cited in García Santo-Tomás, "Introducción", p. 72 [my translation].

43 "Vemos en la facilidad de su vena el natural grande, en la abundancia de sus escritos la mucha imaginativa, en los nervios y disciplina de sus versos el entendimiento y arte tan juntos, tan perfectos … " As cited in Wright, *Pilgrimage to Patronage*, p. 94 [my translation].

44 McKendrick, *Theatre in Spain, 1490-1700*, pp. 72-73.

45 Halliday, *A Shakespeare Companion*, p. 374.

46 Bentley, *The Profession of Dramatist in Shakespeare's Time*, pp. 27-28 (Heywood as cited on p. 27).

47 Halliday, *A Shakespeare Companion*, p. 374; McKendrick, *Theatre in Spain, 1490-1700*, p. 72; Thacker, *A Companion to Golden Age Theatre*, p. 132.

48 The geographic area in which Golden Age theatre had the strongest presence was the Low Countries: more in Álvarez Francés, "Fascination for the 'Madritsche Apollo'"; Blom, "Enemy Treasures"; Blom and Marion, "Lope de Vega and the conquest of Spanish theater in the Netherlands"; Boer, "La representación de la comedia española en Holanda"; Jautze et al., "Spaans theater in de Amsterdamse Schouwburg (1638-1672)"; Sanz Ayán, *Hacer escena*, pp. 90-106; additionally, a detailed account of the performances in the Amsterdam Schouwburg public theatre bwtween 1637 and 1772 is available in the *ONSTAGE* online database (http://www.vondel.humanities.uva.nl/onstage). For studies on the presence of the *comedia* in other European countries see Antonucci, "¿Qué Lope se conocía en la Italia del siglo XVII?"; Botta et al., "Versiones romanas de tres textos de Lope"; Couderc, "Lope de Vega y el teatro francés del siglo XVII"; Sanz Ayán, "To Conquer Paris"; Tercero Casado, "'It's a Spanish *comedia*, and therefore it's better than any other fête'". More on the performance of Spanish drama in colonial America in Ball, *Treating the Public*, pp. 79-95, 100-103, 109-124.

49 McKendrick, *Theatre in Spain, 1490-1700*, p. 72.

50 A summary of the history and styles of the *teatro breve* can be found in Thacker, *A Companion to Golden Age Theatre*, pp. 153-160.

51 Bentley, *The Profession of Dramatist in Shakespeare's Time*, pp. 120-126.

52 Rodríguez Cáceres and Pedraza Jiménez, "Lope de Vega y su teatro ante los hombres de su tiempo", pp. 17-19.

53 Díez Borque, "El negocio teatral de Lope de Vega y Calderón de la Barca", p. 49 [my translation]. More on Lope's life and career in Samson and Thacker, "Introduction: Lope's Life and Work".
54 In a perfect illustration of this point, during a libel lawsuit brought against him in the late 1580s Lope insisted on being described as a secretary for the nobility, and argued that he wrote *comedias* for leisure rather than for money. More in García Reidy, *Las musas rameras*, pp. 107-111.
55 "Verdad es, que yo he escrito algunas vezes / Siguiendo el arte, que conocen pocos, / Mas luego, que salir por otra parte, / Veo los monstruos de apariencias llenos, / Adonde acude el vulgo y las mugeres, / Que este triste exercitio canonizan, / A quel habito barbaro me buelvo, / Y cuando hè de escriuir vna Comedia, / Encierro los preceptos con seis llaves, / Saco à Terencio, y Plauto de mi estudio, / Para que no me den vozes, que suele, / Dar gritos la verdad en libros mu[d]os, / Y escriuo por el arte, que inuentaron, / Los que el vulgar aplauso pretendieron, / Porque como las paga el vulgo, es justo, / Hablarle en necio para darle gusto". Vega, *Arte nvevo De hazer Comedias en este tiempo*, pp. 362 [translation by Marvin Carslon in Vega, "The New Art of Writing Plays", vv. 31-45]. More on this specific passage of the poem in Díez Borque, "Lope de Vega y los gustos del 'vulgo'"; Sánchez Jiménez, "Vulgo, imitación y natural en el *Arte nuevo de hacer comedias* (1609) de Lope de Vega".
56 "fue el poeta más rico y más pobre de nuestros tiempos". As cited in García Reidy, *Las musas rameras*, p. 26 [my translation].
57 Wright, *Pilgrimage to Patronage*, p. 93.
58 The prices dramatists charged companies for their plays rose progressively, both in Spain and in England. In the mid-1580s Gaspar de Porres paid Cervantes forty ducats for two *comedias*; each play earned him approximately five English pounds, which was roughly the same amount Elizabethan dramatists were charging in the early 1590s. In the following decades Lope would ask for two-to-three times as much, and Calderón – who wrote after Lope and at the highest point of inflation – was able to charge around 80 ducats per play, again a similar amount to what the most profitable English dramatists could expect by the 1610s. More in Díez Borque, "El negocio teatral de Lope de Vega y Calderón de la Barca", pp. 49-52; Keenan, *Acting Companies and their Plays in Shakespeare's London*, pp. 58-59; Sanz Ayán and García García, *Teatros y comediantes en el Madrid de Felipe II*, p. 47. For a Spanish-to-English currency conversion chart and explanation, see Brown and Elliott, *A Palace for a King*, p. 257.

INTERLUDE 2
Professional Actresses: To Have and Have Not (and How It Made a Difference)

In addition to contrasting the theatrical cultures of sixteenth- and seventeenth-century England and Spain, this book invites readers to participate in an additional comparative exercise regarding the theatre-making ways of past and present. While much of what these pages describe will make sense to those familiar with contemporary performance practices, there is also a lot that will sound foreign to many ears of the new millennium. One such difference is that whereas authors nowadays rarely write with specific performers or troupes in mind, back then it was customary for dramatists to tailor their work to individual companies. This was the result of the business model of the time, in which troupes often commissioned playwrights to develop new material exclusively for themselves. As a result these plays often reflect the specificities of that company and its performance conditions, ranging from the size of the cast and the design of the venue to the particular roles that played to the strengths of the performers. In other words, much more so than now the dramatic literature from Shakespearean England and Golden Age Spain faithfully embodies the real-life conditions within these two extraordinarily similar playmaking environments, which in turn helps explain the many features English and Spanish plays from this period have in common.

The flip-side is, of course, that the differences and not just the similarities between the English and Spanish theatrical cultures were made equally manifest in their respective dramatic corpora. And among these differences, none was more striking than that of the absence of female performers in England's preeminent commercial theatres, unlike in Spain where the professional actress was a central figure in playmaking society (see pp. 92–96). That one country allowed while the other prevented women from actively participating in the theatrical process had a determining impact on the creation, representation and reception of female characters. This is precisely what this brief interlude explores: building on the information presented in Chapters 3 and 4 as well as through the use of quantitative analysis, the following pages illustrate visually the discrepant levels of protagonism female parts enjoyed in early modern England and Spain's commercial theatre as a consequence of the two countries' disparate attitudes towards professional actresses. By focusing on the amount of words spoken – role length being a reliable yardstick with which to measure protagonism in this form of drama – by female as opposed to male characters in the plays of Shakespeare, Lope de Vega and their peers, it becomes evident that the physical presence of women on the stages of Golden Age Spain's *corrales de comedias* had a significant impact in the stage time and protagonism of these voices that so often were relegated to the margins of story-telling.[1]

The data for this study were taken from *Rolecall: A Database of Characters in Early Modern European Theatre* (http://www.rolecall.eu), an ongoing online database project that provides detailed information for a growing corpus of plays from all across early modern Europe. Here the scope of analysis is limited to English and Spanish plays written with professional adult acting companies and the public stage in mind. This leaves out closet drama, court spectacles and masques, street performances such as Spain's *autos sacramentales*, interludes and other forms of minor theatre, and plays performed by boy companies or amateur troupes. With these parameters in place, I culled and interpreted data from 182 and 410 plays written by English and Spanish dramatists respectively (all titles are listed in Appendix 1, pp. 132–137), and graphically represented in the following

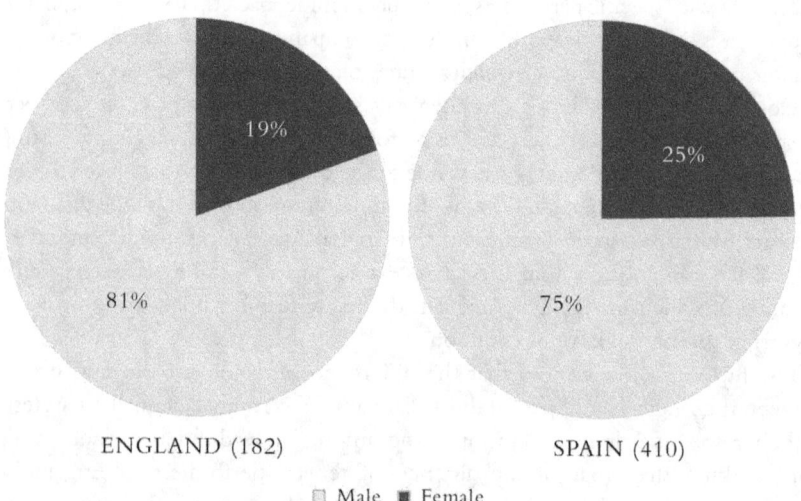

INTERLUDE 2.1 Total proportion of lines allocated to female (dark) and male (light) characters in Shakespearean England and Golden Age Spain's commercial plays

The overall numbers reveal an initial difference between the two corpora: in the English plays, female characters on average speak around 19% of the lines, compared to the 25% of female characters in Spanish *comedias*. In both countries, the dominance of male speech and protagonism reflects a patriarchal social ecosystem in which feminine virtue was defined by a woman's silence and modesty. That said, the 6% margin that separates them, which at first sight may not appear to be too significant, marks a proportional increase north of 30% in female speech in Spanish plays in relation to English ones. This is a substantial difference for two corpora of plays that were written and performed in such similar sociocultural and artistic milieux, and as a result one can expect to find a strong positive correlation between plays with larger shares of female speech and the country that had professional actresses performing those roles as opposed to young, relatively inexperienced cross-dressed boys.

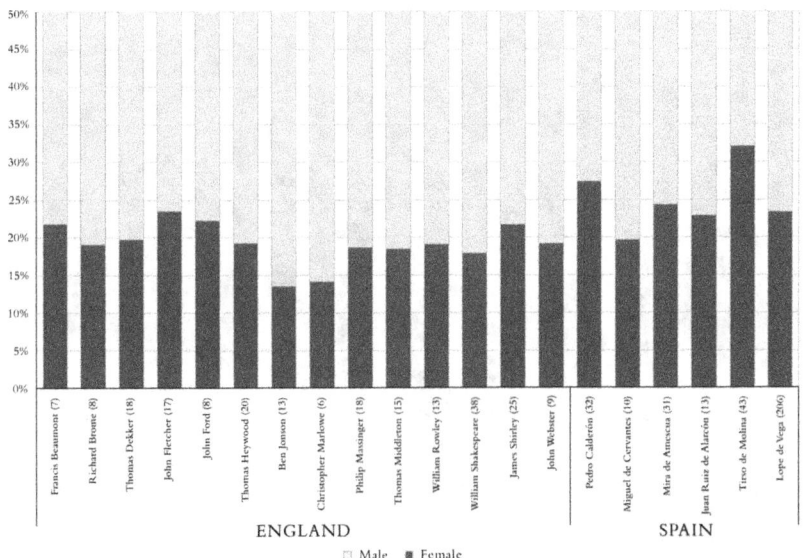

INTERLUDE 2.2 Proportion of lines allocated to female (dark) and male (light) characters in the corpora of Shakespearean England and Golden Age Spain's dramatists (min. five plays)

When one breaks down the corpora into authors, one can see that only four English playwrights crack the 20% barrier of female speech: Francis Beaumont and John Fletcher (who wrote most of their dramatic works together), John Ford and James Shirley. It is important to note that all four wrote primarily for the Jacobean and Caroline indoor playhouses, which had a considerably higher number of female audience members than the open-air theatres in which women had to be chaperoned by male companions.[2] One could attribute their decision to endow female characters with more stage presence at least in some measure to their understanding that they had to address a more diverse theatregoing body than their amphitheatre-oriented colleagues. By contrast, only one Spanish dramatist included in this study dips *under* the 20% barrier. This was Miguel de Cervantes, whose classicist plays were considerably less successful than Lope's and those of his *comedia nueva* acolytes; one cannot but wonder whether this was at least in part because of his lack of sizeable female roles for the nation's fan-favourite actresses.

Another revealing point of analysis is the role dramatic genre plays in determining the levels of protagonism of female characters. The following chart shows all 182 English and 410 Spanish plays classified into comedies, tragedies, tragicomedies (in the modern sense, not the Aristotelian one), mythological/allegorical plays, histories and, in the case of Spain, religious plays:

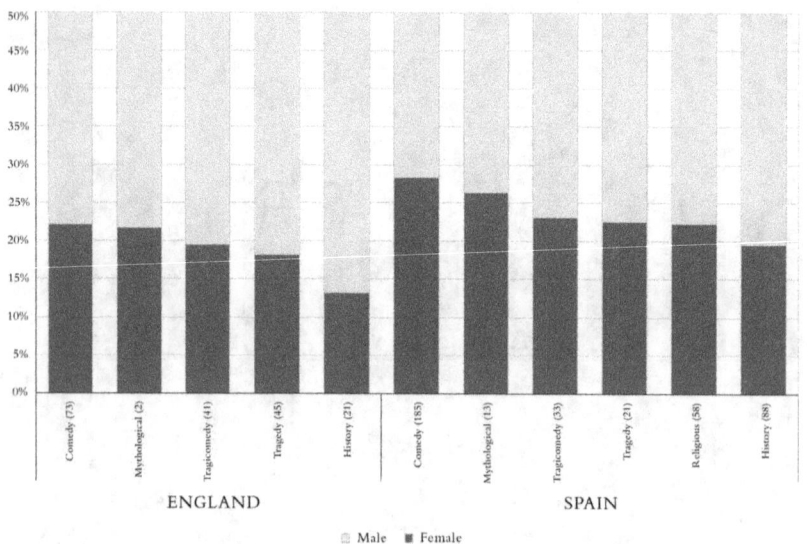

INTERLUDE 2.3 Proportion of lines allocated to female (dark) and male (light) characters in Shakespearean England and Golden Age Spain's commercial plays divided into dramatic genres

In both countries, the comedies and mythological plays proved to be the best vehicles for female presence and agency, followed by tragicomedies, tragedies, – Spain's religious plays, – and in final place the histories. This is not surprising, as many critics have noted the time-tested tradition of having more female-driven plots in comedies than in the habitually male-centric tragedies and history (i.e., oftentimes military) plays. What does stand out, though, is the consistent gap that separates the two corpora in all categories. This graphic yet again reaffirms early modern English and Spanish public drama's underlying sameness barring the single yet significant discrepancy in women's involvement in the creative theatrical process.

The final chart is perhaps the most revealing of them all in this respect. It presents the ten plays with the highest share of female speech from each country, divided into roles and ordered according to their size (moving upward from longest to shortest). Of the ten English plays, in only four of them the character who speaks the most is female; moreover, two of them spend a significant amount of time disguised as a male character, i.e., what would later be known as 'breeches roles' (marked with striped patterns in the chart). However, in nine out of Spain's top-ten *comedias* the character who speaks the most is female, out of which three also take up a man's disguise at some point during the play. In other words, not only do England's most female-driven plays feature considerably fewer female protagonists than Spain's, but also half of those roles speak a considerable number of their lines dressed as men.

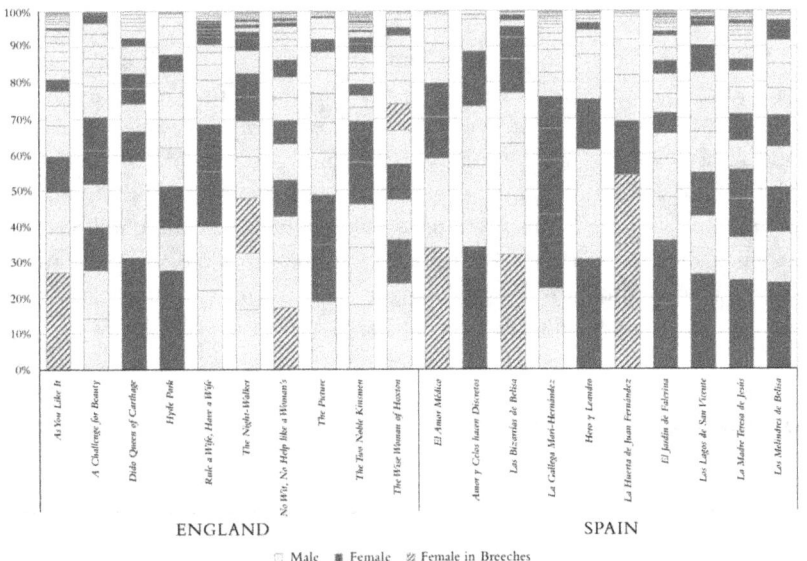

INTERLUDE 2.4 Proportion of lines allocated to female characters (dark), male characters (light) and female characters in breeches (striped) in the ten English and Spanish plays with the largest share of lines spoken by female characters

The visually striking disparity of the chart reflects the broader reality of these two corpora: that there are many more female-led Spanish *comedias* than there are female-led English plays. Appendix 2 (pp. 138–141) lists all the texts analysed from both England and Spain in which the lead character in terms of speech share is female. In only fifteen of the 182 English plays the character who speaks the most is female, which amounts to slightly over 8%. The numbers for Spain are dramatically different: 80 of the 410 studied plays feature a female lead, almost 20% of the total. What is more, on average the Spanish female leads speak a larger share of the plays' lines than their English counterparts (24% to 20%), and many more English female protagonists resort to a male disguise than the Spanish ones (40% to 25%). Clearly there is a stronger correlation between maleness and the ability (or permission) to speak publicly on the pre-1642 English stage than in the *corrales de comedias* of the Spanish Golden Age, where female speech and protagonism were much more widespread and took on a wider array of forms.

Once again, this brief interlude serves as a visual reminder of the influence social and cultural circumstances exerted over the dramatic literature of early modern England and Spain. To read the texts of Shakespeare, Lope de Vega and their peers in a vacuum, without taking into account the contexts and conventions that crucially weighed on their profession as commercial dramatists, prevents the reader from fully understanding why they wrote the plays that they did, and in the way in which they did. With this in mind, one can further explore the connections between female characters' speech in early modern English and Spanish theatre and the two countries' different stances on allowing women to perform publicly on the national stage. It stands to reason that longer and more diverse female roles marked the country that not only had professional actresses, but also allowed women to undertake a wider range of responsibilities within the broader theatrical enterprise. Moreover, it also helps explain why the numbers regarding female protagonism in the plays of these two dramatic traditions become much more similar after 1660, when England lifted the ban on women performing professionally and finally caught up with the playmaking ways of most other early modern European countries.

Appendix 1 List of plays analysed

England	
	Anonymous: Alphonsus, Emperor of Germany.
	Francis Beaumont: The Beggar's Bush★; Cupid's Revenge★; A King and No King★; The Maid's Tragedy★; Philaster; The Wild Goose Chase★; Wit Without Money★. RICHARD BROME. *The Antipodes; The Court Beggar; The Damoiselle; The Jovial Crew; The Late Lancashire Witches★; The Northern Lass; The Queen's Exchange; The Sparagus Garden.*
	Duke of Buckingham (George Villiers): *Monsieur Thomas★*.
	George Chapman: *The Blind Beggar of Alexandria*.
	Henry Chettle: *Patient Grissel★*.
	John Cooke: *Greene's Tu Quoque*.

(*Continued*)

Thomas Dekker: *Blurt, Master Constable*; *The Family of Love*★; *The Honest Whore Pt 1*★; *The Honest Whore Pt 2*; *If it Be Not Good the Devil is in it*; *Lust's Dominion, or the Lascivious Queen*; *Match Me in London*; *Old Fortunatus*; *Patient Grissel*★; *The Roaring Girl*★; *Satiromastix*; *The Shoemaker's Holiday*; *Sir Thomas Wyatt*★; *The Spanish Gypsy*★; *The Virgin Martyr*; *Westward Ho*★; *The Whore of Babylon*; *The Witch of Edmonton*★.

Nathan Field: *The Fatal Dowry*★.

John Fletcher: *The Beggar's Bush*★; *The Chances*; *Cupid's Revenge*★; *The Elder Brother*★; *Henry VIII*★; *A King and No King*★; *The Maid's Tragedy*★; *Monsieur Thomas*★; *The Night-Walker*★; *Philaster*; *Rule a Wife Have a Wife*; *The Tragedy of Rollo, Duke of Normandy*★; *The Tragedy of Thierry, King of France*★; *The Two Noble Kinsmen*★; *The Widow*★; *The Wild Goose Chase*★; *Wit Without Money*★.

John Ford: *The Broken Heart*; *The Fancies Chaste and Noble*; *Love's Sacrifice*; *The Lover's Melancholy*; *Perkin Warbeck*; *The Spanish Gypsy*★; *Tis Pity She's a Whore*; *The Witch of Edmonton*★.

William Haughton: *Patient Grissel*★.

Thomas Heywood: *The Brazen Age*; *A Challenge for Beauty*; *The English Traveler*; *The Fair Maid of the West*; *Fortune by Land and Sea*★; *The Four Prentices of London*; *The Golden Age*; *How a Man May Choose a Good Wife from a Bad*; *If You Know Not Me You Know Nobody Pt 1*; *If You Know Not Me You Know Nobody Pt 2*; *The Iron Age*; *The Late Lancashire Witches*★; *King Edward IV Pt 1*; *King Edward IV Pt 2*; *A Maidenhead Well Lost*; *The Rape of Lucrece*; *The Royal King and the Loyal Subject*; *The Thracian Wonder*★; *The Wise Woman of Hoxton*; *A Woman Killed with Kindness*.

Ben Jonson: *The Alchemist*; *Bartholomew Fair*; *The Case is Altered*; *Catiline His Conspiracy*; *Cynthia's Revels*; *The Devil is an Ass*; *Every Man in his Humour*; *Every Man Out of his Humour*; *The New Inn*; *Sejanus His Fall*; *The Tragedy of Rollo, Duke of Normandy*★; *Volpone*; *The Widow*★.

Thomas Kyd: *The Spanish Tragedy*.

Christopher Marlowe: *Dido, Queen of Carthage*; *Edward II*; *The Jew of Malta*; *The Massacre at Paris*; *Tamburlaine the Great Pt 1*; *The Tragical History of Dr. Faustus (A Text)*.

John Marston: *The Malcontent*★.

Philip Massinger: *The Beggar's Bush*★; *The Bondman*; *The City Madam*; *The Duke of Milan*; *The Elder Brother*★; *The Emperor of the East*; *The Fatal Dowry*★; *The Great Duke of Florence*; *The Maid of Honour*; *A New Way to Pay Old Debts*; *The Old Law*★; *The Picture*; *The Renegado*; *The Roman Actor*; *The Tragedy of Rollo, Duke of Normandy*★; *The Tragedy of Thierry, King of France*★; *The Unnatural Combat*; *The Virgin Martyr*.

Thomas Middleton: *Anything for a Quiet Life*★; *The Changeling*★; *A Chaste Maid in Cheapside*; *A Fair Quarrel*★; *The Family of Love*★; *A Game at Chess*; *Hengist, King of Kent*; *The Honest Whore Pt 1*★; *No Wit, No Help Like a Woman's*; *The Old Law*★; *The Roaring Girl*★; *The Spanish Gypsy*★; *Timon of Athens*★; *Your Five Gallants*; *The Widow*★.

(Continued)

William Rowley: *All's Lost by Lust; The Birth of Merlin; The Changeling*; A Cure for a Cuckold*; A Fair Quarrel*; Fortune by Land and Sea*; A Match at Midnight; A New Wonder, A Woman Never Vexed; The Old Law*; A Shoemaker a Gentleman; The Spanish Gypsy*; The Thracian Wonder*; The Witch of Edmonton**.

William Shakespeare: *A Midsummer Night's Dream; All's Well that Ends Well; Antony and Cleopatra; As You Like It; The Comedy of Errors; Coriolanus; Cymbeline; Hamlet; Henry IV Part 1; Henry IV Part 2; Henry V; Henry VI Part 1; Henry VI Part 2; Henry VI Part 3; Henry VIII*; Julius Caesar; King John; King Lear; Love's Labours Lost; Macbeth; Measure for Measure; The Merchant of Venice; The Merry Wives of Windsor; Much Ado About Nothing; Othello; Pericles; Richard II; Richard III; Romeo and Juliet; The Taming of the Shrew; The Tempest; Timon of Athens*; Titus Andronicus; Troilus and Cressida; Twelfth Night; The Two Gentlemen of Verona; The Two Noble Kinsmen*; The Winter's Tale*.

James Shirley: *The Arcadia; The Ball; The Bird in a Cage; Changes, or Love in a Maze; The Constant Maid; The Coronation; The Duke's Mistress; The Example; The Gamester; The Gentleman of Venice; The Grateful Servant; The Humorous Courtier; Hyde Park; The Lady of Pleasure; Love Tricks, or the School of Complement; Love's Cruelty; The Maid's Revenge; The Night-Walker*; The Opportunity; The Politician; The Royal Master; The Traitor; The Wedding; The Witty Fair One; The Young Admiral*.

John Webster: *A Cure for a Cuckold*; Anything for a Quiet Life*; Appius and Virginia; The Devil's Law-Case; The Duchess of Malfi; The Malcontent*; Sir Thomas Wyatt*; The Malcontent*; Westward Ho*; The White Devil*.

Spain

Pedro Calderón de la Barca: *Afectos de Odio y Amor; El Alcalde de Zalamea; Amado y Aborrecido; Amor, Honor y Poder; Las Armas de la Hermosura; La Aurora en Copacabana; Las Cadenas del Demonio; Casa con Dos Puertas Mala es de Guardar; El Castillo de Lindabridis; La Dama Duende; Darlo Todo y no Dar Nada; La Devoción de la Cruz; El Escondido y la Tapada; El Faetonte; La Fiera, el Rayo y la Piedra; Las Fortunas de Andrómeda y Perseo; El Galán Fantasma; La Hija del Aire, Parte 1; La Hija del Aire, Parte 2; El Jardín de Falerina; Luis Pérez el Gallego; El Mágico Prodigioso; Las Manos Blancas no Ofenden; Mañanas de Abril y Mayo; El Médico de su Honra; El Monstruo de los Jardines; Nadie Fíe su Secreto; No Hay Burlas con el Amor; No Siempre lo Peor es Cierto; El Príncipe Constante; Las Tres Justicias en Una; La Vida es Sueño*.

Miguel de Cervantes: *Los Baños de Argel; La Casa de los Celos; El Cerco de Numancia; La Entretenida; El Gallardo Español; La Gran Sultana; El Laberinto de Amor; Pedro de Urdemalas; El Rufián Dichoso; El Trato de Argel*.

Antonio Mira de Amescua: La Adúltera Virtuosa; *La Adversa Fortuna de Don Álvaro de Luna; La Adversa Fortuna de Don Bernardo de Cabrera; Amor, Ingenio y Mujer; El Animal Profeta; El Arpa de David; La Casa de Tahur; El Clavo de Jael; La Confusión de Hungría; Cuatro Milagros de Amor; El Ejemplo Mayor de la Desdicha; El Esclavo del Demonio; Examinarse de Rey; La Fénix de Salamanca; Galán, Valiente y Discreto; Hero y Leandro; La Hija de Carlos V; La Judía de Toledo; Las Lises de*

(Continued)

Francia; Lo Que Puede el Oír Misa; Lo Que Puede una Sospecha; El Mártir de Madrid; El Más Feliz Cautiverio; La Mesonera del Cielo; No Hay Burlas con las Mujeres; No Hay Dicha ni Desdicha Hasta la Muerte; No Hay Reinar como Vivir; Obligar Contra su Sangre; Los Prodigios de la Vara; La Próspera Fortuna de Don Álvaro de Luna; La Próspera Fortuna de Don Bernardo de Cabrera; El Rico Avariento; La Rueda de la Fortuna; La Tercera de Sí Misma; La Vida y Muerte de la Monja de Portugal.

Agustín Moreto: *El Desdén con el Desdén; El Lindo Don Diego; Santa Rosa del Perú.*

Juan Ruiz de Alarcón: *La Crueldad por el Honor; La Cueva de Salamanca; El Desdichado en Fingir; Los Empeños de un Engaño; Los Favores del Mundo; Ganar Amigos; La Industria y la Suerte; La Manganilla de Melilla; Mudarse por Mejorarse; Los Pechos Privilegiados; La Prueba de las Promesas; Las Paredes Oyen; El Semejante a Sí Mismo; Todo es Ventura.*

Miguel Sánchez: *La Guarda Cuidadosa.*

Tirso de Molina: *Amar por Razón de Estado; Amar por Señas; El Amor Médico; Amor y Celos Hacen Discretos; Antona García; El Aquiles; Averígüelo Vargas; Los Balcones de Madrid; Los Balcones de Madrid (Revised); Bellaco Sois, Gómez; El Burlador de Sevilla; El Castigo del Penséque; Celos con Celos se Curan; La Celosa de sí Misma; El Condenado por Desconfiado; Cómo Han de Ser los Amigos; La Dama del Olivar; Desde Toledo a Madrid; Don Gil de las Calzas Verdes; Doña Beatriz de Silva; La Fingida Arcadia; La Gallega Mari Hernández; La Huerta de Juan Fernández; La Joya de las Montañas; Los Lagos de San Vicente; Marta la Piadosa; El Mayor Desengaño; La Mejor Espigadera; El Melancólico; La Mujer que Manda en Casa; La Ninfa del Cielo; Por el Sótano y el Torno; Quien Calla Otorga; Quien Da Luego Da Dos Veces; Quien no Cae no se Levanta; Las Quinas de Portugal; La República al Revés; La Santa Juana, Parte 1; La Santa Juana, Parte 2; La Santa Juana, Parte 3; Santo y Sastre; Tanto es de lo Más como de lo Menos; La Venganza de Tamar; El Vergonzoso en el Palacio; La Vida de Herodes; La Villana de la Sagra; La Villana de Vallecas.*

Lope de Vega: *El Abanillo; El Acero de Madrid; Acertar Errando; Adonis y Venus; La Adversa Fortuna de Don Bernardo de Cabrera; Al Pasar del Arroyo; El Alcaide de Madrid; El Alcalde Mayor; La Aldehuela; El Amante Agradecido; Los Amantes Sin Amor; Amar como se ha de Amar; Amar, Servir y Esperar; El Amigo Hasta la Muerte; El Amigo por Fuerza; La Amistad y Obligación; El Amor Desatinado; El Amor Enamorado; Amor Secreto Hasta Celos; Amor, Pleito y Desafío; Los Amores de Albanio y Ismenia; Angélica en el Catay; El Animal de Hungría; El Antecristo; El Anzuelo de Fenisa; Arauco Domado por el Excelentísimo Señor Don García Hurtado de Mendoza; La Arcadia; El Arenal de Sevilla; El Argel Fingido y Renegado de Amor; El Asalto de Mastrique por el Príncipe de Parma; Audiencias del Rey Don Pedro; Ay, Verdades, que en Amor; Los Bandos de Sena; Barlaán y Josafat; El Bastardo Mudarra; La Batalla del Honor; Las Batuecas del Duque de Alba; El Bautismo del Príncipe de Marruecos; Belardo el Furioso; La Bella Aurora; La Bella Malmaridada o la Cortesana; Los Benavides; Las Bizarrías de Belisa; El Blasón de los Chaves de Villalba; La Boba para los Otros y Discreta para si; El Bobo del Colegio; El Brasil Restituido; La Buena*

(Continued)

Guarda; La Burgalesa de Lerma; Las Burlas de Amor; Las Burlas Veras; Las Burlas y Enredos de Benito; El Caballero de Illescas; El Caballero de Olmedo; El Caballero del Milagro; La Campana de Aragón; La Carbonera; Carlos V en Francia; El Casamiento en la Muerte; Castelvines y Monteses; El Castigo del Discreto; El Castigo sin Venganza; Los Cautivos de Argel; Los Celos de Rodamonte; La Ciudad sin Dios; Los Comendadores de Córdoba; La Competencia en los Nobles; Con su Pan se lo Coma; El Conde Fernán González; La Contienda de García de Paredes y el Capitán Juan de Urbina; Contra Valor No Hay Desdicha; La Corona de Hungría y la Injusta Venganza; La Corona Derribada y la Vara de Moisés; La Cortesía de España; Las Cuentas del Gran Capitán; El Cuerdo en su Casa; El Cuerdo Loco; La Dama Boba; David Perseguido y Montes de Gelboé; De Amar Sin Saber a Quién; De Cuándo Acá Nos Vino; Del Mal lo Menos; Del Monte Sale; El Desconfiado; La Desdichada Estefanía; El Desposorio Encubierto; El Desprecio Agradecido; La Devoción del Rosario; La Difunta Pleiteada; Dios Hace Reyes; La Discordia en los Casados; La Divina Vencedora y los Famosos Hechos de Meledín Gallinato y Toma de Morón; El Dómine Lucas; Don Juan de Castro, Parte 1; Don Juan de Castro, Parte 2; Don Lope de Cardona; Los Donaires de Matico; La Doncella Teodor; Donde no está su Dueño está su Duelo; En los Indicios, la Culpa; Los Embustes de Celauro; Los Embustes de Fabia; El Enemigo Engañado; Los Enemigos en Casa; La Esclava de su Galán; El Esclavo de Roma; El Esclavo Fingido; Los Esclavos Libres; La Escolástica Celosa; Los Españoles en Flandes; Las Famosas Asturianas; El Favor Agradecido; La Fé Rompida; Las Ferias de Madrid; La Fianza Satisfecha; La Filisarda; La Firmeza en la Desdicha; Las Flores de Don Juan y Rico y Pobre Trocados; La Francesilla; Fuente Ovejuna; La Fuerza Lastimosa; El Galán Castrucho; El Galán de la Membrilla; El Galán Escarmentado; La Gallarda Toledana; El Ganso de Oro; El Genovés Liberal; El Gran Duque de Moscovia y Emperador Perseguido; Las Grandezas de Alejandro; El Grao de Valencia; Los Guanches de Tenerife y la Conquista de Canarias; Guardar y Guardarse; Guerras de Amor y de Honor; Los Guzmanes del Toral; El Halcón de Federico; El Hamete de Toledo; Los Hechos de Garcilaso de la Vega y Moro Tarfe; La Hermosa Alfreda; La Hermosa Ester; La Hermosura Aborrecida; Los Hidalgos del Aldea; Hijo de los Leones; El Hijo por Engaño y Toma de Toledo; El Hijo Sin Padre; El Hijo Venturoso; La Historia de Tobías; El Hombre de Bien; El Hombre por su Palabra; El Honrado Hermano; La Ilustre Fregona; La Imperial de Otón; La Infanta Desesperada; La Ingratitud Vengada; El Ingrato Arrepentido; El Ingrato, Corona de Comedias; La Inocente Laura; La Intención Castigada; Jorge Toledano; Juan de Dios y Antón Martín; El Juez en su Causa; Julián Romero; Las Justas de Tebas y Reina de las Amazonas; El Laberinto de Creta; El Labrador Venturoso; El Lacayo Fingido; Laura Perseguida; El Leal Criado; La Limpieza No Manchada; Lo Fingido Verdadero; Lo Que ha de Ser; Lo Que Pasa en Una Tarde; El Loco Por Fuerza; Los Locos de Valencia; La Locura por la Honra; La Madre de la Mejor; La Madre Teresa de Jesús; El Maestro de Danzar; La Malcasada; El Marido Más Firme; El Marqués de Mantua; Más Pueden Celos que Amor; La Mayor Corona; El Mayor Imposible; La Mayor Victoria; El Mayordomo de la Duquesa de Amalfi; El Mejor Alcalde El Rey; La Mejor

(Continued)

Enamorada, La Magdalena; Los Melindres de Belisa; El Mesón de la Corte; El Molino; La Moza del Cántaro; Las Mudanzas de Fortuna y Los Sucesos de Don Beltrán de Aragón; El Nacimiento de Cristo; Nadie se Conoce; La Necedad del Discreto; La Niña de Plata; La Niñez del Padre Rojas; El Niño Inocente de la Guardia; La Noche de San Juan; No Son Todos Ruiseñores; La Noche Toledana; El Nuevo Mundo Descubierto por Cristóbal Colón; La Octava Maravilla; Las Paces de los Reyes y Judía de Toledo; La Pastoral de Jacinto; Pedro Carbonero; Peribáñez y el Comendador de Ocaña; El Perro del Hortelano; El Perseguido; El Piadoso Aragonés; El Piadoso Veneciano; El Pleito por la Honra o el Valor de Fernandico; Los Pleitos de Inglaterra; El Poder en el Discreto; El Postrer Godo de España; Los Ponces de Barcelona; Por la Puente, Juana; Los Porceles de Murcia; Porfiar hasta Morir; Los Prados de León; El Premio de la Hermosura; El Premio del Bien Hablar; El Premio Riguroso y Amistad Bien Pagada; El Príncipe Despeñado; El Príncipe Inocente; El Príncipe Melancólico; El Príncipe Perfecto, Parte 1; El Príncipe Perfecto, Parte 2; La Próspera Fortuna de Don Bernardo de Cabrera; Quien Todo lo Quiere; La Quinta de Florencia; El Remedio en la Desdicha; La Resistencia Honrada y Condesa Matilde; El Rey por su Semejanza; El Rey por Trueque; El Robo de Dina; Roma Abrasada; San Isidro Labrador de Madrid; Santa Casilda; La Santa Liga; Santo Ángelo; El Santo Negro Rosambuco de la Ciudad de Palermo; La Selva Sin Amor; El Sol Parado; Los Tellos de Meneses; Los Terceros de San Francisco; El Testimonio Vengado; El Toledano Vengado y Celoso Vengado; Los Trabajos de Jacob, Sueños Hay que Verdad Son; Los Tres Diamantes; El Triunfo de la Humildad y la Soberbia Abatida; El Truhan del Cielo y Loco Santo; Ursón y Valentín, Hijos del Rey de Francia; El Valiente Céspedes; El Valor de las Mujeres; Valor, Fortuna y Lealtad de los Tellos de Meneses; El Vaquero de Moraña; El Vaso de Elección y Doctor de las Gentes San Pablo; El Vellocino de Oro; La Vengadora de las Mujeres; La Venganza Piadosa; El Verdadero Amante; La Vida de San Pedro Nolasco; La Villana de Getafe; La Viuda Valenciana; El Villano en su Rincón.

Plays marked with an asterisk (*) were written collaboratively between two or more dramatists.

Appendix 2 List of plays in which the longest speaking role is female

Dramatist	Play Title	Country	Role	Words	%	Breeches	Genre
Tirso de Molina	*Bellaco Sois, Gómez*	Spain	Ana	5355	35.81	Yes	Comedy
Tirso de Molina	*La Huerta de Juan Fernández*	Spain	Petronila	5595	34.83	Yes	Comedy
Tirso de Molina	*Amor y Celos Hacen Discretos*	Spain	Duquesa	4224	34.14	No	History Play
Lope de Vega	*La Boba para los Otros y Discreta para sí*	Spain	Diana	4631	33.88	No	Comedy
Tirso de Molina	*El Amor Médico*	Spain	Jerónima	5503	33.85	Yes	Comedy
Tirso de Molina	*La Ninfa del Cielo*	Spain	Ninfa	4521	32.84	Yes	Religious Play
Lope de Vega	*Las Bizarrías de Belisa*	Spain	Belisa	4461	31.91	Yes	Comedy
Lope de Vega	*Por la Puente, Juana*	Spain	Isabel	3691	31.72	No	Comedy
Lope de Vega	*La Vengadora de las Mujeres*	Spain	Laura	4254	31.59	Yes	Comedy
Christopher Marlowe	*Dido, Queen of Carthage*	England	Dido	4228	31.01	No	Tragedy
Tirso de Molina	*Quien Calla Otorga*	Spain	Aurora	4584	30.71	No	Comedy
Lope de Vega	*Antona García*	Spain	Antona	4508	30.66	No	History Play
Lope de Vega	*La Fé Rompida*	Spain	Lucinda	5432	30.45	Yes	Comedy
Lope de Vega	*La Moza del Cántaro*	Spain	María	3956	29.94	No	Comedy
Antonio Mira de Amescua	*Obligar Contra su Sangre*	Spain	Sancha	3790	29.92	No	History Play
Tirso de Molina	*La Santa Juana, Parte 2*	Spain	Santa	4007	29.84	No	Religious Play
Lope de Vega	*La Esclava de su Galán*	Spain	Doña Elena	4361	29.62	No	Comedy
Antonio Mira de Amescua	*La Judía de Toledo*	Spain	Raquel	4341	29.54	No	History Play
Lope de Vega	*Del Monte Sale*	Spain	Narcisa	4341	29.44	No	Tragicomedy
Pedro Calderón de la Barca	*La Hija del Aire, Parte 2*	Spain	Semíramis	4885	29.42	Yes	Tragedy
Agustín Moreto	*Santa Rosa del Perú*	Spain	Rosa	4540	28.76	No	Religious Play
Lope de Vega	*El Ingrato*	Spain	Infanta	3300	28.61	No	Comedy
Tirso de Molina	*La Santa Juana, Parte 1*	Spain	Santa	5485	28.57	No	Religious Play

Author	Play	Country	Character				Genre
Antonio Mira de Amescua	Cuatro Milagros de Amor	Spain	Lucrecia	3628	28.52	No	Comedy
James Shirley	Hyde Park	England	Mrs Carol	4541	27.71	No	Comedy
Tirso de Molina	La Mejor Espigadera	Spain	Rut	4811	27.39	No	Religious Play
Lope de Vega	El Valor de las Mujeres	Spain	Lisarda	4380	27.38	Yes	Comedy
Antonio Mira de Amescua	No Hay Reinar como Vivir	Spain	Margarita	3182	27.2	No	Comedy
William Shakespeare	As You Like It	England	Rosalind	5804	26.9	No	Comedy
Lope de Vega	Las Burlas y Enredos de Benito	Spain	Infanta	3613	26.58	Yes	Comedy
Antonio Mira de Amescua	Amor, Ingenio y Mujer	Spain	Infanta	3434	26.56	Yes	Comedy
Lope de Vega	El Esclavo Fingido	Spain	Fenis	3982	26.54	Yes	Comedy
Tirso de Molina	Los Lagos de San Vicente	Spain	Casilda	3914	26.24	No	Religious Play
Lope de Vega	La Villana de Getafe	Spain	Inés	4504	26.19	Yes	Comedy
Tirso de Molina	Don Gil de las Calzas Verdes	Spain	Juana	4267	25.37	Yes	Comedy
Lope de Vega	Más Pueden Celos que Amor	Spain	Octavia	3406	25.34	Yes	Comedy
Lope de Vega	El Lacayo Fingido	Spain	Leonora	4444	25.3	Yes	Comedy
Juan Ruiz de Alarcón	Los Empeños de un Engaño	Spain	Teodora	3432	25.26	No	Comedy
Lope de Vega	La Hermosura Aborrecida	Spain	Doña Juana	3999	25.05	Yes	History Play
Tirso de Molina	Quien no Cae no se Levanta	Spain	Margarita	3911	24.82	No	Religious Play
Lope de Vega	La Madre Teresa de Jesús	Spain	Teresa	3406	24.67	No	Religious Play
Antonio Mira de Amescua	Examinarse de Rey	Spain	Margarita	3217	24.46	No	Comedy
Philip Massinger	The Maid of Honour	England	Camiola	4706	24.12	No	Tragicomedy
Lope de Vega	Los Melindres de Belisa	Spain	Belisa	3922	24.11	No	Comedy
Lope de Vega	Marta la Piadosa	Spain	Marta	3626	23.64	No	Comedy
Lope de Vega	Los Terceros de San Francisco	Spain	Isabel	3867	23.64	No	Religious Play
Tirso de Molina	Por el Sótano y el Torno	Spain	Doña Bernarda	3523	23.23	No	Comedy
Lope de Vega	Los Bandos de Sena	Spain	Teodora	3799	23.21	Yes	Comedy
Lope de Vega	Santa Casilda	Spain	Casilda	3301	22.95	No	Religious Play

(*Continued*)

Dramatist	Play Title	Country	Role	Words	%	Breeches	Genre
Lope de Vega	La Buena Guarda	Spain	Doña Clara	3409	22.51	No	Religious Play
Lope de Vega	La Mejor Enamorada, La Magdalena	Spain	Magdalena	2617	22.37	No	Religious Play
Lope de Vega	El Arenal de Sevilla	Spain	Lucinda	3175	22.32	No	Comedy
Tirso de Molina	La Villana de Vallecas	Spain	Violante	4498	22.21	No	Comedy
William Shakespeare	The Merchant of Venice	England	Portia	4721	22.18	Yes	Comedy
Antonio Mira de Amescua	La Tercera de Sí Misma	Spain	Lucrecia	3628	22.18	Yes	Comedy
Thomas Heywood	If You Know Not Me You Know Nobody Part 1	England	Elizabeth	2513	21.29	No	History Play
Tirso de Molina	Averígüelo Vargas	Spain	Sancha	3561	21.15	Yes	History Play
Lope de Vega	El Mesón de la Corte	Spain	Doña Blanca	2703	21.06	Yes	Comedy
Antonio Mira de Amescua	La Vida y Muerte de la Monja de Portugal	Spain	María	2623	21.05	No	Religious Play
Thomas Middleton & William Rowley	The Changeling	England	Beatrice	3865	20.94	No	Tragedy
Lope de Vega	La Noche de San Juan	Spain	Doña Leonor	3147	20.79	No	Comedy
Lope de Vega	El Anzuelo de Fenisa	Spain	Fenisa	3422	20.75	No	Comedy
Lope de Vega	La Malcasada	Spain	Lucrecia	3120	20.68	No	Comedy
Lope de Vega	El Alcalde Mayor	Spain	Rosarda	2991	20.36	Yes	Comedy
Lope de Vega	La Dama Boba	Spain	Finea	3217	20.3	No	Comedy
Thomas Heywood	The Fair Maid of the West, Parts 1 and 2	England	Besse	7224	20.21	Yes	Tragicomedy
Tirso de Molina	La Mujer que Manda en Casa	Spain	Jezabel	2957	19.96	No	Religious Play
Pedro Calderón de la Barca	El Castillo de Lindabridis	Spain	Claridiana	3422	19.94	Yes	Comedy
Lope de Vega	El Animal de Hungría	Spain	Rosaura	3416	19.86	Yes	Tragicomedy
Antonio Mira de Amescua	No Hay Burlas con las Mujeres	Spain	Arminda	3135	19.6	No	Comedy
Miguel de Cervantes	El Laberinto de Amor	Spain	Porcia	3358	19.51	Yes	Tragedy
Lope de Vega	La Burgalesa de Lerma	Spain	Clavela	3324	19.2	No	Comedy

Professional Actresses **141**

Author	Play	Country	Character				Genre
Lope de Vega	El Honrado Hermano	Spain	Julia	3133	19.06	Yes	Tragicomedy
Juan Ruiz de Alarcón	Las Paredes Oyen	Spain	Ana	2710	18.99	No	Comedy
Cristobal de Virués	La Gran Semíramis	Spain	Semíramis	2697	18.73	Yes	Tragedy
Lope de Vega	En los Indicios, la Culpa	Spain	Doña Clara	3014	18.62	No	Comedy
Thomas Dekker & Thomas Middleton	The Roaring Girl	England	Moll	4362	18.33	Yes	Comedy
Lope de Vega	La Corona de Hungría y la Injusta Venganza	Spain	Leonor	2376	18.26	No	Tragicomedy
Pedro Calderón de la Barca	El Jardín de Falerina	Spain	Marfisa	1776	18.19	No	Comedy
Juan Ruiz de Alarcón	Todo es Ventura	Spain	Leonor	2461	18.15	No	Comedy
Lope de Vega	El Juez en su Causa	Spain	Leonida	2916	18.02	Yes	Tragicomedy
Lope de Vega	La Filisarda	Spain	Flora	2370	17.93	No	Comedy
Juan Ruiz de Alarcón	La Manganilla de Melilla	Spain	Alima	2437	17.45	No	History Play
Tirso de Molina	Quien Da Luego Da Dos Veces	Spain	Elena	2397	17.32	Yes	Comedy
Thomas Middleton	No Wit, No Help Like a Woman's	England	Mrs Low-Water	4549	17.24	Yes	Tragicomedy
William Shakespeare	Cymbeline	England	Imogen	4555	16.42	Yes	Tragicomedy
William Shakespeare	All's Well that Ends Well	England	Helena	3653	15.84	No	Comedy
Lope de Vega	La Aldehuela	Spain	María	2430	15.49	No	History Play
Lope de Vega	Las Burlas de Amor	Spain	Reina	2265	15.26	No	Comedy
Lope de Vega	Fuente Ovejuna	Spain	Laurencia	1791	14.93	No	History Play
Tirso de Molina	Doña Beatriz de Silva	Spain	Isabel	2263	14.4	No	History Play
James Shirley	The Maid's Revenge	England	Catalina	2483	13.91	No	Tragedy
Lope de Vega	Los Ponces de Barcelona	Spain	Lucrecia	1965	13.51	No	History Play
James Shirley	The Ball	England	Lucina	2388	13.49	No	Comedy
Thomas Heywood	King Edward IV, Part 2	England	Jane Shore	3169	13.06	No	History Play

Notes

1 This coda builds on a comparative study I conducted recently between the corpora of Shakespeare and Lope de Vega. For more see Amelang, "Playing Gender".
2 Gurr, *The Shakespeare Company*, p. 11; Keenan, *Acting Companies and their Plays in Shakespeare's London*, p. 138.

5
PLAYBOOKS

In 1604, the London-based bookseller Nicholas Ling decided to release a new edition of *Hamlet* only a few months after he and printer Valentine Simmes had first taken Shakespeare's play to the bookstalls. The new version, this time around prepared with the help of James Roberts, came with an eye-catching promise emblazoned on its title page: "Newly imprinted and enlarged to almost as much againe as it was, according to the true and perfect Coppie".[1] Indeed, not only was the 1604 edition considerably longer than its predecessor but it also offered some significant differences in rhetorical quality. These are perhaps best exemplified by the prince's most famous soliloquy:

Hamlet (1603)

To be, or not to be, I there's the point,
To Die, to sleepe, is that all? I all:
No, to sleepe, to dreame, I mary there it goes[2]

Hamlet (1604)

To be, or not to be, that is the question,
Whether tis nobler in the minde to suffer
The slings and arrowes of outragious fortune,
Or to take Armes against a sea of troubles,
And by opposing, end them[3]

The general consensus is that the 1603 rendition was prepared using what book historians describe as a 'memorial reconstruction' manuscript. That is, a bootlegged transcription of the theatrical performance written down from memory by someone present – either an actor or an audience member – who clearly was unable to remember the plot and poetry of the Shakespearean original word for word. The resulting publication is, in Alfred Hart's expert opinion, "an extraordinary destruction of text and vocabulary".[4]

The practice of bootlegging plays was not that unusual in Elizabethan and Jacobean England; in addition to *Hamlet*, four other Shakespeare's plays alone (*Romeo and Juliet*, *Henry V*, *The Merry Wives of Windsor* and *Pericles*) appear to have fallen prey to intellectual thieves who sold their more or less accurate counterfeits to London's printers and publishers. 'Memorial reconstruction' editions of plays can also be found in other European countries from the period, including Spain, and their notoriety is frequently brought up as one of the principal reasons so many dramatists begrudgingly agreed to have their plays published despite the shortcomings of what they loudly proclaimed to be an inadequate medium. As John Marston laments in his address to the reader of *The Malcontent* (1604),

> onely one thing afflicts me, to think that Scænes invented, meerely to be spoken, should be inforcively published to be read, and that the least hurt I can receive, is to do my selfe the wrong. But since others otherwise would doe me more, the least inconvenience is to be accepted.[5]

The invention and widespread use of the moveable type printing press heralded a revolution in performance culture across Renaissance Europe, as public theatre transitioned from an exclusively live form of entertainment to one that could also be enjoyed outside the playhouse as readable compositions. Commercial playbooks were not considered literature *per se*, though. As Marston's complaint evinces, they were conceptualised as performance scripts – 'recorded forms', to use D.F. McKenzie's description – of theatrical events made available to the reading public.[6] This chapter explores the relationship between the playmaking community and the book market in early modern England and Spain. Its concerns range from licensing and censorship practices to the different formats of the publications that filled early modern bookstalls. Before doing so, however, the opening pages comparatively examine the essential nature of commercial playbooks and their correlation with what was presented onstage in the public theatres of these two countries.

Playbook vs Play: Printing Theatre in England and Spain

Much like England's John Marston above, Spain's stand-out playwright Lope de Vega also claimed to be completely uninterested in having his plays printed. It was only in 1614, after other people had released three different twelve-play anthologies of his *comedias*, that he decided to get personally involved and take over the publication process. In an address to readers, Lope professes to have been forced to do so against his better judgement, since "the truth is that the author did not write them in order to have them printed".[7] Three years later, in the preface to yet another collection of his plays, he explains in further detail what motivated him to do so:

> Seeing my plays constantly being printed in such a way that I can hardly recognise them as my own, and that whenever I sought to defend them in court I always lost out to those with greater resources and fortune, I have decided to go ahead and print them myself using my original manuscripts; and while it is true that I did not write them with this intention in mind, taking them from the ears within the playhouse to the confines of a private chamber, I believe it best to do so rather than continue to allow the cruelty with which some tear my work apart.[8]

Echoing Marston's same line of argument, Lope professed not to want to see his *comedias* printed, but that he reluctantly agreed to it as the only way of preventing others from inflicting on them even greater harm. Some readers detect in Marston and Lope's objections to printed playbooks a sincere disapproval of having complex theatrical performances reduced to readable scripts, while others interpret these complaints more as a marketing ploy inspired by the period's lingering stigmatisation of the still relatively novel print industry.[9] However, thanks to the perceived mangling of their plays – not only by bootleggers but by also printers and publishers who were not up to the task – as well as the sheer displeasure over others profiting from their intellectual property, many playmakers overcame their professed contempt for printed theatre and allowed – and in some cases participated in – the publication and commercialisation of their plays.

The concession to transposing plays from the stage to the page was offset by presenting the playbooks as texts unambiguously subordinated to their original function as live entertainment. More often than not the title pages and prefatory material of English and Spanish printed plays boast of the famous acting companies and venues that first brought them to life, thus reminding readers of their essential performativity as well as of their actual performance history. Printed playbooks were theatrical postscripts, a lesser way of enjoying spectacles that found their true form and meaning on the stage. Not all postscripts were equal, of course. The 1604 edition of *Hamlet* presents itself as a more accurate rendition of the Chamberlain's Men's show, using a "true and perfect Coppie" of Shakespeare's text, than the 1603 version. When Lope takes over the publication of his *comedias* in 1614, he leverages his authorial status and asserts on the title page that these renditions – unlike those published by his thieving competitors and predecessors – were *"sacadas de sus originales"* ["based on the original manuscripts"].[10] John Heminges and Henry Condell, the two members of Shakespeare's acting company who compiled and published his collected works in 1623, also guaranteed potential buyers that the anthology was "Published according to the True Originall Copies".[11] Alluring claims of this sort were common in English and Spanish printed playbooks, as they promised readers to bring them closer to the stage despite the inherent limitations of the medium.

The credibility of Heminges and Condell's assertion of originality hinges on the King's Men owning the manuscript originals of Shakespeare's play, which would have been standard practice at the time. However, the fact that the "true and perfect" 1604 version of *Hamlet* is substantially different from that of the "true Originall" of 1623 poses a significant quandary for Shakespearean editors: about 230 lines from the former do not appear in the latter edition, while around 70 lines are missing the other way around. Various theories have been offered to explain this discrepancy. For instance, some scholars contend that the 1623 publishers may have been using a version of the play trimmed and revised for performance by Shakespeare himself. Others point out that, while satisfying on various levels, this proposal remains purely conjectural, and that both the 1604 and 1623 versions – which they interpret as two different abridgments of the longer and complete play – should be considered as equally authoritative.[12] And just as no single theory accounts for how these two alternative print versions of the play came to be, modern editors of *Hamlet* also face the dilemma of which version of text to present as *the* Shakespearean tragedy, since choosing one would painstakingly result in dismissing the other. As Ron Rosenbaum very graphically put it in *The New Yorker*, to pick the 1604 version "is to gain 'the pales and forts of reason' but to lose 'Denmark's a prison', something which no sane bibliophile is willing to endure".[13]

The case of the different 'authoritative' published versions of *Hamlet* is a poignant reminder of the fluid, even schismatic, relationship that existed between what was staged and what ultimately ended up in print. Regardless of the promises made in prefaces and title pages, there is no assurance that the performed play and the printed playbook were one and the same. In fact, many English playbooks openly proclaim their distinctiveness from their staged counterparts, in particular regarding their length. For example, the title page to Ben Jonson's *Every Man Out of his Humour* (1600) trumpets the fact that it contains "more then hath been publikely spoken or acted"; not only was the 1602 version of Thomas Kyd's *The Spanish Tragedy* "newly corrected" and "amended" compared to previous publications, but it had also been "enlarged with new additions of the painters part and others"; John Webster's *The Duchess of Malfi* (1623) is marketed as consisting of the "perfect and exact Coppy, with diuerse things Printed, that the length of the Play would not beare in the Presentment".[14] If one takes these assertions as true, it means that in England either the acting companies cut the original playscripts down during performances or that the dramatists wrote new material specifically for the printed playbook as bonus content. This would help explain why so many of the bootlegged editions that survive are consistently shorter than their subsequent corrected versions, since the prevalent theory is that they were prepared by people familiar with abridged versions of the playtexts and not with their entire originals. It would also account for why there are so many printed plays that easily exceed even the most generous estimations of the time actors would have had at their disposal to perform them publicly. But even if the claims are in fact false and amount to little more than a ruse to sell more copies, they nevertheless show an awareness on the part of the English playmaking community that the printed medium could provide a product different from that offered on the stage, and that the playbook did not have to content itself with being a 'recorded form' of the theatrical event but could thrive as a distinct commodity in its own right.[15]

While one finds identical criticism of bootleggers and proclamations of originality in Shakespearean England and Golden Age Spain's commercial playbooks, there are no claims of *comedias* being 'amended', much less 'enlarged', for print. Indeed, all evidence seems to suggest that what made it on to the stage and into the page were for the most part one and the same. For starters, the length of the substantial amount of surviving numbers of authorial *comedia* manuscripts and their printed counterparts is always very similar, and the differences between the two versions rarely go beyond cleaning up errata and other minor changes.[16] That these are the same versions used for performance can corroborated with the help of the infamous theatrical bootleggers, the *memoriones* or *memorillas* as they were known in Spain. Much like in England, Spain's *memoriones* attended public performances in the nation's *corrales*, and afterward wrote down what they had just heard and seen. Notwithstanding their varying levels of success, the bootlegged versions of *comedias* are always essentially the same length as the authorial manuscripts and/or printed editions; in the case of the more talented *memoriones*, such as Luis Ramírez de Arellano or Diego Martínez de Mora, their copies follow almost word for word the original, a far cry from what the bootlegger of *Hamlet* put Shakespeare's play through.[17] That both the printed and the 'memorial reconstruction' renditions of plays by Lope and his peers are consistently equal in length indicate that they both were prepared using the same authorial performance scripts, whether these were conveyed via the stage or the page.

Not only are the manuscripts – both authorial and bootlegged – of individual *comedias* the same length as their printed playbooks, but *comedias* in general closely resemble each other in size, much more so than the plays from early modern England. The following charts illustrate the length of 224 and 445 English and Spanish public stage plays respectively, without counting any forms of secondary text (prefatory material, stage directions, character names, structural divisions, etc.) and focusing strictly on the words spoken by the characters.

Two differences immediately leap off the page. The first is that the typical English play is considerably longer than the Spanish *comedia*, with the former averaging well above 20,000 words and the latter just short of 15,000.[18] The second, and what matters most here, is the regularity in size Spanish texts show when compared with English ones. Over 78% of *comedias* analysed fall within the 13,000–17,000 word range, indicating a very low deviation from the mean. English plays, on the other hand, show much less concentration: as the charts

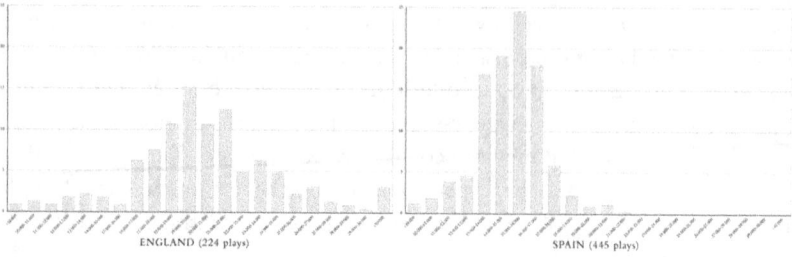

FIGURE 5.1 Length distribution of commercial plays in Shakespearean England (left) and Golden Age Spain (right)

indicate, it takes the interval spanning from 16,000 to 25,000 words – that is, over double the range – to cover a similar percentage of the English corpus (79%). Simply put, Spanish playwrights were much more orderly, in the literal sense, than their English counterparts when plotting the length of their plays, at least as they appear in print. As is so frequently the case, Lope's *Arte nuevo* provides some guidance as to why:

> Four pages for each act should be your aim,
> For twelve best suit the patience and also
> The time of those who come to see the show.[19]

(*Nota bene*: in his translation, Marvin Carlson uses the word 'page' for Lope's '*pliego*'; a *pliego* is a large sheet of paper folded and cut four times into an eight-page booklet). Lope thus advises that *comedias* should follow a very specific length of 96 handwritten pages, for that is what in his opinion is the maximum audiences at the *corrales* can handle. True to form, he himself does not follow his advice to the letter: his extant authorial manuscripts indicate Lope normally wrote in the neighbourhood of 120 pages per play; that is, fifteen *pliegos* instead of twelve, or five *pliegos* per act instead of four.[20] Still, both he and the rest of Spanish dramatists show remarkable consistency in this regard, with a majority of *comedias* analysed falling close to the parameters he set while thinking about what worked best in the nation's public playhouses.

Herein lies the underlying conceptual difference between 'play' and 'playbook' in Shakespearean England and Golden Age Spain. If we are to believe that commercial performances adhered to some degree of scheduled regularity, as Lope's words suggest, then many English printed playbooks must have included material that did not always, or ever, make it onstage. Elizabethan and Jacobean playmakers clearly took advantage, if only nominally and as an advertising tactic, of the possibilities presented by this alternative mode of consuming theatre by offering their readers a product different from what they would have been able to see and hear presented in public. Spanish playbooks, on the other hand, acted much more like McKenzie's 'recorded forms'; in the words of Alejandro García Reidy, "the printed play was subordinated to the performance, as it sought to convey the same joy that would come from visiting the *corrales*, not the distinct kind of pleasure specific to reading".[21]

Despite his initial and well-documented stance against the printing of his plays, Lope was quick to change his mind and soon embraced playbooks as worthy vessels of his art. It was not that his plays should no longer be performed, he explains in the address to the reader of his fourteenth collection (1620), but rather that in addition to going to the *corrales* his fans could now also "enjoy them at their own pace" in the comfort of their homes.[22] A year later, in the prologue to the sixteenth *parte* (1621), Lope takes a more assertive tone in his defense of printed theatre as the proper way of enjoying the rhetorical virtuosity of his plays:

> nobody with half a brain could ever think that most of the women who go to the *corrales*, nor all those ignorants who fill the benches of our theatres, understand the verse, the rhetorical figures, the concepts and proclamations, nor the different poetic styles and allusions.[23]

Lope was not alone in embracing the new medium, and playwrights from both countries quickly became more comfortable with the idea of seeing their plays printed. What is more, some writers started going the extra mile and modified their plays in order better to serve – and expand – their readership. For example, Ben Jonson added notes with historical sources in order to help readers of the 1605 quarto of his play *Sejanus;* for his 1616 collected works he revised all the perfunctory stage directions from previous editions and fleshed them out into proper declarative phrases so as to make them more reader-friendly. Calderón de la Barca also rewrote scenes from some of the *comedias* included in his second *parte* (1637) by replacing the technical references to stage machinery with descriptions that worked better on the page.[24] These adjustments speak to the growing awareness among playwrights that commercial theatre was being increasingly thought of and consumed as literature and not just as audiovisual entertainment, as it moved out of the playhouse and onto the bookshelf. As the rest of this chapter shows, this evolving perception of what printed theatre was – or could be – marked how playbooks were produced, circulated and consumed in the two countries. But before they could reach their readers another step was required: gaining permission from the censors and acquiring the appropriate licenses to do so.

Publication Strategies, Licensing and Censorship

"It is in performance that the plays lived and had their being … performance is the end to which they were created".[25] Stanley Wells' observation regarding Shakespeare's dramatic works can be extended to his contemporaries as well, and not just those from his corner of the world but also colleagues from across the

Channel; the plays performed in England and Spain's public theatres were initially conceived first and foremost as scripts for live entertainment events.[26] And if it were not for the pressure exerted by a prolific coterie of theatrical bootleggers, many playwrights and acting companies claimed they would have been all too happy to leave things that way. But, much to their purported dismay, reading theatre was quickly becoming one of the preferred pastimes in both seventeenth-century England and Spain.[27] While it is true that printed theatre was not the most profitable market share for booksellers – unlike, say, religious sermons and ballads, which enjoyed far greater demand – the sheer abundance of English and Spanish playbooks that survive testify to their ability to attract early modern readers.[28] Various socio-cultural factors and trends including the widespread popularity of commercial theatrical performances, the growth in literacy rates and the increasing affordability of print, combined to create both the appetite as well as the appropriate conditions for the appearance of readable theatre plays in the early modern literary market.[29] Realising that their investments could enjoy a second life in print, many if not most acting companies and impresarios eventually decided to turn the performance texts they owned over to the growing body of lay readers as a way of extending the profitability of their repertoires beyond the confines of the playhouse.

Various factors and strategic calculations lay behind the publication of playbooks. Some companies waited until the novelty of the play wore out to decide that it made financial sense to forfeit their exclusivity over the play and make the script commercially available. This seems to have been the case of Shakespeare's company; according to Lukas Erne's research, the Chamberlain's/King's Men had a "coherent strategy to try to get their playwright's plays into print" some years after staging them, and that they "viewed two of a play's forms of publication – performance and print, the stage and the page, the playhouse and the printing house – as not only compatible but synergetic". Alejandro García Reidy recognises a similar mindset in certain Spanish market-savvy companies and printers as well.[30] In other instances companies from both countries would sell some of their assets, including their prized playscripts, when in financial trouble.[31] And, again as alluded to above, the decision to print a play could also have been prompted by the prior release of a sub-par or bootlegged edition of the same. In any case, there does not seem to have been any single reason why plays ended up being published, even if playwrights coyly complained about seeing their material for the stage transferred to a different – some would say improper – medium.[32]

At least initially, the English and Spanish troupes and impresarios themselves rarely – if ever – directly involved themselves in the printing of playbooks. They preferred instead to sell their manuscripts to printers or booksellers who thought they could turn a profit from them. That is, the dramatists, having handed the playtexts over to the actors and in doing so forfeiting their 'intellectual ownership' over them (pp. 86–87), were not being compensated – and in some instances not even credited – for their own work as it migrated from the stage to the page.

One consequence was that many authors eventually decided to take control and get involved in the printing process as well. Spain's Lope de Vega pioneered this change when he bought some of his manuscripts back from the *autores de comedias* in order to supervise personally their transfer into print.[33] In England the prime example was Ben Jonson, who in 1616 zealously revised, curated and oversaw the print publication of an anthology that included most of his plays and pageants to date (more in the following section). Other dramatists from both countries soon followed suit, which rendered the printing of plays an even more heterogeneous affair in terms of who was behind the enterprise.

Whether a playwright, an acting company or a bookseller took the initative, the next step required of someone seeking permission to print a playbook in either of these countries was to obtain certification from the nations' official censors. In England the ecclesiastical Court of High Commission, presided over by the Archbishop of Canterbury, was responsible for guaranteeing the moral integrity of all printed texts in the country. The Stationers' Company, the livery company (professional guild) that held a monopoly over England's print industry, also had its own set of rules about acceptability for publication. In 1606, the power to license playbooks was transferred from the Court of High Commission to the office of the Master of the Revels, the Crown's appointee in charge of overseeing and censoring celebrations and festivities of all sorts, including public performances.[34] Spain's being a 'composite monarchy' (pp. 9–16) complicated matters, since each territory had its own specific laws regarding printing. Thus, for each title the publisher had to obtain an assortment of individual *privilegios* [licenses], if desired, for its lawful circulation in the numerous Hispanic territories.[35] In the largest kingdom and seat of the monarchy, Castile, there was only one institution in charge of licensing virtually all forms of entertainment and literature: the *Consejo Real de Castilla* [Royal Council of Castile]. This body held the exclusive right to grant licenses to playhouses, acting companies, and performance scripts as well as to any printed publication under its jurisdiction.[36]

After acquiring the appropriate licenses, the publisher would then have to oversee getting the manuscripts printed and into the book market. It remains very telling, however, that the authorities in England did not treat theatrical texts in the same way as other printed publications. When pressed to decide whether printed plays should be regulated by those in charge of overseeing entertainment or those in charge of licensing books, they opted for the former over the latter. That is, while in essence being just another textual artifact, the playbook was not subject to the same rules that applied to the rest of literary products, including other forms of popular fiction. While in Spain – or in Castile, rather – the all-encompassing Royal Council licensed both play and book, the playbook received a somewhat different treatment from the average printed text. For instance, the Council hired other *comedia* writers to be in charge of the censorship and approval process of printed plays, which occasionally caused friction and led to claims of favouritism as well as stoking professional jealousy between competing writers.[37]

The licencing bodies' distinction between book and playbook makes total sense. After all, the latter belonged to, as Andrew Pettegree points out in his panoramic *The Book in the Renaissance*, a subset of literature still in complete subservience to its more influential playhouse counterpart:

> Drama is a strangely hybrid medium. The oral performance has its origin in writing: the manuscript play text. It then takes wing in performance. It may then find a second audience (probably partially overlapping with the first) as literature. This hybrid character is deeply evocative of the fluid, transitional nature of communication in the sixteenth century. This was a world in which print had an important place, but did not yet rule the roost.[38]

This of course would change with time, and nowadays, at a 400 years' distance, we place the English and Spanish dramatists of this generation at the centre of their respective literary canons. Print eventually did rule the roost, and while theatre is still theatre, at a certain point it became literature as well. The initial stages of this paradigmatic shift, from theatre to drama, took place within the book cultures of early modern England and Spain, and were specifically marked – as the following section illustrates – by the formats and means of circulation of printed theatre in the literary marketplaces of these two countries.

The Playbook in the Literary Marketplace

This chapter has so far explored the motives behind the playmakers' decision to release their coveted theatrical scripts publicly for the lay readership, as well as the bureaucratic steps involved in getting their plays into print. What follows is a survey of the different types of playbooks that existed in the early modern English and Spanish literary markets. The material dimension of a book is often a sound indicator of the social respectability of the type of literature it embodies. Physical characteristics of this sort include size and format, paper and ink quality, binding conventions, and whether they were printed or handwritten. Despite their superficial similarities, the differences in the formats and circulation practices of commercial playbooks in Shakespearean England and Golden Age Spain created a ripple effect in the consideration of these two theatrical cultures that can still be felt today.

In England, it would have been very rare to see handwritten playbooks sold in bookstores and stalls. The few play manuscripts for non-professional use appear to have been luxury items produced on demand, such as that made of Thomas Middleton's *Hengist, King of Kent* (c. 1619) bound in vellum with an elaborate title page and ornaments, or the personalised copies of his masques Ben Jonson made for members of the royal family.[39] Manuscript versions of plays were also sold commercially when printed publication proved to be more problematic. This was the case with Middleton's controversial *A Game of Chess* (1624); after this play ended up banned from both stage and page due to its inflammatory political content, the author himself commissioned a series of manuscript copies as a way of side-stepping its prohibition. The same outcome was repeated in the 1650s, during which the closing of the playhouses deprived the nation's commercial dramatists of their regular means of income. In any case, manuscript playbooks were a rare (and also quite expensive) exception to the norm.[40] The vast majority of playbooks sold to England's lay readership were unbound, unadorned and inconspicuous printed formats known as quartos. These notebook-sized editions, which derived their name from the number of times each full sheet of paper had to be folded (four), were not mere ephemera, but neither were they something to write home about; at its best, the quarto is still universally understood as a pedestrian and common format, and immediately linked the genre of printed theatre with the lighter, more casual, and less 'artistic' publications being sold in early modern England's bookstalls.[41]

The year 1616 marked a turning point. This was the year in which, as noted above, Ben Jonson collected and published his plays and pageants in a hefty and somewhat ostentatious collection. The new format Jonson chose, known as the folio, was larger, more meticulously crafted, and used better-quality paper, types and ink than the quarto; it also frequently came bound in goat- or calfskin-leather covers. Up to that point, folios were primarily although not exclusively associated with specific subsets of writing: learned legal and theological texts, elegant publications with illustrations (especially related to the natural sciences), and the literary classics from ancient Greece and Rome. By choosing to release his plays in this format, Jonson was clearly exposing to public notice his high expectations. Roger Chartier contends that in doing so, the dramatist was expressing "a strong desire to achieve the canonical *auctoritas* of the ancient or consecrated poets and to shape the distinctive playwright's authorial persona by means of the printed book".[42] His *Workes*, as the 1616 folio is commonly referred to, thus launched the novelty of theatrical texts being sold as larger and more elegant editions with the expectation of receiving better treatment than the more ephemeral quarto plays. It was soon followed by the 1623 anthology of Shakespeare's plays and the Beaumont and Fletcher collection of 1647. Thomas Heywood, despite his denials, also tried and failed to release a folio of his plays. His experience, as described by Jeremy Lopez, illustrates both the elusiveness as well as the canonising effect of the format:

> Late in his long career, in his preface to the 1631 *1 Fair Maid of the West*, Heywood pointed out that his works had never 'beene exposed to the publike view of the world in numerous sheets, and a large volume' (A4r); and in his preface to the 1632 *2 Iron Age*, he indicated that he had been promised the printing of a single-volume edition of all five *Age* plays, which would include 'an Explanation of all [t]he difficulties, and an Historicall Comment of euery name, which may appeare obscure or

intricate to such as are not frequent in Poetry' (A2v). The *Ages* edition did not pan out, and, in 1633, in the preface to *The English Traveller*, Heywood claimed that it was 'never any great ambition to me, to bee in this kind Volumniously read' (A3r).[43]

Heywood deemed his plays worthy of large volumes with numerous sheets because they were too complex to be enjoyed properly and to their fullest extent in the playhouse alone. They required careful reading accompanied by explanations in the same manner as did other forms of high-brow literature, and as such mere quarto editions would not suffice. A luxury folio, Francis Connor explains, "offered the potential for comprehensiveness, authority, and some promise of canonicity".[44] As time went by and more and more people read plays, either as a substitute for or as a companion to seeing them performed onstage, those dramatists who were fortunate enough to be 'volumniously read' were treated to higher levels of recognition.[45] It is not coincidental that in the decades that followed the English cultural elite celebrated the three authors who had their plays published in folios – Beaumont was thought of as a lesser contributor in Fletcher's more illustrious career – above the rest of their peers, and hailed them as the nation's 'triumvirate of wit'.[46]

If by the mid-1610s England offered basically two different playbook formats, the single quarto and the compilation folio, in Spain the situation was much less straightforward. For starters, it appears that there were more (although still not that many) manuscript *comedias* for popular sale than in England. This was in part a question of total numbers: the remarkable abundance of Spanish plays in general (pp. 115–117) rendered the shelf-life attraction and subsequent demand of specific works much shorter, so publishers would have on occasion preferred to hire scribes to copy them by hand instead of committing to a full print run. Other, more short-term factors also encouraged the circulation of plays in manuscript, including the ban on printing plays in Castile that lasted from 1625 to 1634 and which was circumvented by various means, especially widespread resort to handwritten versions in the literary marketplace.[47] But, exceptional circumstances aside, the immense majority of commercial playbooks appeared in print. As in England, theatrical texts were published as either individual plays or in anthologies, even if the compilation format did not succeed the single play in Spain as neatly as it did in England, since the first publications of each type took place in exactly the same year, 1603.[48] In fact, all evidence suggests that the anthology was the format of choice in the first half of the seventeenth century, and that only in the second half did the single play take over the playbook market. For the sake of narrative symmetry, I will nevertheless begin by describing the printing and selling in Spain of individual plays first.

The most common publication format for Golden Age drama was the *comedia suelta* [single play]. By all standards of comparison, the *suelta* closely resembled the English quarto in terms of size, quality and popularity. The only substantial differences between the two are that *sueltas* were printed in two columns as opposed to one, and that they never opened with a full title page.[49] *Comedias sueltas* were prepared on an individual basis or as part of what were known as *sueltas desglosables* [unbindable single plays], collections of plays printed and sold together which either the vendor or the reader would later take apart to be sold and/or read as single plays. From the printers' standpoint, it was much cheaper to print plays in a bundle regardless of whether they worked well together thematically; from the publishers'/readers', having to unbind the volume and sell/read each play on its own was not too inconvenient if it meant shaving off some of the overhead expenses. This is one of the reasons why most of the surviving individual playtexts from seventeenth-century Spain do not make reference to the printer and bookseller. If any information was ever offered, it would have been printed in the front matter of the collection along with the publication license and other paratextual items that ended up being discarded after the volume was unbound. The other reason is that single playbooks – whether *sueltas* or *sueltas desglosables* – were broadly considered to be ephemeral prints and thus habitually sold through unofficial and often illegal channels. Whereas London's – and by extension England's – lay readership bought most of its entertainment literature, including the quarto and folio playbooks, from the booksellers surrounding St. Paul's Cathedral,[50] Spain's printers were less interested in selling popular literature directly themselves. They often hired *ciegos* and *buhoneros* [street peddlers] to sell their smaller, more ephemeral prints – including *comedias sueltas* – in the local squares and marketplaces.[51] It follows, thus, that producers as well as vendors had little interest in having the *sueltas* traced back to them, preferring instead to keep their names off the product.[52]

The other recognisable format was the collection of plays known as the *parte* [part]. Often – though not always – comprising twelve plays, the *parte* was the dominant playbook type in Spain in the first half of the seventeenth century. *Partes* could feature the works of a single or a variety of dramatists; these latter types are commonly known as the *diferentes* or *escogidas* [picked plays]. Unlike the elegant English folios, *partes* remained unostentatious and quarto-sized. That said, and in contrast with the *sueltas* or the *desglosables*, it was more likely for a purchaser of one of these anthologies to ask the bookseller to bind it (by default all popular texts were sold *en papel* [without covers]). This is not an insignificant difference: as Jaime Moll indicates, early modern Spaniards were aware of what distinguished a book, regardless of format and size, from other types of printed texts.[53] The works of most front-line dramatists of the time appeared in these publications in one way or another. By the end of his extraordinarily productive playwriting career, Lope had produced 25 *partes*; Calderón followed as a distant second with nine, trailed by Tirso de Molina's five and Agustín Moreto's three. Still, a majority of Spain's important playwrights – save two notable exceptions, Antonio Mira de Amescua and Luis Vélez de Guevara – were able to cobble together at least one or two *partes* of their works.[54] As noted above, Lope first became personally involved in the publication of his plays in 1604 with the fourth of his *partes*, the first three having been released without his consent. Throughout his extensive engagement in the printing of his plays, he seems to have focused his attention exclusively on the collected volumes, and never on the *sueltas*. The dramatists who followed Lope's lead also opted to concentrate their efforts on the *partes* and not the single plays. To have one's plays released in an anthology was clearly seen as a mark of prestige among Spain's *comediantes*. The format's visibly authoritative purpose – accompanied by a slightly more careful printing effort and the insertion of proper paratextual front matter – probably indicate that they should be understood as the closest Spanish homologues to Jonson's, Shakespeare's or Beaumont and Fletcher's folios.[55]

Closest, but definitely not the same. When placing these two theatrical book cultures side by side, it is quite clear that the Spanish *parte* was not an exact equivalent of the English folio, and as a result the former did not have the same degree of canonising effect as the latter. Not only were the *partes* smaller, but the quality of the printing materials in Spain was generally speaking not very good. Madame D'Aulnoy, a legendary French writer who visited Madrid in the late seventeenth century, commented that Spanish books were mostly "poorly printed, and the paper is very grey; they are badly bound, more often than not covered with a shabby piece of parchment or a bandanna".[56] Indeed, much of the finer printing of Spanish texts – mainly those of a legal, religious or philosophical nature, what is commonly referred to as the 'international book' – was outsourced to the Low Countries, Italy and France.[57] The *parte* was not among them. Instead, it more closely resembled the typical sort of books printed in Spain: mostly popular in theme and readership, of worse quality in terms of materials, and shorter in length and smaller in size. Additionally, an unmanageable number of collections of plays were published in Spain, hailing from all levels of writers, unlike in England where the folio was reserved as a marker of distinction for a select few. And the fact that some Spanish collections, especially the varied compilations, were often sold with the intention of being ripped apart meant that they ultimately were not the same socio-cultural commodity as was the large, elegant leather-bound dramatic anthology found in Shakespearean England.[58]

The distance between the Spanish *suelta* and *parte*, I contend, was simply not as great as that between the English quarto and folio. It was nonetheless quite significant, and much like its English counterpart the Spanish *parte* contributed to elevating the nation's printed theatre from postscripts of popular entertainment shows to the position of cultural prestige it currently enjoys. This was hardly the only element at play, and the book's conclusion reflects on the different factors that influenced the varied reception of English and Spanish dramatic texts in the centuries that followed. To close, however, this chapter briefly surveys the other ways the print industry became involved in the playmaking process in both Shakespearean England and Golden Age Spain.

Other Documents of Performance

In her *Documents of Performance in Early Modern England* (2009) to which this section's title pays tribute, Tiffany Stern gives a detailed account of the many different types of documents employed in the theatrical productions of Elizabethan and Jacobean England. There were the parts actors used to memorise their lines and cues, the written prologues and epilogues, the music and lyrics, the scrolls (papers delivered onstage, such as letters or proclamations), the book-keepers' playtexts with the stage directions, and a long etcetera. Spain's play-making community was similarly swamped in paperwork, in the literal sense; for instance, Spain's players also worked with *papeles de actor* [acting parts] in exactly the same way as their English counterparts.[59] Most of these documents were for playhouse personnel's eyes only, and would end up 'patched' together – an expression used in Shakespeare's time – into the eventual playbook.[60] As Stern explains, her research explores

> how elemental the 'patch' was to the construction of performance and thence to the construction of playbooks. The dialogue and all that happens within that dialogue exchange was in performance made up of separate manuscripts: learnt actors' parts; backstage-plots; and songs, scrolls, prologues and epilogues all of which might be read onstage, and all of which have their own histories.[61]

The early modern period in general was one abounding in "pieces of paper, scraps of writings and writing instruments", Fernando Bouza explains, "so much so that their presence can be explained as common, even ordinary".[62] Apart from playbooks, many other written and printed documents littered the early modern playgrounds of both England and Spain. In this last section, I draw attention to documents Stern and other scholars examine that did not make it, one way or another, into the playbooks. The reason why these papers were left out of the final commercial product was because they were ancillary and not integral to the performance or reading of the play. Specifically, the following pages discuss the use of playbills, posters, and Elizabethan and Golden Age equivalents to modern programmes and synopses.

In one of his colourful accounts of early modern London life, the water-poet John Taylor narrates how when walking down Fleet Street the actor Nathan Field got stopped by a gentleman asking him which play his company, the King's Men, was putting on that day; Field angrily replied that "he might see what play was to be playd upon every Poste".[63] By the sound of it, playhouse advertising covered the entire city to almost an invasive level, to the point that "theatre had, through the medium of bills, corrupted the pedestrians in the streets of London".[64] Apparently Madrid, Seville and the major theatrical centres of Spain were in a similar situation, and one could not walk across these cities without having the name of Lope de Vega or one of his peers calls out from posters plastered all over the public space.[65] The situation is vividly illustrated in the following epigram, in which an anonymous wit commends two of Madrid's *poetas* in an exercise of good neighbourliness:

> *¡Vítor don Juan de Alarcón*
> *y el fraile de la Merced,*
> *por ensuciar la pared,*
> *y no por otra razón!*

> [All praise don Juan de Alarcón
> and the Friar of La Merced,
> For dirtying our walls
> And for nothing else!][66]

The spaces in which companies posted their advertising were very similar: tethering posts, alehouses, in the environs of the playhouses, the doors of private dwellings and the main shopping streets and squares in the city.[67] The timing for placing these signs was also pretty much the same, waiting until the eve or even the same morning of the performance date so as to avoid confusion with previous shows. Stern adds that, in the case of England, the players would inform the audience of the next day's event at the end of their show and sometimes paraded the streets with drums and trumpets announcing it as 'living' advertisement, something that in all likelihood happened in Spain as well.[68]

All surviving evidence indicates that advertisements for London's theatre, referred to as playbills, were normally printed, in short narrations explaining the nature of the event. The exact wording varied depending on the novelty of the play, the pull of the dramatist's name and other such factors, but for the most part these documents followed a standardised format. This uniformity only increased when the Stationers' Company decided to establish a monopoly for this market to allow only one printer to produce all the playbills for the city's playhouses.[69] In Spain, conversely, the surviving playhouse *carteles* [posters] were handwritten and offered much less information, usually simply indicating the name of the company – or the lead actors or even playwright, depending on who had more name recognition – in big red gothic letters, and the time, date and location in smaller black cursive. When possible, these small manuscript signs would also highlight the novelty of the play, a luring strategy advertising professionals practice even today.[70] Considering the rapid turnover of plays on the stage and the relatively higher prices of printing, it would have made more sense to hire some *amanuenses* [scribes] to "write new signs every day" instead.[71] Most of the printed posters in early modern Spain were reserved for loftier enterprises, such as Inquisition edicts, announcements of poetry competitions, and so on. Indeed, as Antonio Castillo's research shows, the sophistication and medium of the announcement indicated both the status of the event as well as that of the intended receiver, and a run-of-the-mill *comedia* show was nowhere near deserving more than a poorly handwritten sign.[72] That said, printed advertising had its place in Spain's theatrical world, but it was reserved for more special occasions, such as the inauguration of the city's *fiestas* season or for the arrival in town of a new playing company.[73] These more sophisticated printed posters, incidentally, look exactly like the playbills Stern describes, which leads one to wonder whether these few surviving documents from England's entertainment industry were not also signs for special events; after all, theatre was consumed in large proportions by practically illiterate people, and consequently a full narration in small print seems to go against the nature of the popular (and everyday) event supposedly advertised.

Another significant difference in advertising between the two countries is that, according to Stern's research, booksellers in London had the title pages of playbooks posted throughout the city to announce the release in print of one of their plays. This explains why title pages indicated – among other information – where to find the bookstall in which the play was being sold, indications which would have been not necessary for anyone who already owned the product.[74] It is safe to say that this did not happen in Spain, for at least two important reasons. The first is that *comedias sueltas* did not have title pages or front matter that would serve as effective advertisement. The second is that the ephemerality and abundance of Spanish theatre made it unnecessary to advertise specific plays; in special cases in which one *comedia* at one playhouse had fared extremely well, street vendors could simply position themselves near the *corral* and cry out their merchandise.

The final document types to be considered here are the English plot-argument and the Spanish *relación de comedias* [play report]. The plot-argument, or simply argument, was a brief summary of the play whose predecessors were the Greek *hypothesis* and Roman *argumentum*. Arguments were occasionally included as paratextual material at the beginning of playbooks; however, it seems that in Elizabethan and Jacobean England arguments were frequently repurposed to serve as playhouse production programmes, souvenir-like mementos for more expensive performances as well as aids that "accompanied productions thought to need extra elucidation".[75] In her study of the plot-argument, Stern observes similarities between this document and other documents from other European theatre scenes, including the Spanish *relación de comedias* described by Norman Shergold in *A History of the Spanish Stage* (1967).[76] The example *relación* Shergold presents is Lope's *El premio de la hermosura* as performed at Lerma by members of the royalty and members of the court in 1614:

> The description, or *Relación*, shows that the play was performed in a specially constructed open-air theatre on the bank of the river Arlanza, and the scene, compared by the author to the fantasies of the novels of chivalry, had affinities with the décor simultané of the early religious plays in that all the scenery for all the scenes was visible at once. [...] The *Relación* lists the

persons who played the different parts, and describes their costumes. It summarizes the action of the play, which was in three acts, with dances by the Prince and the Queen in two intervals. It ended with a masque, danced by the Queen and court ladies.[77]

Despite the undeniable similarities between the argument and the relación, it seems that the two served completely different purposes. The *relación de comedias* took its name from the more generic *relación*, or *relación de sucesos* [report of events]. A *relación* was a small printed booklet sold by street peddlers that consisted of a brief news report informing the reader of the highlights in politics and international affairs, especially wars.[78] The *relaciones de comedias* were play summaries and excerpts, primarily intended to be read out loud and performed privately by gatherings of friends on festive occasions.[79] They emerged in Andalusia in the seventeenth century – although did not reach the rest of the country until the eighteenth and nineteenth centuries – as a substitute for commercial theatre, since there was a ban on corral performances in Seville between 1679 and 1767. The practice survived this setback, and *relaciones de comedias* soon became highly popular in other regions of the country.[80] Whereas arguments were auxiliary documents of the English stage, the *relaciones de comedias* were closer to substitutes for the professional theatrical event.

Notes

1 Shakespeare, *The Tragicall Historie of Hamlet* (1604), sig. A1r.
2 Shakespeare, *The Tragicall Historie of Hamlet* (1603), sig. D4v.
3 Shakespeare, *The Tragicall Historie of Hamlet* (1604), sig. G2r.
4 Hart, "The Vocabulary of the First Quarto of *Hamlet*", p. 19. More on the 1603 printed edition of Hamlet as a 'memorial reconstruction' text in Stern, "Sermons, Plays and Note-Takers".
5 Marston, *The Malcontent*, sig. A2.
6 McKenzie, *Bibliography and the Sociology of Texts*, p. 12.
7 "aunque es verdad que su autor nunca las hizo para imprimirlas". Vega, *Doze comedias de Lope de Vega … Qvarta parte*, sig. ¶4v [my translation].
8 "Viendo imprimir cada dia mis Comedias, de suerte que era impoßible llamarlas mias, y por los pleytos desta defensa siempre me condenauan los que tenian mas solicitud, y dicha para seguirlos, me he resuelto a imprimirlas por mis originales: que aunque es verdad que no las escriui con este animo, no para que de los oydos del Teatro se trasladaran a la censura de los aposentos, ya lo tengo por mejor, que ver la crueldad con que despedaçan mi opinion algunos intereses". Vega, *Doze comedias de Lope de Vega … Novena parte*, sig. ¶4v [my translation]. The most complete recent study of Lope's involvement in the printed publication of his plays is Alejandro García Reidy's *Las musas rameras*, in particular the last chapter, "Lope de Vega y la reapropriación autorial de su teatro". See also Dixon, *En busca del fénix*, 93-115; García Reidy, "From Stage to Page", 51–60; Moll, *Problemas bibliográficos del libro del Siglo de Oro*, 283–305; Presotto, *Le commedie autografe di Lope de Vega*, pp. 60–62.
9 This trope – whether sincere or not – is recurrent in other seventeenth-century European theatrical cultures. Prefaces similar to Marston's and Lope's are found not only in England (among others by Heywood) and Spain (Calderón) but also in French

classical drama (Molière). More in Chartier, *Publishing Drama in Early Modern Europe*, pp. 28–32; Garcia Reidy, *Las musas rameras*, pp. 370–374, 380–381.

10 Vega, *Doze comedias de Lope de Vega … Qvarta parte*, sig. ¶1r [my translation]. He repeats the exact same message in the title pages of the "*novena*" (ninth), "*dezima*" (tenth) and "*onzena*" (eleventh) collections of his plays as well.

11 Shakespeare, *Mr. William Shakespeares Comedies, Histories, & Tragedies*, sig. A1r.

12 Jenkins, "The Relation between the Second Quarto and the Folio Text in *Hamlet*", p. 75.

13 Rosenbaum, "Shakespeare in Rewrite", p. 71. The historical answer to this editorial conundrum has been to prepare a conflated text which uses the 1604 version as its base layer enriched by emendations and additions taken from or inspired by the other texts. The goal of these types of editions is to reconstruct the 'lost archetype' (to use Rosenbaum's term), the ontological idea of the play, from the material evidence left behind by the playtexts. A less common approach is the one Ann Thompson and Neil Taylor chose in the third (and latest) Arden edition of *Hamlet* (2006, revised in 2016), in which they decided to publish all three available texts back to back to back in two volumes. More in Jenkins, "Introduction", pp. 74–82; Thompson and Taylor, "Introduction", pp. 88–96.

14 Jonson, *The comicall Satyre of Every Man Ovt of his Hvmor*, sig. A1r; Kyd, *The Spanish Tragedie*, sig. A1r; Webster, *The tragedy of the Dutchesse of Malfy*, sig. A2r.

15 There has been a ongoing debate among Shakespearean scholars regarding the length of performances during Shakespeare's lifetime. There are substantial period references to theatrical spectacles running for around two hours, although this description is by now widely accepted as being more metaphoric than precise. Nevertheless, the back-and-forth between those who believe that plays would have kept to somewhat standard duration and those who instead argue that there were no time limitations imposed on performances rages on. A chronological list of recent publications that contribute to this discussion includes Gurr, "Maximal and Minimal Texts"; Orgel, *The Authentic Shakespeare*, pp. 21–47; Erne, *Shakespeare as Literary Dramatist*, pp. 155–197; Hirrel, "Duration of Performances and Lengths of Plays"; Urkowitz, "Did Shakespeare's Company Cut Long Plays Down to Two Hours Playing Time?".

16 Presotto, *Le commedie autografe di Lope de Vega*, pp. 28–31. What one does encounter frequently in Golden Age playscripts are passages that have been blocked out by the players as a way of shortening the original script for particular performances. These cuts nevertheless rarely if ever add up to the degree of difference between the stage and page versions of the same English plays. More in García Reidy, *Las musas rameras*, pp. 308–309; Greer, "Calderón en su laboratorio".

17 More on theatrical bootlegging and the *memoriones* in Golden Age Spain in Greer, "Early Modern Spanish Theatrical Transmission, Memory, and a Claramonte Play", pp. 269–276; Greer, "La mano del copista"; Moll, "El libro en el Siglo de Oro", pp. 52–54; Ruano de la Haza, "An Early Rehash of Lope's *Peribáñez*"; Ruano de la Haza and Allen, *Los teatros comerciales del siglo XVII y la escenificación de la Comedia*, pp. 278–282; Sáez Raposo, "Las aspiraciones creativas de un copista"; Sánchez Mariana, "Los manuscritos dramáticos del Siglo de Oro", pp. 442–443; Tronch Pérez, "A Comparison of the Suspect Texts of Lope de Vega's *La Dama Boba* and Shakespeare's *Hamlet*". Marco Presotto has spearheaded a digital edition of Lope de Vega's comedy *La dama boba*, in which users can consult a variety of print and manuscript editions side by side, including a memorión's rendition of the play; for more see http://www.damaboba.unibo.it.

18 The fact that those seeking to acquire a printing license in Castile had to pay a fee, or *concesión de tasa*, based on the length of the text may help at least partially explain why Spanish comedias tended to be shorter than English plays. More on the licensing

process of playbooks in the following section. I would like to thank Fernando Bouza for suggesting this possible explanation.
19 "Tenga cada acto quatro pliegos solos, / Que doze estan medidos con el tiempo, / Y la parecencia del que està escuchando" [translation by Marvin Carslon in Vega, "The New Art of Writing Plays", vv. 327–329].
20 For more see the editors' notes in Vega, *Arte nuevo de hacer comedias*, pp. 331–332. The primary monographic study on Lope's authorial manuscripts is Presotto, *Le commedie autografe di Lope de Vega*.
21 García Reidy, *Las musas rameras*, p. 367 [my translation].
22 " ... tambien quiero que las gozen con mas espacio, dandoselas imprentas, como las presento esta parte". Vega, *Parte catorze de las comedias de Lope de Vega Carpio*, sig. ¶4v [my translation]. I first read this passage, as well as the one that follows below, in García Reidy, *Las musas rameras*, pp. 376–378. My thanks to Alejandro García Reidy for bringing them to my attention.
23 "nadie se podra persuadir con mediano entendimiento, que la mayor parte de las mugeres que aquel jaulon encierra, y de los ignorantes que assisten a los bancos, entienden los versos, las figuras Retoricas, los concetos y sentencias, las imitaciones, y el graue, o comun estilo". Vega, *Decimasexta parte de las comedias de Lope de Vega Carpio*, sig. ¶2r [my translation].
24 More on Jonson in Amelang, "From Directions to Descriptions"; Dutton, *Ben Jonson: To the First Folio*, pp. 54–63; Syme, "Unediting the Margin". More on Calderón in Fernández Mosquera, "Los textos de la *Segunda parte* de Calderón".
25 Wells and Taylor, *William Shakespeare*, pp. xxxviii.
26 For Wells' Spanish counterpart see Thacker, "'Puedo yo con sola la vista oír leyendo'".
27 Not all scholars agree on the degree of playbooks' popularity, though. In 2005 a public back-and-forth took place among Peter Blayney, Alan Farmer and Zachary Lesser in response to Blayney's 1997 assessment of the concept of popularity. In addition to the fact the concept of 'popularity' is a relative one, what the debate among the three scholars makes abundantly clear is that playbooks in the age of Shakespeare were popular but less well preserved in comparison with more established literature, and that at the same time they were not as visible or forgettable as even more ephemeral genres. For more see (presented chronologically) Blayney, "The Publication of Playbooks"; Farmer and Lesser, "The Popularity of Playbooks Revisited"; Blayney, "The Alleged Popularity of Playbooks"; Farmer and Lesser, "Structures of Popularity in the Early Modern Book Trade". Farmer and Lesser continued to present their research in the 2013 book chapter "What is Print Popularity?".
28 This is particularly true of the smaller and more ephemeral formats, such as quartos and *sueltas*, since their survival rate was significantly lower than for large volumes. As Keith Whinnom explains, "it is obvious enough and is confirmed by modern experience: a large, lavish, expensive tome will be more highly prized and hence better preserved than a small, cheap, possibly unbound volume". Whinnom, "The problem of the 'best-seller' in Spanish Golden-Age Literature", p. 192. D.W. Cruickshank discusses the same issue from the opposite angle when he states that "the mortality-rate of ephemera is rather like that of dwellers in unhygienic slums: it is highest in infancy and childhood". Cruickshank, "'Literature' and the Book Trade in Golden Age Spain", p. 816.
29 More in García Reidy, *Las musas rameras*, pp. 31–36.
30 Erne, "Shakespeare and the Publication of his Plays", pp. 2, 16; García Reidy, "From Stage to Page", p. 53. For more see Erne, *Shakespeare as Literary Dramatist*, pp. 220–244; García Reidy, "Spanish Comedias as Commodities"; Ioppolo, *Dramatists and their Manuscripts in the Age of Shakespeare*, pp. 138–141.
31 García Reidy, *Las musas rameras*, pp. 307–398; Knutson, *Playing Companies and Commerce in Shakespeare's Time*, pp. 63–67.

32 Here I paraphrase Knutson, *Playing Companies and Commerce in Shakespeare's Time*, p. 70.
33 Greer, "Authority and Theatrical Community", pp. 101–107; Moll, "El libro en el Siglo de Oro", pp. 45–47.
34 The Master of the Revels' obligations included attending rehearsals and reading playhouse scripts in order to ensure their propriety. When in 1606 the Office of the Revels was tasked with supervising the playtexts for the press as well, the Master at the time, Edmund Tilney, continued overseeing the performances whereas his second-in-charge George Buc took on the print versions. In 1610 all play-related licensing was delegated to a single individual, Buc, the newly anointed Master of the Revels following Tilney's death that same year (note of warning: Buc's heavy workload ultimately caught up with him and he went mad). Dutton, *Licensing, Censorship and Authorship in Early Modern England*, pp. 10–11. For a concise summary see Keenan, *Acting Companies and their Plays in Shakespeare's London*, pp. 70–74, 77–81.
35 The first edition of Cervantes' *Don Quijote* (1605), for instance, which was printed in Madrid by Juan de la Cuesta, included two different licenses, one in Spanish and one in Portuguese, in order for it to be allowed to be sold in the kingdom of Castile and in the kingdom of Portugal, at the time also part of Philip III's dynastic holdings; see Cervantes, *El ingenioso hidalgo don Quixote de la Mancha*, sigs. ¶2v-¶3v; and Reyes Gómez and González-Sarasa Hernáez, "El taller de Juan de la Cuesta", pp. 304–308, 321–325. More on Spain's licensing process in Bouza, "Los contextos materiales de la producción cultural", pp. 336–338; Cruickshank, "Some aspects of the Spanish book-production", pp. 2–3; Marsá Vila, *La imprenta en los Siglos de Oro*, pp. 47–51; Moll, *Aspectos de la librería madrileña en el Siglo de Oro*, pp. 18–20; Simón Díaz, *El libro antiguo español*, pp. 123–131. For the forgery of *privilegios* [licenses] in early modern Spain see Moll, "El libro del Siglo de Oro", pp. 51–52. For a full account of the history of book licensing in Golden Age Spain and the Habsburg empire see Reyes Gómez, *El libro en España y en América*, pp. 163–389.
36 García de Enterría, *Sociedad y poesía de cordel en el Barroco*, pp. 71–76; Rodríguez Cuadros, "The Art of the Actor", p. 104; Varey, Shergold and Davis, *Los arriendos de los corrales de comedias de Madrid*, p. 11. For a full depiction of the activities of the Council, especially in relation to book licensing, see Bouza, *"Dásele licencia y privlegio"*.
37 In 1622, for example, Juan Ruiz de Alarcón filed a complaint in which he accused his censor, none other than Lope de Vega, of meddling with the publication of one of his plays out of personal animosity. The Council sided with Alarcón, and Vicente Espinel replaced Lope as the text's supervisor. More in Bouza, *'Dásele licencia y privilegio'*, pp. 78–79.
38 Pettegree, *The Book in the Renaissance*, p. 346.
39 Ioppolo, *Dramatists and their Manuscripts in the Age of Shakespeare*, p. 129.
40 Dutton, "The Birth of the Author", pp. 163–164; Love, *Scribal Publication in Seventeenth-Century England*, pp. 65–70.
41 Erne, *Shakespeare and the Book Trade*, ch. 5. Another nuanced exploration that, like Erne's, challenges the inherited assumption that quartos were little more than ephemera is Dane and Gillespie, "The Myth of the Cheap Quarto".
42 Chartier, *Publishing Drama in Early Modern Europe*, p. 54. For an in-depth exploration see Dutton, *Ben Jonson*; other relevant publications include Barbour, "Jonson and the Motives of Print"; Chartier, *The Author's Hand and Printer's Mind*, pp. 166–167; Marcus, *Puzzling Shakespeare*, pp. 22–26.
43 Lopez, *Constructing the Canon of Early Modern Drama*, p. 174.
44 Connor, *Literary Folios and Ideas of the Book in Early Modern England*, p. 12.
45 Michael Dobson traces the beginning of the shift in the perception of English popular drama to the period between the 1680s and the 1730s, when "a new insistence on the separation of 'popular' from 'literary' drama makes itself felt, a separation which is in

part a symptom of the repositioning of the stage in relation to what has been termed the emergent bourgeois sphere, with its increased emphasis on print culture rather than oral". Dobson, *The Making of the National Poet*, p. 100.

46 Shakespeare's and Beaumont and Fletcher's folios, however, were not prepared with the same authorial drive as Jonson's. As Francis Connor's research makes clear, the investors behind these publications were primarily motivated by the prospect of profits rather than the desire to preserve the artistic legacy of the dramatists. Speaking specifically about Shakespeare's folio, Connor describes it as "less a bold, unprecedented production than a natural extension of the capitalist ambitions of the theater from which Shakespeare had made his name". Connor, *Literary Folios and Ideas of the Book in Early Modern England*, p. 124. More on the Shakespeare as well as the Beaumont and Fletcher folios in pp. 123–164. For a summary of the reception of the 'triumvirate of wit' in the second half of the seventeenth century see Dobson, *The Making of a National Poet*, pp. 21–40.

47 Arata, "Notas sobre *La conquista de Jerusalén*", pp. 64–65; Cruickshank, "Some problems posed by *suelta* editions of plays", p. 97; Greer, "Early Modern Spanish Theatrical Transmission" p. 267; Greer, "La mano del copista"; Greer, "Mapa de amanuenses teatrales del siglo XVII", p. 29; Sánchez Mariana, "Los manuscritos dramáticos del Siglo de Oro", p. 441; Vega García-Luengos, "La investigación sobre los formatos", p. 21; Vega García-Luengos, "La transmisión del teatro en el siglo XVII", p. 1296.

48 Vega García-Luengos, "La investigación sobre los formatos", p. 21.

49 For a brief history and taxonomy of the different types of *comedias sueltas* see Cruickshank and Szmuk, "Sueltas".

50 More on London's booksellers in Blayney, "The Bookshops in Paul's Cross Churchyard". Apart from the cathedral grounds, there were other locations in which one could buy popular books. Specifically having to do with theatre, according to Holger Schott Syme's research there were for instance bookstalls strategically located on the way to the playhouses in Shoreditch and Southwark for theatregoers to buy playbooks on their way to and back from a show. More in Syme, "Thomas Creede, William Barkley, and the Venture of Printing Plays", p. 35.

51 Carmen Peraita suggests that the *literatura de cordel*, a sub-type of literature "mainly intended for the female reader, be it lady or maid" and which was often also referred to as *literatura de ciegos* [blind men's literature] in reference to the common condition of many of its vendors, sold better in open access public spaces such as streets or *plazas* since bookstores in Madrid were "unquestionably male-dominated cultural spaces". Indeed, if women wanted to purchase items from a bookstore they often used intermediary male figures to do so, such as their fathers or priests. This gendered interpretation of book-types ties in nicely with how Lope, in *La Dama Boba* ([*A Lady of Little Sense*], 1613), describes the reading list of a typical Golden Age *dama* as one laden with entertainment literature, including his own poetry. The Franciscan friar Juan de la Cerda discusses the problems of women reading fiction in similar fashion: "Some ladies keep themselves entertained by reading these books, and find in them a sweet venom that instigates evil thoughts and makes them lose what little mind they have. It is for this reason that mothers should not make the mistake of letting their daughters taste this scorpion's oil, these diabolical love stories" ["Ay algunas donzellas que por entretener el tiempo, leen en estos libros, y hallan en ellos vn dulce veneno que les incita a malos pensamientos, y les haze perder el seso que tenían. Y por esso es error muy grande de las madres que paladean a sus hijas desde niñas con este azeyte de escorpiones, y con este apetito de las diabólicas lecturas de amor"]. Cerda as cited in Dadson, *Libros, lectores y lecturas*, p. 241 [my translation]; Peraita, "Mar de tinta", pp. 78–79 [my translation]; Vega, *Comedia famosa de la dama boba*, p. 271. More on the literatura de cordel in García de Enterría, "Pliegos de cordel, literaturas de ciego".

52 Cruickshank, "Some problems posed by the *suelta* editions of plays", pp. 97–105; Giuliani, "La Parte de comedias como género editorial", pp. 33–34; González-Sarasa Hernáez, *Tipología editorial del impreso antiguo español*, pp. 230, 400–401; Vega García-Luengos, "La investigación sobre los formatos", pp. 34–37.

53 Moll, "Los surtidos de romances, coplas, historias y otros papeles", p. 47. It is worth pointing out, following François López, that beginning in the second half of the seventeenth-century *partes* had relatively little presence in the playbook market, being reduced instead to "small islands surrounded by the vast ocean of *comedias sueltas*, interludes, farces, laudatory poems, dances, songs, and those *relaciones* [...] that were not written for the *corral* but as a substitute for the theatre". López, "La comedia suelta y compañía", p. 590 [my translation].

54 Vega García-Luengos, "La investigación sobre los formatos del teatro español del siglo XVII", pp. 25–29.

55 As members of the *literatura de cordel* [chapbooks] family, *comedias sueltas* suffered from the perception of being sub-par literature. It was very rare, Carmen Peraita observes, for these lesser publications ever to make it into inventories of private book collections and bookstores. That said, in the most important study of reading practices in Golden Age Madrid José Manuel Prieto Bernabé notes how theatrical texts, especially Lope's *partes*, progressively start appearing in collections and inventories alongside other more conventional forms of literature. Additionally, the team of researchers led by José María Díez Borque has traced a considerable increase of *comedias* in Spanish private libraries by the second half of the seventeenth century. Considering the low survival rate of ephemeral prints from the period, book collectors must have regarded the *partes* as more than just a collection of *sueltas*. For more see Díez Borque, ed., *Literatura, bibliotecas y derechos de autor en el Siglo de Oro*, pp. 15–30, 146–156; Peraita, "Mar de tinta", p. 772; Prieto Bernabé, *Lectura y lectores*, pp. 288–290.

56 "muy mal impresos, su papel es gris; están muy mal encuadernados, cubiertos en su mayor parte por un mal pergamino o por bandana". My translation of D'Aulnoy is based on the translation into Spanish as it appears in Díez Borque, *La vida española en el Siglo de Oro según los extranjeros*, p. 201. For more on Spanish printing and its place in the international book market see Berger, "Del manuscrito a la imprenta", pp. 145–146; Bouza, "Los contextos materiales de la producción cultural", pp. 314–315; Cruickshank, "Calderón y el comercio español del libro"; Cruickshank, "Some aspects of Spanish book-production", pp. 3–16; Griffin, "Itinerant Booksellers, Printers and Pedlars", pp. 43–51; Moll, *Problemas bibliográficos del libro en el Siglo de Oro*, pp. 307–318; Reyes Gómez, *El libro en España y en América*, pp. 227–235.

57 Griffin, *The Crombergers of Seville*, pp. 104–106; Griffin, "Literary Consequences of the Peripheral Nature", pp. 207–210.

58 Quite interestingly, in England there *were* folios that one was expected to rip apart as well. As Francis Connor explains, some literary folios "were sold individually as cheap books that consumers could buy in component parts and bind to their liking". However, this does not seem to have been the case with the collections of Jonson, Shakespeare or Beaumont and Fletcher. More in Connor, *Literary Folios and Ideas of the Book in Early Modern England*, p. 8.

59 Arata and Vaccari, "Manuscritos atípicos, papeles de actor y compañías del siglo XVI", pp. 32–68; Arata, "Notas sobre *La conquista de Jerusalén* y la transmisión manuscrita del primer teatro cervantino", pp. 54–55; Vaccari, "Notas sueltas sobre la relación entre los papeles de actor y el primer Lope de Vega"; Vega García-Luengos, "La transmisión del teatro en el siglo XVII", pp. 1294–1295. For an interesting case of how a company of players patched together a 'fair copy' of a Calderón manuscript in a three-step reading see Bentley, "Del 'autor' a los actores".

60 Stern, *Documents of Performance in Early Modern England*, pp. 1–2.

61 Stern, *Documents of Performance in Early Modern England*, p. 253. More in Palfrey and Stern, *Shakespeare in Parts*, pp. 15–39; Stern, "'I Have Both the Note, and Dittie About Me'"; "'On Each Wall and Corner Poast'"; "'A Small Beer Health to his Second Day'"; "Watching as Reading".
62 Bouza, "Los contextos materiales de la producción cultural", pp. 312 [my translation].
63 As cited in Stern, *Documents of Performance in Early Modern England*, p. 48.
64 Stern, *Documents of Performance in Early Modern England*, p. 48.
65 Díez Borque, *El teatro en el siglo XVII*, p. 31; Fortuño Gómez, "La vida teatral en Barcelona en el siglo XVII", p. 161.
66 As cited in Reyes Peña, "Los carteles de teatro en el Siglo de Oro", p. 105 [my translation]. The two playwrights mentioned are Juan Ruiz de Alarcón and Tirso de Molina (the friar).
67 Reyes Peña, "Los carteles de teatro en el Siglo de Oro", pp. 109–110; Stern, *Documents of Performance in Early Modern England*, pp. 48–51.
68 Reyes Peña, "Los carteles de teatro en el Siglo de Oro", pp. 110–111; Stern, *Documents of Performance in Early Modern England*, pp. 36–37, 47. More on the use of *pregoneros* [criers] and other forms of 'living' advertisement in Spain in García Bernal, "El cartel de fiestas en la configuración de la comunidad urbana en el Barroco", p. 97.
69 Stern, *Documents of Performance in Early Modern England*, pp. 39–42.
70 Reyes Peña, "Los carteles de teatro en el Siglo de Oro", pp. 100–105. The uniformity of *carteles* was guaranteed by the 1608 decree that standardised the information that must be conveyed. In the cases in which less information was required (such as in cities with only one *corral* or one playing company), the posters would logically not need to advertise such things. More in Reyes Peña, "Los carteles de teatro en el Siglo de Oro", p. 106; Reyes Peña, "Nueva entrega sobre carteles del teatro áureo", pp. 838–843.
71 Reyes Peña, "Los carteles de teatro en el Siglo de Oro", pp. 107–109.
72 Castillo Gómez, "A la vista de todos", pp. 85–90; Castillo Gómez, "Desde el muro"; Castillo Gómez, "La letra en la pared".
73 García Bernal, "El cartel de fiestas en la configuración de la comunidad urbana en el Barroco"; Reyes Peña, "Nueva entrega sobre carteles del teatro áureo", pp. 843–844, 855.
74 Stern, *Documents of Performance in Early Modern England*, pp. 55–58.
75 Stern, *Documents of Performance in Early Modern England*, pp. 63–66.
76 Stern, *Documents of Performance in Early Modern England*, p. 66.
77 Shergold, *A History of the Spanish Stage*, pp. 252–254.
78 Chartier, "Del libro a la lectura", p. 320; Moll, *Aspectos de la librería madrileña del Siglo de Oro*, p. 5. More on the *relación de sucesos* in Ettinghausen, "The News in Spain"; García de Enterría (ed.), *Las relaciones de sucesos en España, 1500-1750*.
79 Moll, "Un tomo facticio de pliegos sueltos y el origen de las 'relaciones de comedias'", p. 58; Wilson, "Some Calderonian *Pliegos Sueltos*", p. 140.
80 García de Enterría, *Sociedad y poesía de cordel en el Barroco*, pp. 336–361; Moll, "Un tomo facticio de pliegos sueltos y el origen de las 'relaciones de comedias'", pp. 59–60.

CONCLUSION

The year 2013 was a banner year for devotees of early modern Spanish theatre. In one of his research trips to the archives of the Spanish National Library, the scholar Alejandro García Reidy came across the manuscript of a previously unknown *comedia*. After meticulous palaeographic and stylistic analysis, García Reidy determined that *Mujeres y criados*, as the play is called, was written circa 1613 by none other than Lope de Vega himself.[1] In other words, a new play by one of the most prominent, prolific and performed dramatists in what is widely considered the golden age of European drama had just been unearthed. And yet this rare, even extraordinary discovery received little fanfare outside academic circles and performance communities, or beyond Spain for that matter. It definitely did not enjoy anywhere near the same repercussion as the publication in 2010 of Lewis Theobald's *Double Falsehood*.[2] Theobald claimed to have based his 1727 play on *Cardenio*, a tragicomedy written in 1613 collaboratively by John Fletcher and William Shakespeare that has since been lost. Its release became a major international event: not only was it the first 'Shakespearean' text discovered in a very long time, but it also for the first time established a direct link between two of European literature's most emblematic authors, since the play took its plot from one of the side-stories in Miguel de Cervantes' *Don Quijote* (1605). Its welcome included a multitude of performances, publications and other forms of recognition that only a newly recovered play by Shakespeare could expect. That said, even if one takes Theobald's word for it – and some scholars do not – *Double Falsehood* remains an early eighteenth-century adaptation of a text that in all certainty would have been written primarily by Fletcher, with Shakespeare playing second fiddle in the waning years of his career.[3]

Why were these two recent discoveries received so differently, especially considering the striking aesthetic and cultural similarities between the dramatic traditions to which they belong? One undeniable fact is the almost overwhelming disparity in the number of plays that survive from one and another playwright. As Barbara Fuchs explains,

> the breadth of the Golden Age dramatic corpus conditions its reception. Whereas a lost Shakespeare play would have revolutionised that well-tended field of English, as well as the Shakespeare industry; one more Lope play, when critics can barely attend to his several hundred extant works, does not, on the face of it, alter the shape of the corresponding field of Hispanism, much less of the broader cultural field.[4]

While this point is well taken, the embarrassment of riches that is Golden Age Spanish theatre does not on its own account for the discrepancy in reception by contemporary audiences and readers. Whereas early modern theatre and literature enthusiasts admire Lope as a profoundly talented and prolific dramatist, Shakespeare has become – as Fuchs puts it – a worldwide 'industry' whose appeal and name recognition are universal, far beyond those of any of his Spanish counterparts.

If the theatrical cultures of Shakespeare's England and Golden Age Spain can be characterised as having lived parallel lives, which very broadly speaking is true, their afterlives have been anything but parallel. Unquestionably what most influenced the disparate reception of Shakespearean and Golden Age drama in the centuries that followed were the changing political fortunes of the two nations on the international stage that helped widen the gap between the extent and depth of influence of their respective artistic legacies. During most of the period this book covers, the Spanish monarchy was the principal aspirant to political hegemony in Europe. It controlled large swaths of territory both within the continent as well as in the Americas and the Pacific, alongside Rome it was the spiritual leader of the Counter-Reformation, and Spanish arts and culture were held in high regard across and beyond the Habsburg-controlled territories. The latter included not only its literature but also its widely acclaimed national theatre: playing companies and booksellers all across the continent staged and printed the *comedias* of Lope de Vega and his peers both in the original and in translation. However, Spain's geopolitical strength began to decline in the first half of the seventeenth century, and by the eighteenth century the once-powerful Habsburg monarchy had ceded its position as the predominant force in Europe. This indirectly ended up affecting the popularity of its arts and literature. The plays of Lope and the other dramatists of the Spanish Golden Age that had once been omnipresent across European stages were increasingly perceived as representing a past with very little present, all but disappearing by the early nineteenth century.

The decline of Spain's international prestige and presence roughly coincided with England's ascendance. During the first half of the seventeenth century England was regarded as a country very much on the periphery of Europe's game of thrones, and as such its arts and literature did not have much of an audience outside its borders. The Civil War and Commonwealth of the mid-seventeenth century did not help matters, as England unapologetically isolated itself from the rest of Europe under Cromwell's leadership. Nevertheless, beginning with the Restoration of the monarchy in 1660 England resumed its international profile, aided by a burgeoning domestic economy and a favourable turn in its expansionist endeavours. The eighteenth century witnessed the consolidation of the newly formed Great Britain (1707) as a major Atlantic empire that gradually superceded Spain in cultural as well as political and economic reach. Whether through imposition or by drift, the world began to read English literature – both in the original and in translation – just as it had consumed Spanish writing in previous centuries.

Among the most celebrated English writers as Britain emerged from cultural obscurity were Jonson, Fletcher and Shakespeare. These are, of course, the three Elizabethan-Jacobean dramatists who had their complete works published in large and elegant folio anthologies, a significant factor in their eventual literary canonisation (pp. 153–154). The latter in particular was elevated above all other authors as a symbol of English artistry; as Michael Dobson puts it, beginning in the eighteenth century Shakespeare "has been as normatively constitutive of British national identity as the drinking of afternoon tea".[5] Indeed, in his influential *The Making of the National Poet* (1992) Dobson charts the progressive transformation of Shakespeare's public perception throughout the Restoration and the Enlightenment, from being seen as a talented commercial playwright to becoming a cultural icon and commodity capable of carrying the weight of an imperial power on his shoulders and endowed with a quasi-religious cult-like following of his own. Much of Dobson's argument dwells on how assiduously Shakespeare's plays were adapted and updated to reflect the sensibilities of the moment, thus allowing him to age much more gracefully than other Renaissance and Baroque playwrights did after their time. That said, another development that Dobson stresses throughout his study speaks to England's changing geopolitical fortunes in the late-seventeenth and eighteenth centuries, which he sees as contributing to a growing appreciation around the globe of the country's cultural production. "That Shakespeare was declared to rule world literature at the same time that Britannia was declared to rule the waves", he writes, "may, indeed, be more than a coincidence".[6]

Clearly, the dynamism of a culture is often closely connected to the dynamism of its political fortunes. Spain's downward spiral during the late-Habsburg and early Bourbon years meant that the country's dramatic production, widely celebrated across Baroque Europe, lost favour as the nation's political influence over the continent decreased. On the other side of matters, as England was becoming "more than a nation" Shakespeare was being turned into more than a dramatist, "a literary deity" with his own statue, chapel and jubilee.[7] It is hardly cynical to look to imperial history as a way of at least partially explaining the disparate treatment Shakespeare and his peers have received in comparison with their Spanish homologues. The ebbs and flows of geopolitical supremacy can be easily felt in the amount of attention – and, consequently, praise – given to playwrights from one or another empire.

A telling indicator of Shakespeare's exploding national and international appeal was the substantial number of publications dedicated to dissecting his work and life. Starting with Nicholas Rowe's *The works of Mr. William Shakespear; in six volumes* (1709), eighteenth-century England witnessed the publication of more than twenty distinct anthologies of Shakespeare's plays, as well as the first Shakespearean monographs and biographies.[8] The first collections of Shakespeare's works translated into foreign languages also circulated during the eighteenth century, and he quickly became an influential figure among writers and critics in other countries and cultures. Especially well known were the many German authors associated with the proto-Romantic *Sturm-und-Drang* movement who felt an "intoxicated enthusiasm for Shakespeare" and idolised him to the point of claiming him as their own.[9] There is a through line, a shared DNA, that connects the feelings these eighteenth-century writers felt for Shakespeare with the critical mainstream of the nineteenth and twentieth centuries. The number of critical editions, translations, scholarly studies and biographies of Shakespeare and his plays published throughout the nineteenth century are too numerous to list here, but it is enough to note that they culminated with his enshrinement as the central figure of the so-called canon of western literature. Furthermore, Shakespeare's gravitational pull has served to galvanise the study and appreciation of many of his playwriting peers from the Elizabethan and Jacobean era, and during the past three centuries early modern English dramatists as a collective have enjoyed a position of unusual prominence in literary scholarship.

The same cannot be said for Lope de Vega and most other Spanish writers associated with the *comedia nueva*. The first compendium of Lopean drama did not appear until 1838, as part of the *Tesoro del teatro español* [*The Treasures of Spanish Theatre*], Eugenio de Ochoa's multi-volume anthology of the history of Spanish theatre. Juan Eugenio Hartzenbusch's four volumes of Lope plays for the monumental *Biblioteca de autores españoles* followed in 1853.[10] Neither of these selections, however, benefited from much critical effort; one would have to wait for the anthologies of Marcelino Menéndez Pelayo (1890–1913) and José Luis Cotarelo y Mori and his team (1916–1930) for the first properly curated editions (i.e. with introductions and critical annotations) of Lope's theatre.[11] What is more, the first serious attempt to reconstruct Lope's life since Juan Pérez de Montalbán published in 1636 his pseudo-hagiography of his mentor was published in 1890 as the first volume of Menéndez Pelayo's collection.[12] Interest in the life and works of other prominent seventeenth-century authors meandered in similarly subdued patterns. It took roughly two centuries for Spain's literary and scholarly community to begin seriously to appreciate and celebrate the writers behind the nation's most prolific and successful period of cultural prominence.

Even so, no dramatist from early modern Spain has won canonical consideration within the broader international literary community. Until recently it was quite common to find English-language histories of European theatre that made no reference to the Spanish Golden Age. What little attention it received it was precisely in negative comparison with Elizabethan and Jacobean drama, especially on account of the supposed lack of character development that characterises the *comedia,* more akin to the Italian *commedia dell'arte*'s use of stock characters than to the recognisable humanity with which Shakespeare imbued his dramatis personae.[13] The only author who partly escaped this line of criticism was Calderón, whose writing style was widely perceived as differing markedly from that of the majority of Golden Age playwrights, in particular Lope. Neoclassicist purists of the eighteenth century deemed his dramatic approach more palatable than that of the brunt of the *comedia nueva* corpus. The German Romantics – led by the Schlegel brothers – were especially fond of the philosophical bent to Calderón's plays, and promoted them in the most prestigious circles of European literary erudition; on the other hand, the few who knew of Lope's work considered him to be a semi-barbarian improvisor.[14] Yet even Calderón's plays received but a fraction of the critical interest and admiration that Shakespeare's enjoyed. The only writer from Baroque Spain who warranted any attention similar to that devoted to Shakespeare was Miguel de Cervantes, whose innovations in narrative story-telling and character development earned him widespread acclaim and canonical status.

In short, representatives of the two theatrical cultures that had in their time been described in uncannily similar terms were at this point treated not only as if they belonged to different leagues but as if they played entirely different sports. The publication of anthologies, taxonomies, biographies and monographs that focused on Golden Age theatre beginning in the mid-nineteenth century marked a turning point in the critical reception of Lope, Tirso and the rest of the *comedia nueva* cohort, and many of their plays are now assiduously read and studied all over the world. However, it remains difficult if not impossible for them ever to catch up with the lead Shakespeare – and by extension Elizabethan-Jacobean drama – have maintained from the early eighteenth century through the present. It is hardly surprising that the discovery of a new Lope de Vega play in 2013 was completely overshadowed by the ongoing deliberations regarding whether to brand Lewis Theobald's Shakespeare-adjacent *Double Falsehood* with the stamp of canonicity. Meanwhile, the engine of the Shakespearean industrial machine kept dutifully humming along.

To conclude these parting observations I turn to the stage itself, where contemporary performance practices in my opinion encapsulate perfectly the historical divide that has marked these two dramatic traditions. The institutional and scholarly reverence England has shown for Shakespeare and his peers has translated into such a well-known, rich and sustained presence onstage that it hardly needs mentioning here. This robust performance culture is moreover not limited to England or English-speaking countries alone: much like in the rest of the world, there is a healthy tradition of Shakespearean stagings across continental Europe, not the least in Spain. Indeed, Shakespeare's appeal in Spain has grown to equal and ever surpass that of most of his domestic counterparts to the point that he has been the single most performed dramatist in the Spanish capital since the early 1990s, and the staging of his plays has outnumbered those of Lope, Tirso and Calderón put together.[15] "Shakespeare's unique role in the world canon makes him an unfair point of comparison", Duncan Wheeler notes, "but it is still striking that there have been more productions of his works than of the three chief proponents of Golden Age drama combined".[16] Spanish audiences are thus intimately familiar with the theatre of early modern England, and like practically every other country in the world they partake in the phenomenon known as 'Global Shakespeare'; that is, the assimilation, adaptation and appropriation of Shakespeare's plays into one's own cultural milieu rather than perceiving them as essentially foreign.

Shakespeare's long history of performance in Spain differs ostensibly from the timid presence of the *comedia* on the English stage. Throughout the twentieth century, it was rare for British audiences outside specialist circles even to be aware of the substantial part Spanish theatre played in Europe during the period they celebrated as their own gilded age of drama.[17] Only quite recently, thanks to a series of successful productions, have the plays of Lope and Calderón and their contemporaries started to attract a following among Anglophone audiences after centuries of neglect. The most renowned director of Spanish classical drama in England during this period of buoyancy is Laurence Boswell, who was charged with spearheading the Royal Shakespeare Company's 2004 Golden Age season after having led a similar initiative at the Gate Theatre in London in 1992. In 2013–2014 he organised another well-received season of *comedia* performances at the Ustinov and Arcola theatres in Bath and London. While other noteworthy initiatives and theatremakers have promoted the drama of early modern Spain on English stages in the twenty-first century,[18] the most prominent display so far has been without a doubt the 2004 RSC season, in which England's foremost classical theatre institution performed four *comedias* in translation: Lope's *El perro del hortelano* [*The Dog in the Manger*], Cervantes' *Pedro de Urdemalas* [*Pedro, the Great Pretender*], Tirso's *La venganza de Tamar* [*Tamar's Revenge*] and Sor Juana Inés de la Cruz's *Los empeños de una casa* [*House of Desires*]. The season was met with critical acclaim, and it has often been described as a turning point in the fortunes of the previously undervalued Spanish Golden Age in the British collective imaginary.[19] It must be noted, though, that there have not yet been any signs in these productions of the emergence of a 'Global *comedia*' to match what one frequently sees in the stagings abroad of Shakespeare. Quite the contrary, transnational performances of Golden Age plays often emphasise and even magnify their Spanishness instead of relocating them into different contexts, which speaks to the relative

Conclusion **173**

novelty of Spain's dramatic output for mainstream British audiences.[20] One can expect this to change as spectators become more familiar with these stories, and that evolution and experimentation in British renditions of the *comedia* will thus create yet another point of cross-cultural encounter between two dramatic traditions each of whose individual trajectories is better understood in tandem with the other.

Notes

1. García Reidy, "*Mujeres y criados*, una comedia recuperada de Lope de Vega".
2. Hammond (ed.), *Double Falsehood*.
3. Among the numerous studies of the missing *Cardenio* play – an extraordinarily prolific subject of study within the field of Anglo-Spanish cultural relations – see in particular Bourus and Taylor (eds.), *The Creation and Re-Creation of Cardenio*; Carnegie and Taylor (eds.), *The Quest for Cardenio*; Chartier, *Cardenio between Cervantes and Shakespeare*; Fuchs, *The Poetics of Piracy*, pp. 79–130; Hammond, "*Double Falsehood*"; Payne (ed.), *Revisiting Shakespeare's Lost Play*; Stern, "'The Forgery of some modern Author'?".
4. Fuchs, "'La voluntad jamás permite señor'", p. 59.
5. Dobson, *The Making of the National Poet*, p. 7.
6. Dobson, *The Making of the National Poet*, p. 7.
7. Dobson, *The Making of the National Poet*, p. 227.
8. Wells, *Shakespeare for All Time*, pp. 198–204. A full account of printed editions of Shakespeare's plays in the eighteenth century can be found in Murphy, *Shakespeare in Print*, pp. 311–340. For a brief survey of Shakespeare biographies see Bevington, *Shakespeare and Biography*, pp. 10–12.
9. Wells, *Shakespeare for All Time*, p. 245; Bosman, "Shakespeare and globalization", pp. 286–287.
10. González Canal, "Las ediciones de teatro de la Biblioteca de Autores Españoles", pp. 103–115; Pedraza Jiménez, "Menéndez Pelayo", pp. 88–89.
11. Pedraza Jiménez, "Menéndez Pelayo", pp. 90–94; Romero Tobar, "La edición del teatro de Lope de Vega y su contexto histórico-literario", pp. 45–57.
12. Pedraza Jiménez, "Menéndez Pelayo", p. 87; Samson and Thacker, "Introduction", pp. 2, 8. For a full account of the reception of Lope in post-Baroque Spain see García Santo-Tomás, *La creación del "Fénix"*, pp. 177–225, 248–282.
13. For more on the history behind the critical argument that Spanish playwrights did not develop rounded characters see Ruano de la Haza, "Spanish Classical Theater in Britain and North America", pp. 5–9.
14. Oleza, "Menéndez Pelayo y Lope de Vega", p. 14; Paun de García and Larson, "Introduction", p. 18.
15. Wheeler, *Golden Age Drama in Contemporary Spain*, p. 60.
16. Wheeler, *Golden Age Drama in Contemporary Spain*, pp. 60–61. Moreover, scholars have rightfully pointed out how the Almagro festival – meant to celebrate and promote Spanish classical drama – has occasionally featured more productions of Shakespeare than of any domestic author. More in Gregor, "Contrasting Fortunes", pp. 245–247; Guerrero, "Shakespeare in La Mancha", pp. 29–31.
17. Ruano de la Haza, "Spanish Classical Theater in Britain and North America", pp. 2–3.
18. For a full overview of Anglophone performances of Golden Age plays see Paun de García and Larson, "Introduction".

19 Jeffs, *Staging the Spanish Golden Age*, pp. 175–199. A full retrospective of the RSC Golden Age season, including academic essays as well as interviews with the directors and translators, can be found in Boyle and Johnston (eds.), *The Spanish Golden Age in English*.
20 Gregor, "Contrasting Fortunes", pp. 239–241, 250; Guerrero, "The Exchange of National Authors", p. 331; Wheeler, *Golden Age Drama in Contemporary Spain*, pp. 191–193.

WORKS CITED

Primary Sources

Campbell, Colen, *Vitruvius Britannicus: The Classic of Eighteenth-Century British Architecture* (Mineola, NY: Dover, 2007 [orig. ed. 1715–1725]).
Castillo Solorzano, Alonso de, *Las harpías en Madrid* [ed. Pablo Jauralde Pou] (Madrid: Castalia, 1985 [orig. ed. 1631]).
Cervantes, Miguel de, *El ingenioso hidalgo don Qvixote de la Mancha* (Madrid: Francisco de Robles, 1605).
Cervantes, Miguel de, *Ocho comedias, y ocho entremeses nvevos, Nunca representados* (Madrid: Juan de Villarroel, 1615).
Digges, Leonard, *A Boke Named Tectonicon* (London: Thomas Marshe, 1566).
Earle, William, *Micro-cosmographie, or, A peece of the world discovered in essayes and characters* (London: Edward Blount, 1628).
Fletcher, John, *The Faithfvll Shepheardesse* (London: R. Bonian & H. Walley, 1610).
The Journal of George Fox [ed. Nigel Smith] (London: Penguin, 1998).
Guzmán, Pedro de, *Bienes de el honesto trabajo y daños de la ociosidad: en ocho discursos* (Madrid: Jaques Veruliet, 1614).
Heywood, Thomas, *An Apology for Actors* (London: Nicholas Oakes, 1612).
Howell, James, *Londinopolis an historicall discourse or perlustration of the city of London, the imperial chamber, and chief emporium of Great Britain: whereunto is added another of the city of Westminster, with the courts of justice, antiquities, and new buildings thereunto belonging*, 1657).
Jonson, Ben, *The Comicall Satyre of Every Man Ovt of His Hvmor* (London: Nicholas Ling, 1600).
Jonson, Ben, *The Workes of Beniamin Jonson* (London: Richard Meighen, 1616).
Jonson, Ben, *Bartholomew Fayre: A Comedie* (London: Robert Allot, 1631).
Kyd, Thomas, *The Spanish Tragedie: Containing the lamentable end of Don Horatio, and Belimperia: with the pittifull death of olde Hieronimo. Newly corrected, amended, and enlarged*

Works Cited

with new additions of the painters part, and others, as it hath of late been diuers times acted (London: Thomas Pavier, 1602).

Lyly, John, *Sappho and Phao* (London: Thomas Cadman, 1584).

"The London Journal of Alessandro Magno, 1562" [eds. Caroline Barron, Christopher Coleman and Claire Gobbi] (*London Journal* 9.9, 1983), pp. 136–152.

Mariana, Juan de, "De los espectáculos" in *La dignidad real y la educación del rey (De rege et regis institutione)* [ed.Luis Sánchez Agesta] (Madrid: Centro de Estudios Constitucionales, 1981 [orig. ed. 1599]), pp. 426–438.

Marston, John, *The Malcontent. Augmented by Marston. With the Additions played by the Kings Maiesties servants* (London: William Aspley, 1604).

Pound, Ezra, *ABC of Reading* (London and Boston: Faber & Faber, 1961 [orig. ed. 1934]).

Quevedo, Francisco de, *La vida del bvscon* (New York: G.P. Putnam's Sons, 1917 [orig. ed. 1626]).

Rojas, Agustín de, *El viage entretenido* (Madrid: la viuda de Alonso Martín, 1614).

Shakespeare, William, *The Tragicall Historie of Hamlet, Prince of Denmarke* (London: Nicholas Ling, 1603).

Shakespeare, William, *The Tragicall Historie of Hamlet, Prince of Denmarke* (London: Nicholas Ling, 1604).

Shakespeare, William, *Mr. William Shakespeares Comedies, Histories, & Tragedies* (London: Isaac Jaggard and Edward Blount, 1623).

Stow, John, *A Survey of London, Volume I* [ed. Charles Lethbridge Kingsford] (Oxford: Clarendon Press, 1908).

Stow, John, *A Survey of London, Volume II* [ed. Charles Lethbridge Kingsford] (Oxford: Clarendon Press, 1908).

Stubbes, Philip, *The Anatomie of Abuses* (London: Richard Jones, 1583).

The Marvels of Rome: Mirabilia Urbis Romae, 2nd Edition [ed. and. trans. Francis Morgan Nichols; new ed. Eileen Gardiner] (New York: Italica Press, 1986).

Vega, Félix Lope de, *Arte nvevo De hazer Comedias en este tiempo* in *Rimas de Lope de Vega Carpio. Aora de nvevo Imprimidas. Con el nvevo arte de hazer Comedias deste tiempo* (Milan: Ieronimo Bordon, 1613), pp. 361–376.

Vega, Félix Lope de, *Doze comedias de Lope de Vega Carpio familiar del Santo Oficio. Sacadas de sus originales. Qvarta parte* (Madrid: Miguel de Siles, 1614).

Vega, Félix Lope de, *Doze comedias de Lope de Vega, sacadas de sus originales. Novena parte* (Madrid: Alonso Martín de Balboa, 1617).

Vega, Félix Lope de, *Comedia famosa de la dama boba* in *Doze comedias de Lope de Vega sacadas de sus originales por el mesmo. Nouena Parte* (Barcelona: Sebastián de Cormellas, 1618), pp. 257–276v.

Vega, Félix Lope de, *Parte catorze de las comedias de Lope de Vega Carpio* (Madrid: Juan de la Cuesta, 1620).

Vega, Félix Lope de, *Decimasexta parte de las comedias de Lope de Vega Carpio* (Madrid: Alonso Pérez, 1621).

Vega, Félix Lope de, *The New Art of Writing Plays* [trans. Marvin Carlson] in Barbara Fuchs and G.J. Racz (eds.), *The Golden Age of Spanish Drama* (New York: W.W. Norton & Company, 2018), pp. 377–386.

Vega, Félix Lope de, *Arte nuevo de hacer comedias* [ed. Enrique García Santo-Tomás] (Madrid: Cátedra, 2009).

Vega, Félix Lope de, *Comedias de Lope de Vega. Parte XVI: Tomo I* [coords. Florence D'Artois and Luigi Giuliani] (Madrid: Gredos, 2014).

Vega, Félix Lope de, *Cartas (1604-1633)* [ed. Antonio Carreño] (Madrid: Cátedra, 2018).
Webster, John, *The tragedy of the Dutchesse of Malfy As it was presented priuatly, at the Black-Friers; and publiquely at the Globe, by the Kings Maiesties Seruants. The perfect and exact coppy, with diuerse things printed, that the length of the play would not beare in the presentment* (London: John Waterson, 1623).

Secondary Readings

Abbott, Don, "La Retórica y el Renacimiento: An Overview of Spanish Theory" in J.J. Murphy (ed.), *Renaissance Eloquence: Studies in the Theory and Practice of Renaissance Rhetoric* (Berkeley-Los Angeles: University of California Press, 1983), pp. 95–104.
Albardonedo Freire, Antonio José, *El urbanismo de Sevilla durante el reinado de Felipe II* (Seville: Guadalquivir, 2002).
Albrecht, Jane White, *The Playgoing Public of Madrid in the Time of Tirso de Molina* (New Orleans: University Press of the South Inc., 2001).
Albrecht, Jane White, *Stoicism, Seneca, and Seventeenth-Century Spanish Tragedy* (Potomac MD: Scripta Humanistica, 2012).
Albuquerque García, Luis, *El arte de hablar en público. Seis retóricas famosas del siglo XVI: Nebrija, Salinas, García Matamoros, Suárez, Segura y Guzmán* (Madrid: Visor, 1995).
Allen, John Jay, "El corral de comedias de Almagro" (*Cuadernos de teatro clásico* 6, 1991), pp. 197–211.
Allen, John Jay, "Los corrales de comedias y los teatros coetáneos ingleses" (*Edad de Oro* 5, 1986), pp. 5–19.
Allen, John Jay, "The Disposition of the Stage in the English and Spanish Theatres" in Louise Fothergill-Payne and Peter Fothergill-Payne (eds.), *Parallel Lives: Spanish and English National Drama 1580-1680* (London: Bucknell University Press, 1991), pp. 54–72.
Allen, John Jay, "Documenting the History of Spanish Theatre: Fuentes para la historia del teatro en España" (*The Modern Language Review* 93.4, 1998), pp. 997–1006.
Allen, John Jay, "La importancia de la restauración y la reanimación del Teatro Cervantes" [conference paper] (Vancouver: MLA, 2014).
Allen, John Jay, "El papel del vulgo en la economía de los corrales de comedia madrileños" (*Edad de Oro* 12, 1993), pp. 9–18.
Allen, John Jay, *La Piedra de Rosetta del teatro comercial europeo. El Teatro Cervantes de Alcalá de Henares* (Madrid-Frankfurt: Iberoamericana-Vervuert, 2015).
Allen, John Jay, "Los primeros corrales de comedia: dudas, enigmas, desacuerdos" (*Edad de Oro* 16, 1997), pp. 13–27.
Allen, John Jay, *The Reconstruction of a Spanish Golden Age Playhouse: El Corral del Príncipe 1583-1744* (Gainesville: University Presses of Florida, 1983).
Allen, John Jay, "The Reemergence of the Playhouse in the Renaissance: Spain 1550-1750" in Paul C. Castagno (ed.), *Theatrical Spaces and Dramatic Places: The Reemergence of the Theatre Building in the Renaissance* (Tuscaloosa: University of Alabama Press, 1991), pp. 27–38.
Allen, John Jay, "The Spanish *Corrales de Comedias* and the London Playhouses and Stages" in Frank J. Hildy (ed.), *New Issues in the Reconstruction of Shakespeare's Theatre* (New York: Peter Lang, 1990), pp. 207–235.
Allen, John Jay, "The Teatro Cervantes in Alcalá de Henares: 'To airy nothing, a local habitation and a name'" (*Bulletin of the Comediantes* 64.1, 2012), pp. 147–159.

Allen, John Jay, "The Teatro Cervantes in Alcalá de Henares, Chapter Two: The 1980s" (*Bulletin of the Comediantes* 66.1, 2014), pp. 177–200.
Allen, John Jay, "The World of the *Comedia*" (*Comedia Performance* 4, 2007), pp. 15–34.
Alvar Ezquerra, Alfredo, *El nacimiento de una capital europea: Madrid entre 1561 y 1606* (Madrid: Turner Libros, 1989).
Alvar Ezquerra, Alfredo, "Todo empezó en 1561" (*Torre de Lujanes* 61, 2007), pp. 117–138.
Alvar Ezquerra, Alfredo, "La villa de Madrid vista por los extranjeros en la Alta Edad Moderna" [conference paper] (Madrid: Ciclo de conferencias Madrid, capital europea de la cultura, 3, 1990).
Álvarez Francés, Leonor, "Fascination for the 'Madritsche Apollo': Lope de Vega in Golden Age Amsterdam" (*Arte Nuevo* 1, 2011), pp. 1–15.
Amelang, David J., "Comparing the Commercial Theaters of Early Modern London and Madrid" (*Renaissance Quarterly* 71.2, 2018), pp. 610–644.
Amelang, David J., "A Day in the Life: The Performance of Playgoing in Early Modern London and Madrid" (*Bulletin of the Comediantes* 70.2, 2018), pp. 111–127.
Amelang, David J., "From Directions to Descriptions: Reading the Theatrical *Nebentext* in Ben Jonson's *Workes* as an Authorial Outlet" (*SEDERI Yearbook* 27, 2017), pp. 7–26.
Amelang, David J., "Playing Gender: Toward a Quantitative Comparison of Female Roles in Lope de Vega and Shakespeare" (*Bulletin of the Comediantes* 71.1-2, 2019), pp. 119-134.
Amelang, David J., "¿Qué es un teatro? A vueltas con los corrales de comedias y sus coetáneos ingleses" in Moisés R. Castillo (ed.), *La Vida como Arte: Essays in Memory of John Jay Allen* (Newark, DE: Juan de la Cuesta, 2021), pp. 73–90.
Anderson, Christy Jo, *Inigo Jones and the Classical Tradition* (Cambridge: Cambridge University Press, 2006).
Andrews, Richard, "Resources in Common: Shakespeare and Flaminio Scala" in Robert Henke and Eric Nicholson (eds.), *Transnational Mobilities in Early Modern Theater* (London: Ashgate, 2014), pp. 37–52.
Antonucci, Fausta, "Estructura dramática y función de la polimetría en *La cisma de Ingalaterra* de Pedro Calderón de la Barca" (*Bulletin of the Comediantes* 70.2, 2018), pp. 93–110.
Antonucci, Fausta, "La polimetría en *La dama boba*: funciones poéticas y dramáticas" in Javier Espejo Surós and Carlos Mata Induráin (eds.), *Preludio a La dama boba de Lope de Vega (historia y crítica)* (Pamplona: Universidad de Navarra, 2020), pp. 111–129.
Antonucci, Fausta, "¿Qué Lope se conocía en la Italia del siglo XVII?" (*Criticón* 122, 2014).
Arata, Stefano, "Notas sobre *La Conquista de Jerusalén* y la transmisión manuscrita del primer teatro cervantino" (*Edad de Oro* 16, 1997), pp. 53–66.
Arata, Stefano and Debora Vaccari, "Manuscritos atípicos, papeles de actor y compañías del siglo XVI" (*Rivista di Filologia e Letterature Ispaniche* 5, 2002), pp. 25–68.
Archer, Ian, "The Nostalgia of John Stow" in David L. Smith, Richard Strier and David Bevington (eds.), *The Theatrical City: Culture, Theatre and Politics in London, 1576-1649* (Cambridge: Cambridge University Press, 1995), pp. 17–34.
Arellano, Ignacio, "Lo trágico y lo cómico mezclado: de mezclas y mixturas en el teatro del Siglo de Oro" (*RILCE - Revista de Filología Hispánica* 27.1, 2011), pp. 9–34.
Arteaga Martínez, Alejandro, "El teatro jesuita novohispano: ¿cuál es el estado de la cuestión?" in Luis Fernando Lara, Reynaldo Yunuen Ortega and Marta Lilia Tenorio

(eds.), *de Amicitia Et Doctrina: Homenaje a Maria Elena Venier* (Mexico DF: El Colegio de México, 2007), pp. 77–101.

Astington, John H., *Actors and Acting in Shakespeare's Time: The Art of Stage Playing* (Cambridge: Cambridge University Press, 2010).

Astington, John H., *English Court Theatre, 1558-1642* (Cambridge: Cambridge University Press, 1999).

Astington, John H., "Why the theatres changed" in Andrew Gurr and Farah Karim-Cooper (eds.), *Moving Shakespeare Indoors: Performance and Repertoire in the Jacobean Playhouse* (Cambridge: Cambridge University Press, 2014), pp. 15–31.

Aszyk, Ursula, "' … y pon el teatro, y prevén / lo necesario … ': Hacia una reconstrucción de la puesta en escena original de *Lo fingido verdadero*" in Felipe Pedraza Jiménez, Rafael González Cañal and Elena E. Marcello (eds.), *El corral de comedias: espacio escénico, espacio dramático. Actas de las XXVII jornadas de teatro clásico de Almagro (6, 7 y 8 de julio de 2004)* (Almagro: Universidad de Castilla-La Mancha, 2006), pp. 159–180.

Baker, Susan C. and Judith A. Whitenack, "Desire and Social Order in the *Duchess* Plays of Lope and Webster" (*Pacific Coast Philology* 27.1-2, 1992), pp. 54–68.

Ball, Rachael, "'Beautiful Serpents' and 'Cathedras of Pestilence': Antitheatrical Traditions, Gendered Decline, and Political Crisis in Early Modern Spain and England" (*Sixteenth Century Journal* 46.3, 2015), pp. 541–563.

Ball, Rachael, *Treating the Public: Charitable Theater and Civic Health in the Early Modern Atlantic World* (Baton Rouge: Louisiana State University Press, 2017).

Barbadillo de la Fuente, María Teresa, "Madrid en las obras de Salas Barbadillo" in José Romera, Antonio Lorente and Ana María Freire (eds.), *Ex Libris. Homenaje al profesor José Fradejas Lebrero, Tomo I* (Madrid: UNED, 1993), pp. 239–262.

Barbour, Richmond, "Jonson and the Motives of Print" (*Criticism* 40.4, 1998), pp. 499–528.

Barrie, Robert, "Elizabethan Play-Boys in the Adult London Companies" (*Studies in English Literature, 1500-1900* 48.2, 2008), pp. 237–257.

Barroll, Leeds, *Politics, Plague, and Shakespeare's Theater: The Stuart Years* (Ithaca and London: Cornell University Press, 1991).

Batllori, Miguel et al., "Siglo XVI" in Buenaventura Delgado (ed.), *Historia de la educación en España y América, Vol. 2: La educación en la España Moderna (siglos XVI-XVIII)* (Madrid: Ediciones SM, 1992), pp. 11–401.

Beier, A.L. and Roger Finlay, "The Significance of the Metropolis" in A.L. Beier and Roger Finlay (eds.), *London 1500-1700: The Making of the Metropolis* (London: Longman, 1986), pp. 1–33.

Bejarano Pellicer, Clara, "El oficio de representar y el oficio de la música en Sevilla entre 1575 y 1625" (*Philologia Hispalensis* 27.1-2, 2013), pp. 29–54.

Belsey, Catherine, "Shakespeare's Little Boys: Theatrical Apprenticeship and the Construction of Childhood" in Brian Reynolds and William N. West (eds.), *Rematerializing Shakespeare: Authority and Representation on the Early Modern English Stage* (Houndmills: Palgrave, 2005), pp. 53–72.

Bentley, Bernard P.E., "Del 'autor' a los actores: El traslado de una comedia" in Manuel García Martín, Ignacio Arellano, Javier Blasco and Marc Vitse (eds.), *Estado actual de los estudios sobre el Siglo de Oro. Actas del II Congreso Internacional de Hispanistas del Siglo de Oro* (Salamanca: Universidad de Salamanca, 1993), pp. 179–194.

Bentley, Gerald Eades, *The Profession of Dramatist in Shakespeare's Time, 1590-1642* (Princeton NJ: Princeton University Press, 1971).

Bentley, Gerald Eades, *The Profession of Player in Shakespeare's Time, 1590-1642* (Princeton NJ: Princeton University Press, 1984).
Berger, Philippe, "Del manuscrito a la imprenta: inercia y sinergia" (*Bulletin Hispanique* 106.1, 2004), pp. 143–159.
Berry, Herbert, "Aspects of the Design and Use of the First Public Playhouse" in Herbert Berry (ed.), *The First Public Playhouse: The Theatre in Shoreditch 1576-1598* (Montreal: McGill-Queen's University Press, 1979), pp. 29–45.
Berry, Herbert, *The Boar's Head Playhouse* (Washington D.C.: Folger Books, 1986).
Berry, Herbert, "Where Was the Playhouse in Which the Boy Choristers of St. Paul's Cathedral Performed Plays?" (*Medieval & Renaissance Drama in England* 13, 2001), pp. 101–116.
Bevington, David, *Shakespeare and Biography* (Oxford: Oxford University Press, 2010).
Blank, Daniel, "Actors, Orators, and the Boundaries of Drama in Elizabethan Universities" (*Renaissance Quarterly* 70.2, 2017), pp. 513–547.
Blayney, Peter W.M., "The Alleged Popularity of Playbooks" (*Shakespeare Quarterly* 56.1, 2005), pp. 33–50.
Blayney, Peter W.M., "The Bookshops in Paul's Cross Churchyard" (*Occasional Papers of the Bibliographical Society* 5, 1990).
Blayney, Peter W.M., "The Publication of Playbooks" in John D. Cox and David Scott Kastan (eds.), *A New History of Early English Drama* (New York: Columbia University Press, 1997), pp. 383–422.
Blom, Frans R.E. and Olga van Marion, "Lope de Vega and the conquest of Spanish theater in the Netherlands" (*Anuario Lope de Vega* 23, 2017), pp. 155–177.
Bly, Mary, "Playing the Tourist in Early Modern London: Selling the Liberties Onstage" (*PMLA* 122.1, 2007), pp. 61–71.
Boer, Harm den, "La representación de la comedia española en Holanda" (*Cuadernos de historia moderna* 23, 1999), pp. 113–127.
Bolaños Donoso, Piedad, "Acerca de la ubicación del corral de las Atarazanas" (*Edad de Oro* 16, 1997), pp. 67–87.
Bolaños Donoso, Piedad, "Reescritura de la vida y memoria del corral de comedias de San Pedro (1600-1608)" in Pedro Ruiz Pérez and Klaus Wagner (eds.), *La cultura en Andalucía: Vida, memoria y escritura en torno a 1600* (Estepa: Ayuntamiento de Estepa, 2001), pp. 301–324.
Bolaños Donoso, Piedad, Vicente Palacios, Mercedes de los Reyes Peña and Juan Ruesga Navarro, "El Corral de la Montería de Sevilla: metodología y resultados en su reconstrucción virtual" (*Teatro de palabras* 6, 2012), pp. 221–248.
Bosman, Anston, "Shakespeare and globalization" in Margreta de Grazia and Stanley Wells (eds.), *The New Cambridge Companion to Shakespeare, Second Edition* (Cambridge: Cambridge University Press, 2010), pp. 285–302.
Botta, Patrizia, Aviva Garribba, Massimo Marini and Debora Vaccari, "Versiones romanas de tres textos de Lope" (*Anuario Lope de Vega* 25, 2019), pp. 143–189.
Boulton, Jeremy, "London 1540-1700" in Peter Clark (ed.), *The Cambridge Urban History of Britain Volume 2: 1540-1840* (Cambridge: Cambridge University Press, 2000), pp. 315–346.
Boulton, Jeremy, *Neighbourhood and Society: A London Suburb in the Seventeenth Century* (Cambridge: Cambridge University Press, 1987).
Bourus, Terri and Gary Taylor (eds.), *The Creation and Re-Creation of Cardenio: Performing Shakespeare, Transforming Cervantes* (New York: Palgrave Macmillan, 2013).

Bouza, Fernando, "Los contextos materiales de la producción cultural" in Antonio Feros and Juan Gelabert (eds.), *España en tiempos del Quijote* (Madrid: Taurus, 2004), pp. 309–344.
Bouza, Fernando, *"Dásele licencia y privilegio": Don Quijote y la aprobación de libros en el Siglo de Oro* (Tres Cantos: Akal, 2012).
Bowsher, Julian, "The Rose and its Stages" (*Shakespeare Survey* 60, 2007), pp. 36–48.
Bowsher, Julian, *Shakespeare's London Theatreland: Archaeology, History and Drama* (London: Museum of London Archaeology, 2012).
Bowsher, Julian and Simon Blatherwick, "The Structure of the Rose" in Frank J. Hildy (ed.), *New Issues in the Reconstruction of Shakespeare's Theatre* (New York: Peter Lang, 1990), pp. 55–78.
Bowsher, Julian and Pat Miller, *The Rose and the Globe: Playhouses of Tudor Bankside, Southwark Excavations 1988-91* (London: Museum of London Archaeology, 2009).
Boyle, Catherine and David Johnston (eds.), *The Spanish Golden Age in English: Perspectives on Performance* (London: Oberon, 2007).
Brandon, David and Alan Brooke, *Bankside: London's Original District of Sin* (Stroud: Amberley, 2011).
Brett-James, Norman G., *The Growth of Stuart London* (London: London and Middlesex Archaeological Society, 1935).
Brockey, Liam M., "Jesuit Pastoral Theater on an Urban Stage: Lisbon, 1588-1593" (*Journal of Early Modern History* 9.1-2, 2005), pp. 3–50.
Brown, Jonathan and John H. Elliott, *A Palace for a King: The Buen Retiro and the Court of Philip IV* (New Haven: Yale University Press, 2003 [orig. ed. 1980]).
Brown, Pamela Allen and Peter Parolin, "Introduction" in Pamela Allen Brown and Peter Parolin (eds.), *Women Players in England, 1500-1660: Beyond the All-Male Stage* (Aldershot: Ashgate, 2005), pp. 1–21.
Brown, Pamela Allen and Peter Parolin (eds.), *Women Players in England, 1500-1660: Beyond the All-Male Stage* (Aldershot: Ashgate, 2005).
Browner, Jessica A., "Wrong Side of the River: London's disreputable South Bank in the sixteenth and seventeenth century" [http://www.essaysinhistory.com/articles/2012/96] (*Essays in History* 36, 1994).
Bruaene, Anne-Laura van, "'A wonderfull tryumfe, for the wynnyng of a pryse': Guilds, Ritual, Theater, and the Urban Network in the Southern Low Countries, ca. 1450-1650" (*Renaissance Quarterly* 59.3, 2006), pp. 374–405.
Bruerton, Courtney, "La versificación dramática española en el período 1587-1610" (*Nueva Revista de Filología Hispánica* 10.3–4, 1956), pp. 337–364.
Bryant, William C., "Estudio métrico sobre las dos comedias profanas de Sor Juana Inés de la Cruz" (*Hispanófila* 19, 1963), pp. 37–48.
Burckhardt, Jacob, *The Architecture of the Italian Renaissance* [trans. James Palmes, ed. Peter Murray] (London: Secker & Warburg, 1985).
Burguillo López, Francisco Javier, "En los arrabales de Lope de Vega. El teatro español hacia la comedia nueva (1575-1600)" (*Per Abbat* 8, 2009), pp. 9–25.
Burke, Peter, "Popular Culture in Seventeenth-Century London" in Barry Reay (ed.), *Popular Culture in Seventeenth-Century England* (London & Sidney: Croom Helm, 1985), pp. 31–58.
Burris, Quincy Guy, "'Soft! Here Follows Prose'—*Twelfth Night* II. v. 154" (*Shakespeare Quarterly* 2.3, 1951), pp. 233–239.

Bustamante, Agustín and Fernando Marías, "Algunas consideraciones sobre la casa rural en Castilla en el siglo XVI" in Antonio Cea Gutiérrez, Matilde Fernández Montes and Luis Ángel Sánchez Gómez (eds.), *Arquitectura popular en España. Actas de las jornadas sobre arquitectura popular en España, 1987* (Madrid: CSIC, 1990), pp. 219–228.

Calado, Maria, Margarida de Zoudo Lobo and Vitor Matias Ferreira, "Lisboa" in Manuel Guàrdia, Francisco J. Monclús and José Luis Oyón (eds.), *Atlas histórico de ciudades europeas I. Península ibérica* (Madrid: Alianza, 1994), pp. 95–125.

Canavaggio, Jean, "Sevilla y el teatro a fines del siglo XVI: apostillas a un documento poco conocido" in José María Ruano de la Haza (ed.), *El mundo del teatro español en su Siglo de Oro: ensayos dedicados a John E. Varey* (Ottawa: Dovehouse, 1989), pp. 81–99.

Cantero, Susana, *Dramaturgia y práctica escénica del verso clásico español* (Madrid: Fundamentos, 2006).

Cañadas, Iván, *Public Theater in Golden Age Madrid and Tudor-Stuart London: Class, Gender and Festive Community* (Aldershot: Ashgate, 2005).

Capitán Díaz, Alfonso, *Breve historia de la educación en España* (Madrid: Alianza, 2002).

Carbajo Isla, María, *La población de la villa de Madrid. Desde finales del siglo XVI hasta mediados del siglo XIX* (Madrid: Siglo XXI, 1987).

Carloni Franca, Alida, "La cultura de los corrales sevillanos, a través de la utilización del espacio" in Antonio Cea Gutiérrez, Matilde Fernández Montes and Luis Ángel Sánchez Gómez (eds.), *Arquitectura popular en España. Actas de las jornadas sobre arquitectura popular en España, 1987* (Madrid: CSIC, 1990), pp. 559–570.

Carmona Tierno, Juan Manuel, "Violencia y versificación en *Renegado, rey y mártir* de Cristóbal de Morales" (*Hipogrifo* 4.1, 2016), pp. 183–197.

Carnegie, David and Gary Taylor (eds.), *The Quest for Cardenio: Shakespeare, Fletcher, Cervantes, and the Lost Play* (Oxford: Oxford University Press, 2012).

Castillejo, David, *Spanish Classical Drama: A Classified Survey and Study of 1000 Plays* (London: Oberon, 2011).

Castillo Gómez, Antonio, "A la vista de todos. Usos gráficos de la escritura expuesta en la España altomoderna" (*Scripta. An International Journal of Codicology and Palaeography* 2, 2009), pp. 73–90.

Castillo Gómez, Antonio, "Desde el muro. Formas y mensajes de la escritura expuesta en la ciudad altomoderna" in Gemma Puigvert and Carme de la Mota (eds.), *La investigación en Humanidades* (Madrid: Biblioteca Nueva, 2010), pp. 91–110.

Castillo Gómez, Antonio, "La letra en la pared: usos y funciones de la escritura expuesta en el Siglo de Oro" in Manuel Fernández, Carlos-Alberto González-Sánchez and Natalia Maillard Álvarez (eds.), *Testigo del tiempo, memoria del universo: cultura escrita y sociedad en el mundo ibérico (siglos XV-XVIII)* (Barcelona: Ediciones Rubeo, 2009), pp. 581–602.

Cervera Vera, Luis, *Las mejoras urbanas en el Madrid de Carlos III* (Madrid: Artes Gráficas Municipales, 1989).

Chartier, Roger, *The Author's Hand and the Printer's Mind* [trans. Lydia G. Cochrane] (Oxford: Polity Press, 2014).

Chartier, Roger, *Cardenio between Cervantes and Shakespeare: The Story of a Lost Play* [trans. Janet Lloyd] (Cambridge: Polity Press, 2013 [orig. ed. 2011]).

Chartier, Roger, "Del libro a la lectura. Lectores 'populares' en el Renacimiento" (*Bulletin Hispanique* 99.1, 1997), pp. 309–324.

Chartier, Roger, *Publishing Drama in Early Modern Europe* (London: The British Library, 1999).

Chaytor, Henry J., "The Travels in Spain of Thomas Williams" (*Bulletin of Spanish Studies* 4.14, 1927), pp. 51–67.
Cherry, Brinda, *The Arden Guide to Renaissance Drama: An Introduction with Primary Sources* (London: Bloomsbury, 2017).
Clark, Ira, *Professional Playwrights: Massinger, Ford, Shirley, & Brome* (Lexington: The University Press of Kentucky, 1992).
Clark, Peter, *European Cities and Towns: 400-2000* (Oxford: Oxford University Press, 2009).
Clark, Peter, "The Multi-Centred Metropolis: The Social and Cultural Landscapes of London, 1600-1840" in Peter Clark and Raymond Gillespie (eds.), *Two Capitals: London and Dublin, 1500-1840* (Oxford: Oxford University Press, 2001), pp. 239–264.
Cohen, Walter, "The Artisan Theatres of Renaissance England and Spain" (*Theatre Journal* 35.4, 1983), pp. 499–518.
Cohen, Walter, *Drama of a Nation: Public Theater in Renaissance England and Spain* (Ithaca and London: Cornell University Press, 1985).
Collantes de Terán, Antonio, Josefina Cruz Villalón and Víctor Fernández Salinas, "Sevilla" in Manuel Guàrdia, Francisco J. Monclús and José Luis Oyón (eds.), *Atlas histórico de ciudades europeas I. Península ibérica* (Madrid: Alianza, 1994), pp. 183–209.
Connor, Francis X., *Literary Folios and Ideas of the Book in Early Modern England* (Basingstoke: Palgrave Macmillan, 2014).
Coso Marín, Miguel Ángel, Mercedes Higueras Sánchez-Pardo and Juan Sanz Ballesteros, *El Teatro Cervantes de Alcalá de Henares: 1602-1866. Estudio y documentos* (London: Tamesis, 1990).
Cotarelo y Mori, Emilio, *Bibliografía de las controversias sobre la licitud del teatro en España* [ed. José Luis Suárez García] (Granada: Universidad de Granada, 1997 [orig. ed. 1904]).
Couderc, Christophe, "Lope de Vega y el teatro francés del siglo XVII" (*Anuario Lope de Vega* 23, 2017), pp. 78–103.
Craig, Hugh and Brett Greatley-Hirsch, *Style, Computers, and Early Modern Drama: Beyond Authorship* (Cambridge: Cambridge University Press, 2018).
Crawforth, Hannah, Sarah Dustagheer and Jennifer Young, *Shakespeare in London* (London: Bloomsbury, 2014).
Cressy, David, *Education in Tudor and Stuart England* (London: Edward Arnold, 1975).
Crivellari, Daniele, *Marcas autoriales de segmentación en las comedias autógrafas de Lope de Vega: estudio y análisis* (Kassel: Reichenberger, 2013).
Crivellari, Daniele, "¿Las relaciones piden los romances? Métrica y narración en dos comedias de Lope de Vega (1610)" (*Anuario Lope de Vega* 21, 2015), pp. 1–28.
Cruickshank, Dan, *Spitalfields: The History of a Nation in a Handful of Streets* (London: Windmill Books, 2016).
Cruickshank, D.W., "Calderón y el comercio español del libro" in Kurt Reichenberger and Roswita Reichenberger (eds.), *Manual bibliográfico calderoniano, vol. III* (Kassel: Reichenberger, 1981), pp. 9–15.
Cruickshank, D.W., "'Literature' and the Book Trade in Golden-Age Spain" (*The Modern Language Review* 73.4, 1978), pp. 799–824.
Cruickshank, D.W., "Some aspects of Spanish book-production in the Golden Age" (*The Library* 31 [5th Series].1, 1976), pp. 1–19.
Cruickshank, D.W., "Some problems posed by *suelta* editions of plays" in Michael McGaha and Frank P. Casa (eds.), *Editing the Comedia, Vol. 11* (Michigan: Michigan Romance Studies, 1991), pp. 97–123.

Cruickshank, D.W. and Szilvia Szmuk, "Sueltas" in Frank P. Casa, Luciano García Lorenzo and Germán Vega García-Luengos (eds.), *Diccionario de la comedia del Siglo de Oro* (Madrid: Castalia, 2002), pp. 278–281.

Cruz, Anne J., "Women's Education in Early Modern Spain" in Nieves Baranda and Anne J. Cruz (eds.), *The Routledge Research Companion to Early Modern Spanish Women Writers* (London: Routledge, 2018), pp. 27–40.

Crystal, David, *'Think On My Words': Exploring Shakespeare's Language* (Cambridge: Cambridge University Press, 2008).

D'Evelyn, Margaret Muther, *Venice and Vitruvius: Reading Venice with Daniele Barbaro and Andrea Palladio* (New Haven: Yale University Press, 2012).

Dadson, Trevor, *Libros, lectores y lecturas: Estudios sobre bibliotecas particulares españolas del Siglo de Oro* (Madrid: Arco Libros, 1998).

Dane, Joseph A. and Alexandra Gillespie, "The Myth of the Cheap Quarto" in John N. King (ed.), *Tudor Books and Readers: Materiality and the Construction of Meaning* (Cambridge: Cambridge University Press, 2010), pp. 25–45.

Danson, Lawrence, "The Shakespeare Remix: Romance, Tragicomedy, and Shakespeare's 'distinct kind'" in Anthony R. Guneratne (ed.), *Shakespeare and Genre: From Early Modern Inheritances to Postmodern Legacies* (New York: Palgrave Macmillan, 2011), pp. 101–118.

Davies, Callan, "Elizabethan Commercial Playing at St Paul's" in Shanyn Altman and Jonathan Buckner (eds.), *Old St Paul's and Culture* (Cham: Palgrave Macmillan, 2021), pp. 221–241.

Davies, Callan, *What is a Playhouse?: England at Play, 1520-1620* (New York: Routledge, 2023).

Davis, Charles, "¿Cuántos actores había en el Siglo de Oro? Hacia un análisis numérico del *Diccionario biográfico de actores del teatro clásico español*" (*diablotexto* 4–5, 1997-1998), pp. 61–77.

Davis, Charles and J.E. Varey (eds.), *Actividad teatral en la región de Madrid según los protocolos de Juan García de Albertos, 1634-1660, Vol. 1* (London: Tamesis, 2003).

Davis, Charles and J.E. Varey, *Los corrales de comedias y los hospitales de Madrid: 1574-1615. Estudio y Documentos* (London: Tamesis, 1997).

Delgado, Buenaventura, "Humanismo y Renacimiento" in Buenaventura Delgado (ed.), *Historia de la educación en España y América, Vol. 1: La educación en la Hispania Antigua y Medieval* (Madrid: Ediciones SM, 1992), pp. 617–667.

Delgado, Buenaventura et al., "Siglo XVII" in Buenaventura Delgado (ed.), *Historia de la educación en España y América, Vol. 2: La educación en la España Moderna (siglos XVI-XVIII)* (Madrid: Ediciones SM, 1992), pp. 405–645.

Delicado Puerto, Gemma, *Santas y meretrices. Herederas de la Magdalena en la literatura de los Siglos de Oro y la escena inglesa* (Kassel: Reichenberger, 2011).

Dewar-Watson, Sarah, "Aristotle and Tragicomedy" in Subha Mukerji and Raphael Lyne (eds.), *Early Modern Tragicomedy* (Cambridge: D.S. Brewer, 2007), pp. 15–27.

Díez Borque, José María (ed.), *Literatura, bibliotecas y derechos de autor en el Siglo de Oro: 1600 - 1700* (Madrid-Frankfurt am Main: Iberoamericana-Vervuert, 2012).

Díez Borque, José María, "Lope de Vega y los gustos del vulgo" (*Revista de Estudios Teatrales* 1, 1992), pp. 7–32.

Díez Borque, José María, "El negocio teatral de Lope de Vega y Calderón de la Barca" in José María Díez Borque (ed.), *Teatro español de los Siglos de Oro: Dramaturgos, textos, escenarios, fiestas* (Madrid: Visor, 2013), pp. 37–55.

Díez Borque, José María, *Sociedad y teatro en la España de Lope de Vega* (Barcelona: Bosch, 1978).
Díez Borque, José María, *El teatro en el siglo XVII* (Madrid: Taurus, 1988).
Díez Borque, José María, *La vida española en el Siglo de Oro según los extranjeros* (Barcelona: Ediciones del Serbal, 1990).
Dillon, Janette, *Theatre, Court & City, 1595-1610: Drama & Social Space in London* (Cambridge: Cambridge University Press, 2000).
Dixon, Víctor, *En busca del fénix. Quince estudios sobre Lope de Vega y su teatro* [ed. Almudena García González] (Madrid-Frankfurt: Iberoamericana-Vervuert, 2013).
Dixon, Víctor, "La comedia de corral de Lope como género visual" (*Edad de Oro* 5, 1986), pp. 35–58.
Dixon, Víctor, "The Uses of Polymetry: An Approach to Editing the Comedia as Verse Drama" in Frank Paul Casa and Michael McGaha (eds.), *Editing the Comedia, Vol 1* (Ann Arbor: University of Michigan Press, 1985), pp. 104–125.
Dobson, Michael, *The Making of the National Poet: Shakespeare, Adaptation and Authorship, 1660-1769* (Oxford: Clarendon Press, 1992).
Dodge, Hazel, "Amphitheaters in the Roman World" in Paul Christensen and Donald G. Kyle (eds.), *A Companion to Sport and Spectacle in Greek and Roman Antiquity* (Chichester: Wiley-Blackwell, 2013), pp. 545–560.
Domínguez Matito, Francisco, *El teatro en La Rioja, 1580-1808. Los patios de comedias de Logroño y Calahorra. Estudio y documentos* (Logroño: Universidad de la Rioja, 1998).
Dudley, Donald R., *Urbs Roma: A Source Book of Classical Texts on the City and Its Monuments* (London: Phaidon, 1967).
Dustagheer, Sarah, "Acoustic and visual practices indoors" in Andrew Gurr and Farah Karim-Cooper (eds.), *Moving Shakespeare Indoors: Performance and Repertoire in the Jacobean Playhouse* (Cambridge: Cambridge University Press, 2014), pp. 137–151.
Dustagheer, Sarah, "'And here in London, where I oft have beene': Contrasting Representations of the Early Modern Capital at the Globe and the Blackfriars, 1599-1609" (*Shakespeare Seminar* 8, 2010), pp. 37–43.
Dustagheer, Sarah, "'Our scene is London': *The Alchemist* and Urban Underworlds at the Blackfriars Playhouse" (*Shakespeare Jahrbuch* 147, 2011), pp. 94–104.
Dustagheer, Sarah, *Shakespeare's Two Playhouses: Repertory and Theatre Space at the Globe and the Blackfriars, 1599–1613* (Cambridge: Cambridge University Press, 2017).
Dutton, Richard, *Ben Jonson: To the First Folio* (Cambridge: Cambridge University Press, 1983).
Dutton, Richard, "The Birth of the Author" in Cedric C. Brown and Arthur F. Marotti (eds.), *Texts and Cultural Change in Early Modern England* (Basingstoke: Macmillan, 1997), pp. 153–178.
Dutton, Richard, *Licensing, Censorship and Authorship in Early Modern England* (New York: Palgrave, 2000).
Earle, Peter, "The Middling Sort in London" in Jonathan Barry and Christopher Brooks (eds.), *The Middling Sort of People: Culture, Society and Politics in England, 1550-1800* (Basingstoke: Macmillan, 1994), pp. 159–180.
Egido, Aurora, *El gran teatro de Calderón. Personajes, temas, escenografía* (Kassel: Reichenberger, 1995).
Elliott, John H., "A Europe of Composite Monarchies" (*Past & Present* 127, 1992), pp. 48–71.

Enterline, Lynn, *Shakespeare's Schoolroom: Rhetoric, Discipline, Emotion* (Philadelphia: University of Pennsylvania Press, 2012).
Equipo Madrid, Carlos III, *Madrid y la Ilustración: Contradicciones de un proyecto reformista* (Madrid: Siglo XXI, 1998).
Erne, Lukas, *Shakespeare and the Book Trade* (Cambridge: Cambridge University Press, 2013).
Erne, Lukas, "Shakespeare and the Publication of his Plays" (*Shakespeare Quarterly* 51.1, 2002), pp. 1–20.
Erne, Lukas, *Shakespeare as Literary Dramatist, Second Edition* (Cambridge: Cambridge University Press, 2013 [orig. ed. 2003]).
Es, Bart van, *Shakespeare in Company* (Oxford: Oxford University Press, 2013).
Escobar, Jesús, *The Plaza Mayor and the Shaping of Baroque Madrid* (Cambridge: Cambridge University Press, 2004).
Ettinghausen, Henry, "The News in Spain: Relaciones de sucesos in the Reigns of Philip III and Philip IV" (*European History Quarterly* 14.1, 1984), pp. 1–20.
Facal, Darío, "Sobre *Castelvines y Monteses*" in Félix Lope de Vega (ed.), *Castelvines y Monteses* (Madrid: Editorial Fundamentos, 2005), pp. 9–38.
Farmer, Alan B. and Zachary Lesser, "The Popularity of Playbooks Revisited" (*Shakespeare Quarterly* 56.1, 2005), pp. 1–32.
Farmer, Alan B. and Zachary Lesser, "Structures of Popularity in the Early Modern Book Trade" (*Shakespeare Quarterly* 56.2, 2005), pp. 206–213.
Farmer, Alan B. and Zachary Lesser, "What is Print Popularity? A Map of the Elizabethan Book Trade" in Andy Kesson and Emma Smith (eds.), *The Elizabethan Top Ten: Defining Print Popularity in Early Modern England* (Farnham: Ashgate, 2013), pp. 19–54.
Fernández Guillermo, Leonor, "Aproximaciones a la versificación en la comedia de Lope de Vega (1611-1615)" in Ysla Campbell (ed.), *El escritor y la escena VI: Estudios sobre teatro español y novohispano de los Siglos de Oro* (Ciudad de Juárez: Universidad Autónoma de Ciudad Juárez, 1998), pp. 109–115.
Fernández López, Jorge, "Rhetorical Theory in Sixteenth-Century Spain: A Critical Survey" (*Rhetorica* 20.2, 2002), pp. 133–148.
Fernández Martín, Luis, "Construcción de nueva planta del antiguo teatro de Valladolid 1609-1610" (*Castilla: Estudios de Literatura* 20, 1995), pp. 105–124.
Fernández Mosquera, Santiago, "Los textos de la *Segunda parte* de Calderón" (*Anuario calderoniano* 1, 2008), pp. 127–150.
Fernández Rodríguez, Daniel, "¿Escribió Lope guiones métricos? Métrica y segmentación dramática en *Viuda, casa y doncella*" (*Castilla: Estudios de Literatura* 7, 2016), pp. 38–68.
Feros, Antonio, *Speaking of Spain: The Evolution of Race and Nation in the Hispanic World* (Cambridge, MA: Harvard University Press, 2017).
Ferrer Valls, Teresa, "Bandello, Belleforest, Painter, Lope de Vega y Webster frente al suceso de la Duquesa de Amalfi y su mayordomo" in Vibha Maurya and Mariela Insúa (eds.), *Actas del I Congreso Ibero-asiático de Hispanistas Siglo de Oro e Hispanismo general (Delhi, 9-12 de noviembre, 2010)* (Pamplona: Universidad de Navarra, 2011), pp. 159–175.
Ferrer Valls, Teresa, "La incorporación de la mujer a la empresa teatral: actrices, autoras y compañías en el Siglo de Oro" in Francisco Domínguez Matito and Julián Bravo Vega (eds.), *Calderón. Entre veras y burlas. Actas de las II y III Jornadas de Teatro Clásico de la Universidad de La Rioja (7, 8 y 9 de abril de 1999 y 17, 18 y 19 de mayo de 2000)* (Logroño: Universidad de la Rioja, 2002), pp. 139–160.

Ferrer Valls, Teresa, "La mujer sobre el tablado en el siglo XVII: de actriz a autora" in Felipe B. Pedraza, Rafael González Cañal and Almudena García González (eds.), *Damas en el tablado. Actas de las XXXI Jornadas Internacionales de teatro clásico de Almagro (1-3 de julio 2008)* (Almagro: Universidad de Castilla-La Mancha, 2008), pp. 83–100.

Ferrer Valls, Teresa, "Lope de Vega y la Corte de Felipe IV. El ocaso de una ambición" in José Martínez Millán and Manuel Rivero Rodríguez (eds.), *La Corte de Felipe IV (1621-1665): Reconfiguración de la monarquía católica, Vol. 3: Espiritualidad, literatura y teatro* (Madrid: Polifemo, 2017), pp. 2085–2104.

Ferrer Valls, Teresa, "Prólogo a *El mayordomo de la duquesa de Amalfi*" in Laura Fernández and Gonzalo Pontón (eds.), *Comedias de Lope de Vega. Parte XI: Tomo II* (Madrid: Gredos, 2012), pp. 323–335.

Finkelpearl, Philip J., *John Marston of the Middle Temple: An Elizabethan Dramatist in His Social Setting* (Cambridge: Cambridge University Press, 1969).

Finlay, Roger, *Population and Metropolis: The Demography of London 1580-1650* (Cambridge: Cambridge University Press, 2009).

Finlay, Roger and Beatrice Shearer, "Population Growth and Suburban Expansion" in A.L. Beier and Roger Finlay (eds.), *London 1500-1700: The Making of the Metropolis* (London: Longman, 1986), pp. 37–59.

Fischer, Susan L. (ed.), *Comedias del Siglo de Oro and Shakespeare* (Lewisburg: Bucknell University Press, 1989).

Flórez Asensio, María Asunción, "El Coliseo del Buen Retiro en el siglo XVII: teatro público y cortesano" (*Anales de Historia del Arte* 8, 1998), pp. 171–195.

Florit Durán, Francisco, "'Vuestra oliva es laurel de mi cabeza': Lope de Vega y la búsqueda del Parnaso áulico" (*Anuario de estudios filológicos* 42, 2019), pp. 63–85.

Fortuño Gómez, Vanessa, "La vida teatral en Barcelona en el siglo XVII: las compañías de Juan Martínez, Juan Acacio y Manuel Ángel (1628-1688)" (*Criticón* 99, 2007), pp. 159–166.

Fothergill-Payne, Louise and Peter Fothergill-Payne (eds.), *Parallel Lives: Spanish and English National Drama 1580-1680* (London: Bucknell University Press, 1991).

Friedman, Edward H., "*Romeo and Juliet* as Tragicomedy: Lope's *Castelvines y Monteses* and Rojas Zorrilla's *Los bandos de Verona*" in Susan L. Fischer (ed.), *Comedias del Siglo de Oro and Shakespeare* (Lewisburg PA: Bucknell University Press, 1989), pp. 82–96.

Fuchs, Barbara, *The Poetics of Piracy: Emulating Spain in English Literature* (Philadelphia: University of Pennsylvania Press, 2013).

Fuchs, Barbara, "'La voluntad jamás permite señor': Transnational versions of cross-class desire in Cardenio and Mujeres y criados" in M.A. Katritzky and Pavel Drábek (eds.), *Transnational Connections in Early Modern Theatre* (Manchester: Manchester University Press, 2020), pp. 58–72.

Gadea, Alejandro and Mimma De Salvo, "Jerónima de Burgos y Pedro de Valdés: biografía de un matrimonio de representantes en la España del Seiscientos" (*diablotexto* 4–5, 1997–1998), pp. 143–175.

Gair, W. Reavley, *The Children of Paul's: The Story of a Theatre Company, 1553-1608* (Cambridge: Cambridge University Press, 1982).

García Bernal, José Jaime, "El cartel de fiestas en la configuración de la comunidad urbana del Barroco: ritualización del impreso y escritura de la fiesta" in Antonio Castillo Gómez, James S. Amelang and Carmen Serrano Sánchez (eds.), *Opinión pública y espacio urbano en la Edad Moderna* (Gijón: Ediciones Trea, 2010), pp. 95–116.

García Bernal, José Jaime, *El fasto público en la España de los Austrias* (Seville: Universidad de Sevilla, 2006).

García de Enterría, María Cruz, "Pliegos de cordel, literaturas de ciego" in José María Díez Borque (ed.), *Culturas en la Edad de Oro* (Madrid: Editorial Complutense, 1995), pp. 97–112.

García de Enterría, María Cruz (ed.), *Las relaciones de sucesos en España, 1500-1750. Actas del Primer Coloquio Internacional, Alcalá de Henares, 1995* (Paris - Alcalá de Henares: Universidad de Alcalá, 1996).

García de Enterría, María Cruz, *Sociedad y poesía de cordel en el Barroco* (Madrid: Taurus, 1973).

García de León Álvarez, Concepción, "La construcción del Corral de Comedias de Almagro" in Felipe Pedraza Jiménez, Rafael González Cañal and Elena E. Marcello (eds.), *Francisco de Rojas Zorrilla, poeta dramático: actas de las XXII Jornadas de Teatro Clásico, Almagro 13, 14 y 15 de julio de 1999* (Cuenca: Universidad de Castilla-La Mancha, 2000), pp. 17–38.

García de León Álvarez, Concepción, "El Corral de Comedias de Almagro (1628)" in Andrés Peláez Martín (ed.), *El Corral de Comedias y la Villa de Almagro* (Toledo: Fundación Cultura y Deporte de Castilla-La Mancha, 2002), pp. 15–176.

García García, Luciano, "*The Duchess of Malfi* and *El mayordomo de la duquesa de Amalfi* Revisited: Some Differences in Literary Convention and Cultural Horizon" (*Revista Alicantina de Estudios Ingleses* 12, 1999), pp. 49–60.

García Gómez, Ángel María, "Casa de las comedias de Córdoba: Primer sistema de arrendamientos (1602-1624)" in Luciano García Lorenzo and J.E. Varey (eds.), *Teatros y vida teatral en el Siglo de Oro a través de las fuentes documentales* (London: Tamesis, 1991), pp. 99–109.

García Gómez, Ángel María, "Los espacios teatrales y su campo de irradiación" in Elisa García-Lara and Antonio Serrano (eds.), *Dramaturgos y espacios teatrales andaluces de los siglos XVI-XVII. Actas de las XXVI Jornadas de Teatro del Siglo de Oro* (Almería: Instituto de Estudios Almerienses, 2011), pp. 19–53.

García Reidy, Alejandro, "From Stage to Page: Editorial History and Literary Promotion in Lope de Vega's *Partes de comedias*" in Alexander Samson and Jonathan Thacker (eds.), *A Companion to Lope de Vega* (Woodbridge: Tamesis, 2008), pp. 51–60.

García Reidy, Alejandro, "*Mujeres y criados*, una comedia recuperada de Lope de Vega" (*Revista de Literatura* 75.150, 2013), pp. 417–438.

García Reidy, Alejandro, *Las musas rameras. Oficio dramático y conciencia profesional en Lope de Vega* (Madrid-Frankfurt: Iberoamericana-Vervuert, 2013).

García Reidy, Alejandro, "Spanish *Comedias* as Commodities: Possession, Circulation, and Institutional Regulation" (*Hispanic Review* 80.2, 2012), pp. 199–219.

García Sánchez, Míguel Ángel, *Pobreza, desigualdad y redes sociales en dos ciudades europeas: una comparación entre Madrid y Londres, 1550-1700* [Ph.D. Thesis] (Madrid: Universidad Complutense de Madrid, 2012).

García Sánchez, Míguel Ángel, "Urbanismo, demografía y pobreza en Madrid. La parroquia de San Sebastián, 1578-1618" (*Anales del Instituto de Estudios Madrileños* 43, 2003), pp. 45–84.

García Santo-Tomás, Enrique, *La creación del 'Fénix': Recepción crítica y formación canónica del teatro de Lope de Vega* (Madrid: Gredos, 2000).

García Santo-Tomás, Enrique, "Introducción" in Félix Lope de Vega (ed.), *Arte nuevo de hacer comedias* (Madrid: Cátedra, 2009), pp. 13–127.

Gentil Baldrich, José María, "Sobre la traza oval del Corral de la Montería" (*Periferia* 8–9, 1987), pp. 94–103.

Gerbino, Anthony and Stephen Johnston, *Compass and Rule: Architecture as Mathematical Practice in England, 1500-1750* (New Haven and London: Yale University Press, 2009).

Giuliani, Luigi, "La *Parte de comedias* como género editorial" (*Criticón* 108, 2010), pp. 25–36.

González Cañal, Rafael, "Las ediciones de teatro de la Biblioteca de Autores Españoles" in Guillermo Serés Guillén and Germán Vega García-Luengos (eds.), *Menéndez Pelayo y Lope de Vega: la lucha por el cánon* (Santander: Universidad de Cantabria, 2016), pp. 99–112.

González, José Manuel (ed.), *Cervantes - Shakespeare 1616-2016: Contexto, Influencia, Relación* (Kassel: Reichenberger, 2017).

González, Lola, "El autor de comedias en el siglo XVII. Entre creación literaria y recepción. A propósito de Baltasar de Pinedo" in Manfred Tietz and Marcella Trambaioli (eds.), *El autor en el Siglo de Oro: Su estatus intelectual y social* (Vigo: Academia del Hispanismo, 2011), pp. 129–140.

González-Sarasa Hernáez, Silvia, *Tipología editorial del impreso antiguo español* [Ph.D Thesis] (Madrid: Universidad Complutense de Madrid, 2013).

Giordano Gramegna, Anna, "Actores italianos en España en los siglos XVI y XVII: datos biográficos" (*diablotexto* 4–5, 1997–1998), pp. 177–204.

Granja, Agustín de la, "Comedias del Siglo de Oro censuradas por la Inquisición" in Odette Gorsse and Frédéric Serralta (eds.), *El Siglo de Oro en escena: Homenaje a Marc Vitse* (Toulouse: Presses Universitaires du Mirail, 2006), pp. 435–448.

Granja, Agustín de la, "Un documento inédito contra las comedias en el Siglo XVI: Los *Fundamentos* del P. Pedro de Fonseca" in *Homenaje a Camoens. Estudios y ensayos hispano-portugueses* (Granada: Universidad de Granada, 1980), pp. 173–194.

Greenblatt, Stephen, *Shakespearean Negotiations: The Circulation of Social Energy in Renaissance England* (Berkeley: University of California Press, 1989).

Greenfield, Jon, "Reconstructing The Rose: Development of the Playhouse Building between 1587 and 1592" (*Shakespeare Survey* 60, 2007), pp. 23–35.

Greenfield, Jon and Peter McCurdy, "Practical evidence for a reimagined indoor Jacobean theatre" in Andrew Gurr and Farah Karim-Cooper (eds.), *Moving Shakespeare Indoors: Performance and Repertoire in the Jacobean Playhouse* (Cambridge: Cambridge University Press, 2014), pp. 32–64.

Greer, Margaret Rich, "Authority and Theatrical Community: Early Modern Spanish Theater Manuscripts" (*Renaissance Drama, New Series* 40, 2012), pp. 100–112.

Greer, Margaret Rich, "Calderón en su Laboratorio: La Evidencia de Atajos Comentados y Repartos" (*Anuario calderoniano* 8, 2015), pp. 153–166.

Greer, Margaret Rich, "The Development of National Theatre" in David T. Gies (ed.), *The Cambridge History of Spanish Literature* (Cambridge: Cambridge University Press, 2005), pp. 238–249.

Greer, Margaret Rich, "Early Modern Spanish Theatrical Transmission, Memory, and a Claramonte Play" in Chad M. Gasta and Julia Domínguez (eds.), *Hispanic Studies in Honor of Robert L. Fiore* (Newark, DE: Juan de la Cuesta, 2009), pp. 261–280.

Greer, Margaret Rich, "La mano del copista: Diego Martínez de Mora interpreta a Calderón" (*Anuario calderoniano* 1, 2008), pp. 201–221.

Greer, Margaret Rich, "Mapa de amanuenses teatrales del siglo XVII" in Milagros Rodríguez Cáceres, Felipe B. Pedraza Jiménez and Elena E. Marcello (eds.), *La comedia española en su manuscritos* (Cuenca: Universidad de Castilla-La Mancha, 2014), pp. 17–32.

Greer, Margaret Rich, "*Move over* Shakespeare: el lugar de Lope en el teatro europeo de su tiempo" (*Anuario Lope de Vega* 23, 2017), pp. 318–346.

Greer, Margaret Rich, *The Play of Power: Mythological Court Dramas of Calderón de la Barca* (Princeton: Princeton University Press, 1991).

Greer, Margaret Rich, "Playing the Palace: Space, Place and Performance in Early Modern Spain" in María M. Delgado and David T. Gies (eds.), *A History of the Theatre in Spain* (Cambridge: Cambridge University Press, 2012), pp. 79–102.

Greer, Margaret Rich, "Spanish Golden Age Tragedy: From Cervantes to Calderón" in Rebecca W. Bushnell (ed.), *A Companion to Tragedy* (Malden PA: Blackwell, 2005), pp. 351–370.

Greer, Margaret Rich, "A Tale of Three Cities: The Place of Theatre in Early Modern Madrid, Paris and London" (*Bulletin of Hispanic Studies* 77, 2000), pp. 391–419.

Greer, Margaret Rich and Andrea Junguito, "Economies of the Early Modern Spanish Stage" (*Revista Canadiense de Estudios Hispánicos* 29.1, 2004), pp. 31–46.

Gregor, Keith, "Contrasting Fortunes: Lope in the UK/Shakespeare in Spain" (*Ilha do Desterro* 49, 2005), pp. 235–253.

Gregor, Keith, "Transversal Connections: The Cervantes Quatercentenary in Spain and its Comparison with 'Shakespeare Lives'" (*Multicultural Shakespeare: Translation, Appropriation and Performance* 19.1, 2019), pp. 91–105.

Griffin, Clive, *The Crombergers of Seville: The History of a Printing and Merchant Dynasty* (Oxford: Clarendon Press, 1988).

Griffin, Clive, "Itinerant Booksellers, Printers, and Pedlars in Sixteenth-Century Spain and Portugal" in Robin Myers, Michael Harris and Giles Mandelbrote (eds.), *Fairs, Markets and the Itinerant Book Trade* (London: British Library, 2007), pp. 43–59.

Griffin, Clive, "Literary Consequences of the Peripheral Nature of Spanish Printing in the Sixteenth Century" in Simon Eliot, Andrew Nash and Ian Willison (eds.), *Literary Cultures and the Material Book* (London: The British Library, 2007), pp. 207–214.

Griffith, Eva, *A Jacobean Company and its Playhouse: The Queen's Servants at the Red Bull Theatre (c. 1605-1619)* (Cambridge: Cambridge University Press, 2013).

Griffiths, Paul, "The Structure of Prostitution in Elizabethan London" (*Continuity and Change* 8, 1993), pp. 39–63.

Guerrero, Isabel, "The Exchange of National Authors: Performing Shakespeare in Almagro and Cervantes in Stratford" in Jorge Braga Riera, Javier J. González Martínez and Miguel Sanz Jiménez (eds.), *Cervantes, Shakespeare y la Edad de Oro de la escena* (Madrid: Fundación Universitaria Española, 2018), pp. 319–333.

Guerrero, Isabel, "Shakespeare in La Mancha: Performing Shakespeare at the Almagro Corral" (*SEDERI Yearbook* 27, 2017), pp. 27–46.

Gurr, Andrew, "Maximal and Minimal Texts: Shakespeare v. The Globe" (*Shakespeare Survey* 52, 1999), pp. 68–87.

Gurr, Andrew, "The Move Indoors" in Christine Dymkowski and Christie Carson (eds.), *Shakespeare in Stages: New Theatre Histories* (Cambridge: Cambridge University Press, 2010), pp. 7–21.

Gurr, Andrew, *Playgoing in Shakespeare's London* (Cambridge: Cambridge University Press, 1987).

Gurr, Andrew, *The Shakespeare Company, 1594-1642* (Cambridge: Cambridge University Press, 2004).

Gurr, Andrew, *The Shakespearean Stage 1574-1642, Third Edition* (Cambridge: Cambridge University Press, 1992 [orig. ed. 1970]).
Gurr, Andrew, *The Shakespearian Playing Companies* (Oxford: Clarendon Press, 1996).
Gurr, Andrew, "Why was the Globe Round?" in Laury Magnus and Walter W. Cannon (eds.), *Who Hears in Shakespeare?: Auditory Worlds on Stage and Screen* (Madison, NJ: Fairleigh Dickinson University Press, 2012), pp. 3–16.
Gurr, Andrew and Farah Karim-Cooper, "Introduction" in Andrew Gurr and Farah Karim-Cooper (eds.), *Moving Shakespeare Indoors: Performance and Repertoire in the Jacobean Playhouse* (Cambridge: Cambridge University Press, 2014), pp. 1–12.
Gutiérrez, Carlos M., *La espada, el rayo y la pluma: Quevedo y los campos literarios y de poder* (West Lafayette: Purdue University Press, 2005).
Halliday, F.E., *A Shakespeare Companion 1564-1964* (London: Penguin, 1964).
Hammond, Brean (ed.), *Double Falsehood* (London: Methuen, 2010).
Hammond, Brean, "*Double Falsehood*: The Forgery Hypothesis, the 'Charles Dickson' Enigma and a 'Stern' Rejoinder" (*Shakespeare Survey* 67, 2014), pp. 165–179.
Harding, Vanessa, "City, Capital, and Metropolis: The Changing Shape of Seventeenth-century London" in J.F. Merritt (ed.), *Imagining Early Modern London: Perceptions and Portrayals of the City from Stow to Strype, 1598 -1720* (Cambridge: Cambridge University Press, 2001), pp. 117–143.
Harding, Vanessa, "The Population of London, 1550-1700: A Review of the Published Evidence" (*London Journal* 15, 1990), pp. 111–128.
Hart, Alfred, "The Vocabulary of the First Quarto of *Hamlet*" (*The Review of English Studies* 12.45, 1936), pp. 18–30.
Hart, Vaughan, "Introduction: 'Paper Palaces' from Alberti to Scamozzi" in Vaughan Hart and Peter Hicks (eds.), *Paper Palaces: The Rise of the Renaissance Architectural Treatise* (New Haven: Yale University Press, 1998), pp. 1–29.
Henke, Robert, "Border-Crossing in the *Commedia dell'Arte*" in Robert Henke and Eric A. Nicholson (eds.), *Transnational Exchange in Early Modern Theater* (Aldershot: Ashgate, 2008), pp. 19–34.
Henke, Robert, "'Gentleman-like Tears': Affective Response in Italian Tragicomedy and Shakespeare's Late Plays" (*Comparative Literary Studies* 33.4, 1996), pp. 327–349.
Henke, Robert, "*The Winter's Tale* and Guarinian Dramaturgy" (*Comparative Drama* 27.2, 1993), pp. 197–217.
Henke, Robert and Eric A. Nicholson (eds.), *Transnational Exchange in Early Modern Theater* (Aldershot: Ashgate, 2008).
Henke, Robert and Eric A. Nicholson (eds.), *Transnational Mobilities in Early Modern Theater* (Aldershot: Ashgate, 2014).
Hernández Reyes, Dalia, "El teatro de la Compañía de Jesús en las festividades religiosas de la Nueva España (1600-1630)" (*Bulletin of the Comediantes* 58.1, 2006), pp. 89–102.
Higuera Sánchez-Pardo, Mercedes, Juan Sanz Ballesteros and Miguel Ángel Coso Marín, "Alcalá de Henares: un nuevo corral de comedias. Apéndice documental" (*Edad de Oro* 5, 1986), pp. 73–106.
Hill, Tracey, "'He hath changed his coppy': Anti-Theatrical Writing and the Turncoat Player" (*Critical Survey* 9.3, 1997), pp. 59–77.
Hirrel, Michael J., "Duration of Performances and Lengths of Plays: How Shall We Beguile the Lazy Time?" (*Shakespeare Quarterly* 61.2, 2010), pp. 159–182.
Holmes, Rachel E., "A Widow's Will: Adapting the Duchess of Amalfi in Early Modern England and Spain" (*Studies in Philology* 116.4, 2019), pp. 728–757.

Howard, Jean E., *Theater of a City: The Places of London Comedy, 1598-1642* (Philadelphia: University of Pennsylvania Press, 2009 [orig. ed. 2007]).

Hoxby, Blair, *What Was Tragedy?: Theory and the Early Modern Canon* (Oxford: Oxford University Press, 2017).

Huerta Calvo, Javier, "Teoría y formas dramáticas en el siglo XVI" in Javier Huerta Calvo (ed.), *Historia del teatro español, Vol. 1* (Madrid: Gredos, 2003), pp. 303–316.

Hunt, Maurice, "Romance and Tragicomedy" in Arthur F. Kinney (ed.), *A Companion to Renaissance Drama* (Malden: Blackwell, 2002), pp. 384–398.

Ichikawa, Mariko, "Continuities and Innovations in Staging" in Andrew Gurr and Farah Karim-Cooper (eds.), *Moving Shakespeare Indoors: Performance and Repertoire in the Jacobean Playhouse* (Cambridge: Cambridge University Press, 2014), pp. 79–94.

Ichikawa, Mariko, *The Shakespearean Stage Space* (Cambridge: Cambridge University Press, 2013).

Ihinger, Kelsey J., "The Mirror in Albion: Spanish Theatrical Reimaginings of Queen Elizabeth I and Mary Stuart" (*Bulletin of the Comediantes* 70.1, 2018), pp. 33–57.

Ingram, William, *The Business of Playing: The Beginnings of the Adult Professional Theatre in Elizabethan London* (Ithaca: Cornell University Press, 1992).

Ioppolo, Grace, *Dramatists and Their Manuscripts in the Age of Shakespeare, Jonson, Middleton and Heywood: Authorship, Authority and the Playhouse* (London: Routledge, 2006).

Jautze, Kim, Leonor Álvarez Francés and Frans R.E. Blom, "Spaans theater in de Amsterdamse Schouwburg (1638-1672): Kwantitatieve en kwalitatieve analyse van de creatieve industrie van het vertalen" (*De Zeventiende Eeuw* 32.1, 2016), pp. 12–39.

Jeffs, Kathleen, *Staging the Spanish Golden Age: Translation and Performance* (Oxford: Oxford University Press, 2014).

Jenkins, Harold, "Introduction" in *Hamlet* (London: Thomson, 1982), pp. 1–159.

Jenkins, Harold, "The Relation between the Second Quarto and the Folio Text of *Hamlet*" (*Studies in Bibliography* 7, 1955), pp. 69–83.

Juhász-Ormsby, Ágnes, "Dramatic Texts in the Tudor Curriculum: John Palsgrave and the Henrician Educational Reforms" (*Renaissance Studies* 30.4, 2016), pp. 526–541.

Kagan, Richard L., *Students and Society in Early Modern Spain* (Baltimore and London: Johns Hopkins University Press, 1974).

Kagan, Richard L., "The Toledo of El Greco" in *El Greco of Toledo* (Boston: Little Brown and Co., 1982), pp. 35–73.

Kastan, David Scott and Peter Stallybrass, "Staging the Renaissance" in David Scott Kastan and Peter Stallybrass (eds.), *Staging the Renaissance: Reinterpretation of Elizabethan and Jacobean Drama* (New York: Routledge, 1991), pp. 1–14.

Kathman, David, "Grocers, Goldsmiths, and Drapers: Freemen and Apprentices in the Elizabethan Theater" (*Shakespeare Quarterly* 55, 2004), pp. 1–49.

Kathman, David, "How Old Were Shakespeare's Boy Actors?" (*Shakespeare Survey* 58, 2005), pp. 220–246.

Kathman, David, "The London Playing Bust of the Early 1580s and the Economics of Elizabethan Theater" (*Shakespeare Studies* 45, 2017), pp. 41–50.

Kathman, David, "The Rise of Commercial Playing in 1540s London" (*Early Theatre* 12.1, 2009), pp. 15–38.

Katritzky, M.A., *The Art of Commedia: A Study in the Commedia Dell'Arte 1560-1620 with Special Reference to the Visual Records* (New York: Rodopi BV, 2006).

Katritzky, M.A. and Pavel Drábek (eds.), *Transnational Connections in Early Modern Theatre* (Manchester: Manchester University Press, 2020).

Keenan, Siobhan, *Travelling Players in Shakespeare's England* (Basingstoke: Palgrave Macmillan, 2002).
Keenan, Siobhan, *Acting Companies and Their Plays in Shakespeare's London* (London: Bloomsbury, 2014).
Keene, Derek, "Growth, Modernisation and Control: The Transformation of London's Landscape, c. 1500-c. 1760" in Peter Clark and Raymond Gillespie (eds.), *Two Capitals: London and Dublin, 1500-1840* (Oxford: Oxford University Press, 2001), pp. 7–37.
Keene, Derek, "Material London in Time and Space" in Lena Cowen Orlin (ed.), *Material London, ca. 1600* (Philadelphia: University of Pennsylvania Press, 2000), pp. 55–74.
Keene, Derek, "Metropolitan comparisons: London as a city-state" (*Historical Research* 77.198, 2004), pp. 459–480.
Kernan, Alvin, *Shakespeare, the King's Playwright: Theater in the Stuart Court, 1603-1613* (New Haven: Yale University Press, 1995).
Kesson, Andy, "Playhouses, Plays, and Theater History: Rethinking the 1580s" (*Shakespeare Studies* 45, 2017), pp. 19–40.
Kesson, Andy, "Was Comedy a Genre in English Modern Drama?" (*The British Journal of Aesthetics* 54.2, 2014), pp. 213–225.
Kimbrell, Garth, "Taste, Theatrical Venues, and the Rise of English Tragicomedy" (*Studies in English Literature, 1500-1900* 55.2, 2015), pp. 285–307.
King, Willard F., "The Academies and Seventeenth-Century Spanish Literature" (*PMLA* 75.4, 1960), pp. 367–376.
Kinney, Arthur F., *Shakespeare by Stages: An Historical Introduction* (Oxford: Blackwell, 2003).
Kluge, Sofie, "A Hermaphrodite? Lope de Vega and the Controversy of Tragicomedy" (*Comparative Drama* 41.3, 2007), pp. 297–333.
Knight, Sarah, "Literature and Drama at the Early Modern Inns of Court" in Jayne Elisabeth Archer, Elizabeth Goldring and Sarah Knight (eds.), *The Intellectual and Cultural World of the Early Modern Inns of Court* (Manchester: Manchester University Press), pp. 217–222.
Knutson, Roslyn Lander, *Playing Companies and Commerce in Shakespeare's Time* (Cambridge: Cambridge University Press, 2001).
Knutson, Roslyn Lander, "What was James Burbage *Thinking*???" in Peter Kanelos and Matt Kozusko (eds.), *Thunder at a Playhouse: Essaying Shakespeare and the Early Modern Stage* (Selinsgrove: Susquehanna University Press, 2010), pp. 116–130.
Kozusko, Matt, "Taking Liberties" (*Early Theatre* 9.1, 2006), pp. 37–60.
Laroque, François, *Shakespeare's Festive World: Elizabethan Seasonal Entertainment and the Professional Stage* [trans. Janet Lloyd] (Cambridge: Cambridge University Press, 1993).
Larquié, Claude, "Barrios y parroquias urbanas: el ejemplo de Madrid en el siglo XVII" (*Anales del Instituto de Estudios Madrileños* 12, 1976), pp. 33–63.
Leacroft, Richard and Helen Leacroft, *Theatre and Playhouse: An illustrated survey of theatre building from Ancient Greece to the present day* (London and New York: Methuen, 1984).
Lesser, Zachary, "Tragical-Comical-Pastoral-Colonial: Economic Sovereignty, Globalization, and the Form of Tragicomedy" (*ELH* 74.4, 2007), pp. 881–908.
Loengard, Janet S., "An Elizabethan Lawsuit: John Brayne, his Carpenter, and the Building of the Red Lion Theatre" (*Shakespeare Quarterly* 34.3, 1983), pp. 298–310.
Loftis, John, "Lope de Vega's and Webster's Amalfi Plays" (*Comparative Drama* 16.1, 1982), pp. 64–78.

Loftis, John, *Renaissance Drama in England and Spain: Topical Allusions and History Plays* (Princeton: Princeton University Press, 1987).

Lopez, Jeremy, *Constructing the Canon of Early Modern Drama* (Cambridge: Cambridge University Press, 2013).

López, François, "La comedia suelta y compañía, 'mercadería vendible' y teatro para leer" in Josep Maria Sala Valldaura (ed.), *El teatro español del siglo XVIII* (Lleida: Universitat de Lleida, 1996), pp. 589–603.

López García, José Miguel (ed.) *El impacto de la Corte en Castilla. Madrid y su territorio en la época moderna* (Madrid: Siglo XXI, 1998).

López Grigera, Luisa, *La retórica en la España del Siglo de Oro. Teoría y práctica* (Salamanca: Universidad de Salamanca, 1994).

Love, Harold, *Scribal Publication in Seventeenth-Century England* (Oxford: Oxford University Press, 1993).

Luis Martínez, Zenón and Luis Gómez Canseco (eds.), *Entre Cervantes y Shakespeare: Sendas del Renacimiento/Between Cervantes and Shakespeare: Trails along the Renaissance* (Newark, DE: Juan de la Cuesta, 2006).

Luján Atienza, Ángel Luis, *Retóricas españolas del siglo XVI: El foco de Valencia* (Madrid: Consejo de Educación Superior, 1999).

Lyne, Raphael, "English Guarini: Recognition and Reception" (*The Yearbook of English Studies* 36.1, 2006), pp. 90–102.

Mackay, Ruth, *Life in a Time of Pestilence* (Cambridge: Cambridge University Press, 2019).

Mackinder, Anthony, Lyn Blackmore, Julian Bowsher and Christopher Philpotts, *The Hope playhouse, animal baiting and later industrial activity at Bear Gardens on Bankside: Excavations at Riverside House and New Globe Walk, Southwark, 1999-2000* (London: Museum of London Archaeology, 2013).

Madelaine, Richard, "Material Boys: Apprenticeship and the Boy Actors' Shakespearean Roles" in Lloyd Davis (ed.), *Shakespeare Matters: History, Teaching, Performance* (Newark: University of Delaware Press, 2003), pp. 225–238.

Madrazo, Santos and Virgilio Pinto (eds.), *Madrid en la época moderna: Espacio, sociedad y cultura* (Madrid: UAM-Casa de Velázquez, 1991).

Manley, Lawrence, "Why Did London Inns Function as Theaters?" (*Huntington Library Quarterly* 71.1, 2008), pp. 181–197.

Manley, Lawrence and Sally-Beth MacLean, *Lord Strange's Men and Their Plays* (New Haven: Yale University Press, 2014).

Marcos Álvarez, Fernando, "Los teatros fijos de Badajoz en el siglo XVII" (*Epos* 10, 1994), pp. 233–260.

Marcus, Leah S., "Introduction" in John Webster (ed.), *The Duchess of Malfi* (London: Methuen, 2009), pp. 1–113.

Marcus, Leah S., *Puzzling Shakespeare: Local Reading and Its Discontents* (Berkeley: University of California Press, 1988).

Marías, Fernando, "Teatro antiguo y corral de comedias en Toledo: teoría y práctica arquitectónica en el Renacimiento español" in Luciano García Lorenzo (ed.), *Actas del Congreso Internacional sobre Calderón y el teatro español del Siglo de Oro, Vol. III* (Madrid: CSIC, 1983), pp. 1621–1638.

Marín, Diego, *Uso y función de la versificación dramática en Lope de Vega* (Valencia: Castalia, 1968).

Marín, Francisco José and Rafael Mas, "Madrid" in Manuel Guàrdia, Francisco J. Monclús and José Luis Oyón (eds.), *Atlas histórico de ciudades europeas I. Península ibérica* (Madrid: Alianza, 1994), pp. 31–61.

Marino, Giuseppe, "Del peligro de oír comedias lascivas y asistir a bailes y danzas. Un manuscrito inédito y anónimo sobre las controversias teatrales en España, siglo XVII" (*Bulletin of Hispanic Studies* 92.7, 2015), pp. 775–789.
Marnef, Guido, "Chambers of Rhetoric and the Transmission of Religious Ideas in the Low Countries" in Heinz Schilling and István György Tóth (eds.), *Cultural Exchange in Early Modern Europe. Vol. 1. Religion and Cultural Exchange in Europe, 1400-1700* (Cambridge: Cambridge University Press, 2007), pp. 274–293.
Marsá Vila, María, *La imprenta en los Siglos de Oro* (Madrid: Laberinto, 2001).
McCarthy, Jeanne, "The Influence of Children's Stagecraft: Chapel, School, and Popular Performance in the 1580s" (*Shakespeare Studies* 45, 2017), pp. 87–96.
McDonald, Russ, *Shakespeare and the Arts of Language* (Oxford: Oxford University Press, 2001).
McDonald, Russ, *Shakespeare's Late Style* (Cambridge: Cambridge University Press, 2006).
McKendrick, Melveena, *Theatre in Spain, 1490-1700* (Cambridge: Cambridge University Press, 1989).
McKenzie, D.F., *Bibliography and the Sociology of Texts* (Cambridge: Cambridge University Press, 1999 [orig. ed. 1986]).
McManus, Clare, "Women and English Renaissance Drama: Making and Unmaking 'The All-Male Stage'" (*Literature Compass* 4.3, 2007), pp. 784–796.
McManus, Clare, *Women on the Renaissance Stage: Anna of Denmark and Female Masquing at the Stuart Court (1590-1619)* (Manchester: Manchester University Press, 2002).
McMillin, Scott and Sally-Beth MacLean, *The Queen's Men and Their Plays* (Cambridge: Cambridge University Press, 1998).
McMullan, Gordon, "Shakespearean Tragicomedy and the Idea of the 'Late Play'" in Subha Mukerji and Raphael Lyne (eds.), *Early Modern Tragicomedy* (Cambridge: D.S. Brewer, 2007), pp. 115–132.
Menéndez Peláez, Jesús, *Los Jesuitas y el Teatro en el Siglo de Oro* (Oviedo: Universidad de Oviedo, 1995).
Merritt, J.F., "Introduction: Perceptions and portrayals of London, 1598-1720" in J.F. Merritt (ed.), *Imagining Early Modern London: Perceptions and Portrayals of the City from Stow to Strype, 1598 -1720* (Cambridge: Cambridge University Press, 2001), pp. 1–24.
Miguel Gallo, Ignacio Javier de, *El teatro en Burgos (1550-1752): El patio de comedias, las compañías y la actividad escénica. Estudio y Documentos* (Burgos: Ayuntamiento de Burgos, 1994).
Moll, Jaime, *Aspectos de la librería madrileña en el Siglo de Oro* (Madrid: Comunidad de Madrid, 1985).
Moll, Jaime, "El libro del Siglo de Oro" (*Edad de Oro* 1, 1982), pp. 43–54.
Moll, Jaime, *Problemas bibliográficos del libro del Siglo de Oro* (Madrid: Arco Libros, 2011).
Moll, Jaime, "Los surtidos de romances, coplas, historias y otros papeles" in *De la imprenta al lector: estudios sobre el libro español de los siglos XVI al XVIII* (Madrid: Arco Libros, 1994), pp. 45–55.
Moll, Jaime, "Un tomo facticio de pliegos sueltos y el origen de las 'relaciones de comedias'" in *De la imprenta al lector: estudios sobre el libro español de los siglos XVI al XVIII* (Madrid: Arco Libros, 1994), pp. 57–75.
Morales Padrón, Francisco, *Los corrales de vecinos de Sevilla* (Seville: Universidad de Sevilla, 1974).
Morell Peguero, Blanca, *Mercaderes y artesanos en la Sevilla del Descubrimiento* (Seville: Diputación, 1986).

Morley, S. Griswold, "Strophes in the Spanish Drama Before Lope de Vega" in *Homenaje ofrecido a Menéndez Pidal. Miscelánea de estudios lingüísticos, literarios e históricos*, Vol. 1 (Madrid: Editorial Hernando, 1925), pp. 505–531.

Mouyen, Jean, "Las casas de comedies de Valencia" in José María Díez Borque (ed.), *Teatros del Siglo de Oro: corrales y coliseos en la Península Ibérica* (Madrid: Compañía Nacional de Teatro Clásico, 1991), pp. 91–122.

Mullaney, Steven, *The Place of the Stage: License, Play, and Power in Renaissance England* (Ann Arbor: University of Michigan Press, 1988).

Munro, Lucy, *Children of the Queen's Revels: A Jacobean Theatre Repertory* (Cambridge: Cambridge University Press, 2005).

Munro, Lucy, "Children's Companies and the Long 1580s" (*Shakespeare Studies* 45, 2017), pp. 97–105.

Murphy, Andrew, *Shakespeare in Print: A History and Chronology of Shakespeare Publishing* (Cambridge: Cambridge University Press, 2003).

Nicholson, Eric A., "The Theater" in Natalie Zemon Davis and Arlette Farge (eds.), *A History of Women in the West, Vol. III. Renaissance and Enlightenment Paradoxes* (Cambridge, MA: Harvard University Press, 1993 [orig. ed. 1991]), pp. 295–314.

Noguera Guirao, Dolores, "Elena Osorio: ¿una actriz en la etapa de formación de la comedia barroca?" in Odette Gorsse and Frédéric Serralta (eds.), *El Siglo de Oro en escena: Homenaje a Marc Vitse* (Toulouse: Presses Universitaires du Mirail, 2006), pp. 627–638.

Noguera Guirao, Dolores, "Músicos y compañías teatrales en el Siglo de Oro" (*Edad de Oro* 22, 2003), pp. 309–319.

Oehrlein, Josef, "El actor en el Siglo de Oro: imagen de la profesión y reputación social" in José María Díez Borque (ed.), *Actor y técnica de representación del teatro clásico español* (London: Tamesis, 1988), pp. 17–34.

Oehrlein, Josef, *El actor en el teatro español del Siglo de Oro* [trans. Miguel Ángel Vega] (Madrid: Castalia, 1993 [orig. ed. 1986]).

Oehrlein, Josef, "Las compañías de título: Columna vertebral del teatro del Siglo de Oro. Su modo de trabajar y su posición social en la época" in Christoph Strosetzki (ed.), *Teatro español del siglo de oro: teoría y práctica* (Madrid: Vervuert, 1998), pp. 246–262.

Ojeda Calvo, María del Valle, "Poetas y farsantes: el dramaturgo en los inicios de la Comedia Nueva" in Manfred Tietz and Marcella Trambaioli (eds.), *El autor en el Siglo de Oro: Su estatus intelectual y social* (Vigo: Academia del Hispanismo, 2011), pp. 291–304.

Oleza, Joan, "Menéndez Pelayo y Lope de Vega: la lucha por el canon" in Guillermo Serés Guillén and Germán Vega García-Luengos (eds.), *Menéndez Pelayo y Lope de Vega* (Santander: Universidad de Cantabria, 2016), pp. 13–42.

Oleza, Joan and Fausta Antonucci, "La arquitectura de géneros en la *Comedia Nueva*: diversidad y transformaciones" (*RILCE - Revista de Filología Hispánica* 29.3, 2013), pp. 689–741.

Orgel, Stephen, *The Authentic Shakespeare: And Other Problems of the Early Modern Stage* (London: Routledge, 2002).

Orrell, John, "Building the Fortune" (*Shakespeare Quarterly* 44.2, 1993), pp. 127–144.

Orrell, John, *The Human Stage: English Theatre Design 1567-1640* (Cambridge: Cambridge University Press, 1988).

Orrell, John, "Spanish *Corrales* and English Theaters" in Louise Fothergill-Payne and Peter Fothergill-Payne (eds.), *Parallel Lives: Spanish and English National Drama 1580-1680* (London: Bucknell University Press, 1991), pp. 23–38.

Orrell, John, *The Theatres of Inigo Jones and John Webb* (Cambridge: Cambridge University Press, 1985).

Palfrey, Simon and Tiffany Stern, *Shakespeare in Parts* (Oxford: Oxford University Press, 2007).

Pardo Molina, Irene and Rafael González Cañal, "Prólogo a Los Bandos de Verona" [eds. Felipe B. Pedraza Jiménez and Rafael González Cañal] in Francisco de Rojas Zorrilla (ed.), *Obras completas, Volumen IV. Segunda parte de comedias* (Cuenca: Ediciones de la Universidad Castilla-La Mancha, 2012), pp. 171–203.

Parshall, Peter, "Antonio Lafreri's *Speculum Romane Magnificentiae*" (*Print Quarterly* 23.1, 2006), pp. 3–28.

Passini, Jean, *Casas y casas principales urbanas: el espacio doméstico de Toledo a fines de la Edad Media* (Toledo: Universidad de Castilla-La Mancha, 2004).

Paster, Gail Kern, *The Idea of the City in the Age of Shakespeare* (Athens: The University of Georgia Press, 1985).

Paun de García, Susan and Donald R. Larson, "Introduction: The *Comedia* in English: An Overview of Translation and Performance" in Susan Paun de García and Donald R. Larson (eds.), *The Comedia in English: Translation and Performance* (London: Tamesis, 2008), pp. 1–34.

Payne, Deborah C. (ed.), *Revisiting Shakespeare's Lost Play: Cardenio/Double Falsehood in the Eighteenth Century* (Basingstoke: Palgrave Macmillan, 2016).

Pedraza Jiménez, Felipe B., "Menéndez Pelayo: de la edición académica a los *Estudios sobre el teatro de Lope de Vega*" (*Monteagudo* 17, 2012), pp. 85–96.

Peraita, Carmen, "*Mar de tinta*. Espacios femeninos en la venta de libros y pliegos de cordel en la comedia de Lope de Vega" in Odette Gorsse and Frédéric Serralta (eds.), *El Siglo de Oro en escena: Homenaje a Marc Vitse* (Toulouse: Presses Universitaires du Mirail, 2006), pp. 767–778.

Pérez Díez, José A., "The 'Playhouse' at St Paul's: What We Know of the Theatre in the Almonry" in Shanyn Altman and Jonathan Buckner (eds.), *Old St Paul's and Culture* (Cham: Palgrave Macmillan, 2021), pp. 197–220.

Pettegree, Andrew, *The Book in the Renaissance* (New Haven and London: Yale University Press, 2011).

Pineda Novo, Daniel, *El teatro de comedias del Corral de la monteria del alcazar de Sevilla* (Seville: Guadalquivir, 2000).

Pinto Crespo, Virgilio and Santos Madrazo Madrazo (eds.), *Madrid. Atlas histórico de la ciudad. Siglos IX-XIX* (Madrid: Fundación Caja de Madrid - Lunwerg, 1995).

Porter, Stephen, *Shakespeare's London: Everyday Life in London, 1580-1616* (Stroud: Amberley, 2011).

Presotto, Marco, *Le commedie autografe di Lope de Vega* (Kassel: Reichenberger, 2000).

Prest, Wilfrid R., *The Inns of Court under Elizabeth I and the Early Stuarts, 1590-1640* (Aylesbury: Longman, 1972).

Prieto Bernabé, José Manuel, *Lectura y lectores. La cultura del impreso en el Madrid del Siglo de Oro, 1550-1650, 2 vols.* (Mérida: Editora Regional de Extremadura, 2004).

Rackin, Phyllis, *Shakespeare and Women* (Oxford: Oxford University Press, 2005).

Rappaport, Steve, *Worlds Within Worlds: Structures of Life in Sixteenth-Century London* (Cambridge: Cambridge University Press, 1989).

Rey Hazas, Antonio, "El Madrid literario en la Edad Moderna" in Virgilio Pinto and Santos Madrazo Madrazo (eds.), *Madrid. Atlas histórico de la ciudad. Siglos IX-XIX* (Madrid: Fundación Caja de Madrid - Lunwerg, 1995), pp. 362–373.

Reyes Gómez, Fermín de los, *El libro en España y en América: Legislación y censura. Vol. 1 siglos XV-XVIII* (Madrid: Arco Libros, 2000).
Reyes Gómez, Fermín de los and Silvia González-Sarasa Hernáez, "El taller de Juan de la Cuesta y la impresión del *Quijote*" in Víctor Infantes (ed.), *La primera salida de El ingenioso hidalgo don Quijote de la Mancha (Madrid, Juan de la Cuesta, 1605): La historial editorial de un libro* (Alcalá de Henares: Biblioteca de Estudios Cervantinos, 2013), pp. 293-351.
Reyes Peña, Mercedes de los, "Los carteles de teatro en el Siglo de Oro" (*Criticón* 59, 1993), pp. 99-118.
Reyes Peña, Mercedes de los, "Nueva entrega sobre carteles de teatro áureo" in Odette Gorsse and Frédéric Serralta (eds.), *El Siglo de Oro en escena: Homenaje a Marc Vitse* (Toulouse: Presses Universitaires du Mirail, 2006), pp. 837-855.
Reyes Peña, Mercedes de los and Piedad Bolaños Donoso, "El Patio de las Arcas de Lisboa" in José María Díez Borque (ed.), *Teatros del Siglo de Oro: corrales y coliseos en la Península Ibérica* (Madrid: Ministerio de Cultura, 1991), pp. 265-315.
Rhodes, Neil, *Shakespeare and the Origins of English* (Oxford: Oxford University Press, 2004).
Rico Verdú, José, *La retorica española de los siglos XVI y XVII* (Madrid: CSIC, 1973).
Ringrose, David R., *Madrid and the Spanish Economy, 1560-1850* (Berkeley: University of California Press, 1983).
Ringrose, David R., "The Paradoxes of a Royal City: Madrid and the Transmission of Values in Spanish Culture" in Peter Clark and Herman Van der Wee (eds.), *Cities and Transmission of Cultural Values in the Late Middle Ages and the Early Modern Period* (Brussels: Crédit Communal de Belgique, 1996), pp. 19-33.
Ringrose, David R., "A Setting for Royal Authority: The Reshaping of Madrid, Sixteenth to Eighteenth Centuries" in Gary B. Cohen and Franz A.J. Szabo (eds.), *Embodiments of Power: Building Baroque Cities in Europe* (New York: Berghahn, 2008), pp. 230-248.
Río Barredo, María José del, *Madrid, Urbs Regia: La capital ceremonial de la Monarquía Católica* (Madrid: Marcial Pons, 2000).
Robertson, James, "Stuart London and the Idea of a Royal Capital City" (*Renaissance Studies* 15.1, 2001), pp. 37-58.
Rodríguez Cáceres, Milagros and Felipe Pedraza Jiménez, "Lope de Vega y su teatro ante los hombres de su tiempo" in Milagros Rodríguez Cáceres and Felipe Pedraza Jiménez (eds.), *El Siglo de Oro habla de Lope* (Madrid: Ministerio de Cultura - Instituto Nacional de las Artes Escénicas y de la Música, 2011), pp. 15-34.
Rodríguez Cuadros, Evangelina, "The art of the actor, 1565-1833: From moral suspicion to social institution" in María M. Delgado and David T. Gies (eds.), *A History of the Theatre in Spain* (Cambridge: Cambridge University Press, 2012), pp. 103-119.
Rodríguez-Badendyck, Cynthia, "The Neglected Alternative: Shakespeare's *Romeo and Juliet* and Lope de Vega's *Castelvines y Monteses*" in Louise Fothergill-Payne and Peter Fothergill-Payne (eds.), *Parallel Lives: Spanish and English Drama, 1580-1680* (Lewisburg PA: Bucknell University Press, 1991), pp. 91-107.
Rogers, Gayle, "Ezra Pound, 'lopista'" (*Anuario Lope de Vega* 22, 2016), pp. 217-237.
Romero Tobar, Leonard, "La edición del teatro de Lope de Vega y su contexto histórico-literario" in Guillermo Serés Guillén and Germán Vega García-Luengos (eds.), *Menéndez Pelayo y Lope de Vega* (Santander: Universidad de Cantabria, 2016), pp. 43-58.

Romero-Díaz, Nieves and Lisa Vollendorf (eds.), *Women Playwrights of Early Modern Spain: Feliciana Enríquez de Guzmán, Ana Caro Mallén, and Sor Marcela de San Félix* [trans. Harley Erdman] (Tempe: Arizona Center for Medieval and Renaissance Studies, 2016).

Rosenbaum, Ron, "Shakespeare in Rewrite" (*The New Yorker*, 13 May 2002), pp. 68–77.

Ruano de la Haza, José María, "An Early Rehash of Lope's *Peribañez*" (*Bulletin of the Comediantes* 35, 1983), pp. 5–29.

Ruano de la Haza, José María, "Una nota sobre la cazuela alta del corral del Príncipe" (*Bulletin of the Comediantes* 41.1, 1989), pp. 45–49.

Ruano de la Haza, José María, *La puesta en escena de los teatros comerciales del Siglo de Oro* (Madrid: Castalia, 2000).

Ruano de la Haza, José María, "Spanish Classical Theater in Britain and North America" (*Romance Quarterly* 52.1, 2005), pp. 2–12.

Ruano de la Haza, José María and John J. Allen, *Los teatros comerciales del siglo XVII y la escenificación de la Comedia* (Madrid: Castalia, 1994).

Ruge, Enno, "Having a Good Time at the Theatre of the World: Amusement, Antitheatricality and the Calvinist Use of the Theatrum Mundi Metaphor in Early Modern England" in Björn Quiring (ed.), *'If Then the World a Theatre Present ... ': Revisions of the Theatrum Mundi Metaphor in Early Modern England* (Berlin-Boston: De Gruyter, 2014), pp. 25–38.

Rutter, Tom, "Repertory Studies: A Survey" (*Shakespeare* 4.3, 2008), pp. 336–350.

Sacks, David Harris, "London's Dominion: The Metropolis, the Market Economy and the State" in Lena Cowen Orlin (ed.), *Material London, ca. 1600* (Philadelphia: University of Pennsylvania Press, 2000), pp. 20–54.

Sáez Raposo, Francisco, "Las aspiraciones creativas de un copista: La intervención de Diego Martínez de Mora en *Un castigo en tres venganzas*" (*Anuario calderoniano* 3, 2010), pp. 321–332.

Salkeld, Duncan, *Shakespeare Among the Courtesans: Prostitution, Literature, and Drama, 1500-1650* (Farnham: Ashgate, 2012).

Samson, Alexander, "Cervantes on the 17th century English Stage" in J.A.G. Ardila (ed.), *The Cervantean Heritage: Influence and Reception of Cervantes in Britain* (Oxford: Legenda, 2009), pp. 206–222.

Samson, Alexander, "Distinct Drama? Female Dramatists in Golden Age Spain" in Xon de Ros and Geraldine Hazbun (eds.), *A Companion to Spanish Women's Studies* (London: Tamesis, 2011), pp. 157–172.

Samson, Alexander, "Exchanges: Time to Face the Strange" in Helen Hackett (ed.), *Early Modern Exchanges: Dialogues Between Nations and Cultures, 1550-1750* (London: Ashgate, 2015), pp. 243–250.

Samson, Alexander, "A Fine Romance: Anglo-Spanish Relations in the Sixteenth Century" (*Journal of Medieval and Early Modern Studies* 39.1, 2009), pp. 65–94.

Samson, Alexander, "'Last Thought Upon a Windmill': Fletcher and Cervantes" in J.A.G. Ardila (ed.), *The Cervantean Heritage: Influence and Reception of Cervantes in Britain* (Oxford: Legenda, 2009), pp. 223–233.

Samson, Alexander and Jonathan Thacker, "Introduction: Lope's Life and Work" in Alexander Samson and Jonathan Thacker (eds.), *A Companion to Lope de Vega* (Woodbridge: Tamesis, 2008), pp. 1–12.

Sánchez Escribano, Federico and Alberto Porqueras Mayo, *Preceptiva dramática española del Renacimiento y el Barroco, 2da edición* (Madrid: Gredos, 1972 [orig. ed. 1965]).

Sánchez, José, *Academias literarias del Siglo de Oro español* (Madrid: Gredos, 1961).
Sánchez Jiménez, Antonio, "Vulgo, imitación y natural en el *Arte nuevo de hacer comedias* (1609) de Lope de Vega" (*Bulletin of Hispanic Studies* 88.7, 2011), pp. 727–742.
Sánchez Mariana, Manuel, "Los manuscritos dramáticos del Siglo de Oro" in *Ex Libris. Homenaje al profesor Fradejas Lebrero, vol. 1* (Madrid: UNED, 1993), pp. 441–452.
Sánchez Rubio, Mª Antonia, "Mesón de la Fruta y Teatro de Rojas de Toledo" (*Docencia e Investigación: Revista de la Escuela Universitaria de Magisterio de Toledo* 25.10, 2000), pp. 185–215.
Sanders, Julie, "'In the Friars': The Spatial and Cultural Geography of an Indoor Playhouse" (*Cahiers Élisabéthains* 88, 2015), pp. 19–33.
Santos de la Morena, Blanca, "Lope y la tragedia 'al estilo español': hacia *El castigo sin venganza*" (*Dicenda. Cuadernos de Filología Hispánica* 32, 2014), pp. 73–82.
Sanz Ayán, Carmen, *Hacer escena: Capítulos de historia de la empresa teatral en el Siglo de Oro* (Madrid: Real Academia de la Historia, 2013).
Sanz Ayán, Carmen, "More Than Faded Beauties: Women Theater Managers of Early Modern Spain" (*Early Modern Women: An Interdisciplinary Journal* 10.1, 2015), pp. 114–121.
Sanz Ayán, Carmen, "To Conquer Paris: Spanish Actresses at the Court of Louis XIV (1660-1674)" in Anne J. Cruz and María Cristina Quintero (eds.), *Beyond Spain's Borders: Women Players in Early Modern National Theaters* (London and New York: Routledge, 2017), pp. 49–65.
Sanz Ayán, Carmen and Bernardo J. García García, *Teatros y comediantes en el Madrid de Felipe II* (Madrid: Editorial Complutense, 2000).
Scammacca del Murgo, Agnese, "Gli amanti di Verona tra Lope de Vega e William Shakespeare" (*Artifara* 15, 2015), pp. 185–212.
Schofield, John, "The Topography and Buildings of London, ca. 1600" in Lena Cowen Orlin (ed.), *Material London, ca. 1600* (Philadelphia: University of Pennsylvania Press, 2000), pp. 296–321.
Schoone-Jongen, Terence G., *Shakespeare's Companies: William Shakespeare's Early Career and the Acting Companies, 1577–1594* (Farnham: Ashgate, 2008).
Sentaurens, Jean, "Los corrales de comedias de Sevilla" in José María Díez Borque (ed.), *Teatros del Siglo de Oro: corrales y coliseos en la Península Ibérica* (Madrid: Compañía Nacional de Teatro Clásico, 1991), pp. 69–90.
Sentaurens, Jean, "De artesanos a histriones: la tradición gremial como escuela de formación de los primeros actores profesionales. El ejemplo de Sevilla" (*Edad de Oro* 16, 1997), pp. 297–303.
Sentaurens, Jean, "Séville dans la seconde moitié du XVIe siècle: population et structures sociales. Le recensement de 1561" (*Bulletin Hispanique* 77, 1975), pp. 321–390.
Sentaurens, Jean, *Seville et le théatre, de la fin du Moyen Age à la fin du XVIIIe siècle* (Bordeaux: Presses Universitaires de France, 1984).
Shapiro, Michael, *Children of the Revels: The Boy Companies of Shakespeare's Time and Their Plays* (New York: Columbia University Press, 1977).
Shergold, N.D., "Documentos sobre Cosme Lotti, escenógrafo de Felipe IV" in Karl-Hermann Körner and Klaus Rühl (eds.), *Studia Iberica. Festschrift für Hans Flasche* (Bern: Francke, 1973), pp. 589–602.
Shergold, N.D., "Ganassa and the *Commedia dell'Arte* in Sixteenth-Century Spain" (*Modern Language Review* 51.3, 1956), pp. 359–368.

Shergold, N.D., *A History of the Spanish Stage: From Medieval Times Until the End of the Seventeenth Century* (Oxford: Clarendon Press, 1967).
Shergold, N.D. and J.E. Varey, *Los Autos sacramentales en Madrid en la época de Calderón: 1637-1681. Estudios y Documentos* (Madrid: Ediciones de Historia, Geografía y Arte, 1961).
Sidney, Philip, *The Defence of Poesie* (London: William Ponsonby, 1595).
Simón Díaz, José, *El libro antiguo español: análisis de su estructura* (Madrid: Ollero & Ramos, 2000).
Smith, Bruce R., *The Acoustic World of Early Modern England: Attending the O-Factor* (Chicago: University of Chicago Press, 1999).
Smith, Dawn L., "Text, Stage, and Public in Webster's *The Duchess of Malfi* and Lope's *El mayordomo de la Duquesa de Amalfi*" in Louise Fothergill-Payne and Peter Fothergill-Payne (eds.), *Parallel Lives: Spanish and English Drama, 1580-1680* (Lewisburg PA: Bucknell University Press, 1991), pp. 75–90.
Smith, Irwin, *Shakespeare's Blackfriars Playhouse: Its History and Its Design* (New York: New York University Press, 1964).
Smout, Clare, "Actor, Poet, Playwright, Sharer ... Rival? Shakespeare and Heywood, 1603-4" (*Early Theatre* 13.2, 2010), pp. 175–189.
Southern, Richard, *The Medieval Theatre in the Round: A Study of the Staging of the Castle of Perseverance and Related Matters* (London: Faber & Faber, 1975 [orig. ed. 1957]).
Southern, Richard, *The Staging of Plays before Shakespeare* (London: Faber & Faber, 1973).
Stern, Tiffany, *Documents of Performance in Early Modern England* (Cambridge: Cambridge University Press, 2009).
Stern, Tiffany, "'The Forgery of some modern Author'?: Theobald's Shakespeare and Cardenio's *Double Falsehood*" (*Shakespeare Quarterly* 62.4, 2011), pp. 555–593.
Stern, Tiffany, "'I Have Both the Note, and Dittie About Me': Songs on the Early Modern Page and Stage" (*Common Knowledge* 17.2, 2011), pp. 306–320.
Stern, Tiffany, "'On each Wall and Corner Poast': Playbills, Title-pages, and Advertising in Early Modern London" (*English Literary Renaissance* 36, 2006), pp. 57–85.
Stern, Tiffany, "'A ruinous monastery': the Second Blackfriars Playhouse as a place of nostalgia" in Andrew Gurr and Farah Karim-Cooper (eds.), *Moving Shakespeare Indoors* (Cambridge: Cambridge University Press, 2014), pp. 97–114.
Stern, Tiffany, "Sermons, Plays and Note-Takers: *Hamlet* Q1 as a 'Noted' Text" (*Shakespeare Survey* 66, 2013), pp. 1–23.
Stern, Tiffany, "'A Small-Beer Health to His Second Day': Playwrights, Prologues, and First Performances in the Early Modern Theater" (*Studies in Philology* 101.2, 2004), pp. 172–199.
Stern, Tiffany, "The theatre of Shakespeare's London" in Margreta de Grazia and Stanley Wells (eds.), *The New Companion to Shakespeare, Second Edition* (Cambridge: Cambridge University Press, 2010), pp. 45–59.
Stern, Tiffany, "Watching as Reading: The Audience and Written Text in Shakespeare's Playhouse" in Laurie Maguire (ed.), *How to Do Things with Shakespeare* (Oxford: Blackwell, 2008), pp. 136–159.
Stokes, James, "The Ongoing Exploration of Women and Performance in Early Modern England: Evidences, Issues, and Questions" (*Shakespeare Bulletin* 33.1, 2015), pp. 9–31.
Stoll, Anita K. (ed.), *Vidas paralelas: el teatro español y el teatro isabelino, 1580-1680* (London: Tamesis, 1993).

Stone, Lawrence, "The Residential Development of the West End of London in the Seventeenth Century" in Barbara C. Malament (ed.), *After the Reformation: Essays in Honour of J.H. Hexter* (Manchester: Manchester University Press, 1980), pp. 167–211.

Straznicky, Marta, "Private drama" in Laura Lunger Knoppers (ed.), *The Cambridge Companion to Early Modern Women's Writings* (Cambridge: Cambridge University Press, 2009), pp. 247–259.

Streete, Adrian, *Protestantism and Drama in Early Modern England* (Cambridge: Cambridge University Press, 2009).

Súarez García, José Luis, "Enemigos del teatro en el Siglo de Oro: el padre Juan de Mariana" in Ysla Campbell (ed.), *El escritor y la escena III: estudios en honor de Francisco Ruiz Ramón : actas del III Congreso de la Asociación Internacional de Teatro Español y Novohispano de los Siglos de Oro (9-12 de marzo de 1994, Ciudad Juárez)* (Ciudad Juárez: Universidad Autónoma de Ciudad Juárez, 1995), pp. 119–133.

Súarez García, José Luis, "La licitud del teatro en el reinado de Felipe II: textos y pre-textos" (*XXI Jornadas de teatro clásico, Almagro*, 1998), pp. 219–251.

Subirá, José, *El gremio de representantes españoles y la cofradía de Nuestra Señora de la Novena* (Madrid: Instituto de Estudios Madrileños, 1960).

Sullivan, Henry W., *Tragic Drama in the Golden Age of Spain: Seven Essays on the Definition of a Genre* (Kassel: Reichenberger, 2018).

Syme, Holger Schott, "Thomas Creede, William Barkley, and the Venture of Printing Plays" in Marta Straznicky (ed.), *Shakespeare's Stationers: Studies in Cultural Bibliography* (Philadelphia: University of Pennsylvania Press, 2013), pp. 28–46.

Syme, Holger Schott, "Unediting the Margin: Jonson, Marston, and the Theatrical Page" (*English Literary Renaissance* 38.1, 2008), pp. 142–171.

Tercero Casado, Luis, "'It's a Spanish *comedia*, and therefore it's better than any other fête': Empress Margarita María and Spanish Cultural Influence on the Imperial Court" in Anne J. Cruz and María Cristina Quintero (eds.), *Beyond Spain's Borders: Women Players in Early Modern National Theaters* (London and New York: Routledge, 2017), pp. 91–109.

Thacker, Jonathan, *A Companion to Golden Age Theatre* (London: Tamesis, 2010 [orig. ed. 2007]).

Thacker, Jonathan, "Lope de Vega, Calderón de la Barca and Tirso de Molina: Spain's Golden Age drama and its legacy" in María M. Delgado and David T. Gies (eds.), *A History of the Theatre in Spain* (Cambridge: Cambridge University Press, 2012), pp. 36–56.

Thacker, Jonathan, "'Puedo yo con sola la vista oír leyendo': Reading, Seeing, and Hearing the *Comedia*" (*Comedia Performance* 1, 2004), pp. 143–173.

Thomas, Hugh (ed.), *Madrid: A Travellers' Companion* (London: Constable, 1988).

Thompson, Ann and Neil Taylor, "Introduction" in *Hamlet, Revised Edition* (London: Methuen, 2016 [orig. ed. 2006]), pp. 1–168.

Thomson, Leslie, "Staging on the Road, 1586-1594: A New Look at Some Old Assumptions" (*Shakespeare Quarterly* 61.4, 2010), pp. 526–550.

Tittler, Robert, *Architecture and Power: The Town Hall and the English Urban Community c. 1500-1640* (Oxford: Clarendon Press, 1991).

Tomlinson, Sophie, *Women on Stage in Stuart Drama* (Cambridge: Cambridge University Press, 2005).

Tootalian, Jacob, "Without Measure: The Language of Shakespeare's Prose" (*Journal for Early Modern Cultural Studies* 13.4, 2013), pp. 47–60.

Tosh, Will, *Playing Indoors: Staging Early Modern Drama in the Sam Wanamaker Playhouse* (London: Bloomsbury, 2018).
Tribble, Evelyn, "Marlowe's Boy Actors" (*Shakespeare Bulletin* 27.1, 2009), pp. 5–17.
Tronch Pérez, Jesús, "A Comparison of the Suspect Texts of Lope de Vega's *La dama boba* and Shakespeare's *Hamlet*" in José Manuel González and Holger Klein (eds.), *Shakespeare Yearbook XIII. Shakespeare and Spain* (Lewiston: The Edwin Mellen Press, 2002), pp. 30–57.
Turner, Henry S., *The English Renaissance Stage: Geometry, Poetics, and the Practical Spatial Arts 1580-1630* (Oxford: Oxford University Press, 2006).
Urkowitz, Steven, "Did Shakespeare's Company Cut Long Plays Down to Two Hours Playing Time?" (*Shakespeare Bulletin* 30.3, 2012), pp. 239–262.
Vaccari, Debora, "Notas sueltas sobre la relación entre los papeles de actor y el primer Lope de Vega" in Xavier Tubau (ed.), *"Áun no dejó la pluma": Estudios sobre el teatro de Lope de Vega* (Bellaterra: Universitat Autònoma de Barcelona, 2009), pp. 11–49.
Varey, John E., "Memory Theaters, Playhouses, and *Corrales de Comedias*" in Louise Fothergill-Payne and Peter Fothergill-Payne (eds.), *Parallel Lives: Spanish and English National Drama 1580-1680* (London: Bucknell University Press, 1991), pp. 39–53.
Varey, John E. and Charles Davis, "The Corral del Príncipe in 1609" (*Bulletin of Hispanic Studies* 70, 1993), pp. 53–63.
Varey, J.E. and N.D. Shergold, *Teatros y comedias en Madrid: 1600-1650. Estudio y documentos* (London: Tamesis, 1971).
Varey, J.E., N.D. Shergold and Charles Davis (eds.), *Los arriendos de los corrales de comedias de Madrid: 1587-1719. Estudio y documentos* (London: Tamesis, 1987).
Vega García-Luengos, Germán, "La investigación sobre los formatos del teatro español del siglo XVII en la imprenta" (*Bibliologia* 4, 2009), pp. 21–45.
Vega García-Luengos, Germán, "La transmisión del teatro en el siglo XVII" in Javier Huerta Calvo (ed.), *Historia del teatro español, 2 vols.* (Madrid: Gredos, 2003), pp. 1289–1320.
Vickers, Brian, *The Artistry of Shakespeare's Prose* (London: Methuen, 1968).
Villalba Pérez, Enrique, "Notas sobre la prostitución en Madrid a comienzos del siglo XVII" (*Anales del Instituto de Estudios Madrileños* 34, 1994), pp. 505–519.
Villalba Pérez, Enrique, *¿Pecadoras o delincuentes? Delito y género en la corte (1580-1630)* (Madrid: Calambur, 2004).
Vince, Ronald, "Historicizing the Sixteenth-Century Playhouse" in Paul C. Castagno (ed.), *Theatrical Spaces and Dramatic Places: The Reemergence of the Theatre Building in the Renaissance* (Tuscaloosa: University of Alabama Press, 1991), pp. 39–50.
Vitse, Marc, "Polimetría y estructuras dramáticas en la comedia de corral del siglo XVII: el ejemplo de *El burlador de Sevilla*" in Ysla Campbell (ed.), *El escritor y la escena VI: Estudios sobre teatro español y novohispano de los Siglos de Oro* (Ciudad de Juárez: Universidad Autónoma de Ciudad Juárez, 1998), pp. 45–61.
Vitse, Marc, "Teoría y géneros dramáticos en el siglo XVII" in Javier Huerta Calvo (ed.), *Historia del teatro español, Vol. 1.* (Madrid: Gredos, 2003), pp. 717–755.
Walthaus, Rina and Marguérite Corporaal (eds.), *Heroines of the Golden Stage. Women and Drama in Spain and England, 1500-1700* (Kassel: Reichenberger, 2008).
Ward, Joseph P., "The Taming of the Thames: Reading the River in the Seventeenth Century" (*Huntington Library Quarterly* 71.1, 2008), pp. 55–75.
Weimann, Robert, *Shakespeare and the Popular Tradition in the Theater: Studies in the Social Dimension of Dramatic Form and Function* [ed. Robert Schwarz] (Baltimore: Johns Hopkins University, 1978 [orig. ed. 1967]).

Weis, René, "Introduction" in William Shakespeare (ed.), *Romeo and Juliet* (London: Bloomsbury, 2012), pp. 1–116.

Weissbourd, Emily, "Spain and the Rhetoric of Imperial Rivalry in Webster's *The Duchess of Malfi*" in Barbara Fuchs and Emily Weissbourd (eds.), *Representing Imperial Rivalry in the Early Modern Mediterranean* (Toronto: University of Toronto Press, 2015), pp. 217–232.

Wells, Stanley, *Shakespeare for All Time* (London: Macmillan, 2002).

Wells, Stanley and Gary Taylor (eds.), *William Shakespeare: The Complete Works* (Oxford: Clarendon Press, 1988).

Wesley, John, "Rhetorical Delivery for Renaissance English: Voice, Gesture, Emotion, and the Sixteenth-Century Vernacular Turn" (*Renaissance Quarterly* 68.4, 2015), pp. 1265–1296.

West, William, "The Idea of a Theater: Humanist Ideology and the Imaginary Stage in Early Modern Europe" in Jeffrey Masten and Wendy Wall (eds.), *Renaissance Drama XXVIII: The Space of the Stage* (Evanston: Northwestern University Press, 1999), pp. 245–287.

Wheeler, Duncan, *Golden Age Drama in Contemporary Spain: The Comedia on Page, Stage and Screen* (Cardiff: University of Wales Press, 2012).

Whinnom, Keith, "The Problem of the 'Best-Seller' in Spanish Golden-Age Literature" (*Bulletin of Hispanic Studies* 57, 1980), pp. 189–198.

White, Martin (dir.), *The Chamber of Demonstrations: Reconstructing the Jacobean Indoor Playhouse* [script by Martin White] (Ignition Films, 2007).

White, Martin (dir.), *Renaissance Drama in Action: An Introduction to Aspects of Theatre Practice and Performance* (London and New York: Routledge, 1998).

White, Martin (dir.), "'When Torchlight Made an Artificial Noon': Light and Darkness in the Early Modern Playhouse" in Andrew Gurr and Farah Karim-Cooper (eds.), *Moving Shakespeare Indoors: Performance and Repertoire in the Jacobean Playhouse* (Cambridge: Cambridge University Press, 2014), pp. 115–136.

White, Martin (dir.), "William Poel's Globe" (*Theatre Notebook* 53.3, 1999), pp. 146–162.

Wickham, Glynne, *Early English Stages 1300 to 1660, Volume Two: 1576 to 1660, Part I* (London: Routledge, 2002 [orig. ed. 1963]).

Wickham, Glynne, Herbert Berry and William Ingram (eds.), *English Professional Theatre, 1530-1660* (Cambridge: Cambridge University Press, 2000).

Williams, Laura, "'To Recreate and Refresh Their Dulled Spirits in the Sweet and Wholesome Ayre': Green Space and the Growth of the City" in J.F. Merritt (ed.), *Imagining Early Modern London: Perceptions and Portrayals of the City from Stow to Strype, 1598 -1720* (Cambridge: Cambridge University Press, 2001), pp. 185–213.

Williamsen, Vern G., "A Commentary on 'The Uses of Polymetry' and the Editing of the Multi-Strophic Texts of the Spanish Comedia" in Frank Paul Casa and Michael McGaha (eds.), *Editing the Comedia, Vol 1* (Ann Arbor: University of Michigan Press, 1985), pp. 126–145.

Wilson, Edward M., "Some Calderonian *Pliegos Sueltos*" in *Homenaje a J.A. Van Praag* (Amsterdam: L.J. Veen's Uitgeversmaatschappij N.V., 1956), pp. 140–144.

Wilson, John Dover, *Life in Shakespeare's England: A Book of Elizabethan Prose* (Harmondsworth: Penguin, 1962).

Winston, Jessica, *Lawyers at Play: Literature, Law, and Politics at the Early Modern Inns of Court, 1558-1581* (Oxford: Oxford University Press, 2016).

Wright, Elizabeth R., *Pilgrimage to Patronage: Lope de Vega and the Court of Philip III, 1598-1621* (London: Associated University Presses, 2001).

Wright, George T., "An Almost Oral Art: Shakespeare's Language on Stage and Page" (*Shakespeare Quarterly* 43.2, 1992), pp. 159–169.

Wright, George T., *Shakespeare's Metrical Art* (Berkeley: University of California Press, 1988).

Wrightson, Keith, "'Sorts of People' in Tudor and Stuart England" in Jonathan Barry and Christopher Brooks (eds.), *The Middling Sort of People: Culture, Society and Politics in England, 1550-1800* (Basingstoke: Macmillan, 1994), pp. 28–51.

Yachnin, Paul, "The Reformation of Space in Shakespeare's Playhouse" in Angela Vanhaelen and Joseph P. Ward (eds.), *Making Space Public in Early Modern Europe: Performance, Geography, Privacy* (Abingdon: Routledge, 2013), pp. 262–280.

Yates, Frances A., *Theatre of the World* (Chicago: University of Chicago Press, 1969).

Zofio Llorente, Juan Carlos, *Gremios y artesanos en Madrid, 1550-1650. La sociedad del trabajo en una ciudad cortesana preindustrial* (Madrid: CSIC, 2005).

Zofio Llorente, Juan Carlos, "Trabajo y emigración en el Madrid de los siglos XVI y XVII" (*Torre de Lujanes* 62, 2008), pp. 97–110.

Zorach, Rebecca, *The Virtual Tourist in Renaissance Rome: Printing and Collecting the Speculum Romane Magnificentiae* (Chicago: University of Chicago Press, 2008).

Digital Projects

Records of Early English Drama [http://reed.utoronto.ca], accessed 18/6/2022.

TC/12: Red del Patrimonio Teatral Clásico Español [https://tc12.uv.es/], accessed 18/6/2022.

ONSTAGE: Online Datasystem of Theatre in Amsterdam from the Golden Age to the present [https://www.vondel.humanities.uva.nl/onstage], accessed 18/6/2022.

Amelang, David J. (coord.), *Rolecall: A Database of Characters in Early Modern European Theatre* [http://www.rolecall.eu]), accessed 18/6/2022.

Amelang, David J. (coord.), *SdOCORRALES: Corrales de Comedias del Siglo de Oro Español* [http://www.sdocorrales.com], accessed 18/6/2022.

Bolaños Donoso, Piedad, Mercedes de los Reyes Peña, Vicente Palacios and Juan Ruesga Navarro (coords.), *Grupo de investigación teatro Siglo de Oro* [http://www.investigacionteatrosiglodeoro.com], accessed 18/6/2022.

Ferrer Valls, Teresa (coord.), *Diccionario biográfico de actores del teatro clásico español (DICAT)* [DVD-ROM] (Kassel: Reichenberger, 2008).

Kesson, Andy (coord.), *Before Shakespeare: The Beginnings of London Commercial Theatre, 1565-1595* [http://www.beforeshakespeare.com], accessed 18/6/2022.

Oleza, Joan (coord.), *ArteLope: Base de Datos y Argumentos del teatro de Lope de Vega* [https://artelope.uv.es/], accessed 18/6/2022.

Presotto, Marco (coord.), *La Dama Boba: Edición Crítica y Archivo Digital* [http://damaboba.unibo.it/], accessed 18/6/2022.

INDEX

acoustics 46, 56, 57–59, 75
actresses 45, 86, 92–96, 127–132
Admiral's Men 84
Alcalá de Henares 34, 54, 63
Alleyn, Edward 79, 82, 84
Almagro 34, 44–45, 63
America 11, 117, 168
animal baiting 12, 13, 18, 19, 48, 50
apprentices 83, 86, 93
Aristotle 110–111, 130
Athens 8
Aulnoy, Madame D' 156
autos sacramentales 63, 64, 76, 91, 113, 115, 116, 117, 128

Badajoz 21, 54
Bandello, Matteo 110
Bath 172
Beaumont, Francis 124, 129, 132, 153, 154, 156, 164, 165
Beeston, Christopher 82
Boaistuau, Pierre 110
Boccaccio, Giovanni 123
Boswell, Laurence 172
Brayne, John and Margaret 16, 45–46, 47, 48, 50
Bristol 13, 33–34, 89
Brooke, Arthur 110
Buc, George 163
Burbage, James 16, 45–46, 48, 50
Burbage, Richard 79, 80, 83

Burgos 21, 40, 54
Burgos, Jerónima de 98

Calahorra 54
Calderón de la Barca, Pedro 2, 14, 61–62, 63–64, 105, 116, 119, 124, 125, 134, 149, 155, 160, 171, 172
Cambridge (University) 105
Camillo, Giulio 45
Campbell, Colen 66
Caro, Ana 119–120
Cary, Elizabeth 119–120
Castile 13, 21, 35, 36, 52, 91, 92, 151, 154, 161, 163
Catholics 104, 115
Cervantes, Miguel de 5–6, 14, 83, 105, 115, 125, 130, 134, 163, 167, 171, 172
Charles V 14, 20
Chaucer, Geoffrey 1, 19
Chamberlain's Men (a.k.a King's Men) 48, 52, 68, 82, 84, 85, 86, 89, 145, 146, 157
children companies 29–30, 54, 82–83, 87–88, 92–96; Blackfriars/Chapel/Queen's Revels/Revels 87, 88, 90; Paul's 87, 88, 90
Church of England 25
Cicero 103
Cisneros, Alonso de 79, 92, 97, 98
Ciudad Rodrigo 54
Civil War (England) 12, 169
Clifton, Henry 82–83, 88

Clifton, Thomas 82–83, 88
Cofradía de la Novena 84
Cofradías (Soledad and Pasión) 27
commedia dell'arte 2, 6, 44–45, 46, 48, 55, 94, 171
Consejo de Castilla (Council of Castile) 94, 151, 163
Cromwell, Oliver 64, 169
Condell, Henry 82, 145
Cordoba 50, 70
corral de vecinos 21–23, 34, 39, 52
Counter-Reformation 104, 168
Crosse, Henry 26
Cruz, Juana Inés de la 172

Daniel, Samuel 124
Davies of Hereford, John 12
Day, John 124
Dekker, Thomas 37, 116, 133
Digges, Leonard 65–66
Donne, John 85
Dublin (Werburgh Street Playhouse) 13, 34

Earle, John 83
entremeses 106, 108, 113
Evans, Henry 88

Farrant, Richard 31, 87–88
Field, Nathan 133, 158
Fletcher, John 112, 116, 124, 129, 133, 153, 154, 156, 164, 165
Fonseca, Pedro de 40
Ford, John 129, 133
Fox, George 35
Fludd, Robert 45
France 2, 6, 46, 68, 93, 124, 156, 160–161

Ganassa *see Naselli, Alberto*
Germany 170, 171
Góngora, Luis de 14
grammar schools 103–106
Greece 8, 46, 49, 82, 103, 104, 107, 110, 111, 112, 113, 153
Greene, Robert 83, 105
Greene, Thomas 82
Guzmán, Pedro de 26

Hartzenbusch, Juan Eugenio 170
Henry VIII 19, 31, 123–124
Heminges, John 82, 85, 145–146
Henslowe, Philip 51

Heywood, Thomas 49, 67, 81, 82, 83, 99, 105, 116, 133, 153–154, 160
Howell, James 8

Italy 2, 6, 8, 12, 44–46, 48, 60, 61, 65–66, 108, 109, 111, 123, 156

James I 81, 82, 90, 119
Jesuits 26, 39, 93, 104–106
Jones, Inigo 50, 61, 65–66
Jonson, Ben 45, 61, 80, 82, 105, 119, 133, 146, 149, 151, 152, 153, 156, 164, 165, 169

King's Men *see Chamberlain's Men*
Kyd, Thomas 133, 146

Lafréry, Antoine 49
Latin 49, 55, 81, 87, 103–105
Lerma, Duke of 14, 28, 91
licensing (playbooks) 149–152, 155, 161–162, 163
lighting 47, 62–63, 64, 71
Ling, Nicholas 143
Lisbon 11, 15; Pateo das Arcas 21, 35, 54, 68, 70
London: Boroughs: (City of London 10, 11, 12, 17, 18, 19, 20, 26, 27, 29, 30, 31, 32, 58, 62, 74; Clerkenwell 38, 41; Dulwich 82; Mile End 16; Shoreditch 14, 16–17, 19, 24, 26, 29, 30, 31, 46, 47, 49, 89, 164; Southwark 17, 18–20, 24, 38, 51, 89, 164); Inns of Court 17, 31, 32, 105; Liberties 19–20, 27, 31, 32; Performance Inns (Bell Inn, Bell Savage Inn, Bull Inn, Cross Keys Inn) 17; Playhouses: (Blackfriars 29–32, 39, 58, 59, 61, 62, 74–76, 82–83, 87–88, 90; Boar's Head 51–52; Cockpit/Phoenix 32; Curtain 16, 17, 19, 29, 30, 31, 52; Globe 18, 42, 44, 46, 50, 52, 58, 59, 62, 65, 67, 68, 69, 70, 75; Hope 67; Newington Butts 17; Porter's Hall 32; Red Bull 51–52, 68; Red Lion 16, 47, 66; Rose 18, 51–52, 65, 67; Salisbury Court 32; Swan 18, 67; St Paul's 29–32, 41, 74, 88, 90; Theatre in Shoreditch 16, 19, 29, 30, 31, 45–46, 47, 49; Whitefriars 32)
Lotti, Cosimo 50, 61
Low Countries (a.k.a Netherlands) 12, 124, 156
Lyly, John 30, 54, 105

Madrid: Buen Retiro Palace 76;
  Playhouses: (Burguillos 21; Coliseo 76;
  Cruz 21, 23, 63, 67, 73, 75–76; Lobo
  21; Pacheca 21, 44, 48, 60; Príncipe 21,
  23, 63, 73, 75–76); Parish of San
  Sebastián 23–25, 39, 74
Magno, Alessandro 9
Mariana, Juan de 26, 93
Marlowe, Christopher 105, 123, 133
Marston, John 90, 133, 144–145
Martínez de Mora, Diego 147
Massinger, Philip 116, 133
Master of the Revels 28, 85, 89, 151, 163
Mayne, Jasper 97
Menéndez Pelayo, Marcelino 170
Middleton, Thomas 105, 123, 133, 152–153
Mira de Amescua, Antonio 134–135, 155
Molière 2, 160–161
Moreto, Agustín 135, 155
Moryson, Fynes 83
Mulcaster, Richard 104
Munday, Anthony 39

Naples 9, 11
Naselli, Alberto (a.k.a Ganassa) 44, 48, 60, 94
Nashe, Thomas 45, 105
Netherlands see Low Countries

O, Mariana de la 94
Ochoa, Eugenio de 170
Ovid 110
Oxford (University) 105

Pacheco, Francisco 115
Palladio, Andrea 65–66
Parigi, Giulio 50, 65
Paris 9, 11; Hôtel de Bourgogne 68
particulares 74
Pérez de Montalbán, Juan 116, 118, 170
Philip II 10, 27, 96
Philip III 10, 14, 81, 82, 163
Philip IV 69, 76
Porres, Gaspar de 125
Portugal 15, 91–92, 116–117, 163
posters 157–159, 166
Pound, Ezra 1
Prescot 13, 33, 34, 89
Prynne, William 93
Puritans 25–26, 93

Quevedo, Francisco de 14, 81, 83, 95

Racine, Jean 2
Ramírez de Arellano, Luis 147
Reformation 12
relaciones de comedias 159–160
Remón, Alonso 116
Restoration 64, 96, 169
Roberts, James 143
Rojas, Agustín de 50, 78, 79–80, 83, 97, 115
Rome 8, 11, 67, 46, 49, 82, 110, 111, 113, 153, 168; Colosseum 49
Rowe, Nicholas 170
Royal Shakespeare Company 172
Rueda, Lope de 14, 20, 92, 94, 98, 121
Ruiz de Alarcón, Juan 135, 158, 163, 166

Salamanca 54, 105
Salas Barbadillo, Alonso de 37
Schlegel, Friedrich and August Wilhelm 171
Seneca 103, 114
Seville 11, 14, 15–16, 20, 21, 22–23, 25, 32–33, 34, 40, 44–45, 50, 61, 64, 79, 83, 90, 91, 92, 98, 100, 115, 157, 160;
  Playhouses: (Alcoba, Atarazanas, Coliseo, Don Pablo, Don Pedro, Doña Elvira, Montería, San Vicente)
Serlio, Sebastiano 46, 48
Sessa, Duke of 102
Shakespeare, William 1–2, 4, 5, 17, 18, 55, 61, 64, 81, 82, 84, 86, 87, 102, 105, 107, 109, 110–113, 119, 122, 123–124, 128, 132, 134, 143–146, 147, 149, 153, 156, 165, 167–172
Shirley, James 124, 129, 134
Sidney, Philip 112–113
Simmes, Valentine 143
Stow, John 13–14, 18, 19, 36, 37
Stubbes, Philip 25–26

Téllez, Gabriel see Tirso de Molina
Terence 103, 114, 118
The Hague 11
Theobald, Lewis 167, 171
Tilney, Edmund 163
Tirso de Molina 14, 78, 105, 116, 124, 135, 155, 166, 171, 172
Toledo 8, 10, 14, 15, 34, 35, 36, 40, 91, 92, 95, 98; Mesón de la Fruta 21, 54
Toro 54

tragicomedy 110–115, 130
Turia, Ricardo de 114, 115

universities 28, 53, 80, 104–105, 107, 112, 114

Vaca, Mariana 94
Valdés, Pedro de 98
Valencia 10, 14, 15, 40, 61, 91–92; Casa de la Olivera 21, 50, 53–54, 70; Casa del Santets 21
Valladolid 10, 14, 15, 20, 21, 37, 40, 54, 70, 91
Vega, Lope de 1–2, 14, 37, 55, 62, 78, 81, 96, 97, 102–103, 105, 109, 110, 113–114, 115, 117–119, 128, 130, 132, 135–137, 144–145, 147–149, 151, 155–156, 158, 160–161, 163, 164, 165, 167–168, 170–173

Vélez de Guevara, Luis 123, 155
Vicenza (Teatro Olimpico) 66
Vienna 11
Virgil 103
Vitruvius 46

Webster, John 62, 110, 134, 146
Westminster 9, 11, 17, 18, 31, 32, 35
White, Thomas 26
Williams, Thomas 64
Wroth, Mary 119–120
Wynn, Richard 96

York 13, 33, 34, 89

Zamora 21, 54
Zayas, María de 119–120

For Product Safety Concerns and Information please contact our EU representative GPSR@taylorandfrancis.com
Taylor & Francis Verlag GmbH, Kaufingerstraße 24, 80331 München, Germany

www.ingramcontent.com/pod-product-compliance
Lightning Source LLC
Chambersburg PA
CBHW051357290426
44108CB00015B/2048